Terror and the Postcolonial

Blackwell Concise Companions to Literature and Culture
General Editor: David Bradshaw, University of Oxford

This series offers accessible, innovative approaches to major areas of literary study. Each volume provides an indispensable companion for anyone wishing to gain an authoritative understanding of a given period or movement's intellectual character and contexts.

Published

Modernism	Edited by David Bradshaw
Feminist Theory	Edited by Mary Eagleton
The Restoration and Eighteenth Century	Edited by Cynthia Wall
Postwar American Literature and Culture	Edited by Josephine G. Hendin
The Victorian Novel	Edited by Francis O'Gorman
Twentieth-Century American Poetry	Edited by Stephen Fredman
Chaucer	Edited by Corinne Saunders
Shakespeare on Screen	Edited by Diana E. Henderson
Contemporary British Fiction	Edited by James F. English
English Renaissance Literature	Edited by Donna B. Hamilton
Milton	Edited by Angelica Duran
Shakespeare and the Text	Edited by Andrew Murphy
Contemporary British and Irish Drama	Edited by Nadine Holdsworth and Mary Luckhurst
American Fiction 1900–1950	Edited by Peter Stoneley and Cindy Weinstein
The Romantic Age	Edited by Jon Klancher
Postwar British and Irish Poetry	Edited by Nigel Alderman and C. D. Blanton
Middle English Literature	Edited by Marilyn Corrie
Terror and the Postcolonial	Edited by Elleke Boehmer and Stephen Morton
Postcolonial Literature	Edited by Shirley Chew and David Richards

Terror and the Postcolonial

Edited by Elleke Boehmer and
Stephen Morton

WILEY-BLACKWELL
A John Wiley & Sons, Ltd., Publication

This edition first published 2010

Blackwell Publishing was acquired by John Wiley & Sons in February 2007. Blackwell's publishing program has been merged with Wiley's global Scientific, Technical, and Medical business to form Wiley-Blackwell.

Registered Office
John Wiley & Sons Ltd, The Atrium, Southern Gate, Chichester, West Sussex, PO19 8SQ, United Kingdom

Editorial Offices
350 Main Street, Malden, MA 02148-5020, USA
9600 Garsington Road, Oxford, OX4 2DQ, UK
The Atrium, Southern Gate, Chichester, West Sussex, PO19 8SQ, UK

For details of our global editorial offices, for customer services, and for information about how to apply for permission to reuse the copyright material in this book please see our website at www.wiley.com/wiley-blackwell.

Library of Congress Cataloging-in-Publication Data

Terror and the postcolonial : a concise companion / edited by Elleke Boehmer and Stephen Morton.
p. cm. — (Concise companions to literature and culture)
Includes bibliographical references and index.
ISBN 978-1-4051-9154-8 (hardcover : alk. paper) 1. Commonwealth literature (English)—History and criticism. 2. Terrorism in literature. 3. Colonies in literature. 4. Postcolonialism in literature. 5. Postcolonialism. 6. Terrorism-Social aspects-Commonwealth countries. I. Boehmer, Elleke, 1961– II. Morton, Stephen, 1972–

PR9080.5.T46 2009
820.9-dc22

2009009387

A catalogue record for this book is available from the British Library.

Set in 10/12.5pt Meridien by Graphicraft Limited, Hong Kong
Printed and bound in Malaysia by Vivar Printing Sdn Bhd

01 2010

Contents

Notes on Contributors

Bashir Abu-Manneh is Assistant Professor of English at Barnard College, New York, and the author of several articles in journals such as *Interventions*, *New Formations*, and *Monthly Review*. He is writing a book on the Palestinian novel and nationalism.

Elleke Boehmer is well known for her research in international writing and postcolonial theory, and is the author of the world best-seller *Colonial and Postcolonial Literature: Migrant Metaphors* (1995, 2005), the monographs *Empire, the National and the Postcolonial, 1890–1920* (2002) and *Stories of Women* (2005), and of the acclaimed edition of Robert Baden-Powell's *Scouting for Boys* (2004). Elleke Boehmer is the Professor of World Literature in English at the University of Oxford. Her most recent books are *Nelson Mandela* and *Nile Baby* (both 2008).

Emma Brodzinski is a Senior Lecturer in the Department of Drama and Theatre at Royal Holloway, University of London. She has a background in theatre-making and applied theatre practice. She is also a dramatherapist and has worked in both National Health Service and private settings. In collaboration with Helen Nicholson and Katie Normington she has recently published a book examining devised theatre entitled *Making a Performance: Devising Histories and Contemporary Practices* (2007). She is also currently writing a publication for Palgrave on theatre in health and care, and is engaged in a research project jointly funded by the AHRC, ESRC, Arts Council, and DTI, which examines creativity in the health and care workforce.

Robert Eaglestone is Professor of Contemporary Literature and Thought at Royal Holloway, University of London. His publications include *Ethical Criticism* (1997), *Doing English* (3rd ed. 2009), and *The Holocaust and the Postmodern* (2004), and four edited books including *J. M. Coetzee in Context and Theory* with Elleke Boehmer and Katy Iddiols. He is the series editor of *Routledge Critical Thinkers.*

Derek Gregory is Distinguished University Scholar and Professor of Geography at the University of British Columbia at Vancouver. He is a Fellow of the British Academy and of the Royal Society of Canada and was awarded the Founder's Medal of the Royal Geographical Society in 2006. He is the author of several books including *The Colonial Present: Afghanistan, Palestine, Iraq* (2004) and *Violent Geographies: Fear, Terror and Political Violence* (edited with Allan Pred) (2007). His research focuses on political and cultural geographies of modern war, the subject of his forthcoming *War Cultures.*

Louise Hardwick is a Postdoctoral Fellow at Homerton College, Cambridge, and a graduate of Trinity College, Oxford. Her doctoral thesis examines the significance of childhood narratives in the development of Francophone Caribbean literature (Patrick Chamoiseau, Maryse Condé, Raphaël Confiant and Dany Laferrière), and she has published on Condé, Confiant and Joseph Zobel. She is the editor of a forthcoming volume on approaches to crime in French literature and visual culture.

Peter Heehs is an American historian based in Pondicherry, India. He writes on modern Indian history, and Indian spirituality and religion. Much of his work focuses on the Indian political and spiritual leader Sri Aurobindo. His publications include *The Lives of Sri Aurobindo* (2008), *The Bomb in Bengal* (1993 and 2004), *Nationalism, Terrorism, Communalism* (1998), and more than 40 articles in journals and magazines.

Alex Houen is a University Lecturer in Modern Literature at Cambridge University. He is the author of *Terrorism and Modern Literature: From Joseph Conrad to Ciaran Carson* (2002), and numerous articles on modern literature, theory, and politics.

Achille Mbembe, born in Cameroon, and educated at the Sorbonne in Paris and at the Institut d'études politiques (IEP), Paris, is Research Professor in History and Politics at the University of Wiwatersrand, South

Africa. He is the author of several books on African history and politics, most notably *On the Postcolony* (2001).

Stephen Morton is a Senior Lecturer in English at the University of Southampton. He has written widely on postcolonial literature and theory, and is the author of *Gayatri Chakravorty Spivak* (2003), *Gayatri Spivak: Ethics, Politics and the Critique of Postcolonial Reason* (2006), *Salman Rushdie: Fictions of Postcolonial Modernity* (2007), and is the co-editor of *Foucault in an Age of Terror: Biopolitics and the Defence of Society* (2008). He is currently working on a monograph on *Colonial States of Emergency in Literature and Culture 1905–2005*.

Stuart Price is Principal Lecturer in Media, Film and Journalism at De Montfort University, Leicester. He is the author of *Discourse Power Address* (2007), and has also produced material on politics and security, including "Missiles in Athens, Tanks at Heathrow" (*Social Semiotics*, 2008: 18/1). Forthcoming work includes *Brute Reality: Structures of Representation in the "War on Terror"* (2010). Current research encompasses a study of public disorder in Greece following the death of the teenager Alexandros Grigoropoulos.

Ranka Primorac is a Teaching Fellow at the University of Southampton. She has written widely about Zimbabwean literatures and cultures, and is the author of *The Place of Tears: The Novel and Politics in Modern Zimbabwe* (2006) and co-editor of *Versions of Zimbabwe* (2005) and *Zimbabwe in Crisis* (2007). Her edited collection *African City Textualities* is forthcoming with Routledge in 2009. Her research interests are centered on narrative constructions of space-time, the social functioning of literary fictions, city cultures and texts, and postcolonial/literary theory.

Neluka Silva is Professor in English and Head of Department at the University of Colombo, Sri Lanka and a visiting lecturer for the Postgraduate Diploma in Peace and Conflict Studies of the University of Bradford Sri Lanka program. She is also a creative writer and has been involved in the Sri Lankan theatre in English for over 20 years. Her research interests include cultural production in South Asia; Gender, Peace, and Conflict issues; and Contemporary Theatre.

Sujala Singh is a Senior Lecturer in English at the University of Southampton. Her publications include essays in *Wasafiri, Critical*

Survey, New Formations, and *Kunapipi,* and she is currently completing a monograph on *Postcolonial Children: Representing the Nation in South Asian Literature*.

Alex Tickell is a Senior Lecturer in English at the University of Portsmouth. His publications include *Arundhati Roy's The God of Small Things* (2007), a critical edition of *Selections from "Bengaliana"* by Shoshee Chunder Dutt (2005), and articles in journals such as the *Journal of Commonwealth Literature, Ariel,* and *Postcolonial Studies.* He is currently working on a monograph on Violence, Terror, and Insurgency in Indian-English Writing.

Vron Ware is currently a Research Fellow at the Centre for Research on Socio-Cultural Change and the Centre for Citizenship, Identities and Governance, based at the Open University. Previous publications include *Beyond the Pale: White Women, Racism and History* (1992), *Out of Whiteness: Color, Politics and Culture* (2002), and *Who Cares About Britishness? A Global View of the National Identity Debate* (2007).

Robert J. C. Young is Julius Silver Professor of English and Comparative Literature at New York University. He was formerly Professor of English and Critical Theory at Oxford University. He has published *White Mythologies: Writing History and the West* (1990, new edition 2004), *Colonial Desire: Hybridity in Culture, Theory and Race* (1995), *Postcolonialism: An Historical Introduction* (2001), *Postcolonialism: A Very Short Introduction* (2003), and *The Idea of English Ethnicity* (2008). His edited books include *Untying the Text* (1981), and, with Derek Attridge and Geoffrey Bennington, *Poststructuralism and the Question of History* (1987). He is also General Editor of *Interventions: International Journal of Postcolonial Studies,* and was a founding editor of the *Oxford Literary Review.* His work has been translated into 20 languages, and he is currently writing a book on translation.

Acknowledgments

The editors would like to express their gratitude to the School of Humanities and the English Department at the University of Southampton for their generous financial contribution towards the costs of translation and permissions for this book; and to the British Academy, the Canadian High Commission, and HARC (Humanities and Arts Research Committee) at Royal Holloway, University of London for their support of the two workshops on Terror and the Postcolonial at Royal Holloway, University of London (RHUL) and Southampton University in 2006. We would also like to express our gratitude to colleagues and graduate students at RHUL and at the University of Southampton for their participation and critical feedback on the workshops. In particular we would wish to thank Alice Christie, then in the English Department office at RHUL, for her sterling help with the workshop accounts and administration. We thank the English Faculty, University of Oxford, for kind support with the indexing process.

We owe a big debt of gratitude to Professor Susheila Nasta of the Open University, Editor of *Wasafiri*, for hosting the special issue "Cultures of Terror" (July 2007), co-edited with Elleke Boehmer, in which earlier versions of three of the essays collected here first appeared.

The editors would also like to thank Routledge for permission to reprint the following articles: Derek Gregory, "Vanishing Points: Law, Violence, and Exception in the Global War Prison," in Derek Gregory and Allan Pred (eds.), *Violent Geographies: Fear, Terror and Political Violence* (New York: Routledge, 2007), pp. 205–36; Robert Eaglestone, "'The age of reason was over . . . an age of fury was dawning': Contemporary Fiction and Terror," *Wasafiri* 22:2 (2007), pp. 19–22; Ranka Primorac, "The Poetics of State Fiction in Twenty-First Century Zimbabwe," *Interventions* 9:3 (2007), pp. 434–50; Vron Ware, "The White Fear Factor," *Wasafiri* 22:2 (2007), pp. 51–6; Bashir Abu-Manneh, "Israel in the US Empire," first published in Priyamvada Gopal and Neil Lazarus (eds.), *After Iraq: Reframing Postcolonial Studies, new formations* 59 (London: Lawrence and Wishart, 2006); Elleke Boehmer, "Post-colonial Writing and Terror," *Wasafiri* 22:2 (2007), pp. 4–7.

Our partners Steven Matthews and Susan Kelly have offered unfailing support across the many days and hours we have spent on this absorbing and ongoing "Terror and the Postcolonial" project: our gratitude to them is boundless.

Introduction: Terror and the Postcolonial

Elleke Boehmer and
Stephen Morton

As If Invoked, Like Dracula

Terror, postcolonial or otherwise, induces affect, as a number of essays in this book describe. Among the affective repercussions of acts of terror are extreme fear, galvanizing shock, vengeful anger, displacement, and, perhaps above all, paranoia – the belief that having struck once, terror will do so again, at the same place, like lightning. Or, even if it has not appeared before, the deep paranoia associated with terror is that, once conceived, once entertained in the mind, terror will inexorably arise, somewhere, and attack the body, whether national, social, or individual, just as Dracula attacks, with his type of watchfulness and cunning.

That day, 7/7/2005, "London's 9/11" (with apposite, necromantic rhyme), it certainly did seem to this book's editors that our theoretical engagement with terror and terrorism, defiant and skeptical as it was, had in some way called forth the configuration of terrorist events that manifested all about us. North, east, west of our meeting that day in the heart of London, bombs exploded, the repercussions of which we almost immediately felt; the aftershocks of which pulled through us, forming as we did part of a vast, moving crowd. Thus drawn in, it was as if our academic investigations – especially because they *were* skeptical and against current neo-imperial orthodoxies concerning the unquestioned rightness of the war on terror – had mysteriously invoked these outrages, even conjured them into being.

We had fixed the July 7 date some months before, for a meeting in Senate House to discuss the overall shape and tenor of two workshops we were planning, to which we had given the name this book now bears as its title: *Terror and the Postcolonial.* The workshops, funded in part by the British Academy, as well as by the Canadian High Commission, HARC at Royal Holloway, and the Southampton English Department, set out to address a range of questions concerning the links between postcolonial writing and theory, and the phenomenon of terror. We asked, for example, why it was that the post/colonial state sought to propagate terror? And in what ways did West/non-West divisions underpin the rhetoric of terrorism and its "real world" manifestations? How did postcolonial concepts of, for example, resistance and worldliness contribute to our understanding of contemporary terror? And how might we set about redefining the human in a situation of terror?

For the two of us located at separate institutions, Stephen Morton at the University of Southampton, Elleke Boehmer, then at Royal Holloway, University of London, the Institute of English Studies in Senate House in Bloomsbury seemed an excellent, central place to meet. This was especially the case as we had invited a few other colleagues, now among the contributors to this volume, to participate in the meeting. We were keen to gauge their different insights into the risks and difficulties involved in organizing a series of terror workshops that would seek to analyze contemporary developments while retaining historical and ethical perspective, and foreground the terror phenomenon without making of it a spectacle. In the event our colleagues never made it to Senate House that morning. They were turned away at stations proximate to London, instructed that "something had happened" in the capital and it was best not to continue on their journey.

Setting out a little earlier than the others, to confer before the discussion proper began, we two workshop conveners were geographically closer to Bloomsbury – though we hadn't yet met – when a strange electricity made itself felt in the air. At just after nine o'clock in the morning we were, as we remember, so close to what was soon identified as the epicenter of the unfolding developments that universal confusion still reigned about the unnamed (and unnamable) "event" that had, to us palpably, taken place. All that was clear was that the Underground was being evacuated and the grille gates at the entrances to stations being shut, but the police could not or would not yet explain to the puzzled public why this was. They were taking precautions, was all they said; there could have been an electrical fault, so they were recommending that people travel by London bus instead. (By this point, at 8.50 a.m., three bombs of the four that were to go off that day had already exploded – at Edgware Road, Aldgate, and deep in the Underground, not far from Russell Square station.) There was something amiss somewhere, some red alert, that much was evident, and the police were responding with extreme distraction.

Shuffling out of Euston Station alongside hundreds of other Tube evacuees, one of the editors, Elleke, saw a red-faced policewoman haring over to a police car slewed crazily up against a curb on Euston Road, crying "where, where, where?" Stephen, walking up to Senate House from Waterloo Station, saw the streets emptying as if by magic. As he wandered past police cordons near Bloomsbury, and beneath the whirring of helicopters, he could not help but think of Iraq, where similar scenes and sounds were daily being played out. He wondered about the connections, causal, rhizomic, and otherwise, that linked the carnage and confusion in those streets to these. (Bilal Abdulla, who two years later, in June 2007, allegedly laid car bombs in central London, certainly claimed that his motive was to introduce the effect of living in Iraq to the British public: he wanted to give Britons "just the taste, the taste of fear") (Attewill 2008: 4).

Meanwhile Elleke, who had successfully avoided being pressed on to one of the waiting red Routemaster buses, was heading down Tottenham Court Road from the north. Around 9.30, as she exited a Starbucks coffee shop on Tottenham Court road with a takeaway coffee in hand, a man leaving at the same time, a step in front, expressed out loud his opinion, to anyone who might be listening, that "it's got to be a terrorist attack." (About 20 minutes later, at 9.47, another Tube evacuee, Hasib Hussain, who had followed police directions with his lethal backpack still intact, denoted the fourth bomb on the number 30 double-decker bus, in Tavistock Square, not far from the statue of Gandhi, and about as far from Euston Station as the Starbucks shop.) By now mobile phones were no longer working; strangers were muttering to one another in the street that there was no signal to be had; and queues began forming at phone booths in the snaking, ambling way reminiscent of the pre-mobile-phone era.

Though in terms of physical proximity we editors could probably have heard the Tavistock explosion, we did not in reality (though retrospective memories are of course full of screaming sirens and dull thuds). But as soon as we met in the darkened rooms of the Institute of English Studies, where Warwick Gould, the Director, offered stoical good cheer, as well as a radio, we began remarking on the strange quirks of fate and odd juxtapositions that were marking the morning. Throughout Senate House the blinds had been pulled down as another "precaution," one of the many moments in the day when people responded to the events with obvious "Blitz"-type defenses. Elleke recalled how, years before, she had left a South Africa gripped by a state of emergency imposed by the apartheid regime – a country where terror attacks were daily expected, and counter-terroristic responses routine. And now, here, in the timeless heart of London, the atmosphere of emergency and non-specific alarm was being repeated, as if with hyperbolic force.

An aimless and remarkable day then ensued. Bar the occasional screaming of ambulances and police cars, London fell gradually silent. Shops closed, smaller public buildings were evacuated, the British Library shut its doors at noon. Vast and largely speechless crowds were on the move, trying to get home, reach loved ones, escape the city, process their fear. Small huddles of individuals stood clustered outside electrical shops, or wherever there were televisions that showed the unspooling events. People barely spoke, in order not to miss crucial information when it came. News channels began slowly to piece together a story of sorts: of "London's 9/11," the calamity that had in many quarters been expected, on this day timed perhaps to coincide with the G8 summit at Gleneagles, where Tony Blair, a key propagator of the Iraq War, was presiding.

Everywhere we editors turned on our long walk through London that day the communications and transport infrastructure was stopped, closed, locked down. The worst thing was not being able to phone home and worrying about family and friends. Until much later, when we eventually found ourselves on last trains rattling emptily out of the capital, the concept of getting home seemed the ultimate impossibility, here on this bright summer's day in a surreal, *flâneur*'s London without traffic. Now, a strange quiet after-echo appeared to hang in the air following each footfall one made. It was as if the silence around one (the absence of cars, double-decker buses, taxis) was already creating an atmosphere of reverence, intoning the tiny imperceptible pauses, moments of hush, that would begin by slow accumulation to mark this inconceivable and (for many) infinitely painful Thing that had happened.

And so – leaving Senate House, wandering directionless from place to place, stopping at the Quaker building where everyone was either drinking or serving cups of hot tea, trekking down Marylebone Road in the direction of Paddington – we editors could barely name the term which had occasioned our being here today. Terror. *Terror*? For us the word was so blatant, so raw, as to be close to unmentionable; so bizarrely coincidental, we couldn't begin at the time to confront what these unfolding events meant to us. It resembled a case of delayed decoding in a Conrad novel: like his narrator Marlow in *Heart of Darkness* we were aware and yet not aware that "arrows" (that is, terror, the knowledge of a terror attack) were coming at us from all directions (Conrad 1995: 76–8).

As this analogy suggests, the terror we experienced that day felt to us invoked, called up, and we, interpellated by it. Truly it seemed as if we had brought this thing upon us and so could not call it by its name, its common-or-garden street name – terrorism; a terror attack – lest we risk further ensnaring. Briefly, Elleke wondered whether she would continue for the rest of her life to find herself locked into repeat patterns of terror events, as if postcolonial existence meant being shuttled like this from one terror zone to another – as bizarrely anticipated in her novel about Irish-South African terrorism *Bloodlines* (Boehmer 2000). Still preoccupied by the relationship between the war in Iraq and these London events, Stephen reflected on the metaphorical language of foes within and without that the state mobilized to justify its recourse to security measures, metaphors which aided and abetted the very acts of terrorism they claimed to repress.

We also could not avoid comparing the sight of the streaming crowd of hundreds upon hundreds walking the long straight road from Euston Station to Paddington (and skirting the Edgware Road's no-go zone), to images we'd seen of crowds on the move elsewhere in the world: 1947 Partition, China's Long March. The analogy of the Blitz and the Blitz spirit did indeed press everywhere on our senses – in those widely made and shared cups of tea, in the rueful toughing-it-out smiles perfect strangers exchanged with one another. Shades of T. S. Eliot's *The Waste Land*, too, were unmistakable, in the crowds flowing (whether over London Bridge or everywhere else), in the intimations of a ruined city. Terror effects, projected outwards, hurtling, bringing pain, anger, fear, were already transferring into the quotidian in these concrete, predictable ways, translating into the stories and images we were outlining for one another, about the day we'd shared, ever since that moment when, at 8.50 a.m., London life had seemingly changed.

Elleke Boehmer and Stephen Morton

Terror, the Colony and the Postcolony

Terror; counter-terrorism; terrorism; war on terror; Islamic terrorists; terror cells; solutions to terror: the vocabulary of terror has in recent years become the bass note to Western government rhetoric, if not to political and journalistic discourse more broadly. "One person's terrorist is the next person's freedom fighter" is an oft-heard truism (Walter 1969: 5), which implicitly concedes that we all perceive some overpowering horror against which our counter-terroristic standards, our values of freedom and heroism, are defined. For early twenty-first-century Western societies, it seems, terror represents the ultimate fear, the unsaid that can only be condemned, never condoned; and one of the few near-taboo subjects of comedy. The Iraqi journalist Muntadar al-Zaidi, who threw his shoes at the former US President George W. Bush during a press conference in 2008 in a high-risk gesture of defiance, may seem to offer a counterpoint to this taboo by targeting a figure associated with the "war on terror"; however, the incident predictably led to his arrest and imprisonment.[1] The subjective violence of the real world, writes Žižek, the violence that takes the form of mass murders, genocide, and rape, masks the underlying objective violence of capital, systemic, anonymous, that informs "real-life developments and catastrophes" throughout (Žižek 2008: 10–11).

Yet how do we understand this phenomenon of terror, that seems at once so contemporary and so age-old and constant; at once systemic, yet convulsive; so archetypal, but of its nature so evanescent? Is terror a historical force that flashes up at moments of crisis in the inchoate forms of the sublime; or is it by its very nature heterogeneous and chameleon-like, a form of auto-immunity, taking expression from the methods and approaches of its individual terroristic exponents? Is terror chaos or crisis; catachresis or cataclysm; a gradually unfolding process or single spontaneous instant, if with long-lasting painful effects (Walter 1969: 5)? The *Oxford English Dictionary* distinguishes between terror as the emotional state, as might be attributed to a tale of terror; and terrorism, or a system of terror, as when a person or group adopts a policy of intimidation intended to strike with terror those against whom it is adopted. Yet this latter free-floating, liberal understanding of terrorism denies the fundamental point that terrorism as political violence is the ground upon which sovereignty is in many cases defined in the colonial present.

Within the overarching context of this post-9/11 world, *Terror and the Postcolonial* posits a relationship between three terms: terror, the colony, and what has been called the "postcolony" – which refers to the effective continuation of the authority structures of the colony in the post-imperial nation despite "flag independence." The colonial forms of present-day terror or the *terror of the postcolonial*, we editors submit, demands a turn (back) to certain modes of imperial history in order to understand and to explicate these apparent continuities. In particular "postcolonial terror" requires that we turn back to the colonial archive of violence and repression, to records of the colonial formations of sovereignty, policing, and surveillance, which find such prominent afterlives in counter-terroristic formations today. Moreover, postcolonial terror reminds us of resistance to these (post)colonial formations – resistance that historically has taken a variety of different forms, including sedition, sabotage, insurgence, and, of course, armed conflict, themes that several of the essays collected here explore.

Despite the alleged concern of postcolonial studies with such matters as colonial power and anti-colonial resistance – that is, with terroristic repercussions of the colonial within our contemporary, postcolonial condition – it is noteworthy, however, that postcolonial studies has to date largely neglected the back-history of today's postcolonial or late colonial terror. Although terror appears endemic to how power operates in the so-called postcolony, postcolonial histories, and cultural and literary studies, have devoted close-to-minimal energy to the scrutiny of contemporary imperialism, and the traditional colonial and terroristic forms it takes. Terror may well be a dominant form through which the colonial is reiterated in the postcolonial world; yet, bar the exceptions represented by names like Achille Mbembe and Derek Gregory, this is an issue that postcolonial studies till very recently has been hesitant to confront. Related to this, postcolonial scholars also tend to skirt around perhaps one of the most pressing postcolonial issues of our age, the contemporary neo-imperial hegemony of the United States (though the election of Senator Barack Obama as 44th President may have an interesting impact on that global notoriety). Hence, in the editors' opinion, the importance of a collection of essays that examines the intercalations of terror with not only colonial but also postcolonial processes and representations.

True, the surfeit of scholarly books on terrorism produced in response to the incidents of September 11, 2001, and the subsequent declaration of the "war on terror," suggest that terrorism has not only been constituted as an object of contemporary knowledge, but also that it defines the twenty-first-century Western zeitgeist. Yet there are significantly fewer studies that probe the deeper histories of the present, and address what is in fact at stake in the constitution of terrorism as an object of knowledge in the social sciences and humanities.[2] Such studies might in principle confront – yet in fact sidestep – such questions as: How do we interpret the colonial contours we discern within the dimensions of present-day terror? What exactly does the emerging field of terrorism studies reveal about the political and cultural values of contemporary Western culture and its histories of violence? Might our growing body of terroristic knowledge work in ways that are complicit with postcolonial counter-terrorism? To what extent does an academic preoccupation with terror and terrorism provide intellectual and rhetorical support for the continuation of a war on terror without a foreseeable end – a war that is in many respects impossible and unfeasible, waged on an abstract concept, "terror"? This book seeks to address urgent yet relatively neglected questions such as these, that might be encapsulated in the following bluntly expressed ethical concern: What is the critical vocation of postcolonial studies during and beyond the "war on terror"?

By approaching the question of a critical vocation for postcolonial studies with respect to terror, *Terror and the Postcolonial* offers a response to the critical task outlined by Priya Gopal and Neil Lazarus in their 2006 special issue of the journal *New Formations* on postcolonial studies "after Iraq." This task is "to work towards the production of a new 'history of the present' which takes on both the history of imperialism and the history of resistance to imperialism in the long twentieth century" so as to reassert the postcolonial critic's radical calling (Gopal and Lazarus 2006: 9). As the two co-editors suggest, the so-called war on terror demands that postcolonial studies interrogate and re-interrogate the histories of violent colonial occupation, and also resistances to such forms of occupation, and the terroristic or subterroristic shapes and rhetoric these histories and forms have taken. Such a retrospective analysis necessitates, too, a reassessment of the continuities between historical formations of colonial sovereignty, policing and the use of force, and their reappearance in the current wars in Iraq, Afghanistan, and Northern Pakistan, as well as in Europe and the United States. Forms of reappearance also include the establishment of detention camps or "spaces of exception" at Guantánamo Bay, Abu Ghraib and other locations, as Derek

Gregory's work discusses, and the introduction of emergency police powers in cities like London to justify the shoot-to-kill treatment of suspected suicide bombers (see Stuart Price). As with the detention camps, the latter is a development that blurs the boundaries between the rule of (international) law and the declaration of a state of martial law.

It would seem therefore that postcolonial studies "after Iraq," or "beyond" the war on terror, entails espousing and adopting some of the more radical critical practices that it has to offer. For the editors of the essay collection *Postcolonial Studies and Beyond* (Loomba et al. 2005: 1–2), this is something still profoundly worth doing – where those radical practices involve analyzing the colonial past in relation to "the new empires of our times"; the "world-systems of modern capitalism" to "newer transnational networks." With their forthright assertion that postcolonial studies respond to the imperialist forms of today's globalization by supplying it with "a historical conscience – and consciousness" (p. 9), the contributors to the volume agree, too, that the anti-imperial, decolonizing agenda of postcolonialists has become ever more pressing. In particular the collection is concerned to re-examine and re-evaluate the oppositional methodologies of the postcolonial: materialist, idealistic, progressively transnational, "post-Occidental," humanist. It wishes to acknowledge that the rapid pace at which globalization is revealing its imperialism has not always in postcolonial studies carried over into a reawakening of its anti-Eurocentric critical strain, or to a close investigation of its collusion with the decentered and "kaleidoscopic" cultural forms of world capitalism (pp. 14–15).

Postcolonial Studies and Beyond does not raise terror as a primary concern, not even in its capacity as a foundation of power in the colony: this type of critique is evidently not part of its "postcolonial beyond." Yet it is interesting to observe that the subject of terror as it is expressed in the contemporary globalized world does in fact provide a prime occasion for the radical, apparently oppositional, postcolonial methodologies advocated by the editors to come into operation in mutually co-operative and interactive ways. For example, the terroristic violence through which modern states randomly assert their authority, and through which globalizing forces propagate themselves, demands attention to how local experience is linked into the broadest structures of global power – that is, demands an intermeshing of conventional subject-area binaries. It also involves challenging the simplistic dichotomies of the anti-modern as being the main alternative to the modern (in that terror can be the instrument of both), and of the national as rigidly counterpoised to the transnational (as these may collaborate in their deployment of terroristic practices). In other words, to turn again to Žižek, tracing the taken-for-granted colonial antecedents of present-day terror offers powerful ways of showing up the invisible "objective violence" of society: it exposes the systemic violence that supplies the "zero-level standard" against which subjectively violent acts of terror are perceived (Žižek 2008: 1–6).

Terror, the Logic of Unilateral Orientalism

The reticence of academic postcolonial studies ever since Fanon as regards terror may be explained in part by the ways in which the discourse of terrorism is historically overdetermined by Western imperialism, as our repeated juxtaposition of the terms "terror," "colonial," and "postcolonial" underlines. So, in an essay published in the Egyptian newspaper *Al-Ahram*, entitled "Punishment by Detail" (2002), Edward Said presciently noted how, in the Western media, there was "such repetitious and unedifying attention paid to Palestinian suicide bombing that a gross distortion in reality has completely obscured what is much worse: the official Israeli . . . evil that has been visited so deliberately and so methodically on the Palestinian people" (Said 2002). This sentence is significant, first, because it clarifies the way in which a discourse of terrorism serves the political interests of the (in this case Israeli) state and its policies towards its others (Palestinians) – and also of course of the US state that supports it. But it also gestures at a historical relationship between imperialism and the discourse of terrorism. For the "gross distortion in reality" that Said diagnoses in the Western media's representation of suicide bombing is a contemporary example of what Said calls "orientalism" in his influential eponymous 1978 study: a "distribution of geopolitical awareness into aesthetic, scholarly, economic, sociological, historical and philological texts" (1978: 12).

Already in 1988, in an essay entitled "The Essential Terrorist," Said observed how terrorism had "displaced Communism as public enemy number one" in American public discourse; and how this elevation of terrorism had "deflected careful scrutiny of the government's domestic and foreign policies" (p. 149).[3] Citing a book by the then Israeli ambassador to the United Nations, Benjamin Netanyahu, Said described how Netanyahu's definition of terrorism was flawed because it depended "a priori on a single axiom: 'we' are never terrorists; it's the Moslems, Arabs and Communists who are" (p. 152). Similarly, for the South African apartheid regime, opponents of the state such as Nelson Mandela were labeled as terrorists whereas the regime's supporters were hailed as brave defenders of law and order (Boehmer 2007). These were the axioms, the deadly orientalist logic, through which state repression at the time was justified and defended.

In criticizing the discourse of terrorism, Said is not of course denying that acts of terrorism take place and that their effects are abhorrent. Rather he is questioning the way in which the discourse of terrorism is used by powerful states such as the United States and its allies to describe and condemn violent acts of resistance to imperial occupation, instead of addressing the violence of imperial occupation itself. The discourse of terrorism, in other words, couched in familiar orientalist metaphors, is another way of framing the anti-colonial other and legitimating the colonial self by contrast. As in Nasser Hussain's *The Jurisprudence of Emergency*, on British colonial law in India, where in the colony fatal tensions between the rule of civil law and absolute state sovereignty arose (Hussain 2004: 6–7), colonialism produced discourses of otherness to move toward a suspension of the law (Sharpe 1993).

A further example of the orientalist aspects of the contemporary discourse of terrorism emerges in how the fearsome yet faceless figure of the terrorist is invoked as the cause of the expansion of US and of British military power in the twenty-first century – and as requiring transnational disciplinary measures. Yet the war in Afghanistan and the military occupation of Iraq – two expressions of such disciplinary measures – are at the same time, as we well know, fully motivated by the military, political, and economic interests of the United States and Britain. Related disciplinary measures against terrorists also include American and British support for Israel's occupation of the West Bank and Lebanon, and, on the domestic front, the extension of detention laws and surveillance procedures and the suspension of habeas corpus. In all these cases the threat of the (post)colonial terrorist is presented as a primary trigger for retaliatory action. This causal logic forms a striking instance of what Spivak calls "metalepsis": where an effect of colonial discourse (here, the terrorist) is presented as a cause; or where a focus on the emotional-aesthetic connotations of terror is made logically to override awareness of the imperial interests that produced the terrorism.

The Aestheticization of Terror

In a discussion of Kantian and Burkean theories of the sublime, Terry Eagleton asserts that "sublime eruptions like the French Revolution could be admired as long as they were aestheticized, contemplated from a secure distance" (2005: 47). Similarly, Gene Ray in *Terror and the Sublime in Art and Critical Theory* has argued that the rethinking of the sublime as trauma after the events of Auschwitz and September 11, 2001 must be understood as a problem (2005: 7). For both, the experience of terror is problematically refracted into the aestheticized contemplation of the sublime – a refraction and displacement with which postcolonial critical attentions to terror may similarly be complicit.

The vicarious experience of terrorism as a spectacle, which evokes shock and fear, has also preoccupied theorists such as Jean Baudrillard and Slavoj Žižek in their commentaries on "9/11," though in ways that are more involved with the aesthetics of such spectacles than otherwise. For Baudrillard, the vision of the World Trade Center in flames after the attacks of September 11 produced the now-famed sensation of spellbound fear amongst the public (Baudrillard 2002). Yet, although he allows a complicit relationship between aghast audience and horrifying spectacle, at the same time Baudrillard cannot help but frame the terroristic event as an aesthetic phenomenon analogous to the category of terror in aesthetic theories of the sublime, as in Edmund Burke and Immanuel Kant (Žižek 2002). Relatedly, Slavoj Žižek's comparison of the Middle East to the desert of the Real in the Wachowski brothers' film *Matrix* (1999), in his essay "Welcome to the Desert of the Real!" (2002), collaborates with the aestheticization of terror described by Eagleton in favor of examining the geopolitical determinants of terrorism as a discourse – or that with which we hope this book is most intensely preoccupied.

Instead of treating terror as a mere contemporary aesthetic or postmodern philosophical category, the contributors to this volume follow postcolonial theorists such as Paul Gilroy, Gayatri Spivak, and Luke Gibbons in interrogating the category and experience of terror from the standpoint of the colonized and the abject of history. After all, for the colonial subject, terror was no aesthetic experience or feeling, but a brutal material and corporeal experience of sovereign power in the raw. As Achille Mbembe writes both in these pages and elsewhere, citing Fanon, all aesthetic connotations of terror are complicated by the violent, terroristic exercise of sovereign power in the European colony. Indeed, terrorism, understood as political violence (pitted against the anti-colonial insurgent or "savage" who must be civilized), constitutes the rock-bottom ground of sovereignty in the colony. From this it becomes clear that European aesthetic theory partakes in a contiguous foundation, based as it often is on the construction, and then screening out, of the non-European other as a figure of fear and terror. As in Luke Gibbons's case for the political dimensions of Burke's aesthetic theory of the sublime, "the sublime is present in all its terrifying force" when illegitimate political institutions "rule by fear alone" (2002: 7).

Texts on Terror: Honest Fundamentalists

Although postcolonial studies may to date have failed to examine in a sustained, systematic way how the foundations of colonial rule are based in terror, and how state terror models anti-colonial insurgency, postcolonial literature for its part has grappled vigorously with questions concerning imperial violence and colonial sovereignty. The role of literary, dramatic, and filmic texts to decode and explicate the contradictory operations of terror is widely explored in these pages, as are, if more implicitly, the ways in which terror may be mediated to consciousness through metaphor. So, in J. M. Coetzee's 1980 novel *Waiting for the Barbarians,* for example, the reader is exposed to the relationship between violence, law, and the colonial state, as brought to the fore in the Magistrate's reflections on his position in relation to the acts of torture that he witnesses and experiences. At an early point in the novel the Magistrate asserts that "there is nothing to link" him "with torturers" (Coetzee 1980: 48). After his own experience of torture, however, he realizes that the distinction between the normal rule of law and the violent practices of interrogation carried out under the legal order of empire is untenable. "I was not, as I liked to think," he thinks, "the indulgent pleasure-loving opposite of the cold rigid Colonel. I was the lie that Empire tells itself when times are easy, he the truth that Empire tells when harsh winds blow" (p. 148). The Magistrate is a "lie," in other words, because the rule of law that he symbolizes is the condition of possibility for the emergency powers which allow Colonel Joll to torture the barbarians, rather than a safeguard against such practices. When the Magistrate says that Colonel Joll "is here under the emergency powers, that is enough," he obfuscates the relationship between the rule of law and the emergency powers (p. 1). He does not question the origins of the emergency powers, and his own position as the guardian of the Empire's legal order, for to do so would be to acknowledge that the emergency powers are produced by the very juridical order that he represents.

In a similar vein, the narrator Changez in Mohsin Hamid's much-discussed 2007 novel *The Reluctant Fundamentalist* offers a series of reflections on the justification for the wars in Iraq and Afghanistan. He observes how "a common strand seemed to unite these conflicts, and that was the advancement of a small coterie's concept of American interests in the guise of a fight against terrorism, which was defined to refer only to the organized and politically motivated killing of civilians by *killers* not wearing the uniforms of killers" (Hamid 2007: 178). Here, Changez not only offers an insightful criticism of the way in which the meaning of terrorism is defined by narratives of counter-terrorism to justify the state's use of military force; he also demonstrates that the word itself masks the ways in which the US-led war on terror serves American economic and geopolitical interests at the expense of human lives in Iraq, Pakistan, and Afghanistan. He observes: "the lives of those of us who lived in lands in which such killers also lived had no meaning except as collateral damage" (p. 178). The precarious character of civilian life in Pakistan during the US war in Afghanistan is further borne out by Changez's story of a boy who was allegedly involved in a plot to assassinate an American development worker. This boy, as Changez explains, "had disappeared – whisked away to a secret detention facility, no doubt, in some lawless limbo between [America and Pakistan]" (p. 182).

If, as Hamid suggests, the "war on terrorism" masked an imperialist agenda, this imperialist agenda is inextricably entwined with the history of neoliberal globalization and America's place within it. Indeed, it is significant that Changez's disaffection with America at the end of *The Reluctant Fundamentalist* is also a form of disaffection with his position as a market fundamentalist in the American corporate financial firm Underwood Samson. As Žižek also perceives, systemic, invisible terror is closely bound up with, indeed imprinted by, the operations of neoliberal capitalism.

The Colonialism of Terror; the Terror of the Postcolonial: Essays

Although the editors' planned discussion on terror that July 7 day never happened, the Terror and the Postcolonial workshops themselves went off successfully, on April 26 and June 30, 2006, as if to confirm a widely felt need for the kind of exploratory discussions on postcolonial terror that they had invited. The chapters that make up this book are based on the diverse papers given respectively at Royal Holloway, University of London and the University of Southampton, at these two workshops. Though distinctions and gradations of emphasis between the two interlinked events are difficult to pinpoint, the first cluster of papers, on April 26, concentrated on theories of terror and violence, and instances of colonial and postcolonial resistance, whereas the papers given on June 30 were possibly more situated and contextualized. In this volume, however, this binary division is overridden in favor of an arrangement into three parts: first, essays exploring *theories* of colonial and postcolonial terror; second, essays investigating *histories* of post/colonial terror; and, third, essays discussing the *generic forms* through which terror is articulated. What connects all the chapters, however, is this central question, approached from a number of different angles: What is postcolonial about present-day terror; or, put slightly differently, how is terror colonialist or neo-imperialist?

The collection opens with Achille Mbembe's essay, "The Colony: Its Guilty Secret and Its Accursed Share," which sets the keynote of the book, and of its first section on theory, by addressing the postcolony as a debased mirror of the colony, and as saturated with terror. Drawing on the political thought of Hegel, Fanon, Bataille, and others, Mbembe maps the postcolony, the social space left after colonial power has formally retreated, as a place of death, convulsed by trauma, governed by orgies of destruction and necromancy, whose history is mediated as psychic loss. The colony's base-line experience, or "accursed share," Mbembe writes, is the ubiquitous operation of terror, with which even fantasy life is complicit. In the postcolony, terror effects, far from being cauterized or exorcised, are repeated as the arbitrary rule of the leader, or displaced in the form of abjection. This means, however, that in Mbembe's terms the totalizing experience of death is a foundational space for African subjectivity. He who inflicts terror himself, having once been its victim, is the quintessential contested subject of the postcolony. The line of flight out of this situation, as is the case also in Robert Young's essay, lies in the resurrection of the dead through proper memorialization, and in the realization that some lost things can never be restored.

Derek Gregory in "Vanishing Points: Law, Violence, and Exception in the Global War Prison" continues the concern with the postcolony as the site where colonial terror is reiterated. The essay focuses in particular on the imagery and legal status of the war prisons in Abu Ghraib and Guantánamo Bay, 2001–6. With reference to Michel Foucault's work on biopower and governmentality, and Giorgio Agamben's on the state of exception, Gregory argues that the contemporary law of war lies at the vanishing point of international law. The space of the war prison is a space of exception produced through the law: it is therefore a space that is both inside and outside the law. Citing from documents that legitimated the practice of torture in Abu Ghraib and Guantánamo Bay, the chapter concludes with an examination of how the overtly imperial leader President George Bush acted both as a sovereign figure outside the law, and as a figure who rewrote international law.

In "Sacrificial Militancy and the Wars around Terror" Alex Houen is concerned with how opposed sides fighting in current wars of terror have become caught up in mutual exchanges of sacrifice. While various Islamic groups have increasingly used and defended so-called "suicide bombing" as a form of sacrificial martyrdom, the Bush administration has been forced to invoke "sacrifices" when justifying its continuing investment in the "war against terror." That is not to say that we are witnessing the growth of the same form of sacrifice universally – indeed, the wars of terror could be better described as wars concerning whose particular mode of sacrificial militancy is most powerful and legitimate. Nor can these various modes of sacrifice be seen as fundamentally religious, argues Houen, for sacrificial militancy has frequently been used to establish new intimacies for a community between its media, religion, politics, and economics. What makes a community's use of sacrifice particular is thus the social syntheses it produces, and Houen outlines how this has taken place differently in Iran, Palestine, Afghanistan, and the USA. Having made reference to a range of thinkers – including Talal Asad, Ali Shariati, Martin Heidegger, and Georges Bataille – the chapter closes by arguing that media depictions of sacrificial militancy frequently continue the work of sacrifice in reifying death and transcendence for public consumption.

Vron Ware's "The White Fear Factor" explores the links between the racial fears of the postcolonial Western world and the response of terror. The essay begins with a meditation on the contemporary image of a Stop sign in a Johannesburg neighborhood, on which "being afraid" is spray-painted. Drawing on the work of Zygmunt Bauman and Ghassan Hage, it proceeds to argue that terror has become a byword for various phenomena, such as the fear of asylum seekers and cultural strangers. Fueled by increasing economic inequalities, the solipsism and paranoia deriving from the "war on terror" threatens to obscure the connection in the West between postcolonial racism and the fear of the poor and dispossessed. Reflecting on these themes in the aftermath of Hurricane Katrina, the chapter turns to Forster's portrayal of the fragility of colonial order threatened by rumors of an assault on a white woman. It evokes the figure of Adela Quested in *A Passage to India* as a "young girl fresh from England," as it considers white fear of the other as a post/colonial legacy.

"Postcolonial Writing and Terror" is Elleke Boehmer's account of terror as that which is involved in the attempt by the dispossessed to clamber on to the tracks of modern history. Rounding off Part I of the book on theories of terror, the essay explores the interconnections between the act of terror and the experience of modernity, given that terrorism, in its incarnation as anarchism, and its manifestation as dynamite explosion, was born with the late nineteenth-century modern world. Drawing on Walter Benjamin and Achille Mbembe, Boehmer considers whether, far from being an irruption of the barbaric or primitive, the terroristic act in the once-colonized world represents a pressurized if not desperate attempt by marginalized groups to seize hold of the rights and privileges of modernity. Looking forward to Robert Young's essay in the section on "Genre," the essay further considers how postcolonial novels have plotted ways of moving beyond and/or reconciling the terroristic act. Though the moment of terror is incomprehensible to perception, yet writers come to terms with that moment through the temporal continuities and predictive, teleological patterns of story.

"Revolutionary Terrorism in British Bengal," Peter Heehs's meticulously historicized essay on terrorism in Bengal in the first decades of the twentieth century, represents an appropriate doorway into the second section of the book, in which terror events and developments invite historical contextualization. The "moment in and out of time" of the terror act is here described in relation to lead-ins and follow-ons, causes and consequences, narrative progressions and reiterations. By tracing the chronology of terror in British Bengal as a form of modern resistance to colonial rule – as distinct from pre-modern "traditional violence" in response to local grievances – Heehs presents violent resistance, operating alongside the broader non-violence movement, as an important factor behind the freedom struggle's success in India. Looking beneath the surface of standard histories of India's nationalist movement, the body of the essay examines the genesis, structure, and activities of Bengal's revolutionary terrorist societies.

Despite Bengal terrorism not being very effective or well organized, Heehs suggests that Bengal's propagators of terror did over the years succeed in applying an anti-colonial pressure complementary to that of the non-violence movement. He also points out that their approaches and techniques took path-breaking forms still recognizable in terrorism today (organized small-group activity, training programs, revolutionary propaganda).

Alex Tickell's "Excavating Histories of Terror: Thugs, Sovereignty, and the Colonial Sublime" maintains the focus on India by interpreting British nineteenth-century responses to Indian *thuggee* as precursors to counter-terroristic practices in the present day. The essay engages with David Rapoport's reading of the Indian ritual crime of *thuggee* as a form of early "religious terrorism," and traces the influence of Rapoport's historiography of terror in the burgeoning field of terrorism studies. It asks how postcolonial approaches might be used in a cross-disciplinary critique of the politicization of difference in terrorism studies, and suggests that the colonial anti-*thuggee* campaign of the 1830s should be analyzed, more accurately, as a nodal moment in the development of a modern terror-politics, which used fear, exceptional juridical powers, and the aesthetics of the sublime to consolidate colonial sovereignty in the subcontinent. Revisiting the primary texts of the anti-*thuggee* campaign, and reviewing developments in the historiographic scholarship on *thuggee*, Alex Tickell joins Vron Ware in arguing for a renewed postcolonial critical awareness of the connection between colonial anxiety (manifested in subjective instabilities such as mimicry, and a slippage between self and other) and the integral place of fear in a wider colonial politics of policing, repression, and counter-insurgency.

Stephen Morton in "Terrorism, Literature, and Sedition in Colonial India" extends the concern with form-giving terror events in the Indian subcontinent into an account of the representation in fiction of the organized terrorism of the early twentieth century, also described by Heehs, and, in particular, of state responses to it. The essay considers how Edmund Candler's novel *Siri Ram, Revolutionist* describes both terrorist attacks *and* sedition laws in British India after the planned 1905 partition of Bengal, looking in particular at how the revolutionary insurgent's political consciousness and commitment to the cause of national independence are represented. With reference to sedition trials, colonial police memoirs, and the 1918 Rowlatt Report, Morton probes the extent to which the figures of the terrorist and the sedition-monger entail a fictional refraction of the British Empire's counter-insurgency strategies in early twentieth-century India.

Shifting the focus to the Middle East, an often-cited locale of mediatized terror, and to the fine continuities between colonial terror and the terror of the present day, Bashir Abu-Manneh in "Israel in the US Empire" starts by examining how American support for Israeli colonialism has shaped the formation of Israel's cultural and political identity. The essay focuses on the work of several post-Zionist historians and sociologists in order to argue that much of this scholarship disavows Israel's role in Western imperialism and valorizes the United States as an ideal political model for Israel to emulate. Abu-Manneh then proceeds to argue that since 1967, US imperialism and Israeli colonialism have worked in tandem to produce both Israeli and American nationalist outcomes. By analyzing the dynamics, limitations, and major consequences of US support for Israel, the essay shows how ongoing American interests in the Middle East have become consistent with supporting the Jewish state and defending its colonialist objectives. In short, Israel has been crucial in the realization of the American Empire in the Arab world, and, conversely, Israeli dependency on American support has had a profound impact on its state ideology and society.

According to Ranka Primorac, Zimbabwe's "patriotic history" – its official state ideology of the new millennium – conforms to Achille Mbembe's theorization of a postcolonial "master fiction" as the attempt on the part of the post-independence state to create its own world of meaning, which then seeks to govern the production of all other social meaning. Her essay, "The Poetics of State Terror in Twenty-first-century Zimbabwe," is preoccupied with the ideological and generic properties of this postcolonial "master fiction" as it is expressed in Zimbabwe. She claims that in narrative terms this state fiction corresponds to an "adventure narrative of ordeal," an accumulation of distinct narrative segments with separate official designations, expressed in the form of both popular fictions and official histories. These teleological adventure fictions, inscribing a one-dimensional trajectory propelling the population from their once-free past to a newly liberated future (and eliding the sacrificial present), perform a powerful rationalizing function that is insidious and complex for all that it also appears transparent. It has, she argues, served to underpin the terror unleashed on Zimbabwean citizens in recent years, yet remains locked in a deadly opposition, a war of words with its imagined interlocutor – the national enemy, Europe, white people, the other within.

Stuart Price's thoroughgoing study of the Jean Charles de Menezes police shooting on the London Underground on July 21, 2005, "The Mediation of 'Terror': Authority, Journalism, and the Stockwell Shooting," examines British media representations of that event in the context of the failed bombing attempt on the capital's transport system and its subsequent media reportage. It explores how the mainstream media classified the event, based on the mobilization of established themes. It also argues that the national press was dependent upon authoritative sources, unaccountable centers of power that exist within Britain's contemporary surveillance society. In response to the challenges of an emergent meaning, or a meaning that has not yet been determined, such as the circumstances of the de Menezes shooting, the chapter explores how the press depended on official statements and unreliable eyewitness reports, treated as truthful because of their claim to authenticity.

For Robert Young in "Terror Effects," as also for Vron Ware in her essay, terror exists through its repetitive and transhistorical yet always shocking effects – anxiety, fear, extreme apprehension. Through its focus on the narrative genres of terror, which appropriately opens the book's third section, on Genre, Robert Young's essay tracks the operations of such terror effects in literature in so far as they gradate between world and self, the state and the psyche, the nation and the imagination, in a range of writers – Austen, Conrad, and Michael Ondaatje, amongst others. How real world and fantasy fold into one another through terror effects is demonstrated powerfully in Gothic novels such as Mary Shelley's *Frankenstein*, but also in the sublime, terror's "psychic intensification," as definitively described by Edmund Burke. Here the response of pure terror is not merely performed, but generated in the reader through that performance. By tracking the formal permutations of terror in the novel from the time of its pure embodiment as Gothic to the representation of terror as suspense and farce, Young asks whether such narrative mediations of terror allow us to move out of or beyond terror. Especially in worlds where terror seems ubiquitous (as in Sri Lanka, or Zimbabwe) how do we refuse its effects? In the postcolony – defined for Mbembe by the pervasiveness of terror – is there an alternative to arbitrary violence and the relentless infliction of trauma? To address this question Young turns to the terror-ridden context of Sri Lanka, as represented in Ondaatje's novel *Anil's Ghost*, where alternatives to terror are found in the always-still-dangerous commitment to non-violence, androgyny, and the post-human. Although for Young terror does not take a special form in the colonial context, colonial terror is a particularly virulent form of aestheticized state terror. Yet in the postcolony, he suggests, the locus of terror is further complicated by the use of violence against the state by its opponents as well as by the practice of state terror. It is this generalization of terror which, in Young's reading of Ondaatje, permeates the psychic as well as the political life of the postcolony and thwarts the possibility of a meaningful response to the causal logic of terror.

Further extending the focus on the terror-saturated context of Sri Lanka, Neluka Silva in her chapter "'Gendering' Terror: Representations of the Female 'Freedom Fighter' in Contemporary Sri Lankan Literature and Cultural Production" focuses on the representation of the female suicide bomber and women's participation in the insurgency struggle in Sri Lanka, in the play *The Forbidden Area* and in Sri Lankan television drama, pointing out how nationalist politics and religion collude. Silva addresses the extent to which the figures of the female suicide bomber and the female insurgent depart from essentialist assumptions about femininity, and, in so doing, her essay raises important questions about whether the female suicide bomber's act of death is (in the words of Neloufer de Mel) an act of victimhood or a sign of agency.

For Sujala Singh in "Terror, Spectacle, and the Secular State in Bombay Cinema," the tension between the abstraction that is "India" and the lived, non-straightforward, conflicted encounters of "becoming Indian," are evocatively played out within the melodramatic genre of popular Bombay cinema of the 1990s. Specifically, the essay looks at how the supposed secular ideal of nationhood is negotiated in two films that highlight perceived threats to such an ideal through the figure of the terrorist and in portrayals of fleeting glimpses of state terror: *Dil Se* (1998) and *Mission Kashmir* (2000). The primary question the chapter seeks to address is this: How does the genre of Bombay "masala" cinema, with its mix of romance, politics, tourism, and terrorism, deliver an account of contemporary terror through a vision of a secular-universalist nation-state at a time when the very foundations of a secular polity in India have been under threat? The terrorists in both films figure unsurprisingly as aberrations, estranged from normal social structures and existing outside of normative filmic codes of heterosexual romance and family values, and the essay examines whether and at what cost they are reintegrated into the bosom of the nation-state. Sujala Singh concludes by asking whether these films, in their striving toward a nationalist vision of India, expose secularism itself as a fragile concept, enshrined in the constitution but never fully realized.

Robert Eaglestone's " 'The age of reason was over . . . an age of fury was dawning': Contemporary Fiction and Terror" considers how a range of contemporary Anglophone novels have reflected the war on terror: Ian McEwan's *Saturday*, Salman Rushdie's *Shalimar the Clown*, and Jonathan Safran Foer's *Extremely Loud and Incredibly Close*, and, as a coda, Martin Amis's short story "The Last Days of Muhammad Atta." Each of these texts clearly engage with the mélange of anxiety and anger that make up the West's fuzzy understanding of the current crisis, with its multiple and interwoven arcs (the "War on Terror," 9/11, and the wars in Iraq and Afghanistan, bombings across the globe, and so on). Yet, as the essay proceeds to suggest, the novels, despite their many merits, fail to address precisely the issues to which they lay claim. Yet this failure does not mean that we should ignore them: it is exactly their failure that makes us aware of the limits of current Western understandings of the crisis, and, perhaps also, of the contemporary limits of the novel's form itself.

Emma Brodzinski's essay "Bodies of Terror: Performer and Witness" examines the ways in which trauma is registered in two theatrical responses to terrorist acts by Laurie Anderson and Walid Raad. Through an examination of these live art events, the chapter explores the compulsion to reiterate trauma; the complex negotiation of fear and pleasure that may be engendered; and the possibilities for healing, resolution, and social critique – for both artist and audience – which may result. The position of the essay at the close of *Terror and the Postcolonial* is therefore fitting. Beginning with a discussion of Laurie Anderson's post-9/11 performance *Happiness* (2002), Brodzinski argues that Anderson's refusal to use visual images and her foregrounding of the voice's materiality during her performance creates a space for the audience to process the trauma of the terrorist attacks. The chapter then turns to the New York-based Lebanese artist Walid Raad's performance *My Neck Is Thinner Than a Hair*, and examines how Raad's application of a theatrical methodology conveys the trauma of the constant car bomb onslaughts in Beirut that raged for 15 years during the Lebanese Civil War (1975–90). In conclusion the chapter argues that both performances represent personalized responses to terrorist activity, which use cathartic theater to process affective experiences.

Notes

1 The fact that Muntadar al-Zaidi was held in police custody and charged with assaulting a visiting head of state exemplifies the way in which such symbolic acts of subversion are contained.

2 One exception to such a tendency is the anthology *The Other Side of Terror: An Anthology of Writings on Terrorism in South Asia*, edited by Nivedita Majumdar (New Delhi: Oxford University Press, 2009).

3 In "The Essential Terrorist" Said also argued that the scholarship on terrorism is "brief, pithy, totally devoid of the scholarly armature of evidence, proof, argument" (p. 150).

References

Arendt, Hannah. (1970) *On Violence*. London: Allen Lane.

Attewill, Fred. (2008) "Car bombs were a 'taste of fear,'" *Metro* (November 13).

Bataille, Georges. (1990) "Hegel, Death and Sacrifice," *Yale French Studies* 78: 9–28.

Battersby, Christine. (2003) "Terror, Terrorism and the Sublime," *Postcolonial Studies* 6(1): 67–89.

Baudrillard, Jean. (2002) "L'Esprit du Terrorisme," *South Atlantic Quarterly* (Spring) 101(2): 403–15.

Boehmer, Elleke. (2000) *Bloodlines*. Cape Town: David Philip.

Boehmer, Elleke. (2005) "Postcolonial Terrorist: The Case of Nelson Mandela," *Parallax* 37: 46–55.

Boehmer, Elleke. (2007) "Postcolonial Writing and Terror," *Wasafiri* 22(2): 4–7.

Coetzee, J. M. (1980) *Waiting for the Barbarians*. London: Secker and Warburg.

Conrad, Joseph. ([1899] 1995) *Heart of Darkness*. Introduction by Robert Hampson. London: Penguin.

Eagleton, Terry. (2005) *Holy Terror*. Oxford: Oxford University Press.

Fanon, Frantz. (1968) "Concerning Violence," *The Wretched of the Earth*, trans. C. L. Markmann. New York: Grove Press, pp. 35–106.

Gibbons, Luke. (2002) *Edmund Burke and Ireland*. Cambridge: Cambridge University Press.

Gopal, Priyamvada, and Neil Lazarus. (2006) "Editorial," *New Formations* 59.

Hamid, Mohsin. (2007) *The Reluctant Fundamentalist*. London: Hamish Hamilton.

Hussain, Nasser. (2004) *The Jurisprudence of Emergency: Colonialism and the Rule of Law*. Ann Arbor: University of Michigan Press.

Loomba, Ania, Suvir Kaul, Matti Bunzl, Antoinette Burton, and Jed Esty, eds. (2005) *Postcolonial Studies and Beyond*. Durham, NC, and London: Duke University Press.

Ray, Gene. (2005) *Terror and the Sublime in Art and Critical Theory*. New York: Palgrave.

Said, Edward W. (1978) *Orientalism: Western Conceptions of the Orient*. London: Routledge and Kegan Paul.

Said, Edward. (1988) "The Essential Terrorist," *Blaming the Victims: Spurious Scholarship and the Palestinian Question*, edited by Edward W. Said and Christopher Hitchens. London: Verso, pp. 149–58.

Said, Edward W. (2002) "Punishment by Detail," *Al-Ahram*, August, 8–14, 2002. (Accessed March 19, 2009). http://weekly.ahram.org.eg/2002/598/op2.htm

Sen, Amartya. (2006) *Identity and Violence: The Illusion of Destiny*. New York: W. W. Norton & Co.

Sharpe, Jenny. (1993) *Allegories of Empire: The Figure of Woman in the Colonial Text*. Minneapolis: University of Minnesota Press.

Walter, Eugene Victor. (1969) *Terror and Resistance: A Study of Political Violence*. Oxford: Oxford University Press.

Žižek, Slavoj. (2002) "Welcome to the Desert of the Real!," *South Atlantic Quarterly* (Spring) 101(2): 385–9.

Žižek, Slavoj. (2008) *Violence: Six Sideways Reflections*. London: Profile.

Part I

Theories of Colonial and Postcolonial Terror

Chapter 1

The Colony: Its Guilty Secret and Its Accursed Share[1]

Achille Mbembe

The following essay distances itself, in many respects, from the preoccupations generally invoked in debates on memory, history, and forgetting (including colonial history). My concern is not to pinpoint the status of memory in historiographic operations and processes of knowledge in general, and I am even less concerned with unraveling relations between collective and individual memory. It has become evident that the distances (but also the connections) between memory as a sociocultural phenomenon and history as epistemology are complex, and the intersections between historical and mnemonic discourses are manifest.[2] By contrast, the concern here is to reflect upon ways of considering how *the colony* inscribes itself into the contemporary African imagination. This manner of defining the subject has obvious limits. African forms of mobilizing the memory of the colony vary according to the period, the stakes involved, and the precise situations evoked. As for the modes of representing the colonial experience itself, these range from active commemoration to forgetting, passing via nostalgia, fiction, and reappropriation, all diverse forms through which the past becomes instrumental in current social struggles – or, a more serious consequence, becomes used as a means to destroy the political connection altogether.[3]

Contrary to such instrumentalist readings of the colonial past, however, I will demonstrate that memory (just like recollections, nostalgia, or forgetting) is fundamentally composed of *psychic images*. This is the manner all these elements take, as they resurface in the representative field. These images are composed of absent objects, of formative, original experiences that occurred in the past – the image enabling the presence of absence. Therefore, what is important in memory, recollections, and forgetting, is not so much "truth," but rather gaps, "lies," erasures, and blackouts, things which cannot easily be articulated, slips and the failure to recall simple acts, all of which may be summed up as the reluctance to confess. As powerful representational complexes, memory, recollection, and forgetting are, strictly speaking, symptomatic acts. They only glean meaning through their relation to a secret. They thus emerge as the product of psychic work and the critique of time – which are two fundamental processes of the cure from the past.

I am, then, particularly interested in those aspects of the African remembrance of the colony which render the latter a place of loss. In canonical African texts (literature, philosophy, political essays, art, music, and cinema), the colony appears first and foremost as a place of loss, which, in turn, makes it possible to establish a debt between the ex-colonized subject and the ex-colonizer. Indeed, all this is not unrelated to the very nature of the colonial potentate and the manner in which he operated two levers which were, on the one hand, the functions of terror (the colony's accursed share) and on the other, the functions of fantasy (its guilty secret). Then again, representing the memory of the colony does not only require an engagement with psychic work and its losses; it also requires a critique of time and artifacts that claim to be the last substitutes for the very substance of time (statues, monuments, effigies). I will consider literature as an example of this African critique of time, one of the instances (alongside dance, music, celebrations, trance, and possession) when memory, imagination, and forgetting become entwined to such an extent that distinctions between the symbolic and the real, the individual and the collective, are abolished.[4] Finally, I will examine the connections between skulls (in statues, effigies, and colonial monuments which are found in many public squares in Africa today) and the question of the *proper name* (auto-recognition), which, as we know, occupies such a central place in modes of African self-writing.

Remembering the Potentate

In African self-writing, *the colony* is depicted as an original scene which does not merely occupy a space of remembrance, as if reflected in a mirror.[5] It is also represented as one of the significant matrices of language, operating on the past and the present, identity and death. It is pictured as an original body giving flesh and weight to subjectivity, and is not just remembered, but continues to inflect lived experience, viscerally, long after its formal disappearance.[6] In doing so, Africans grant it the attributes of an inaugural power, with its own *psyché*, the double of the living body, "a likeness which is taken to be the real body, which has its exact same appearance, the same clothing, gestures and voice,"[7] although it all the while participates in a shadow whose essence is effervescence – which only strengthens its morphogenous power.

If then, through their literature, music, religions, and cultural artifacts, Africans have developed a phenomenology of *the colony* which recalls, in many respects, what psychoanalysis terms "the mirror experience," is this not a direct result of the fact that this scene appears to play out both the confrontation between the colonized subject and his mirror image and the relation of imprisonment which binds his descendants to the horrific image and the demon of the alter ego in the mirror, his totem? More radically, in canonical African texts, the colony always appears as the scene where the ego was stripped of its tenor and replaced by a voice which has the peculiarity of being embodied through a sign which negates, revokes, inhibits, suspends, and removes any impulse of authenticity. In African discourse, this is the reason why remembering *the colony* almost always involves remembering a primordial decentering between ego and subject.

This original diffraction generally leads to the deduction that *the authentic ego appears to have been altered*. An unknown ego has assumed the place of the real ego, thus making the African, in spite of himself, the carrier of secret significations, obscure intentions, and something uncanny that unbeknown to him directs his existence, conferring a demonic aspect upon certain features of his psychic and political life. The West, it is then alleged, is entirely *guilty* for this internal fracture. The process of the psychoanalytic cure, from this point onwards, will aim to put an end to this psychic lesion. However, to escape from *that* (the colony as a figure of haunting and discordance) would demand that an original symbolic matrix be reinstated in the subject, capable of preventing the parceling out of the African body. Once this had been achieved, the former colonized subject could be born into a world that was his own in every respect, and the madness to which the mirror experience led, would, at last, be exorcised.[8]

It can hardly be surprising that such a central place has been accorded to *the colony* in discourses on the construction of the African "ego," or even that the colony has been selected as such a crucial experience in the accession to subjectivity. This can in part be attributed to the nature of the colonial potentate and also to the manner in which Africans undertake the critique of time. The case of the colonial potentate merits further consideration. In his lifetime, Frantz Fanon demonstrated that the colony should be considered as a power formation endowed with its own relatively specific sensorial life. In order to function, this power formation had to be connected to a fantasmatic device – without this, any repeat attempts at the original colonial act would have been doomed to failure. This archaic act – the *accursed share* of the colony – had its origins in sacrificial reason. In other words, the deep roots of the colony can be sought in the totalizing experience of death, even at the expense of life, which we recognize as being a major trait of European history, its social operations of production and accumulation, its composition into states, its wars, its religious and artistic productions.[9]

Fanon also emphasized that the life of the colony is not only made up of pulsations and tensions – a vigorous life, in a quasi-permanent state of erection – but also that the colonial potentate maintained power through two contradicting processes of logic, which, when placed together, had the effect of utterly canceling out any possibility of the emergence of an autonomous subject under colonial conditions. The first consisted of not accepting difference, in spite of appearances, and the second, of refusing similarities. In this respect, the colonial potentate was a narcissist.[10] Simultaneously desiring that the colonized subject resemble him, and at the same time forbidding this resemblance, the potentate rendered the colony the quintessential "anti-community," an "outside-place" [*hors-lieu*] where, paradoxically, division and separation represented the only manner of "living-together" [*être-avec*], and where the principal form of communication between colonial subjects and their masters (that is to say, violence) would without fail reiterate the sacrificial bonds in place and ratify the generalized exchange of death briefly alluded to above.[11]

If there is one domain in which all these paradoxes can most clearly be observed, it is, according to Fanon, in the link between medicine (*caring*) and colonialism (*wounding*).[12] The body which, at times, is enclosed, "stripped, shackled, forced to toil, beaten, deported, put to death" is the same which, at other times, is "cared for, educated, clothed, fed and paid."[13] In the colony, the subject receiving such care is the same who, elsewhere, is subjected to disfiguration.[14] Yet, within the processes of the cure, he is allocated the role of human detritus, mere scrap and residue, a deprived subject relentlessly wounded, because (or so the thinking goes) in the past he was literally dishonored, in the manner of the slave under the plantation regime.[15] The figure par excellence of vulnerability and stripped dignity, captured from time to time in snatched phrases describing a disparate and derisory humanity, he now only answers to abjection and to the same forms of misery to which he has been reduced.[16] As a consequence, instead of inspiring empathy, his suffering and his cries provoke nothing more than disgust. In this balance between caring and wounding there appears, in all its violence, the paradox of the "commandment," a grotesque and brutal power which aims to draw together the attributes of logic (*reason*), fantasy (*arbitrary*), and cruelty.[17] Whether it concerns acts of destruction (such as wars, massacres, and even genocides) or acts of self-preservation, the wrath directed at indigenous peoples or manifestations of power against them using objects and machines recall purely sexual activities, including sadistic forms (such as torture[18]), and the thrusting propulsions of the "commandment" are inseparable from the way in which the colonial potentate regards himself as a racial potentate, at war with other "races," as Hannah Arendt amongst others has described.[19]

The colonial potentate reproduces himself by constantly attacking the humanity of the colonial subject, multiplying the wounds on the colonized body and also assaulting his brain: "because it is a systematic negation of the other, a concerted effort to deny the other the slightest attribute of humanity, colonialism forces the cornered, dominated population to constantly ask themselves: 'what is my true nature?' " It is enough, says Fanon, "to study, to appreciate the number and the depth of the wounds inflicted upon a colonized subject during just one day spent under the colonial regime" to understand the magnitude of pathological tendencies this oppression produces.[20] Yet the colonized subject does not suffer from these "pathological tendencies" alone: the colonizer cannot escape them either. For one as for the other, the symbol henceforth contains "all the efficiency and the significance of the symbolized."[21] Moreover, "commanding" requires, above all, the ability to impose silence upon the indigenous people. His body, as Fanon so clearly recognized, must become his tomb. The "commandment" does not merely seek to cause prejudice in the name of "civilization." The commandment must go hand in hand with the will to humiliate the indigenous inhabitant, to insult him, to make him suffer, whilst gaining a certain satisfaction from this suffering and the pity or the disgust it will eventually cause. And if, in the end, it is necessary to take his life, his death must occur as deep down in the dirt as is possible.[22]

Yet, over and above this, too, the colonial potentate attempts to create an unsullied new world upon the debris of the one he first found there. He seeks to make the world he has found conform to a logic of his liking. Engaging in this task requires an enormous amount of affect and energy.[23] Whether the aim is to modify agricultural systems, to deal with concepts of money and value, to transform domestic structures, to clothe the colonized subject, or to care for the indigenous people, it may be summed up as the desire to transform the subject into a new "moral subject"; the colony finds no shame in its fantasies, and hardly seeks to conceal them.[24] And this is why the act of colonizing bears the traces of Dionysius. The heady combination of voluptuousness, frenzy and cruelty, intoxication and dreams which accompanies colonial deeds and gestures can only be understood in relation to that kind of enchantment which is, at the same time, agitation and tumult. Is it not also composed of the majority of those characteristics which Nietzsche believes he discerns in Greek tragedy?: "that phenomenon by which pleasure is stirred from pain itself, and jubilation draws forth the gasps of the torture victim," whilst "at the crescendo of joy, the cry of horror rings out, or a plea is made, consumed by desire, for an irreparable loss."[25] This "irreparable loss" is the feeling experienced by the colonized subject of a *disempowerment of the self* – the loss of the proper name which will in future accompany any recollection of this event. It is the motif of loss that, in African self-writing, is used to justify the inscription of the colony and its memory under the political sign of debt.

Parallel to this accursed share, whose origins lie in terror, the colony is a prodigious machine generating desires and fantasies. Seduction and terror are the resources skillfully managed and administered by the potentate. The administration of terror and the management of seduction are both carried out through a certain modulation of truth and lies, a certain rationing of emoluments and rewards, and the production of objects which are alternately moving or stupefying but always spectacular and ceremonial, which the stupefied colonized subject will struggle to forget.[26] In this respect, colonial domination requires an enormous investment of emotional expenditure. This emotional economy must inform everything that bears the stamp of life and death, abundance and plenitude, in short, *wealth*. The desire for wealth must worm its way entirely into the body of the colonized subject and take up residence in every nook and cranny of his psyche. Thus the potentate tries to force the indigenous subject to renounce the objects and desires to which he is attached, and to substitute new idols in their place, the law of new merchandise, the price of new values, a new order of truth.

However, he creates this new order in such a way that it glistens with the possibility of abundant material wealth. The touchstone of the potentate's fantasmatic lever is the idea that there is *no limit to riches and propriety, and thus no limit to desire*. This notion of an *imaginary with no symbolic* is the "guilty secret" of the colony and explains the power of the colonial potentate. It is also not inconceivable that the success of this "imaginary with no symbolic" may be explained by the fact that it has profound echoes with, and is anchored in, autochthonous symbolic categories. This applies to instances of excess and *doubling*, or to the existence of monstrous figures and ambivalent creatures, which, having assimilated the role of the fetish, transform into fearsome masters of the forces of dark and night, capable, for this very reason, of the Archimedean feat of raising the world. This also applies to the case of the tribal chiefs who go from drinking beer from the skulls of one of their predecessors one day, to being symbolically put to death through the intermediary of a substitute human victim the next, when, delivered of any tribal ties, they feel no need to affirm their sexual potency by having sexual relations with a sister or to marry a young niece from their own matrilineal family.

The fact that there is hardly any limit to desire can also be explained by the distribution of diverse categories of spirits, each corresponding to the logic of juxtaposition, permutation, and multiplicity. It is imperative, says Luc de Heusch, "to unite all of these fully or partially developed characteristics in the same symbolic structure, case by case: royal incest, anthropology, the assimilation of the king to a witch doctor, the interdicts which surround him, and even regicide," all aspects which "define a formidable magic power which undoes the border between culture – from which the chief becomes separated at the moment of his sacralization – and his vested power in nature as sovereign."[27] The same goes for the enchanted objects which are said to hold dangerous powers and which therefore function in the same way as the accursed share of royalty, because their secret is to participate in the "resurrection of things." Just like the Atlantic slave trade, colonization heralds the arrival of Africans in a new era characterized by the frenetic pace of desire and pleasure – irresponsible desire and mindless pleasure.[28] The colonized subject, like the slave trader before him, is fascinated and entranced by the idol which lurks behind the mirror, the vision of the mirror image of fabrics and loincloths, rum, guns and ironmongery, roads, monuments, railways, and hospitals. But to acquire these new goods, he must adopt a posture of unwavering servitude toward the potentate.

He must take up his place in a relation of debt – the debt of utter dependency upon his master. He must also force himself to adopt a pedagogic system intended to inculcate him with the passions of venality, vanity, and cupidity. As much pulses of inclination as they are deliberately cultivated pulses, vanity, venality, and cupidity constitute the three privileged manifestations of this position of servitude toward the master, and the cult of the potentate. A long detour will always be necessary, then, before these new material goods or even the promise of citizenship may be enjoyed, and the possibility of the fulfillment of new desires is always, without fail, postponed. This is the reason why the colony always contains a neurotic dimension as well as a ludic one, occasioned by unpredictable circumstances, a radical ambivalence whose importance has been underestimated by scores of analysts. Does it not cause the colonized subject to inhabit a world of dreams which, overnight, may be transformed into a nightmare? This dialectic of the dream that, at any moment, may veer into a nightmare is one of the driving forces of the potentate, but it is also his Achilles heel. In many respects, African nationalisms are the product of the conflict between these dreams and the frustration borne out of the impossibility of actually satisfying them.

If the colony does have a guilty secret, it is without doubt *the subjugation of the native by his own desire*. On the colonial stage, it is this subjugation by desire which, finally, renders the colonized subject "out of himself" [*hors de soi*], lured by the empty illusion of the image and witchcraft. In allowing himself to be led in this manner, he penetrates another being, and from then on he experiences his work, language, and life as so many processes of sorcery and willful disguise. It is precisely because of this experience of sorcery and estrangement that a profusion of fantasies originated from the colonial encounter. It stirred up desires which both the colonized and the colonizers had to conceal from themselves, and which, consequentially, for this very reason, were repressed and pushed into the unconscious.

Following on from this discussion, the memory of the colony in African literature inscribes it into a mythology of debt by emphasizing the losses Africa is believed to have suffered during the detour of this oppressive encounter. This debt has two supposed levels of operation, primarily as a debt of procreation (development; work not done), and secondly, as a debt of hospitality (immigration; relations not undertaken). In both cases, discourses on loss and debt aim to induce the effects of guilt. The African world that emerges from the colony is said to be a world of loss – a loss caused by murder. The culprit of this murder should be, then, not only wracked by guilt, but also indebted to those whose natural rights he has violated.

The colony's memory, then, assumes the allure of a *psychic work,* whose final objective is the cure. The cure consists, generally speaking, of bringing two types of secrets evoked by Freud in his *Inquiétante étrangeté* to a conscious level: those of which we are aware, but try to hide, and those of which we are not aware, because they do not reveal themselves directly to our consciousness. In the African (con)text, these two types of secret actually fuse into one. Beyond violence and cruelty, the colony's guilty secret is that, in the indigenous imaginary, the colony acts as a locus of enchantment. The African text refuses to admit that the enigma of a loss rooted in desire is the principal cause of the loss of the proper name. It is this enigma which explains the "gaping void" (Lacan) with which African self-writing is so concerned. It is this enigma which also notifies and ratifies loss. In these conditions, an authentic practice of the cure for Africans would consist of liberating them of this guilty secret, by recognizing "the other within" once and for all, and by considering this "detour of alterity" as the foundation stones of a new kind of self-knowledge – a knowledge which must be divided, *a knowledge of distanciation and its representation.* The fact that a considerable psychic burden continues to be attributed to the colony in processes of self-construction is, strictly speaking, a consequence of a reluctance to confess: both to the subjugation by desire of African peoples and to the fact that they have allowed themselves to be duped, seduced, and deceived by the "transparent manipulator of the imaginary mechanism,"[29] the colony.

The Critique of Time and the Aesthetics of Recollection

I have just observed that Africans recall the colonial potentate as a cause of original distress, yet at the same time, they refuse to confess the role of unconscious investments in the colony as a machine which generates desire. All this may probably be explained by the manner in which they draw on the critique of time. Indeed, what is time, and what should be understood by this category? In the penultimate chapter of his *Phénoménologie de la perception*, Merleau-Ponty speaks of it as what we encounter, inevitably, on the path which leads to subjectivity.[30] He further comments that time is "the most general character of psychic processes" – by this, we may understand two things: that on the one hand, an intimate connection exists between time and subjectivity, composed of a series of psychic events; and that on the other, time and the subject communicate from within – and that, therefore, to analyze time is to have access to the concrete and intimate structure of subjectivity.

Merleau-Ponty's comments on time could be easily extended to memory, and even to recollections, all the more so because memory and recollections are fundamental manifestations of the past (its traces, its remains and fragments) in the consciousness, whether the latter be rational consciousness or a dreamlike, oneiric consciousness. The following remarks are concerned with demonstrating how, by considering evidence beginning with the literary archive, it is possible to explain why the refusal to confess (as identified above) occurs. The discussion aims to identify the cognitive and expressive parameters with which the African critique of time is put in place and develops, in a general manner, the memory of the colony and by extension, of the potentate.

The fact that, in Africa, the languages of recollection largely rely on the critique of time is amply illustrated by the literary text. Everything in the African novel seems to indicate that, here, time is not a process that could simply be recorded in the form of a "succession of the now," for example. In other words, there is no time in itself. Time is born of a connection which is contingent, ambiguous, and contradictory and is established with objects, the world and even the body and anything identical to it (the double). Moreover, as Merleau-Ponty indicates, time (and the same goes for memory) is born of a certain way in which we view ourselves, others, the world, and all that is invisible. It is formed from a certain *presence*, which bonds each of these realities together.

The African novel also clearly demonstrates that time always has a connection with its doubles, illustrated by the fact that to participate in time is always, in part, to no longer know the drives of one's own ego. It entails the "doubling of the ego, the division of the self, the permutation of the ego."[31] In the writings of Amos Tutuola, Sony Labou Tansi, as well as Dambudzo Marechera, Yvonne Vera or even Yambo Ouologuem, time is experienced through attention to the senses (sight, hearing, touch, smell, taste). Memory and recollections actually trigger a whole organ structure, a whole nervous system, a whole economy of emotions at whose center the body, and all that which excites it, must be placed. These novels also demonstrate how recollections may be accessed through dance and music, or even through a game of masks, trance, and possession.[32] There is, therefore, no memory that, at a given moment, cannot find expression through the universe of sense, imagination, and multiplicity. So it is that in several African countries confronted by the drama of war, the memory of death is directly inscribed upon the wounded or mutilated body of the survivor, and it is from these bodies and their infirmities that the event is recalled and remembered. Through this coupling of imagination, memory, and the body, the understanding of time proceeds both semantically and pragmatically.

That said, the critique of time as it is presented in contemporary African fiction also teaches us that time is always uncertain and provisory. It changes permanently and its forms are constantly varying. It therefore always represents a heterogeneous, irregular, and fragmented region of human experience. This being the case, the relationship of the subject to time is a relationship which, if not aiming to evade both the past and the future, at the very least aims to liberate and subsume them.[33] This is not to imply, however, that the distinction between before and after, past and future, does not exist. The present, being the present, pulls in two directions, the past and the future – or, more radically, attempts to abolish both. This explains the literary predilection for a time which might be called paradoxal, because a true present tense can only be achieved through a total severance from both past and future.[34] It is a temporal state of differential durations, governed by two laws: time lag and simultaneity (co-occurrence). Consequently, the African novel always talks of time and its flux in the plural. Literary writing is therefore preoccupied with describing the transmutational processes of time, the very way in which time forms in layers.[35]

Yet memory and recollections only gain meaning in relation to the idea that time is actually a sort of *anti-chamber to reality*.[36] In this anti-chamber lie things which are unseen, unexpected, or, even more radically, "hidden possibilities," all kinds of potentialities which are both creative and destructive, an invisible and hidden world, which constitutes the true face of reality and without which this same reality may find no redemption.[37] This surface becomes the interface for the journey from reality to fantasy, from the wrong side to the right side,[38] for the conversion of one way of being into another.[39] In these conditions, remembering primarily becomes a means of distributing difference and bringing about a *doubling*, precisely because there is always an essential *time lag* between the connections of the various temporal unities to the event.[40]

However, the event does not simply happen. Once again, it is necessary to be able to decode and express it – whence the importance of divinatory procedures.[41] But how may an "event" be expressed, without recourse to a general association of words and images, certain words serving as empty forms which are filled with images, and others only owing their existence to being vehicles for signs – to which, however, they must not merely be reduced? The recollection, therefore, exists solely as an intersection between an event, words, signs, and images. This intersection can then lead to rituals. The nigh impossibility of disassociating words, signs, and images not only allows the event to be expressed, but, more radically, allows it to be revealed, as an epiphany.[42] When invoking these processes of recollection, the psychoanalytic cure allows images to vary and be substituted and interchanged. Following this method, an extremely complex relation is established between the meaning/the significance and the designation, or rather what I would term the manifestation.

As for the subject who remembers, they inevitably become a contested subject. This contestation arises from an inaugural event: the loss of the proper name. This loss is rendered all the more traumatic because it is accompanied by a profound destabilizing of knowledge, a destruction of common meaning, and a radical uncertainty concerning the ego, time, the world, and language. This state of radical uncertainty – unpredictability – forms the objective structure of the very event, but also informs its narration and the way it is related. It renders any attempts to establish a fixed identity impossible. In African novels, it partially explains the very close relationship between the loss of the proper name (the destruction of a measure) and the descent into madness, the trigger for a life plagued by convulsions, or even resulting in suicide.[43]

In this context, remembering always requires an operation that transcends the limits of core linguistic capabilities.[44] So we see that authors adopt many simultaneous languages of time, even of the body, in that, as is the case in Tutuola, each body always penetrates another and coexists with it, if not in its entirety, at least in its essential regions.[45] Yet this mode of remembering is actually little more than a stutter, when what is needed is a discourse – a discourse on identity or the events of the past. The same type of process occurs when attempting to recall the postcolonial potentate, that resplendent manifestation of a time with neither past nor future, or even of a failed time, whose meaning, despite constant resuscitative attempts, only emerges through psychic cracks and dispelled fears.[46]

An example taken from the first chapter of *La Polka* by Kossi Efoui illustrates this point. The novel opens with the seated narrator describing his view of a quiet road. Before we are even aware of the narrator's name, his senses are invoked: in this precise example, it is sight which is privileged. But what is it that is seen, apart from a pile of ruins, "sections of collapsed walls, their doors and windows stripped bare by fire" (p. 9)? From these objects emerges the theme of ruin – the temporality of ruin and destruction. Time reveals itself through its capacity to leave traces of a primordial event – a destructive event, whose major signifier is fire. Time is then experienced and seen and read in the landscape. Before memories are formed, there is sight. To remember is literally to see the physical traces left upon *a place's body* by the events of the past.

However, no *place's body* is completely unconnected to the human body. Life itself must be "embodied" in order to be recognized as reality. The novelist pays particular attention to the face and form of the human body, emphasizing that they have been redrawn "by a certain brutality introduced into their gaze." He is careful to mention the bodies and faces of women, men, and animals in the same sentence, all rendered identical in their immobility, caused by one event whose irruption was signified by brutality. The distinction between species and genders thus becomes blurred. This shared appearance, this resemblance, will henceforth link them together. The face itself closely resembles the mask: "men and animals alike share the same dazed mask" (p. 9).

I have already outlined how sight may precede naming. In fact, sight and naming respond to each other through echo. The act of naming revives the gaze, and vice versa. One cannot exist without the other, and both link back to the voice, the gesture, and finally to life itself. Subsequently, the time of ruin is, according to the novelist, the moment when the "gestures of life are no longer followed by the gaze" (p. 10). This is when bodies stiffen and the voice, its timbre and rhythm, becomes ever changing. It goes from quivering, to harsh and rasping. At times, it is even "asthmatic." It can then be observed that "after a time, each word [emitted by the voice] is a false emission," as from now on, the voice is "without meaning," severed in two (p. 11). As speech no longer knows "how to catch up with, or seize hold of, the current moment" – in other words, time is no longer tangible – time must take refuge "in the troubled movement between before, after and return." Time resides "beyond the words of life" (p. 12). It might be added that the event itself is constructed of time placed beyond the words of life.

In the novel *La Polka*, the body is a site of memory par excellence. At times, the body appears not to belong to anyone in particular. It belongs to what we might call the *many*. This is a common scene in bars after dark, when men seek the anonymous debauchery of alcohol and girls: "The whores come and go, flirtatiously twirling around each man in turn – how much for this ass?" (p. 38). Amongst the heat of bodies and the stifling air "there are those who grope . . . those who pinch . . . the sailors who suggestively slap and then those who are just there to watch" (p. 38). And, reigning supreme, there is the female body: "the girls know how to channel their energy to each part of the body as required. First a smile, then they jiggle their breasts . . . Then they start again, smiling, catching an interested eye – how much for this ass? The gaze, as soon as it is caught, wanders towards the buttocks. The girl extinguishes her smile and it is her legs that now do the work" (p. 38). It is as though everything inevitably comes down to generalized copulation (pp. 54, 111).

In *La Polka*, the body is predisposed to disguise and display. This is how it gains much of its beauty: floral headdresses, long gloves laced with ribbons, all kinds of decorations – pearls strung around the girls' bare necks, golden bells wrapped around the dancing musicians' ankles. Yet such ceremony is never far removed from death. On top of a hearse of woven palm ribs stands one of "the living-dead, dressed all in white, motionless." It is the carnival mascot (p. 58). But a constant risk hangs over the body of the crowd. It is the risk of being reduced to nothing more than bodies which are "emaciated and stumbling, which no garment will ever again flatter" (p. 58). Even more dangerously, they are condemned to move outside time and even outside themselves:

> the night was spent fighting against the stricken impulses of our internal organs inside our bodies: stomachs overcome, now feeling nothing where once they had known pangs of hunger and thirst, tongues lolled back towards the glottis, arms hanging limp at our sides, shoulders sloping and fearful eyes in the back of our heads. Suddenly, mouths are flung open, wide open, not to utter a cry but in anticipation of a burp, a stream of vomited intestines or a brutal ejection, bone after bone, as the entire carpentry of the body is wrenched out. Bone after bone, long

> bones, short bones, flat bones, bones that seem deceptively round or knobbly, all are flung through this gaping mouth in a rosary of vertebrae, until the flaccid skin caves in, turns inside out and falls slack. The body is in suspense, in free-fall, on epilepsy alert. (p. 59)

In *La Polka,* this gigantesque corporeal shudder is not unrelated to dying or even bereavement. The problem, according to the novelist, is that memories do not necessarily arise from death: "how can these impressions of death around us help us to generate memories? Each death reduces the memory of names, as if all those lives were classified cases" (p. 64). From now on, "the dazed mask is donned whenever everything fades away, until all that is left is the hint of an ultimate image which searches for a place somewhere between before and after" (p. 65). Time may also rebel, refusing to run out and conspiring to catch us in its trap.

Process of the Cure; Question of the Proper Noun

Statues, effigies, and colonial monuments all play on this very function – the trap. In spite of their differences, they are all linked back to three names. And strictly speaking, they are all objects. They are constructed of any number of materials: marble, granite, bronze, steel and so on. Considered as objects, they are inert blocks, looming down on a fixed point, apparently mute. On the whole, these objects depict the form of a human body or beast (such as a horse carrying a conqueror). They represent the dead. Through them, death becomes an object, a skilled work. Finally, these dead were, at a given moment in their lives, subjects, and it is this element that the statues seek to convey. There are hardly any statues that fail to demonstrate this fusion of objectality, subjectivity, and mortality. What is more, there are hardly any statues that do not seek to turn back time. Colonial statues and effigies testify, almost without exception, to this mute genealogy, through which the subject is projected beyond death, which, in turn, is projected beyond the object intended to both occupy the place of the subject, and the place of death, at the same time.

Alongside these designated statues are other objects, monuments, and infrastructures: railway stations, colonial governors' palaces, bridges, military camps, and fortresses. In the French colonial empire, most of these works date from the twentieth century, that is to say, from the postwar period. In purely aesthetic terms, this was a time when, beyond the emergence of secularization, art's mission was still conceived in a para-religious mode. Art must be used to heal the West of its unhappy memories and its new fears, or so the belief ran.[47] It thus participates in a heroic narrative. It must call upon dormant powers whilst simultaneously reintroducing, in its own way, a type of celebration and showiness. In the colonies, this celebration took a savage turn. These creations and other infrastructures (palaces, museums, bridges, monuments, and so forth) are not only new kinds of fetishes. Often, their creation required the profanation of sepulchers. The skulls of deceased kings had to be displayed, their coffins dismantled. All treasures which accompanied the bodies were removed from the sepulchers (jewels, piasters, chains, and so on) before the pillaged funereal objects could be displayed in museums.[48] This turning of the dead, or ransacking, was intended to induce a trance-like state in the colonized subjects, obliging them, from then on, to celebrate a "Godless sacrifice." The symbolic economy of the colony then becomes, in this context, a grand economy of giving without receiving. A kind of exchange takes place around these works and these infrastructures which arises from sumptuary loss. Objects considered as non-exchangeable (bridges, museums, palaces, infrastructures) are yielded to the indigenous peoples by a brutal authority, during a process of savage celebration where body and substance become entwined.

It is therefore vital to connect these multiple significations of colonial statues and monuments – which are still the centerpieces of African public squares, long after declarations of independence have been made – with structures of power and domination. The *remains* of the potentate, they are signs of the physical and symbolic struggle which the colonial power was forced to lead against the colonized subject. It is known that a long-lasting domination must not only inscribe itself onto the bodies of its subjects, but must also leave its marks upon the space they inhabit, as well as leaving indelible traces in their imaginary. This domination must envelop the subjugated people and hold them in a more or less permanent state of trance, intoxication, and convulsion – incapable of thinking for themselves with any perspicacity. This is the kind of domination that it took to bring them to think, act, and behave as though they were perpetually caught in an unbreakable spell. It follows, then, that subjugation must be written into the very fabric of everyday life, as well as into the structures of the unconscious. The potentate must inhabit the subject, to the extent that the latter can never truly exercise his powers of sight, hearing, feeling, touch, movement, speech, travel, imagination; he cannot even dream unless it is in reference to the master signifier who forever looms over him, forcing him to stutter and stagger.[49]

The colonial potentate will not deviate from this rule. At every stage of his everyday life, the colonized subject was constrained by a series of submissive rituals, each more prosaic than the last. For example, he could be ordered to quake, to cry, and to tremble, to prostrate himself, shivering, in the dust, to go from place to place, singing, dancing, and experiencing his domination as a providential necessity. This was indeed the case during the inauguration of various monuments, the unveiling of commemorative plaques, during anniversaries and other celebrations which united colonizers and colonized.[50] This negative consciousness (of not being anything without the master, of owing everything to the master, who sometimes assumed a parental role) must exercise its influence upon every moment of his life, liberating it of any trace of free will.[51] It is evident, then, that in this context, colonial statues and monuments were not meant to be aesthetic artifacts designed to embellish towns or the everyday condition in general. The whole undertaking was designed, from start to finish, to provide manifestations of despotic absolutism, whose basis was already discernible in the way in which colonial wars, wars of "pacification," were waged, or even in the way in which armed kidnappings were countered.[52] These powers of transvestism were the sculptural extension of a form of racial terror.[53] At the same time, they were a spectacular expression of the powers of destruction and suppression, which, from its conception to its fall, drove the colonial enterprise.

But, above all, no domination can exist without a kind of *cult of spirits* – in this case the hound-spirit, the hog-spirit, the rabble-spirit,[54] and so on, so characteristic of all imperialism, past and present. In turn, this cult of spirits requires, from start to finish, a manner of evoking the dead – a necromancy and a geomancy. In this respect, statues and colonial monuments truly belong to this double universe of necromancy and geomancy. They constitute, strictly speaking, the characteristic emphases of this hound-spirit, this hog-spirit, this rabble-spirit which drove colonial racism as well as colonial power – and all that followed it: the *postcolony*. They are the shadow or the graph which outlines its profile in a space (African space) that can never be violated or despised too greatly.

For, given these faces of "death without resurrection," it is easy to understand what the colonial potentate was: a typically *funereal* power, so often reifying the deaths of the colonized and denying their lives any shred of value.[55] The majority of these statues depict the ancient dead who fell in wars of colonial conquest, occupation, and "pacification" – the evil dead, elevated through vain pagan beliefs into protective divinities. The ongoing presence of the evil dead in public places ensures that the principles of murder and cruelty which they personified will continue to haunt the memory of the formerly colonized people, saturating their imaginary and their everyday places, causing within them a bizarre eclipse of consciousness, and preventing them, ipso facto, from thinking with any perspicacity. The role of statues and colonial monuments is, then, to resurrect the dead, who, during their lives, tormented African existences, often with a double-edged sword. These statues function as rites, evoking the very dead who had regarded African humanity as worthless – and for this reason, they had not the slightest scruple about the wanton spilling of African blood.

If it is true, as Hegel suggests, that each statue is inhabited by a god,[56] which divinity do the colonial statues of Africa celebrate, if not the one who declared that going to war with "inferior races" was necessary for the advancement of "civilization"? Instead of stripping away animal connotations, statues of humans actually attempt to preserve a belief which refuses to die. The fact that so many of these monuments are dedicated to the glory of soldiers and the military indicates the extent to which the colonial unconscious has grown accustomed to massacres. These monuments of death convey it all: the celebration of a foreign nationalism, fearsome and all-conquering; the celebration of conservative values inherited from the anti-Enlightenment and most emphatically put into place in the colonies, the privileged sites of experimentation, before they once again came to prominence under Nazism, fascism, and communism; the celebration of the ideologies of inequality which were spawned by social Darwinism.

It is a testimony to the power of the secret I have evoked above that these masks of terror, made-up to resemble human faces, continue, as I have said, to occupy a central space in African towns, and despite the fact that no sepulcher worthy of that name exists for the numerous oppressed Africans throughout history. For, in practice, nothing in the attitude of postcolonial African nationalisms was simple or univocal where the relics of colonialism were concerned. Numerous colonial myths have been adapted and interiorized into apparently autochthonous cults and rituals. By contrast, during the mass of conflicts linked to decolonization or even favored during the political struggles experienced by some countries in the 1970s and 1980s, a certain number of countries tried to liberate themselves of the symbols of

European domination and to imagine other modes of organizing their public space. The first step in clearly delineating their new status within humanity was to abandon the very names they had been dressed up in during the time of conquest and occupation.

The idea was that, finally, starting with their names, they would once again possess not only themselves, but also by extension the world, which had for so long dispossessed them. Along the way, they renewed ties of continuity with a past history that the colonial parenthesis had interrupted. In granting the former colonial entity of the Gold Coast the new name of Ghana (the former West African empire), or again, by changing from Rhodesia to Zimbabwe, and Haute Volta to Burkina Faso, African nationalism sought above all to regain mastery over itself and the world and, along the way, to catalyze the coming of a "god" hidden amongst us. But we also know that this concern with the "proper noun" is not unambiguous. For reasons that are more or less apparent, Dahomey (the name of a former slave kingdom on the West African coast), became Benin. Other countries sought to redesign their urban landscapes by rebaptizing some of their towns. Salisbury became Harare in Zimbabwe. Maputo was substituted for Lourenço Marques in Mozambique. Leopoldville became Kinshasa. Fort Lamy changed to Ndjamena, whilst Fort Fourreau became Kousseri, and so on. Generally speaking, however, the great architectural landmarks of the colonial period were preserved. So it is that today, it is possible to take a stroll along Lumumba Avenue in Maputo whilst admiring, along the way, the buildings bordering the avenue which are the essence of Art Deco transplanted by the Portuguese to their colony. The Catholic cathedral is, for its part, the indication of a religious acculturation which did nothing to prevent the emergence of a pronounced cultural syncretism. And so it is that in Maputo, Karl Marx, Mao Tse-tung, and Lenin cohabit with Nyerere, Nkrumah, and other prophets of black liberation. Whenever the revocation of colonial signs has occurred, it has always been a highly selective process.

It is in the ex-Belgian Congo that the embeddedness of colonial and nationalist forms has perhaps reached the highest degree of ambiguity. Here, "nativism" assumed the place of racist logic, and in doing so it restored the major idioms of colonial discourse and ordered them in accordance with the same symbolic economy as before: the mortifying adoration of the potentate – only now, the potentate was postcolonial. Under the pretext of authenticity, the country was dressed up with a new name, Zaire. Paradoxically, the origins of this name were not to be found in any ancestral tradition, but were rather due to the Portuguese presence in the region. Then, in order to penetrate the oneiric universe of his subjects and be able to torture them more absolutely, the postcolonial potentate decided, just like the *Bula Matari* (the colonial state) before him, that he must be represented in stone and marble. Yet the lay cult bestowed upon the autocrat not only took the form of enormous statues, mighty and grotesque, wrought in cruel metal. It also required an entire emotional economy to be set up, a mixture of seduction and terror, modulating at its will the virile and the amorphous, the true and the false, using the eye and the ear as one would use orifices whose function is to viscerally open up the whole body to the discourse of an "African potentate," who is also, just like the colonial potentate, inhabited by the hound-spirit, the hog-spirit, the rabble-spirit.

South Africa presents another configuration, a mixture of innovations and inertia, in a country where, not long ago, the last state-enforced system of racism since World War II was still thriving. Since the end of white supremacy in 1994, the official names of rivers, mountains, valleys, townships, and large cities have hardly changed. The same goes for public squares, boulevards, and avenues. Even today, it is possible to head to the office via Verwoerd Avenue (named after the architect of apartheid), to dine in a restaurant situated on John Vorster Boulevard, drive along Louis Botha Avenue and attend mass in a church situated at the corner of two roads, each named after some shady character of the iron years of the racist regime. Pompously mounted on enormous horses, the sinister and reddening army of Pretorius, Kruger, Cecil Rhodes, Lord Kitchener, Malan, and others has a number of statues deployed on the principal squares of large towns. Perched atop one of the hills of the capital, Pretoria, is the Voortrekker Monument, a kind of cenotaph, as baroque as it is grandiose, erected to the glory of Boer tribalism and celebrating the marriage of the Bible and racism.

It would seem that there is not a single petty white adventurer, whether a gold or diamond seeker, a pirate, torturer, hunter, ex-employee of the Bantu administration, or ex-prison governor who does not have an alley named in his honor in one or another of the country's towns. All of these truly despicable and shifty individuals, who during their lifetimes unfailingly veered toward all that is low and abject (racism), can to this very day be found throughout the country, littered across its surface, like errant souls and disappointed shadows which history has rejected. They have all left traces here, either on the African bodies which they visited through burns or flagellations (an eye torn out here, a leg broken there, in mutilations, repressions, incarcerations, torture, and massacres), or in the memories of the widows and orphans who survived such violence and brutality. From the country's toponymy, the names of towns and numerous townships, streams and rivers, lakes, parks, and mountains, it would be quite plausible to believe you were somewhere in some forgotten corner of Holland, England, or deepest Germany, rather than in Africa. And what is worse, certain other names are literally constructed of insults directed at the original inhabitants of the country (Boesman-this, Hottentot-that, Kaffir-so-and-so). The long humiliation of black people, and their invisibility, is still traced upon the surface of this territory in golden letters, even if it is not visible in certain museums.

Paradoxically, the fact that these former colonial landmarks have been kept does not mean that the symbolic landscape of South Africa has been void of transformation. In actual fact, the decision to keep these colonial names has gone hand in hand with one of the most remarkable contemporary experiments concerning the processes of memory and reconciliation. Of all the African countries, South Africa is the one leading the most systematic reflections on the relationships between memory and forgetting – truth, reconciliation with the past, and reparation. The idea here is not necessarily to destroy monuments whose former purpose was to diminish the humanity of others, but to acknowledge the past as a base, from which a new and different future can be created. This supposes that the executioners, who, in the past, were blind to the terrible suffering they had inflected upon their victims, will today undertake to tell the truth about what happened – and thus will unambiguously renounce dissimulation, repression, or denial, in return for forgiveness. Yet this also requires the "victims" to accept the fact that reaffirmation of the power of life, in both day-to-day activities and in the organization of institutions and power, is the best method of celebrating victory over an unjust and cruel past.

Here lies the significance of other processes of memorialization which are currently being carried out. So we see the appropriate shrouding of the bones of those who fell in the struggle; the erection of funeral steles marking the very places where they fell; the consecration of religious and therapeutic rituals destined to "heal" survivors of anger and the desire for vengeance; the creation of numerous museums (Museum of Apartheid, Hector Peterson Museum) and parks destined to celebrate a common humanity (Freedom Park); the flourishing of the arts (music, fiction, biographies, poetry); the promotion of new architectural forms (Constitution Hill); and, first and foremost, great efforts to put one of the most liberal constitutions in the world into practice in everyday life.

The case of the Cameroon could have been added to those already mentioned. Gripped by an orgyesque commotion for over a quarter of a century, this country represents, for its part, the *anti-model* of the relationship of a community to its trespasses, and particularly to the people whose deaths were the result of the very act of attempting to create history. For here, a temporal consciousness is the absolute last concern of the state, and indeed of society itself. Still suffering from the acute need to survive, as well as from the mines of corruption and venality, many people in Cameroon do not realize that this temporal and historical consciousness is a fundamental characteristic of our humanity. They do not see that a country which "doesn't give a damn" about its dead cannot sustain a politics of life. It can only promote a mutilated life – a life on borrowed time.

Conclusion

The memory of colonization is hardly a happy one. But contrary to a tradition anchored in Africa's consciousness of victimization, destruction was not the only thing to arise from the colonial *œuvre*. Colonization itself was far from being an infernal machine. It is evident that, from beginning to end, it was shot through with lines of flight. The colonial regime dedicated most of its energies either to attempting to control these flights, or to using them as a constitutive dimension, even a decisive dimension, of its auto-regulation. It is impossible to understand anything about the way in which the colonial potentate was placed in power, how he became contorted, how he was partially destroyed or metamorphosed into something else, without recognizing these flights as the quintessential forms conflict assumed.

The colony was a place of terror and horror – this goes without saying. And the losses suffered by African societies due to this encounter with the West are, in most cases, immeasurable – this, too, is an evident truth. The fact that the majority of these losses are irremediable only heightens the tragedy of their history. There are objects, and also figures and values, which can no longer be recovered, and Africans must, henceforth, live in these conditions – these truths occupy a large part of the reality of the situation. The question, today, is of knowing how to recognize sites where the memory of that phenomenon which, in essence, represented a mixture of terror, desire, and fear, may be constructed.[57] As we have seen in South Africa, this begins through a meditation on the ways of transforming the physical absence of those who were lost, returned to dust by the sun of trespass, into an interior presence. To remember the colony, then, is to meditate upon this absence and thus to allow the theme of the sepulcher its full force, recognizing it as a supplement to life which is essential for the resurrection of the dead, at the intersection of poetics and politics.

Translated by Louise Hardwick

Notes

1 Translator's note: the title makes reference to Georges Bataille, "The Accursed Share" [*La part maudite précédé de La notion de dépense*] (Paris: Éditions de Minuit, 1967). All translations of secondary sources are my own.
2 For discussion of these kinds of issues, see Ricoeur (2000). In the African case in particular, see Jewsiewicki (1988), and also Jewsiewicki (1993).
3 Chrétien and Triaud (1999); Cole (2001); Ranger (2005).
4 Rouget (1990); de Heusch (2006: ch. 1); Bastide (1972).
5 Khanna (2003).
6 Mbembe (2000a).
7 Vernant (1990: 29).
8 On this subject, F. Eboussi Boulaga speaks of "the reconciliation which the Muntu seeks" – a manner of indicating "agreement with himself," "the design of living with oneself and for oneself through meditation on having and doing," "the courage of being, doing and creating oneself." He recognizes that this quest "is not the dream of a paradise lost, the pursuit of a fantasy, of a compact or monolithic unity," but the ability to live amongst the world's diversity; Boulaga (1979: 229).
9 See Bataille (1967); Arendt (1964), in particular the chapter on "race and buraucracy"; Junger (1990); Levinas (1997).
10 Rosolato (1987: 30).
11 Fanon expresses this impossibility of "community" in the following manner: "Colonialism is not a thinking machine or a body with the gift of reasoning. It is violence towards nature, and can only bow before greater violence." He also comments: "for the colonized subject, life can only surge forth from the decomposing corpse of the colonizer" in Fanon (1961: ch. 1).
12 Fanon (1961: ch. 5); Fanon (1959: ch. 4).
13 Bayart (2005: 208); Vergès (2001).
14 Fanon (1952).

15 Hartman (1997); Savitt (2002).
16 Vaughan (1990); Hunt (1999).
17 Mbembe (2000b: ch. 4).
18 Alleg (1958).
19 Arendt (1964); see in particular the chapter on "race and bureaucracy." See also Grandmaison (2005).
20 Fanon (1961: 240).
21 Freud (1985: 251).
22 See, for example, the account of the assassination of the Cameroon nationalist leader Ruben Um Nyobè, and the profanation of his corpse, in Mbembe (1986: 13–17). See also De Witte (2000: 223–78).
23 See, for example, de Arriaga (1968).
24 On colonization as an experience of subjectivation, see Bayart (2005: 197–250). See also Comaroff and Comaroff (1997: chs. 3–8 in particular).
25 Nietzsche (1977: 34).
26 Oyono (1960); Beti (1974).
27 See de Heusch (1986), particularly the chapter discussing the "roi sur la scène sacrificielle." See also de Heusch (2000).
28 Miller (1988).
29 An expression used by Gérard Guillerault: see Guillerault (2003: 142).
30 Merleau-Ponty (1945: 469).
31 Freud (1985: 236).
32 Amongst the other vectors of memory, Catherine Coquery-Vidrovitch includes sacred woods, the tombs of Muslim saints, mosques, and even certain masks and dances. See Coquery-Vidrovitch (1999: 378–9).
33 Tchak (2001).
34 Kourouma (1998).
35 Tutuola (2000).
36 See in particular Tansi (1981a); Tansi (1988); as well as Tansi (1981b) and (1995).
37 Couto (1996).
38 Translator's note: an echo of Camus's *De l'envers à l'endroit*.
39 Tansi (1983).
40 Tutuola (2004).
41 Kourouma (2000).
42 Tansi (1985).
43 Kane (1961).
44 See, for example, Vera (2002), and also Tansi (1995); Tansi (1997).
45 Mbembe (2003).
46 Mabanckou (2005).
47 Dorléac (2004).
48 Nativel and Raison-Jourde (1999) in Jean-Pierre Chrétien and Jean-Louis Triaud's *Histoire d'Afrique. Les enjeux de mémoire*. In the same collection, see also Odile Goerg (1999a).

49 Mbembe (1996a).
50 Goerg (1999: 201–7).
51 Mbembe (1996b).
52 Pélissier (1978); Pélissier (1979); Pélissier (2004); Anderson (2005).
53 For a theorization of this terror, see de Tocqueville (1988).
54 Translator's note: the original French term operates on a further, untranslatable, level of meaning, also signifying mischievousness.
55 Hussain (2003); Barkat (2005).
56 Hegel (1991).
57 Taussig (1986).

References

Alleg, H. (1958) *La Question*. Paris: Éditions de Minuit.

Anderson, David. (2005) *Histories of the Hanged. The Dirty War in Kenya and the End of the Empire*. New York: Norton.

Arendt, Hannah. (1964) *The Origins of Totalitarianism*. New York: Harcourt Brace and Jovanovich.

de Arriaga, Pablo José. (1968) *The Extirpation of Idolatry in Peru*. Lexington: University of Kentucky Press.

Barkat, Sidi Mohammed. (2005) *Le corps d'exception. Les artifices du pouvoir colonial et la destruction de la vie*. Paris: Editions d'Amsterdam.

Bastide, Roger. (1972) *Le rêve, la transe et la folie*. Paris: Flammarion.

Bataille, Georges. (1967) "The Accursed Share" [*La part maudite précédé de La notion de dépense*]. Paris: Éditions de Minuit.

Bayart, Jean-François. (2005) *Le gouvernement du monde. Une critique politique de la globalization*. Paris: Fayard.

Beti, Mongo. (1974) *Perpétue et l'habitude du Malheur*. Paris: Buchet/Chastel.

Boulaga, F. Eboussi. (1979) *La crise du Muntu. Authenticité africaine et philosophie*. Paris: Présence africaine.

Camus, Albert. (1986 [1937]) *De l'envers à l'endroit*. Paris: Gallimard.

Chrétien, Jean-Pierre and Jean-Louis Triaud, eds. (1999) *Histoire d'Afrique. Les enjeux de la mémoire*. Paris: Karthala.

Cole, Jennifer. (2001) *Forget Colonialism? Sacrifice and the Art of Memory in Madagascar*. Berkeley: University of California Press.

Comaroff, John L. and Jean Comaroff. (1997) *Of Revelation and Revolution. The Dialectics of Modernity on a South African Frontier*, Volume 2. Chicago: Chicago University Press.

Coquery-Vidrovitch, Catherine. (1999) "Lieux de mémoire et occidentalisation," in Jean-Pierre Chrétien and Jean-Louis Triaud (eds.), *Histoire d'Afrique. Les enjeux de mémoire*, pp. 378–9. Paris: Karthala.

Couto, Mia. (1996) *Les baleines de Quissico*. Paris: Albin Michel.

De Witte, Ludo. (2000) *L'assassinat de Lumumba*. Paris: Karthala.

Dorléac, Laurence Bertrand. (2004) *L'ordre sauvage. Violence, dépense et sacré dans l'art des années 1950–1960*. Paris: Gallimard.

Efoui, Kossi. (1998) *La Polka*. Paris: Seuil.

Fanon, Frantz. (1952) *Peau noire, masques blancs* [Black skin, white masks]. Paris: Seuil.

Fanon, Frantz. (1959) *L'an V de la révolution algérienne*. Paris: Maspero.

Fanon, Frantz. (1961) *Les damnés de la terre* [The wretched of the earth]. Paris: Maspero.

Freud, Sigmund. (1985) *L'inquiétante étrangeté et autres essays* [The uncanny and other essays]. Paris: Gallimard.

Goerg, Odile. (1999a) "Le site du Palais du gouverneur à Conakry. Pouvoirs, symboles et mutations de sens," in Jean-Pierre Chrétien and Jean-Louis Triaud (eds.), *Histoire d'Afrique. Les enjeux de la mémoire*, pp. 389–404. Paris: Karthala.

Goerg, Odile, ed. (1999b) *Fêtes urbaines en Afrique. Espaces, identités et pouvoirs*. Paris: Karthala.

Grandmaison, Olivier Lecour. (2005) *Coloniser. Exterminer. Sur la guerre et l'État colonial*. Paris: Fayard.

Guillerault, Gérard. (2003) *Le miroir et la psyche*. Paris: Gallimard.

Hartman, Saidiya V. (1997) *Scenes of Subjection: Terror, Slavery, and Self-Making in Nineteenth-Century America*. Oxford: Oxford University Press.

Hegel, Georg. (1991) *Phénoménologie de l'Esprit*. Paris: Aubier.

de Heusch, Luc. (1986) *Le sacrifice dans les religions africaines*. Paris: Gallimard.

de Heusch, Luc. (2000) *Le roi de Kongo et les monstres sacrés*. Paris: Gallimard.

de Heusch, Luc. (2006) *La Transe*. Bruxelles: Éditions Complexe.

Hunt, Nancy Rose. (1999) *A Colonial Lexicon of Birth Ritual, Medicalization, and Mobility in the Congo*. Durham: Duke University Press.

Hussain, Nasser. (2003) *The Jurisprudence of Emergency. Colonialism and the Rule of Law*. Ann Arbor: University of Michigan Press.

Jewsiewicki, Bogumil. (1988) "Mémoire collective et passé présent dans les discours historiques populaires zaïrois," in *Dialoguer avec le léopard? Pratiques, savoirs et actes du peuple face au politique en Afrique noire contemporaine*. Paris: L'Harmattan.

Jewsiewicki, Bogumil. (1993) *Naître et mourir au Zaire. Un demi-siècle d'histoire au quotidian*. Paris: Karthala.

Junger, Ernst. (1990) *L'État universel* suivi de *La mobilisation totale*. Paris: Gallimard.

Kane, Cheikh Hamidou. (1961) *L'aventure ambiguë*. Paris: Julliard.

Khanna, Ranjana. (2003) *Dark Continents: Psychoanalysis and Colonialism*. Durham: Duke University Press.

Kourouma, Ahmadou. (1998) *En attendant le vote des bêtes sauvages*. Paris: Seuil.

Kourouma, Ahmadou. (2000) *Allah n'est pas oblige*. Paris: Seuil.

Levinas, Emmanuel. (1997) *Quelques réflexions sur la philosophie de l'hitlérisme*. Paris: Éditions Payot & Rivage.

Mabanckou, Alain. (2005) *Verre cassé*. Paris: Seuil.

Mbembe, Achille. (1986) *La naissance du maquis dans le Sud-Cameroun (1920–1960). Histoire des usages de la raison en colonie*. Paris: Karthala.

Mbembe, Achille. (1996a) "La 'chose' et ses doubles dans la caricature camerounaise," *Cahiers d'études africaines* 36(1–2): 141–2.

Mbembe, Achille. (1996b) *La naissance du maquis dans le Sud Cameroun (1920–1960). Histoire des usages de la raison en colonie*. Paris: Karthala.

Mbembe, Achille. (2000a) "À propos des écritures africaines de soi," *Politique africaine* 77. Translated by Steven Rendall as "African Modes of Self-Writing," *Public Culture* 14(1) (2002): 239–73.

Mbembe, Achille. (2000b) *De la postcolonie. Essai sur l'imagination politique dans l'Afrique contemporaine*. Paris: Karthala, 2000; published in 2001 as *On the Postcolony* (Berkley: University of California Press).

Mbembe, Achille. (2003) "Politiques de la vie et violence spéculaire dans la fiction d'Amos Tutuola," *Cahiers d'études africaines* 43(4): 172.

Merleau-Ponty, Maurice. (1945) *Phénoménologie de la perception* [Phenomenology of perception]. Paris: Gallimard.

Miller, Joseph C. (1988) *Way of Death. Merchant Capitalism and the Angolan Slave Trade, 1730–1830*. Madison: University of Wisconsin Press.

Nativel, Didier and Françoise Raison-Jourde. (1999) "Rapt des morts et exhibition monarchique. Les contradictions de la République colonisatrice à Madagascar," in Jean-Pierre Chrétien and Jean-Louis Triaud (eds.), *Histoire d'Afrique. Les enjeux de mémoire*, pp. 173–95. Paris: Karthala.

Nietzsche, Friedrich. (1977) *La naissance de la tragédie* [The birth of tragedy]. Paris: Gallimard.

Oyono, Ferdinand. (1960) *Une vie de boy*. Paris: Julliard.

Pélissier, René. (1978) *Les guerres grises. Résistance et révoltes en Angola, 1845–1941*. Montamets: Editions Pélissier.

Pélissier, René. (1979) *La colonie du Minotaure. Nationalismes et révoltes en Angola, 1926–1961*. Montamets: Editions Pélissier.

Pélissier, René. (2004) *Les campagnes coloniales du Portugal, 1844–1941*. Paris: Pygmalion.

Ranger, Terence. (2005) "Rule by Historiography: The Struggle Over the Past in Contemporary Zimbabwe," in Robert Muponde and Ranka Primorac (eds.), *Versions of Zimbabwe. New Approaches to Literature and Culture*, pp. 217–43. Harare: Weaver Press.

Ricoeur, Paul. (2000) *La mémoire, l'histoire, l'oubli*. Paris: Seuil.

Rosolato, Guy. (1987) *Le sacrifice. Repères psychanalytiques*. Paris: Presses universitaires de France.

Rouget, Gilbert. (1990) *La musique et la transe. Esquisse d'une théorie générale des relations de la musique et de la possession*. Paris: Gallimard.

Savitt, Todd L. (2002) *Medicine and Slavery. The Diseases and Health Care of Blacks in Antebellum Virginia*. Urbana: University of Illinois Press.

Tansi, Sony Labou. (1981a) *La vie et demie*. Paris: Seuil.

Tansi, Sony Labou. (1981b) *L'État honteux*. Paris: Seuil.
Tansi, Sony Labou. (1983) *L'anté-peuple*. Paris: Seuil.
Tansi, Sony Labou. (1985) *Les sept solitudes de Lorsa Lopez*. Paris: Seuil.
Tansi, Sony Labou. (1988) *Les yeux du volcan*. Paris: Seuil.
Tansi, Sony Labou. (1995) *Le commencement des douleurs*. Paris: Seuil.
Tansi, Sony Labou. (1997) *L'autre monde. Écrits inédits*. Paris: Éditions Revue Noire.
Taussig, Michael. (1986) *Shamanism, Colonialism and the Wild Man*. Chicago: University of Chicago Press.
Tchak, Samy. (2001) *Place des fêtes*. Paris: Seuil.
de Tocqueville, Alexis. (1988) *De la colonie en Algérie*. Bruxelles: Editions Complexe.
Tutuola, Amos. (2000) *L'ivrogne dans la brousse*. Paris: Serpent à Plume.
Vaughan, M. (1990) *Curing Their Ills. Colonial Power and African Illness*. Cambridge: Polity Press.
Vera, Yvonne. (2002) *Papillon brûle*. Paris: Fayard.
Vergès, Françoise. (2001) *Abolir l'esclavage: une utopie coloniale. Les ambiguïtés d'une politique humanitaire*. Paris: Albin Michel.
Vernant, Jean-Pierre. (1990) *Figures, idoles, masques*. Paris: Julliard.

Chapter 2

Vanishing Points: Law, Violence, and Exception in the Global War Prison

Derek Gregory

> *When one hears about another person's physical pain, the events happening within the interior of that person's body may seem to have the remote character of some deep subterranean fact, belonging to an invisible geography that, however portentous, has no reality because it has not yet manifested itself on the visible surface of the earth.*
>
> Elaine Scarry, *The Body in Pain: The Making and Unmaking of the World*

Power, Space, and Visibility

The "vanishing points" that I seek to identify in this essay can be brought into preliminary view through three figures and two sites. The three figures are a hooded man, a masked philosopher, and an outlaw president, none of whom is quite what he seems. The two sites are the US Naval Station at Guantánamo Bay and Abu Ghraib prison in Iraq: and neither of these is quite what it seems either.

A Hooded Man, a Masked Philosopher, and an Outlaw President

In the middle of October 2003 Haj Ali al-Qaisi, the former *Mukhtar* – community leader – of al Madifai, a district west of Baghdad, was arrested by US troops on his way to work. He was hooded, handcuffed, and taken to Abu Ghraib prison, where he was asked about Saddam Hussein, Osama bin Laden, and the insurgency. "They wanted me to become their eyes in the region," he said. But he protested that he knew nothing, and he was left to kick his heels in a large tent compound. Ten days later he was taken to Cage 49 in Cell-block 1. There he was interrogated daily, and frequently made to spend the night hanging by his handcuffs from the crosspiece of the bars in his cage. Finally, he was told that he had exhausted the patience of his captors. Forced up on a box, electrodes were attached to his fingers. Again he was asked for names of insurgents, and again he protested that he did not know any. Silence. He could see the flashes of cameras through the rough hood. Then he felt the first electrical shocks: "My eyes felt like fire, my whole body shook; I lost feeling in my tongue and bit it. I fell down; my tongue was bleeding. They took the hood from my face and a doctor came to me. He opened my mouth with his foot and put some water in my mouth and said, 'He is OK. Shock him some more.'" He endured two more sessions before being returned to the tent compound. He says he vomited when he saw the sun. He was released in January 2004 and told that it had all been "a mistake." For some considerable time al-Qaisi was believed to be the hooded man in the iconic photograph from Abu Ghraib, but it now seems that this was another prisoner who was subjected to similar treatment. According to a terse deposition from Abdou Hussain Saad Faleh, he was forced to stand on a box "with no clothing, except a blanket. Then a tall soldier came and put electrical wires on my fingers and toes and on my penis, and I had a bag over my head. Then he was saying, 'Which switch is for electricity?'"[1]

Some commentators have exploited the uncertain identification of "the hooded man" to discredit al-Qaisi's testimony and his work for the Association of the Victims of American Occupation Prisoners, while Faleh's testimony – like that of other victims – is shuffled off into an appendix to one of the official investigations. But their voices need to be heard, for the fact remains that the war prison described by victims like these is a far cry from the modern carceral regime described by "the masked philosopher," Michel Foucault. It is a strange hybrid. It is not a prisoner-of-war camp, since its central operation is the continued interrogation of prisoners taken during the "war on terror," most of whom are denied the status of prisoners of war; yet many of its sites are inspected by the International Committee of the Red Cross, which is required to visit all prisoners held as a result of armed conflict or military violence. Neither is it an ordinary prison, since its inmates have been captured by security forces and placed outside the normal legal process, and the regime to which they are subjected is not an intrinsically correctional one; yet they are subject to stringent surveillance and moved through a hierarchy of spaces depending on their co-operation with their captors. In what follows I suggest that the war prison (like the "war on terror" more generally) can be understood as a dispersed series of sites where sovereign power and bio-power coincide.[2]

It was Foucault who distinguished these two modalities of power, but Italian philosopher Giorgio Agamben claims that Foucault failed to locate the "vanishing point" to which these "perspectival lines" converged, "a hidden point of intersection between the juridical-institutional and the bio-political models of power." In fact, however, Foucault was acutely aware of their contradictory combination, and argued that they coincided within the paroxysmal space of the Third Reich. This is the same constellation identified by Agamben, who describes the point of intersection between the two as the production of bare life – "life exposed to death" – and treats the concentration camp in general and Auschwitz in particular as the paradigmatic space of political modernity.[3] Here I treat the global war prison as neither a paroxysmal nor a paradigmatic space but as a potential space of political modernity, which is given form and force through a profoundly colonial apparatus of power that the metropolitan preoccupations of Foucault and Agamben more or less erase.

One of the crucial differences between these philosophical projects is that Foucault focused on strategies through which the normal order contains and confines "the outside" (the sick, the mad, the criminal) whereas Agamben focuses on strategies through which "the outside" is included "by the suspension of the juridical order's validity – by letting the juridical order withdraw from the exception and abandon it." This "space of the exception," Agamben argues, is produced through martial law and a state of emergency, which then become the ground through which sovereign power constitutes and extends itself. It is here that we encounter "the outlaw president." Three days after the terrorist attacks on the Pentagon and the World Trade Center on September 11, 2001, President George W. Bush declared a National Emergency "by reason of [those] attacks and the continuing and immediate threat of further attacks on the United States." This was followed by a further declaration on September 23, 2001 to deal with "the unusual and extraordinary threat to the national security, foreign policy and economy of the United States" by "grave acts of terrorism and threats of terrorism committed by foreign terrorists." The emergency has been renewed in each subsequent year, and Agamben suggests that Bush "is attempting to produce a situation in which the emergency becomes the rule": in which "provisional and exceptional measures" are transformed into "a technique of government." The cascade of National Emergencies did not begin with Bush; he has continued seven previous National Emergencies and declared eight others.[4] But what attracts Agamben's attention, and what distinguishes the double emergencies declared in September 2001, is their proximity to a supposedly new kind of war (the "war on terror") and the legal formularies that have been mobilized around it.[5] Although it has become a commonplace to describe this as a "war on law," however, I seek to show that it is also a war fought through the law ("law as tactic," as Foucault might say). While the Bush administration shows manifest disdain for domestic and international laws, it neither dismisses nor disregards them.[6] This matters because it means that law is a site of political struggle not only in its suspension *but also in its formulation, interpretation and application.*

Guantánamo and Abu Ghraib

The Bush administration produced two different "exceptional" geographies to account for – and pry apart – its operations at Guantánamo Bay and Abu Ghraib. In the first case, Guantánamo was construed as a legally constituted space of the exception. It was selected because the Department of Justice believed that the location of the Naval Station – as "foreign territory, not subject to US sovereignty" – would militate against any attempt to use federal courts to obtain a writ of habeas corpus on behalf of enemy aliens held prisoner there. Other legal protections were withdrawn when the President determined that neither al-Qaeda nor Taliban prisoners qualified as prisoners of war under the Geneva Conventions. In the second case, in contrast, Abu Ghraib was declared a crime scene, the incidents there held to be offenses against both US military and international law, and official inquiries were conducted that issued in reprimands, disciplinary actions, and (in the case of enlisted soldiers) courts-martial. What happened at Abu Ghraib was glossed as unacceptable but un-American, appalling but an aberration, inexcusable but an exception.

The different meanings of exception that were invoked depend on the articulation of two different space-times. "Guantánamo" signifies not only an ambiguous space – a grey zone over which the United States claims jurisdiction but not sovereignty – but also a place of indeterminate time: "As a territory held by the United States in perpetuity over which sovereignty is indefinitely deferred, the temporal dimensions of Guantánamo's location make it a chillingly appropriate place for the indefinite detention of unnamed enemies in what the administration calls a perpetual war against terror."[7] Conversely, "Abu Ghraib" is made to appear as a precise punctuation in time and space: the abuse of prisoners was supposedly confined to Tier 1A of the so-called "Hard Site" of the Baghdad Central Correctional Facility, and it occurred in a number of isolated incidents during the night shift from October through December 2003. Thus one site is produced as an exception by being located beyond the law; the other is produced as an exception by being localized within the law.

I want to contest all these partitions by showing that "Guantánamo" and "Abu Ghraib" are connected by the intersections of sovereign power and bio-power that are realized through a series of spaces that fold in and out of them.

Agamben and Auschwitz

In describing these connections as "foldings" I am using Agamben's topological vocabulary, but my mapping is guided by two critical considerations. One concerns the state of exception and extra-territorialization – the volatile geographies produced through geopolitics and international law – and the other concerns witnessing and the apparatus of violence. Both arise from Agamben's reflections on Auschwitz, and while I do not seek to collapse "American Empire" into the Third Reich I do want to urge recognition of its proto-fascist potentialities.

Exception and extra-territorialization

Agamben's description of sovereign power and the state of exception is almost always framed by a single state. His brief history of the state of exception in Europe and the United States is shaped by the exigencies of war, but the emphasis is on suspensions of national law during states of emergency declared by France, Germany, Italy, Britain, and the United States.[8] In treating the camp as the exemplary locus of the modern space of exception, Agamben notes that concentration camps first emerged in colonial spaces of exception in Cuba and South Africa, but he passes over these to focus on Nazi concentration camps and, in particular, Auschwitz. Yet Auschwitz, like the other five extermination camps that were dedicated to the horrifying production of what Agamben calls the "German biopolitical body," *was within Nazi-occupied Poland.* Agamben has drawn parallels between the legal status of prisoners in these camps and prisoners in Guantánamo: their situations, so he says, are formally – "paradigmatically" – equivalent. To adjudicate such a claim, however, and to connect the metaphysics of power to its material inscriptions, it is necessary to ask how the state of exception is mediated by the connections between war, military occupation, and *international* law.

Agamben is silent on this question, whereas one of his principal provocations, the German jurist Carl Schmitt, wrote passionately about war, military occupation, and international law. He saw an intimate connection between the state of exception within a state's territory and belligerent occupation where, in practice, "the occupied population is subject to the holder of undifferentiated power without even the protection afforded to it indirectly by pure international law, for it is not a legal subject."[9] He knew what he was talking about, given his own complicity with the Nazi regime, but his argument raises a question that is central to any critical analysis of the "war on terror." If the *state* of exception is also a *space* of exception, as Agamben insists, then in these situations surely the exception depends on the articulation of *multiple* spaces of political-juridical violence and an ex-ception, a "taking outside," through the *extra-territorial* inscriptions of colonizing power?

International law is no stranger to the inflections of colonialism and imperialism, and it is scarcely surprising that the perverse and paradoxical spatiality that Agamben attributes to the exception should be compounded by the spatialities of international law. International law is decentered, without a unitary sovereign to ground or guarantee its powers; its provisions are distributed through a congeries of conventions, treaties, and organizations. For this reason, nineteenth-century legal philosopher John Austin famously declared that international law is not really law at all: laws could only be "properly so called" if they were "commands of a sovereign," which made international law merely "law by close analogy."[10] After World War II one of Schmitt's sharpest interlocutors extended this view (though to different ends) to suggest that "if international law is at the vanishing point of law, the law of war is perhaps even more conspicuously at the vanishing point of international law." And more recently, Lieutenant-Colonel William Lietzau, Special Advisor to the General Counsel of the US Department of Defense, extended even that view to propose that "the global war on terror" is at "the vanishing point of the law of war."[11] Taken in sequence, these three telescoping perspectives direct the politico-legal gaze through an extended series of vanishing points toward "non-places" for "non-people": sites like Guantánamo and Abu Ghraib.

Witnessing and the apparatus of violence

Those visual metaphors raise a second set of questions: What happens when those sites become sights? The question is raised most powerfully by the images from Abu Ghraib, but despite the iconic status of both Guantánamo and Abu Ghraib – or, rather, because of it – we need to remember that these are spaces of both constructed and *constricted* visibility and that most of what happens there continues to be shielded from the public gaze. The images that entered public cultures around the world multiplied with extraordinary speed. They attracted the attention of cartoonists, graphic designers, sculptors, and artists, and in the fall and winter of 2004 many of the photographs from Abu Ghraib were displayed at the International Center of Photography in New York and the Andy Warhol Museum in Pittsburgh.

What are we to make of this image frenzy? Cultural critics have raised myriad questions about the connections between the images and other photographic regimes in the United States but the most urgent centered on the complex affiliations between aesthetics and politics.[12] In this case these are complicated by the fact that both sides in the "war on terror" deploy images as strategic devices, and by the strong supposition that, had it not been for the minimalist release of the Abu Ghraib images, neither the Pentagon nor the White House would have taken much notice of reports of prisoner abuse and torture. That the images have been aestheticized seems beyond doubt, then, but in many cases and contexts it seems no less clear that they also carry a political charge. And yet: I have come to agree with Mark Danner when he suggests that the photographs eventually came to stand in the way of an adequate understanding of what happened. The public gaze was directed toward the images, not the process and policy behind them. Critical attention was focused on acts isolated as a series of stills and frames rather than on the apparatus that produced them.[13]

These concerns intersect with Agamben's reflections on Auschwitz and the ethics of bearing witness. He distinguishes two senses of "witness": one is juridical, and concerns third-party testimony to establish the facts of the matter in a trial, whereas the other derives from first-hand experience that radically estranges its testimony from law that "is solely directed toward judgement, independent of truth and justice." This distinction opens into a lacuna, because those who survived Auschwitz are witnesses in neither sense. They were scarcely third-party observers, but neither can they substitute for the first-hand testimony of those millions who died in the camps. Agamben confronts the absence – "the untestifiable, that to which no one has borne witness" – through the figure of the *Muselmann* ("the Muslim"), the abject prisoner who moved in the indeterminate shadows of life and death, in a space where "humanity and non-humanity" constantly passed through each other. He thus reads the *Muselmann* as a "perfect cipher" for the camp itself, the bearer of its secret performative geography.[14]

In a passionate commentary, however, Jay Bernstein suggests that what is lost from view, as a constitutive moment in Agamben's itinerary of reductions to bare life, is the complex of institutions, practices, and people through which human beings were transformed into *Muselmänner*: the gas chambers, the guards, the huts, the watch-towers, the railways, the police, the round-ups, in short the whole apparatus of violence of the Reich itself.

> At no point does [Agamben's] account veer off from the space of impossible sight to the wider terrain: from the victim to the executioners, to the nature of the camps, to the ethical dispositions of those set upon reducing the human to the inhuman. Just the inhuman itself fills Agamben's gaze, and hence ours; such is the *pure* desire to bear witness.

Bernstein's concern is that Agamben transforms the act of witnessing into an aesthetic act that re-stages what he calls "the pornography of horror" through its abstraction. For Bernstein, this aestheticization betrays "one of the deepest strains in Agamben's thought" by "suppressing the very ethical space it means to elaborate." If this is so, then what are we left with? What remains? This is Bernstein's answer: "Not the chambers or Auschwitz, not a place or set of practices, not the apotheosis of a complex historical trajectory, just the result of it all. With this we can hear the shutter of Agamben's philosophic camera snap open and closed. Click!"[15]

In order to pre-empt the closure that Bernstein so acutely identifies – "Click!" – it is vitally important to recover the lines of sight (flight?) that converge on these "vanishing points" and to reconstruct the spaces that fold in and out of the sites of their captivity. "Torture" derives from the Latin *torquere* meaning "to twist," and under the sign of our colonial modernity torture not only twists bodies – piling them on top of one another, shackling them to bed frames, standing them on boxes – but also twists space and time. To explicate this requires in turn the topology of sovereign power, and hence of the state of exception, to be understood as a performance, a doing. Only in this way do I think it possible to show (first) how "Guantánamo" has been produced through a series of juridical divisions, a sort of parsing of legal sentences, and (second) how "Guantánamo" and other spaces were folded into "Abu Ghraib" and beyond. I have briefly reintroduced the scare quotes to emphasize that neither is reducible to a single space: both are prisons but their cages and bars are not able to contain the practices that are inscribed through them. In explaining why this is the case, I also hope to show that law and violence are not opposed but hold each other in a deadly embrace.[16]

Guantánamo Bay

Critics have described the Bush administration as waging a "war on law," and the President has provided them with substantial evidence. "International law?" he responded to a reporter in December 2003. "I'd better call my lawyer. I don't know what you're talking about by international law."[17] More particularly, it has become common to treat the US prison complex at Guantánamo Bay as a "lawless place" that is "beyond the reach of national and international law"; a place where sovereign power has been mobilized "outside the rule of law"; a wild zone subject to "a lawless and prerogatory power," where "the law is effectively suspended in both its national and international forms" and where sovereign power is extended "in excess of the law." Agamben himself describes the state of exception as "a kenomatic state," a vacant space limned by the "emptiness of law."[18] I want to change the landscape these claims bring into view by rattling the chain that yokes colonialism, violence, and the law at Guantánamo and then tracing the legal and paralegal production of Guantánamo as a staging post for the "war on terror." En route, it will become clear that Bush does indeed know what "international law" is about – and that he has repeatedly called his lawyers.

Colonialism, violence, and the law

Colonialism frequently operates under the imprimatur of law, both in the past and the present, and its violent assaults on land, liberty, and life are regularly authorized and articulated through legal formularies. The legislative and interpretive fields, the actions of rulers and judges, are thus suffused with violence. If their metropolitan operation "takes place in a field of pain and death," as Robert Cover once presciently observed, then how much more anguished is their colonial mode of address; if their normal powers are "realized in the flesh," as he also remarked, then how much more painful is their emergency invocation.[19]

Guantánamo Bay bears the marks of these ligatures between colonialism, violence, and the law. Its modern history has been shaped by military encounters between three imperial powers – Spain, the United States, and the Soviet Union – and by enduring military occupation. Cubans rose against their Spanish occupiers in 1868–78, 1879–80, and 1895–8. Alarmed by the success of the revolutionaries in the final War of Independence, the Spanish military governor sought to cut off their popular support through a policy of *reconcentración*. Hundreds of thousands of peasants were forcibly relocated into concentration camps, where many of them were left to starve to death. American public opinion was inflamed by these atrocities, but the desire for military intervention was also motivated by thoroughly instrumental economic and strategic interests. In fact the United States had made repeated attempts to purchase Cuba from Spain in the closing decades of the nineteenth century, and it was only after the last of these offers had been rejected in 1897 that Washington, buoyed by the rising tide of public opinion, found a pretext and in 1898 declared war on Spain. This too was an image war. Photographs of the effects of Spain's counter-insurgency operations heightened public condemnation of its oppressive colonial regime. And, as Daniel Ross wryly observes, "the American prize for its outrage at Spanish concentration camps in Cuba has become the right to run its own camp on the same territory."[20]

When peace was concluded later that year Spain relinquished all its overseas possessions, but Cuba remained under American military occupation for three more years. In 1901 the United States stipulated its conditions for Cuban independence through provisions set out in the Platt Amendment to the appropriations bill in Congress that authorized the continued financing of the occupation. These reserved to the United States the right to intervene in the future "for the preservation of Cuban independence" and, to that end, required Cuba to sell or lease to the United States "lands necessary for coaling or naval stations."[21] Accordingly Guantánamo Bay was leased from Cuba in February 1903 "for the time required for the purposes of coaling and naval stations" and the United States was permitted "to do any and all things necessary to fit the premises for use as coaling and naval stations only, and for no other purpose." The lease could only be terminated with the consent of both parties or through the unilateral abandonment of the base by the United States. Its central provision read thus:

> While on the one hand the United States recognizes the continuance of the ultimate sovereignty of the Republic of Cuba over the above described areas of land and water, on the other hand the Republic of Cuba consents that during the period of the occupation by the United States of said areas under the terms of this agreement the United States shall exercise complete jurisdiction and control over and within said areas.

The language, as Kaplan argues, imposes a hierarchy between recognition and consent, "rendering Cuban sovereignty over Guantánamo Bay contingent on the acknowledgment of the United States, in exchange for which Cuba agrees to cede sovereignty over part of the territory it never controlled." The lease also locates Guantánamo in an ambiguous space between the "ultimate sovereignty" of Cuba and the "complete jurisdiction" of the United States.[22]

In 1959, following the revolution, the government of Cuba tried unsuccessfully to terminate the lease, and since then it has maintained that the presence of American armed forces on Cuban soil is an illegal occupation. At the height of the Cuban missile crisis in October 1962, President John F. Kennedy rejected Secretary of Defense Robert McNamara's proposal that the USA should offer to withdraw from Guantánamo as a quid pro quo for the removal of Soviet medium-range missiles and bombers from the island. On the contrary, the base's perimeter was strengthened as a symbolic frontier between capitalism and communism, and Guantánamo remained under American occupation. In subsequent years the base provided logistical support for US military interventions in the Caribbean and Central America. From 1991 to 1994 detention camps were constructed there for 36,000 refugees from the military coup in Haiti who were denied entry to the United States, and again in 1994–5 21,000 Cubans seeking asylum in the United States were imprisoned there. The construction of the camps violated the terms of the lease, which allowed the land to be used only as a coaling or naval station. A prison camp is at best an extralegal appendix to the original agreement, and yet it became the central mission of the base.

When Kaplan describes Guantánamo as "haunted by the ghosts of empire," then, she is surely correct. She also suggests that its history reveals "a logic grounded in imperialism, whereby coercive state power has been routinely mobilized beyond the sovereignty of national territory and outside the rule of law." Much of that is accurate too; but the base has also emerged through a long process of legal argument, and it subsists through legal formularies – bundles of memoranda and minutes, acts and amendments, treaties and the terms of the lease itself – that, taken together, have produced a legal impasse: a stand-off between the United States (which insists it has a legal right to occupy Guantánamo) and Cuba (which has declared the continued occupation illegal). For this reason it seems necessary to add that the space of Guantánamo also derives from law at a standstill. It is a zone of indistinction where the legalized and the extralegal cross over into one another.[23]

Producing Guantánamo

The Bush administration has made much of the presumptive novelty of the "war on terror," but the selection of Guantánamo as a prison camp, the designation of its inmates as "unlawful combatants," and the delineation of a regime of interrogation do not depart from the templates that shaped the base's colonial history and their mobilization of legal protocols. In particular, Fleur Johns argues that:

> The plight of the Guantánamo detainees is less an outcome of law's suspension or evisceration than of elaborate regulatory efforts by a range of legal authorities. The detention camps are above all works of legal representation and classification. They are spaces where law and liberal proceduralism speak and operate *in excess*.[24]

For far from the reactivation of the prison camps at Guantánamo signaling the retreat of law from the field of battle, there was a vigorous debate between the Departments of Defense and Justice and the State Department over the prosecution of the "war on terror."

The immediate objective was to place selected prisoners taken during the war in Afghanistan beyond the reach of any federal district court that might entertain a habeas corpus petition.[25] Here the ambiguous status of Guantánamo conferred a distinct advantage over other sites that were considered, like the US bases on Midway and Wake, which were included within the federal district of Hawaii. For Guantánamo was "neither part of the United States nor a possession or territory of the United States" and yet the United States exercised "complete jurisdiction" over the base. The reactivation of Guantánamo thus produced precisely the space envisaged in the President's Military Order of November 13, 2001, in which it would be possible to detain and try suspects "for violation of the laws of war and other applicable laws" while simultaneously suspending "the principles of law and rules of evidence generally recognised in the trial of criminal cases in the United States district courts."[26] These provisions, elaborated through a series of detailed memoranda, allowed a convergence between sovereign power and governmentality through what Judith Butler describes as "a law that is no law, a court that is no court, a process that is no process." She sees this as an instrumental, expedient, paralegal tactic, in which both detention and trial are determined by discretionary judgments that "function within a manufactured law or that manufacture law as they are performed."[27]

The imperative of indefinite detention, extending the emergency ad infinitum, jibed against a second objective that interrupted its limbo through the counter-imperative of speed.[28] This is where battle was joined between the Departments of Defense and Justice on one side and the State Department on the other. The first group argued that the "war on terror" had inaugurated a new paradigm that required interrogators "to quickly obtain information from captured terrorists and their sponsors," and in their view this rendered "obsolete [the] Geneva [Convention]'s strict limitations on questioning of enemy prisoners." That being so – and law officers in the State Department protested that it was not so – interrogations would have to be conducted beyond the prosecutorial reach of both the federal War Crimes Act and the Geneva Conventions. Accepting the advice of Defense and Justice, Bush declared that none of the provisions of the Geneva Conventions applied to al-Qaeda prisoners. He also accepted that he had the authority "under the Constitution to suspend [the] Geneva [Conventions] as between the United States and Afghanistan," and his favored legal advisors outlined several ways in which he might do so. But Bush preferred the simpler expedient of deeming Taliban prisoners to be "unlawful combatants" who did not qualify as prisoners of war under the Geneva Conventions.[29] There are established procedures to determine the status of prisoners taken during armed conflict, but the White House insisted that these were only to be invoked where there was doubt. And in the view of the President's inner circle, there could never be any doubt.[30]

Here was sovereign power at its most naked, and when the first prisoners arrived at Guantánamo Bay in January 2002, it was equally clear that they were to be reduced to bare life. All legal protections had been visibly withdrawn from them. Photographs of their transportation and incarceration at once displayed and reinforced their reduction to something less than human. They seem to have been published "to make known that a certain vanquishing had taken place, the reversal of national humiliation, a sign of successful vindication."[31] The prisoners had been chained, gloved, ear-muffed and masked throughout their 27-hour flight, and arrived soaked in their own bodily waste. Otherwise, the chairman of the Joint Chiefs of Staff explained, they would "gnaw through hydraulic lines at the back of a C-17 to bring it down." As they slowly shuffled down the ramp in their jumpsuits, one reporter wrote: "[They] don't look natural. They look like giant bright orange flies." Then were led off to their makeshift steel-mesh cages at Camp X-Ray.[32]

A senior CIA analyst concluded that fewer than 10 per cent of the prisoners who were transferred to Guantánamo were "high-value" terrorists. Most of them were minor players or indeed wholly innocent people who had been turned in to settle old scores or to receive bounties of thousands of dollars.[33] Yet our horror ought not to be measured by the innocence or guilt of the prisoners – which is a matter for the very judicial process denied to them – but by the calculated withdrawal of subjecthood from all of them. The legal determinations of the location of Guantánamo Bay worked in concert with the imaginative geographies of the "war on terror" to produce what Butler calls "a zone of uninhabitability":

> The exclusionary matrix by which subjects are formed requires the simultaneous production of a domain of abject beings. . . . The abject designates here precisely those "unlivable" and "uninhabitable" zones of social life which are nevertheless densely populated by those who do not enjoy the status of the subject, but whose living under the sign of the 'unlivable' is required to circumscribe the domain of the subject.

> This zone of uninhabitability will constitute the defining limit of the subject's domain.[34]

If the prisoners were "bodies that mattered," to continue to speak with Butler, then in Washington measures were being contemplated to ensure that they mattered *only* as bodies: as biopoliticized bare life. Throughout the discussion that follows, it needs to be remembered that the Bush administration repeatedly insisted that prisoners would be treated in a manner "consistent with" the Geneva Conventions. Such a claim relegates the treatment of prisoners to a matter of policy not law; it is not an acknowledgment that the actions of the United States are *subject to* the Geneva Conventions, and this lexical slippage creates a space of executive discretion (Schmitt's "decision") that would otherwise be (and as a matter of fact *is*) closed by international law.[35]

In fact, as Corine Hegland remarks, "even as the CIA was deciding that most of the prisoners at Guantánamo didn't have much to say, Pentagon officials were getting frustrated with how little the detainees were saying."[36] In the summer of 2002 Alberto Gonzales, then Counsel to the President and now Attorney-General, was busily considering advice from the Department of Justice about the bearing of the international Convention Against Torture and Other Cruel, Inhuman and Degrading Treatment or Punishment as implemented by title 18 (Part I, Chapter 113C) of the United States Code on the conduct of interrogations outside the United States. Under §2340A of the Code, "whoever *outside* the United States commits or attempts to commit torture" or conspires to commit torture is guilty of a criminal offense (my emphasis). This presented the White House with a real prisoner's dilemma, of course, because Guantánamo had been selected as a site of indefinite detention because it was *outside* the United States. But the Department of Justice pointed out that the relevant provisions of the Code defined the United States as "all areas under the jurisdiction of the United States," including all places and waters "continental or insular." And according to the lease the United States exercised "complete jurisdiction" over the base. Through this contorted legal geographing, Guantánamo was *outside* the United States in order to foreclose habeas corpus petitions from prisoners held there and *inside* the United States in order to forestall prosecutions for torturing them. As Voltaire put it, "Those who can make you believe absurdities can make you commit atrocities."

The memorandum also provided an intricate parsing of definitions of "torture" which not only raised the bar at which the conjunction of violence and pain turned into torture but made this threshold the property of the torturer. First, "only the most extreme forms of physical or mental harm" would constitute torture: severe pain that would "ordinarily" be associated with "death, organ failure or serious impairment of bodily functions," or severe mental suffering that produced "prolonged mental harm." This allowed "a significant range of acts that though they might constitute cruel, inhuman or degrading treatment fail to rise to the level of torture." Second, a defendant could only be convicted if these consequences were a known and intended outcome of his or her actions: "Where a defendant acts in good faith, he acts with an honest belief that he has not engaged in the proscribed conduct." If these sophistries were not enough, Gonzales was assured that "criminal statutes" could not infringe on the President's "complete" and "ultimate" authority as Commander-in-Chief over the conduct of war, including the interrogation of prisoners.[37]

This memorandum had been prepared with CIA rather than military interrogations in mind, but the lines were already becoming blurred. In October 2002 the Joint Chiefs of Staff were presented with recommendations from the Joint Task Force charged with conducting "Department of Defense/Interagency" interrogations at Guantánamo to allow a graduated series of increasingly "aggressive" techniques to be used against prisoners who had "tenaciously resisted" current methods. Category I techniques involved direct questioning, yelling, and deception; Category II techniques involved the use of stress positions, hooding, removal of clothing, and forced shaving, and the induction of stress through aversion ("such as fear of dogs"); Category III techniques involved convincing the prisoner that death or severe pain were imminent for him and/or his family, "exposure to cold weather or water," and "use of a wet towel and dripping water to induce the misperception of suffocation." The Department of Defense authorized the first two categories and noted that while all the techniques in the third category may be "legally available" their approval was not warranted "at this time."

If the skeletal list of approved techniques seems unremarkable, even banal, this is the result of two strategic omissions. First, the list contained no *limits* on the use of these techniques, and in a remarkably pointed exchange the General Counsel for the Navy, Alberto Mora, urged William Haynes, the General Counsel for the Department of Defense, "to think about the techniques more closely." "What did 'deprivation of light and auditory stimuli' mean? Could a detainee be locked in a completely dark cell? And for how long? A month?

Longer? What precisely did the authority to exploit phobias permit? Could a detainee be held in a coffin? Could phobias be applied until madness set in?"

Seen thus, Mora insisted, there was no clear line between the approved techniques and torture.[38] Second, the list was concerned entirely with instruments and provided no consideration of their *effects*. Since the end of World War II the United States has developed a consistent interrogation protocol that centers on sensory deprivation and self-inflicted pain. According to historian Alfred McCoy, "the method relies on simple, even banal procedures – isolation, standing, heat and cold, light and dark, noise and silence – for a systematic attack on all human senses." Early experiments showed that subjects could stand only two or three days of being goggled, gloved, and muffled in a lighted cubicle, while forced standing for 18–24 hours produced "excruciating pain" as ankles swelled, blisters erupted, heart rates soared, and kidneys shut down. These "no-touch" techniques leave no marks, but they create "a synergy of physical and psychological trauma whose sum is a hammer-blow to the fundamentals of personal identity": they deliberately ravage the body in order to "un-house" the mind.[39]

In January 2003, Secretary of Defense Donald Rumsfeld withdrew his permission for the use of Category II techniques and convened a Working Group to prepare an assessment of "Detainee Interrogations in the Global War on Terrorism." Its final report was not circulated to those who, like Mora, had been critical of the original recommendations. In effect, the Pentagon was now pursuing what Jane Mayer describes as a "secret detention policy" whose guidelines followed the memorandum of the previous August to the letter. The report found that, because Guantánamo is within the United States for the purpose of title 18, "the torture Statute does not apply to the conduct of US personnel at GTMO." It reaffirmed the inadmissibility of the Geneva Conventions and, in reaffirming the ultimate authority of the President, made an astonishing reversal of the precedent set by the Nuremberg tribunals: "The defense of superior orders will generally be available for US Armed Forces personnel engaged in exceptional interrogations except where the conduct goes so far as to be patently unlawful" (remember that those last two words had been eviscerated by the law officers favored by the White House). The report suggested a range of 35 interrogation techniques from "asking straightforward questions" and providing or removing privileges through hooding, "mild physical contact" and dietary or environmental manipulation, to "exceptional" measures that included isolation, 20-hour interrogations, forced shaving, prolonged standing, sleep deprivation, "quick, glancing slaps," removal of clothing, and "use of aversions" ("simple presence of dog"). Rumsfeld approved 24 of them. Although he withheld approval of all the "exceptional" measures other than isolation, however, the list of authorized techniques contained none of the crucial limitations. There was thus considerable latitude for coercive interrogation to slide through cruel, inhuman, and degrading treatment into outright torture. If this were not enough, Rumsfeld also accepted that "interrogators [must be] be provided with reasonable latitude to vary techniques" for reasons that included the degree of resistance and "the urgency of obtaining information."[40]

I have no way of knowing how much extra "latitude" that final clause was intended to allow; I simply make two observations. First, testimony from prisoners, soldiers, and interrogators makes it clear that the red lines (such as they were) were repeatedly crossed. There have been consistent reports of enforced nudity; exposure to extremes of temperature; deprivation of adequate food, water, and pain medication; induced disorientation through loud music, strobe lighting, and sleep deprivation; menacing by dogs; prolonged short-shackling in fetal positions; sexual taunting and assault; immersion in toilet bowls to induce fear of drowning; and isolation for months at a time.[41] Secondly, notwithstanding the techniques proscribed for military intelligence, since March 2002 the CIA had been authorized to use six "enhanced" techniques, which included forcing prisoners to stand, handcuffed and shackled, for more than 40 hours; forcing them to stand naked in a cold cell for prolonged periods and frequently dousing them with cold water; and simulated drowning ("waterboarding"). The CIA ran its own prison within the GTMO complex (at Camp Echo), but the CIA and the military frequently worked in concert because Guantánamo was the designated operating base for a Joint Interagency Interrogation Facility.[42]

During the summer of 2005, when Senator John McCain proposed an amendment to the Defense Appropriation Bill that would ban cruel, inhuman, or degrading treatment or punishment of anyone in US custody anywhere, the Vice-President insisted that the CIA should be exempt – it required "extra latitude" (that word again) – and the White House vigorously rejected any such measure that would "restrict the President's authority [not ability] to protect Americans from terrorist attack." The bill passed the Senate 90–9 and the House 308–122, but when the President reluctantly signed the Detainee Treatment Act into law at year's end he added a defiant signing statement insisting that he would interpret its provisions in a manner consistent with "constitutional limitations on the judicial power" and his own executive powers to protect national security, and he made it clear that he reserved the right to waive those restrictions in "special situations." Thus the hermeneutic circle – the mutuality of interpretation – was hammered flat until it fitted the Oval Office.[43] But it turns out that the Act contained its own Catch-22. In March 2006 lawyers for the Department of Justice reminded a district court judge that, under the provisions of the Act, prisoners at Guantánamo only had the right to appeal their designation as enemy combatants – not to seek protection against their treatment there. As Human Rights Watch put it, "The law says you can't torture detainees at Guantánamo, but it also says you can't enforce that law in the courts."[44]

Abu Ghraib

Abu Ghraib had been a "vanishing point" since its construction by British and Dutch contractors in the 1960s. After the coup that brought the Ba'ath Party back to power in 1968, mass arrests, torture, and imprisonment of opponents of the regime resumed, and political prisoners were consigned to Abu Ghraib even before it officially opened in 1970. The prison was under the control of the Directorate of General Security, and was the scene of some of the worst excesses of Saddam Hussein's regime. Within its walls prisoners were routinely beaten, broken, and degraded, stripped, chilled, and electrocuted. Thousands were put to death, sometimes two or three hanging from the scaffold at the same time, their bodies buried in unmarked graves.

This history is immensely important, but not because it can be invoked to excuse what happened after the American rehabilitation of Abu Ghraib in the summer of 2003. Far worse atrocities took place there under Saddam Hussein, but it is grotesque to hold up his regime as a standard to judge the ill treatment and torture of Iraqi prisoners by their American captors. Neither is it important because there is a direct parallel between Saddam's Iraq and Bush's Iraq. Instead, this history matters for the lives it remembers, and for the memories that were reawakened by the reopening of the prison under American administration. After the cruise missiles, the cluster bombs, and the killings, I doubt that many people's fears were dispelled by the large sign that replaced Saddam's portrait at the main gate: "America is a friend of all Iraqi people."

The decision to fold the invasion and occupation of Iraq into the "war on terror" produced another series of fraught intersections between violence and the law. On the one side, coalition forces were surprised by the widespread resistance to continued military occupation, and their aggressive counter-insurgency operations served only to intensify the insurgency. The collection of executable intelligence was placed at the center of this spiral. But the possibilities for interrogation were circumscribed by the President's acknowledgment that, unlike Afghanistan, the Geneva Conventions would be applied to prisoners captured in Iraq. On the other side, therefore, the rapidly improvised detention regime in Iraq exerted extraordinary pressure on the provisions of international law. There were two crucial questions: How far was it possible to "enhance" interrogation methods in Iraq without violating the letter of the law, and – if this provided insufficient "latitude" – was it possible to transfer prisoners out of Iraq to other sites under the control of the United States or its allies and accomplices? I treat these considerations in turn. I begin by plotting the spiral of insurgency and counter-insurgency in Iraq, and then I turn to the architecture of an emerging carceral archipelago.[45] Between these two parametric geographies lies the hideous intimacy of the torture chamber, and it is at this vanishing point that I end.

Insurgency and counter-insurgency

The insurgency in Iraq has many roots and takes many forms, and its complex, adaptive geography cannot be reduced to a single map. The failure of the occupying powers to comprehend the scale of dislocation and distress brought about by the combination of Saddam, sanctions, and war was a major cause. Millions of Iraqis had suffered terribly under Saddam and rejoiced at the downfall of his regime, but thousands had also died as a direct result of sanctions and two US-led wars, so that there was scarcely a family that had not been touched by America's wings of death too. Shortages of electricity, water, and medical supplies, the breakdown of public order, the economic dislocation, and the enforced privatization of the economy all heightened a common sense of grievance, especially in the central and southern regions of the country. Then there were the thousand and one daily humiliations of occupation: the ceaseless surveillance, the armored patrols, the checkpoints, the body searches, the midnight raids, the sheer inability or unwillingness to understand. Time and time again American troops fired on unarmed demonstrators calling for an end to the occupation; civilians were seriously injured or killed when troops opened fire during raids on houses and markets; countless others were humiliated, beaten, and even killed at checkpoints. Excuses were offered as explanations; apologies were rare, investigations perfunctory. These were all landmarks of occupation agonizingly familiar from the Israeli occupation of Palestine.[46]

President Bush declared the end of major combat operations in May 2003, but by the summer it was difficult to distinguish occupation from war. In Baghdad there were daily attacks on troops patrolling the streets, and in the so-called "Sunni Triangle" mortars and rocket-propelled grenades were used to ambush convoys and attack checkpoints. The coalition launched ever more aggressive military operations in June and July, involving thousands of troops backed by tanks, helicopter gunships, and aircraft. These massive deployments resulted in the deaths of hundreds of Iraqis and the detention of thousands more, all of which increased popular resentment of the occupation.[47] The opposition was many-stranded, at once spontaneous and organized, non-violent and militarized. As the summer wore on, demonstrations and riots spread across the Shi'a south, with thousands marching in Basra, Najaf, and other cities to demand an end to the occupation. There was the real possibility of the opposition turning into a national resistance movement in which SunniS and Shi'ites would fight side by side. While the Americans were slow to realize this, others were not. Iraq is part of the heartland of Islam, and the US occupation turned it into a new field of struggle for political Islam. Abu Mos'ab al Zarqawi, leader of a Salafi terrorist group with a base in northern Iraq, chose this moment to launch an armed jihad against both the coalition forces ("the far enemy") and the Shi'a ("the near enemy") in order to nullify the prospect of a unified, nationalist, and above all secular resistance. In August his group was responsible for two spectacularly deadly attacks: a massive truck bomb exploded at the United Nations mission, murdering the head of the delegation and more than 20 other people; and at the end of the month a car packed with explosives crashed into the Imam Ali mosque in Najaf, murdering more than 100 Shi'ites, including the spiritual leader of the Supreme Council of the Islamic Revolution.[48] That month there were an average of 12 attacks a day on American forces. This rose to 15 in early September; by the beginning of October there were more than 25 a day; and at the end of that month 33 a day. Large areas of Baghdad were declared "hostile," and the guerrilla war expanded beyond the Sunni heartland into the north and the Shi'a south. The situation was rapidly sliding out of control.

All of this bears directly on Abu Ghraib, which has been portrayed as a place of chaos outside the "normal" order. By the winter of 2003–4 more than 8,000 prisoners were crammed inside its compounds. Facilities were poor, and overcrowding increased the pressures; the detainees seethed with resentment, and riots and escapes were common. Military investigations and the media reported that Abu Ghraib was seen by those who worked there as "the forgotten outpost," poorly defended and constantly rocked by mortar attacks. It was variously described as "a prison on the brink," a howling chaos, a "hellish place" (for the guards, not the prisoners). In short, it was made to appear as a sort of twilight zone where the boundary between order and disorder was constantly slipping away, patrolled by exhausted and jumpy reservists, outnumbered and ill prepared for their duties, who labored under inadequate resources and ineffective supervision. Beyond the perimeter and its watchtowers, however, the rest of Iraq was descending into chaos too. In response, the level of military violence was ratcheted up and "pressure increased to obtain operational intelligence on the enemy's identity, support systems, locations, leadership, intelligence sources, weapons and ammunition caches, and centers of gravity." It was decided that a more "aggressive" structure of human intelligence collection and analysis was imperative.[49]

And so Abu Ghraib was not exceptional at all. It was the gravity of the situation *outside* Abu Ghraib that was used to license the horrors *inside* Abu Ghraib: not because the prison was "out of place," removed from the surveillant eyes of a high command preoccupied with the insurgency beyond its perimeter, *but because the US military folded the prison into its counter-insurgency operations.* This connection is extremely important, because otherwise the violence of torture obscures the violence of invasion, incarceration, and occupation. As our eyes are drawn to the hideous images from Abu Ghraib they are drawn away from the atrocities committed by the US military in places like Fallujah. As other forms of military violence are marginalized by the "exceptional" violence of torture, so the politico-military project of domination becomes contorted into the image of "liberation."

The carceral archipelago

In May 2003, the Department of Defense sent a team to Iraq to assess its detention system. Abu Ghraib had been virtually emptied when

Saddam issued a general amnesty in October 2002, and after the war – like most other Iraqi prisons – it was heavily damaged and extensively looted. Only three prisons were operational, with a combined capacity of just 500 prisoners. At Abu Ghraib two compounds had been totally destroyed and all the others were badly damaged, but two cell-blocks were suitable for immediate renovation. Out of the 21 sites the team visited, the team considered Abu Ghraib "closest to an American prison." They not only attached a priority to its reconstruction; they also supervised the work. As the new Baghdad Central Correctional Facility, Abu Ghraib was to serve two purposes. It was intended as a temporary prison for criminal prisoners until a new Iraqi government took office and a new prison was established elsewhere. These prisoners began to arrive in June and were confined in tent-blocks rimmed by razor wire. It was also to serve as the primary place of detention for the US Army's "security detainees," who began to arrive as soon as the renovations of the cell-blocks were completed in August.

It was not long before anxious Iraqis gathered at the gates of the prison seeking information about the thousands of men and women who had been arrested by the military. Most met with little success, and petitioners and prisoners became lost in an administrative labyrinth. By then, according to journalist Seymour Hersh, decisions to align detention and interrogation operations in Iraq with those elsewhere in the "war on terror" had been made at the highest reaches of the administration. The Vice-President subcontracted execution to the Secretary of Defense who had the system engineered by his Under Secretary of Defense for Intelligence Stephen Cambone. Rumsfeld's capacity for micro-management is well-known – "the 8,000 mile screwdriver" – but it is extraordinarily difficult to trace the torque. The official investigations that have been made public contain much huffing and puffing about the problems of information flowing up the chain of command – "how were they to know?" – but provide no rigorous examination of the ways in which reverse flows helped set the conditions for what happened at Abu Ghraib and elsewhere. Those flows include memoranda, directives, and orders, together with more informal understandings, but they also include speeches from the White House, the Department of Defense, and the military that consistently described America's enemies as outlaws, barbarians, and monsters. Is it any wonder that American forces subjected their Iraqi captives to brutal and dehumanizing treatment? They had been told repeatedly that this was a war against Evil incarnate, so that they were not fighting enemies so much as casting out demons. The fate of those imprisoned at Abu Ghraib was not decided by a few "rotten apples" at the bottom of the barrel: it was the fruit of a vast poison orchard assiduously cultivated by the President and his under-gardeners.[50]

The central strategy for interrogation and intelligence that they devised had three elements. The first was the designation of prisoners. Although President Bush had accepted that the Geneva Conventions would apply in Iraq, their provisions were stretched to the very limit by designating most of the prisoners held after the nominal end of hostilities as "security detainees" or "security internees" (the terms were interchangeable) rather than "prisoners of war." Of the 5,000 prisoners in its custody in May 2003, the United States recognized only 500 as prisoners of war. "Security detainee" was a technical term of particular significance because it allowed the full protection of the Geneva Conventions to be withdrawn from such prisoners for the duration of the armed conflict where "absolute military security so requires." This determination was invoked in a letter dated December 24, 2003, which was drafted by the Office of the Staff Judge Advocate and signed by Brigadier-General Janice Karpinski, the officer commanding the 800th Military Police Brigade at Abu Ghraib, in reply to serious concerns about detention and interrogation operations contained in interim reports from the ICRC (International Committee of the Red Cross): "While the armed conflict continues, and where 'absolute military security so requires', security internees will not obtain full G[eneva] C[onvention] protection."[51]

This provision is contained within Article 5 of the Fourth Geneva Convention. But in its commentary the ICRC makes it clear that this can only be applied "in *individual* cases of an *exceptional* nature, when the *existence of specific charges* makes it almost certain that penal proceedings will follow," and only to those who can be shown to be a continuing threat to security. It is not a catchall clause to allow the prolonged detention of thousands of people for endless interrogation.[52] Yet the letter under Karpinski's signature insisted on the "military necessity" of holding security detainees for their "significant intelligence value," and senior officers regularly repeated the same objectives. In the course of his inspection of detention and corrections operations in Iraq in November 2003, however, Major-General Donald Ryder, the Provost Marshal General, had found that 117 prisoners of war, 101 "high value detainees," and 3,400 security detainees were still in US custody, and he cited numerous cases "where Iraqis at most expressed displeasure or ill-will" at the occupation "and have been held for several months." The intensifying counter-insurgency rapidly boosted the number of security detainees, even though it was reliably estimated that 85–90 percent of those held were in the wrong place at the wrong time and "were of no intelligence value." Perversely, this increased their vulnerability: their very innocence "made them more likely to be abused, because investigators refused to believe they could have been picked up on such arbitrary grounds."[53] The ICRC describes Article 5 as a "regrettable concession to state expediency," and warns with chilling prescience that "what is most to be feared is that widespread application of the Article may eventually lead to the existence of a category of civilian internees who do not receive the normal treatment laid down by the Convention but are detained under conditions which are almost impossible to check."[54]

The second element in the strategy was to "enhance" methods of interrogation. In September 2003, a 30-member military team arrived in Iraq to conduct an assessment of "counter-terrorism interrogation and detention operations." With the encouragement and support of the Department of Defense, and Under Secretary Cambone in particular, the team was led by Major General Geoffrey Miller, Commander of JTF Guantánamo. His report recommended an immediate transition from "tactical" to "strategic" interrogation with a focus on the "rapid exploitation" of prisoners for "actionable intelligence." As at Guantánamo, detention and interrogation were to be integrated so that the one would "set conditions" for the other: "It is essential that the guard force be actively engaged in setting the conditions for successful exploitation of the internees." Miller recommended the introduction of "new approaches and operational art" developed at Guantánamo, which elsewhere he called a central "laboratory for the war on terror," and he provided details of the standard operating procedures that had been instituted there. An expert team from Guantánamo worked at Abu Ghraib from October through December, "to assist in the implementation of the recommendations," and by November "the real changes began to show."[55]

By that stage rumors of renewed abuse and torture at the prison were circulating widely in Iraq. Since April the ICRC had made a number of oral and written reports to the coalition complaining of consistent ill-treatment of prisoners and serious violations of international humanitarian law. After 29 visits to 14 internment facilities between March and November, delegates had seen enough to protest that the methods of physical and psychological coercion, "that in some cases might amount to torture," formed a "standard operating procedure"

– a systematic apparatus of abuse – that included beating, stripping, and hooding prisoners, the use of prolonged stress positions, photographing prisoners naked, and having them humiliated still further by female guards. Several officers admitted that "it was part of the military intelligence process" to hold prisoners "naked in a completely dark and empty cell for a prolonged period [and] to use inhumane and degrading treatment, including physical and psychological coercion" to "secure their cooperation." In January 2004, Major-General Antonio Taguba confirmed "numerous acts of sadistic, blatant and wanton criminal abuse" so pervasive and repetitive that they were "systemic."[56]

Hersh concludes that "Abu Ghraib had become, in effect, another Guantánamo."[57] According to subsequent investigations, however, the procedures recommended by Miller were intended to be no more than "starting-points," and Miller and other senior officers claimed that it was clearly understood that they could not be implemented without modification "because, unlike Afghanistan and Guantánamo, the Geneva Conventions applied in the Iraq theater." The categorization of most prisoners as "security detainees" considerably closed that gap between the permissible procedures, however, and the connections established between the two carceral regimes through Miller's report and the expert team contracted the distance still further. In fact, by September 2003 JTF-7 had decided that the latitude provided for the treatment of security detainees was insufficient. Reverting to the designation of prisoners from the war in Afghanistan, Sanchez argued that "unlawful combatants" were present in Iraq too and that, in accordance with the President's Memorandum of February 7, 2002, they were not entitled to *any* of the protections of the Geneva Conventions. He then authorized 29 interrogation techniques, of which 12 went beyond those described in Army Field Manual 34–52, and five of those exceeded the techniques approved for Guantánamo. CENTCOM viewed these additional methods as "unacceptably aggressive," and in mid-October Sanchez rescinded his directive "and disseminated methods only slightly stronger than those in Field Manual 34–52." Even so, his new memorandum remained as close as possible to the Guantánamo template provided by Miller. Interrogation operations were to be "conducted in close cooperation with the detaining units" and interrogators had to have "reasonable latitude" (again) to vary their techniques depending on both the prisoner and "the urgency with which information must be obtained."[58] In March 2004 Miller was transferred from Guantánamo to assume command of US prison operations in Iraq.

The circuits connecting Afghanistan, Guantánamo, and Iraq were more than words and paper. Interrogators circulated and interrogation techniques "migrated" from one theater to another, and it gradually became clear that similar abuses were widespread in both Afghanistan and Iraq. The ICRC reported a consistent pattern of brutality during arrest and transfer in Iraq, and this was subsequently shown to have extended throughout the detention system and to have started before and continued after the torture at Abu Ghraib. One officer and two NCOs testified that "the torture of detainees took place almost daily" throughout their deployment at FOB Mercury, for example, 20 kilometers east of Fallujah, from September 2003 through April 2004. Many of those most closely involved had been attached to Special Services in Afghanistan, where they had witnessed CIA interrogations, and they brought knowledge of those techniques with them to Iraq. These revelations were particularly significant because they showed that torture was not the product of a small number of ill-trained, undisciplined support troops but extended to front-line regiments, including "some of the best-trained, most decorated and highly respected units in the US Army." Special Operations units were active in Iraq too. Task Force 6–26 occupied an Iraqi military base at Baghdad International Airport, for example, designated as Camp Nama, and converted its former torture chambers into "interrogation rooms." There, according to Department of Defense, CIA, and FBI witnesses, prisoners were kept in darkness, beaten with rifle butts, stripped naked "and had cold water thrown on them to cause the sensation of drowning." From these and other reports it is evident that Abu Ghraib was no aberration.[59]

The third element of the interrogation and intelligence strategy was to outsource these operations. Inside Iraq the practices I have just described were plunged deeper into the shadows by the use of private contractors. The US occupation would be impossible without 20,000 contractors undertaking tasks that were once the preserve of the military. They were intimately involved in the preparation and execution of the invasion – Peter Singer calls them "the coalition of the billing" – and the demand for their services soared as the occupation wore on. Thirty contractors were hired for interrogations at Abu Ghraib: the Titan Corporation (San Diego) supplied interpreters and CACI International (Arlington) supplied interrogators. This strategy was more than a matter of outsourcing and profiteering, because it enabled the actions of contractors to be removed from any public ledger where they could be called to account. They were not part of the military chain of command and so were not subject to military justice; the Coalition Provisional Authority also explicitly excluded them from the provisions of Iraqi law. Indeed, no contractors operating anywhere in Iraq have been indicted, prosecuted, or punished for anything; the only corporate inquiry into the events at Abu Ghraib was conducted by CACI which, as Singer says, "unsurprisingly found that CACI had done no wrong." (Equally unsurprising, CACI also provides the US government with training videos on ethics.) In short, private contractors were – and remain – free to operate in a zone of absolute indistinction between the legal and the extralegal.[60]

Outsourcing reaches far beyond Iraq. Abu Ghraib was wired to a global network of prisons and detention centers run by the US military, the CIA, and allied intelligence services.[61] In March 2004 the White House wanted to know if it could forcibly transfer prisoners from Iraq so that they could be held indefinitely and subjected to even more extreme methods of interrogation. Forcible transfers are explicitly proscribed by the Geneva Conventions, whose architects had before them the policies of mass deportation and the enforced disappearance of individuals into the *Nacht und Nebel* programs carried out by the Nazis. But this did not deter the legal cartographers in the Department of Justice. Their counter-argument appealed to Iraq's immigration law, which, unlike virtually every other law on Iraq's statute books, apparently could not be repealed or suspended by the occupying power. This provided for anyone entering the country illegally (the "foreign fighters" who had joined the insurgency, not the thousands in US Army uniforms) to be imprisoned or deported. It seems unlikely that the drafters of the original law entertained the prospect that these measures could be coincident, but Guantánamo and its replicant sites made it possible for the United States to deport and imprison in a single gesture.[62]

This program dovetailed with a system of "extraordinary renditions" organized by the CIA. The Clinton administration had authorized the clandestine program after the bomb attacks on the World Trade Center in 1993 but nominal safeguards were attached to the process. Every abductee was supposed to have been convicted in absentia or to have been charged with a criminal offense that would lead to a judicial trial; each rendition required individual review and approval. The Bush administration dramatically expanded the program after 9/11 and removed most of those requirements. The central objective was to shackle indefinite detention to extreme interrogation. According to Jane Mayer, what started as a program aimed at a small, discrete set of suspects was thus widened to include a larger and looser target population of "unlawful combatants" for whom any pretense of judicial process was abandoned. The objective was to put such people "outside the protection of the law" altogether and place them "completely in the power of their captors."[63] It is estimated that 100–150 people have been rendered under the revised program and taken to jails in Egypt, Jordan, Libya, Morocco, Saudi Arabia, Syria, and Uzbekistan: all of which have been criticized by the State Department for gross violations of human rights. Equally cynically, the program uses the law to violate the law. Renditions are carried out using civilian rather than military aircraft to take advantage of the Chicago Convention on International Civil Aviation (1944), which makes it unnecessary for non-scheduled, non-commercial civil aircraft to seek permission to pass through the airspace of other states or to land at civilian airports. The aircraft usually belong to a number of shell companies (companies that exist on paper only) to take advantage of commercial law: "You can set them up quickly," one former CIA agent explained, and "dismantle them when they are exposed." These slippery maneuvers are necessary because enforced disappearances are expressly prohibited under international law, which further imposes on all states an absolute and unconditional ban on transferring people to states where they risk torture. The token gesture of compliance made by the United States is really a sign of utter contempt: it claims to seek assurances about the treatment of those subject to rendition, and US diplomats are nominally in charge of monitoring compliance. But the Director of the CIA, Porter Goss, openly admits that, "Once they are out of our control, there's only so much we can do . . .": which is of course precisely the point.[64]

Some prisoners remain firmly under US control, however, because the CIA also has its own covert prison system that was also authorized by President Bush after 9/11. These so-called "black sites" open and close at different times, and prisoners are regularly flown from one to another for interrogation that exceeds the boundaries of federal and international law. At Abu Ghraib there was a formalized Memorandum of Understanding with the military over the CIA's "ghost detainees" who were held in isolation on Tier 1A of the Hard Site. They were not identified by name or registered and they were moved around the prison to hide them from ICRC delegations. At least one prisoner died in CIA custody at Abu Ghraib.[65] Other black sites have been identified in Afghanistan and Pakistan; in Qatar and Yemen; on the British Indian Ocean Territory of Diego Garcia; in

Thailand (which was closed in 2003); at Guantánamo (which was closed in 2004 when federal courts began to exercise jurisdiction over prisoners there); and in the Czech Republic, Poland, and Romania (which were all closed in November 2005 following widespread outrage in Europe). All these sites are under direct US control where, to take Goss at his weasel word, there is plainly a great deal that the United States can do.[66]

The very language of "extraordinary rendition," "ghost prisoners," and "black sites" implies something out of the ordinary, spectral, a twilight zone: a serial space of the exception. But this performative spacing works *through* the law to annul the law; it is not a "state" of exception that can be counterpoised to a rule-governed world of "normal" politics and power. It is, at bottom, a process of *juridical* othering that involves three overlapping mechanisms: the creation of special rules that withdraw legal protections and permit the torture of what Ruth Jamieson and Kieran McEvoy call "juridical others"; the calculated outsourcing of war crimes to regimes known to practice torture; and the exploitation of extra-territorial sites where prisoners are detained and tortured at the pleasure of sovereign power. These strategies are not novel, however, and they did not begin with 9/11. Neither are they exclusively American strategies; the agencies of many other states have been complicit in the process. What is new is the way in which the vanishing points that they so assiduously produce are selectively but deliberately brought into fleeting view – in a calculated gesture of intimidation – and the way in which they reveal the totalizing will to power that lies at the crucial intersections of sovereign power and biopolitics.[67] In all these ways, as Kaplan concludes, the Bush administration has sought to redraw the borders of the law in order "to create a world in which Guantánamo is everywhere."[68]

In fact, the wheel has turned full circle, and Afghanistan has turned into a major hub in the global system of clandestine detention centers. "Prisoner transports criss-cross the country between a proliferating network of detention facilities," and this prefigures what two reporters describe as "a radical plan to replace Guantánamo Bay." The intention, so they claim, is to produce a global prison network beyond the reach of American or European judicial process. By the summer of 2005 negotiations were under way to transfer 50–70 percent of the prisoners under the jurisdiction of the Department of Defense at Guantánamo to Afghanistan, Saudi Arabia, and Yemen, where they would be incarcerated in purpose-built jails financed and constructed by the United States. Once again, it was claimed that the State Department would assume responsibility for "monitoring agreements to make sure prisoners were not mistreated." It beggars belief that occasional diplomatic visits announced in advance could be regarded as effective monitoring when so many officers working inside Abu Ghraib claimed not to have known what was happening day after day under their own noses.[69]

Torture chambers

The renovated cellblocks at Abu Ghraib ("the Hard Site") set the stage for a convergence between the US war machine and the US prison industry. The United States jails over two million of its citizens; around half of those prisoners are African-American, and many of them are Muslims: estimates suggest they make up 10–20 percent of the total prison population. Federal and state prisons have long been sites of crucial encounter between Islam and those versions of America that exclude its Muslim "other." In this system, racialized brutality and intramural violence are more or less sanctioned, and humiliation and abuse have become ritualized and routinized.[70] As Michelle Brown remarks, prisons are thus "liminal spaces both inside and outside the boundaries of constitutional law." Is it so surprising that two of the ringleaders at Abu Ghraib should have been corrections officers back home? This does not excuse their actions, of course, still less the carceral system that makes them possible. Brown's point is that the ideology of crime and punishment and the prosecution of the "war on terror" are both conducted in a language of retribution that, at the limit, reduces its "object-other" to a pure embodiment of the force of sovereign power: to bare life.[71]

The parallels between the two are indeed close, but the space between them needs to be retained because what happened at Abu Ghraib was more than a foreign replay of the odious domestic regime of incarceration. Abu Ghraib was in the middle of a war zone where the US Army was deploying ever more force and not only failing to suppress the insurgency but also increasing opposition to its occupation. In contradistinction to the triumphant mastery displayed in the photographs of the first prisoners arriving at Guantánamo, therefore, Allen Feldman reads the images from Abu Ghraib as recording "ceremonies of nostalgia" that betray a longing for the power that was so visibly slipping away. Through these rituals, he argues,

> The perpetuators re-acquire, if only in an allegorical idiom, their former sense of mastery and command in a situation that is rapidly lurching beyond their grasp. . . . [The] hooded and faceless bodies that are being manipulated and posed are merely emblems of a collective, recalcitrant Iraqi body politic that has to be dissected as the treacherous social surface of an occupied Iraq.[72]

This reminds us that the torture chamber is a setting for the aggrandizement of power, and that its affirmation is likely to become more frenzied as it is mocked or threatened. Elaine Scarry suggests that:

> The torturer's questions objectify the fact that he has a world, announce in their feigned urgency the critical importance of that world, a world whose asserted magnitude is confirmed by the cruelty it is able to motivate and justify. Part of what makes his world so huge is its continual juxtaposition with the small and shredded world objectified in the prisoner's answers . . . It is only the prisoner's steadily shrinking ground that wins for the torturer his swelling sense of territory.[73]

Conversely, as the vortex of insurgency and counter-insurgency intensified, perhaps it seemed to these soldiers and their accomplices that, outside the confines of the cell-block where their command was undisputed, the ground of the US Army was steadily shrinking as the insurgency asserted its own "swelling sense of territory" (and sovereignty). The degradation, humiliation, and sheer cruelty were, in their hideous way, a petty reversal of that greater reversal. That the attempts to engorge their enfeebled sense of power played on an elaborately Orientalized fantasy of feminized Arabs and of political militants as products of a failed heterosexuality enables Jasbir Puar to link torture in a metonymic chain that culminates in a climactic assertion of a heteronormative nationalism. "The bonding ritual of the carnival of torture – discussing it, producing it, getting turned on by it, recording it, disseminating the proof of it, gossiping about it – [becomes] the ultimate performance of patriotism." No wonder it is the last refuge of the scoundrel.[74]

Scarry makes another suggestion that helps make sense of the larger canvas that was folded in to Abu Ghraib when she notes that the questions and answers in the torture chamber are "a prolonged comparative display, an unfurling of world maps." This speaks directly to the project of interrogation and intelligence. Some commentators have sought to explain what happened there by blaming it on ignorance: "Soldiers were immersed in Islamic culture," one military psychiatrist wrote, "a culture that many were encountering for the first time."[75] Yet the scenes that were recorded in the cell-blocks revealed a display of knowledge as well as power. They combined many of what Arab cultures see as utterly shameful acts in a montage of incandescent horror: "the display of naked flesh; the use of dogs and dog-like treatment in human company; the removal of space between people and forced contact, grovelling and prostration; physical and intimate touching by strangers; nudity and sexual exposure before other men; homosexual contacts; the humiliation of men in front of women; filth; enslavement."[76] This was not happenstance. Neither were the techniques invented by the torturers. Written testimony and photographs shows that prisoners' arms were often stretched behind their backs and shackled to the bars in a high-stress position that is known as a "Palestinian hanging" from its use by the Israeli secret service in the occupied territories; it contributed directly to the death of Manadel al-Jamadi in CIA custody at Abu Ghraib. The crucified position into which the hooded man was forced is called "the Vietnam," an extraordinarily painful method studied by the CIA and used by interrogators in South Africa and South America. It strains credibility to believe that such tableaux of intense humiliation and pain – a theater of cruelty if ever there was one – were nothing more than the artless staging of a handful of reservists from small-town America.

That said, one has to confront the rictus of delight shown on the faces of those hometown, Homeland soldiers. They were not just triumphant; they were exultant. Michael Taussig makes the sharp point that "it is not the victim as animal that gratifies the torturer, but the fact that the victim is human, thus enabling the torturer to become the savage." In other words, torture requires its victims to be less than human, so that the degradation can continue – the specter of "the monster" stalks the torture chamber – but it also requires them to be human: otherwise sexual gratification is withheld from the torturer. A space that is at once inside and outside the political-juridical order is a space where these doubled subjects can be conjured into being, paraded and subjugated. Here, in the most intimate recesses of the space of the exception, we finally come face to face with the other specter that haunts these splattered cell-blocks. For here, in Taussig's vital paraphrase of Benjamin, "mimesis occurs by a colonial mirroring of otherness that reflects back onto the colonists the barbarity of their own social relations, but as imputed to the savage they yearn to colonize."[77]

After Words

Iraqis responded to the images from Abu Ghraib with understandable outrage, and much of their anger was focused on the colonial mirroring that Taussig describes: the Janus-face of occupied Iraq, preaching liberation while practicing degradation. But one of the most telling responses that I have seen comes from the weblog of "Riverbend," a young Iraqi woman in Baghdad:

> Seeing those naked, helpless, hooded men was like being slapped in the face with an ice cold hand. I felt ashamed to be looking at them – like I was seeing something I shouldn't be seeing and all I could think was, "I might know one of those faceless men . . ." I might have passed him in the street or worked with him. I might have brought groceries from one of them or sat through a lecture they gave in college . . . any one of them might be a teacher, gas station attendant or engineer . . . any one of them might be a father or grandfather . . . each and every one of them is a son and possibly a brother."[78]

These are haunting words. The practices at Guantánamo, Abu Ghraib, and elsewhere are saturated with a colonial past that is reactivated in our colonial present, and I hope that in making them visible I have helped to undercut the pernicious claim that terror and torture always refer to the actions of others, never to ourselves. Seen thus, as Philip Kennicott says, the images from Abu Ghraib are unexceptional: "In different forms, they could be pictures of the Dutch brutalizing the Indonesians; the French brutalizing the Algerians; the Belgians brutalizing the people of the Congo." When we look at these images, he concludes, we should see ourselves because they are *ours*: "Every errant smart bomb, every dead civilian, ever sodomized prisoner, is ours."[79] This seems exactly right to me. But Riverbend's anguish suggests another way to see ourselves in these images: for they are also *us*. There has never been a greater need to untwist the separations between "us" and "them" than the present moment of danger. For as the viral "war on terror" proliferates across the globe, and as regimes around the world invoke "national security" to suppress human rights, we are all, potentially, *homines sacri*. Our vulnerability is differentially distributed – scored by class, gender, sexuality, "race," and other markers – but it is also *shared*. We could all end up on other boxes in other prisons, arms outstretched and wires attached to our trembling bodies.

Acknowledgments

This essay was written in 2006; the original version was first published in Derek Gregory and Allan Pred (eds.), *Violent Geographies: fear, terror and political violence* (Routledge, 2007); an extended version that addresses the response of the Obama administration to the abuses described in these pages will appear in Derek Gregory, *War Cultures*.

I am grateful to Matthew Farish, David Nally, and Matthew Sparke for helpful comments.

Notes

1 Coppola (2005); Webster (2005); Zernike, (2006); "Translation of Statement Provided by Detainee 18470," in Greenberg and Dratel (2005: 526).
2 See Reid (2005: 241).
3 The central texts are Foucault (1977); Foucault (1978); Foucault (2003: 260); Agamben (1998: 6); Agamben (1999); Agamben (2005).
4 Relyea (2005).
5 Agamben (1998); Agamben (2005: 2, 22).
6 Indeed, both neoliberalism and neoconservatism work to disparage existing laws and juridical practices (the insistence on the supreme power of the "unitary executive," the assault on "activist judges," the drive to "deregulation") and also to introduce new ones that restrict democratic politics, roll back human rights, and reify the market.
7 Kaplan (2005: 837).
8 Agamben (2005: 11–22).
9 Stirk (2004: 530).
10 Austin (1995: 254). It would not be difficult to argue that the United States now seeks to arrogate to itself precisely that sovereign role.
11 Lauterpacht (1952: 382); Lietzau (2002: 79).
12 Sontag (2004); Mitchell (2005).
13 Danner (2004: xiii, 9, 40, 47).
14 Agamben (1999: 17–18, 41, 47).
15 Bernstein (2004: 3, 7, 14). See also Mills (2005: 218 note 4).
16 Cf. "The sovereign is the point of indistinction between violence and law, the threshold on which violence passes over into law and law passes over into violence"; Agamben (1999: 32). This does not exhaust my reservations about Agamben's project. I also want to emphasize the multiple ways in which the reductions of people to bare life are contested: in this case, by the prisoners themselves, and by a host of other actors inside and outside the Bush administration and inside and outside the United States.
17 Sands (2005: xii); "President discusses year-end accomplishments in Cabinet meeting" (2003).
18 Kaplan (2003: 91–2); Kaplan (2005: 832); Butler (2004: 51, 56, 64); Agamben (2005: 6, 86).

19 Cover (1986); Hussain (1999); Hussain (2003).
20 Pérez (1983: 55–6); Ferrer (1999); Ross (2004: 128).
21 The Platt Amendment was abrogated in 1934, when a new treaty was signed between the United States and Cuba, but this did not affect the lease of Guantánamo.
22 Pérez (1986); de Zayas (2003); Kaplan (2005: 836).
23 Kaplan (2005: 832, 836); cf. Agamben (2005: 48), who describes the state of exception as both "an emptiness *and standstill* of law" (my emphasis).
24 Johns (2005: 614).
25 A writ of habeas corpus orders a prisoner to be brought before a court to determine whether s/he has been imprisoned lawfully. Congress granted all federal courts jurisdiction under title 28 of the United States Code to issue such writs to release from custody prisoners held by state or federal agencies in violation of the Constitution.
26 Greenberg and Dratel (2005: 25–8, 29–37). In June 2004, however, the Supreme Court ruled that it had jurisdiction over Guantánamo to hear habeas corpus petitions from those imprisoned there. This landmark ruling was subsequently challenged by the Detainee Treatment Act (2005) that, inter alia, limited jurisdiction to the validity of the decision to detain a non-citizen as an "enemy combatant"; see pp. 72–3. It also reaffirmed that, "For the purposes of this section, the term 'United States', when used in a geographic sense, . . . does not include the United States Naval Station, Guantánamo Bay, Cuba."
27 Butler (2004: 58, 62). Johns (2005) radicalizes this interpretation: for her, Guantánamo Bay is "more cogently read as the jurisdictional outcome of attempts to *domesticate* the political possibilities occasioned by the experience of exceptionalism." The regime at Guantánamo Bay, so she suggests, "is dedicated to producing experiences of having no option, no doubt and no responsibility."
28 Butler says much less about this second imperative, though she does acknowledge that the withdrawal of legal protections from the prisoners and their indefinite detention are effected through their constitution as "less than human" (2004: 75–6, 98). Johns is silent on the question.
29 Greenberg and Dratel (2005: 38–79, 67, 69, 81–117, 102, 129, 134).
30 Watkins, (2005); de Zayas (2003); Aldrich (2002).
31 Butler (2004: 77).
32 See Rose (2004a); Gregory (2004: 66).
33 Golden and Van Natta (2004); Faul (2005); Sengupta (2006); Golden (2006). A detailed independent review revealed that most prisoners at Guantánamo were arrested neither in Afghanistan nor by US troops but were seized in Pakistan by Pakistani authorities. The Bush administration has dismissed their claims of innocence by characterizing them as well-trained liars but, as Corine Hegland observes, "if a well-trained liar looks like an innocent man, what does an innocent man look like if

not a well-trained liar?" See her "Who Is at Guantánamo Bay?" (2006a), "Guantánamo Grip" (2006b), and "Empty Evidence" (2006c).

34 Butler (1993: 3).

35 Rodley (2005: 55); Butler (2004: 80–1).

36 Hegland (2006c).

37 Greenberg and Dratel (2005: 172–217, 218–22, 202–3). On this basis you wonder how Saddam Hussein could ever be brought to trial for war crimes. For a devastating critique of these and related claims by Bush's lawyers, see Paust (2005).

38 Greenberg and Dratel (2005: 228, 223, 237); "Statement for the Record: Office of General Counsel Involvement in Interrogation Issues" (2004). Memorandum from Alberto J. Mora, General Counsel of the Navy to Vice-Admiral Albert Church, Inspector General, Department of the Navy, July 7, 2004.

39 McCoy (2006: 8, 35, 46).

40 Greenberg and Dratel (2005: 241–85, 265–6, 286–359: 291; 360–5: 365); "Statement for the Record" (2004); Mayer (2006).

41 See, for example, Rose (2004b); Carrell (2005); "Detention in Afghanistan and Guantánamo Bay: Statement of Shafiq Rasul, Asif Iqbal and Rhuhel Ahmed" (2004); "Guantánamo and Beyond"; "Testimony of Guantánamo Detainee Jumah al-Dossari" (2005); Oliver (2005).

42 Priest and Higham (2004); Jehl (2005a); Ross and Esposito (2005).

43 White (2005a); Savage (2006).

44 White and Leonnig (2006).

45 Klemens et al. (2003).

46 Gregory (2004: 225–47); Chehab (2005: 129–47).

47 Conetta (2005); Finlan (2005).

48 Napoleoni (2005: 157–60).

49 Saunders (2004a); Higham, White, and Davenport (2004); Jehl and Schmitt (2004); Fay–Jones Report in Greenberg and Dratel (2005: 998).

50 Hersh (2004: 59–60). "To fight in the name of humanity does not eliminate enmity; it only makes one's enemy the representative or embodiment of the inhuman": Norris (2004); Gregory (2004).

51 www.abc.bet.au/4 corners/content/2004/s1143841.htm, June 7, 2004.

52 "Convention IV Relative to the Protection of Civilian Persons in Time of War," Geneva, August 12, 1949 [full text and commentaries] (my emphases), at www.icrc.org.

53 "Report on Detention and Corrections Operations in Iraq" (2003: 27, 54); Borger (2004); Jehl (2004).

54 "Convention IV," commentary.

55 Greenberg and Dratel (2005: 451–9, 1062–66).

56 Ibid., pp. 391–2, 416.

57 Hersh (2005: 41).

58 Greenberg and Dratel (2005: 912, 1035–38).

59 Human Rights Watch (2005); Schmitt and Marshall (2006). See more generally Amnesty International (2006a).
60 Singer (2004a); Singer (2004b). The use of proxies for state violence – mercenaries and private military firms – is a common strategy of distancing the state from the perpetrators of its crimes: Jamieson and McEvoy (2005: 512–14).
61 Priest and Stephens (2004a).
62 Greenberg and Dratel (2005: 373–4).
63 Human Rights Watch (2004); Mayer (2005a); Amnesty International (2006b).
64 Grey (2004); Priest (2004); Hirsh, Hosenball, and Barry (2005); Jehl and Johnston (2005); Priest (2005a); Shane, Grey, and Williams (2005; Amnesty International (2006c).
65 White (2005b); Mayer (2005b).
66 Priest (2005b); Sevastopulo et al. (2005); Freeman (2005); White (2005c); Harding (2005); "European Investigator Says US 'Outsourced' Torture," *Associated Press* 24 January 2006.
67 Jamieson and McEvoy (2005: 515, 521); Parry (2005).
68 Kaplan (2005: 854).
69 Engelhardt (2004); Priest and Stephens (2004b); Borger (2005); Steele (2005); Jehl (2005b); Levy and Scott-Clark (2005); White and Wright (2005).
70 Zoll (2005).
71 Brown (2005: 989). The interpolation of Agamben is mine not Brown's. Her argument turns on the way in which the Hard Site at Abu Ghraib followed the logic of the self-contained "supermax" prison in the United States, where exclusion, segregation, and isolation – the removal of all ordinary human interaction – are used as managerial strategies under the sign of "security" (pp. 986–8).
72 Feldman (2004: 340).
73 Scarry (1987: 36).
74 Puar (2005); see also Puar and Rai (2002).
75 Greenberg and Dratel (2005: 448).
76 Saunders (2004b).
77 Taussig (1987: 83, 134).
78 Riverbend (2004).
79 Kennicott (2004); Harpham (2004).

References

Agamben, Giorgio. (1998) *Homo Sacer: Sovereign Power and Bare Life*. Stanford: Stanford University Press.

Agamben, Giorgio. (1999) *Remnants of Auschwitz: The Witness and the Archive*. New York: Zone Books.
Agamben, Giorgio. (2005) *State of Exception*. Chicago: University of Chicago Press.
Aldrich, G. H. (2002) "The Taliban, Al Qaeda and the Determination of Illegal Combatants," *American Journal of International Law* 96: 891–8.
Amnesty International. (2006a) *Beyond Abu Ghraib: Detention and Torture in Iraq*. Amnesty International, March.
Amnesty International. (2006b) *Rendition and Secure Detention: A Global System of Human Rights Violations*. Amnesty International, January.
Amnesty International. (2006c) *Below the Radar: Secret Flights to Torture and Disappearance*. Amnesty International, April.
Austin, John (1995 [1832]) *The Province of Jurisprudence Determined*, ed. Wilfred E. Rumble. Cambridge: Cambridge University Press.
Bernstein, J. M. (2004) "Bare Life, Bearing Witness: Auschwitz and the Pornography of Horror," *Parallax* 10(1): 2–16.
Borger, Julian. (2004) "'Cooks and Drivers Were Working as Interrogators,'" *Guardian*, May 7.
Borger, Julian. (2005) "US Plans Permanent Guantánamo Jails," *Guardian*, January 3.
Brown, Michelle. (2005) "'Setting the Conditions' for Abu Ghraib: the Prison Nation Abroad," *American Quarterly* 57: 973–97.
Butler, Judith. (1993) *Bodies That Matter: On the Discursive Limits of "Sex."* New York: Routledge.
Butler, Judith. (2004) "Indefinite Detention," *Precarious Life: The Powers of Mourning and Violence*. London and New York: Verso.
Carrell, Severin. (2005) "US Guards at Guantánamo Tortured Me, Says UK Man," *Independent*, April 24.
Chehab, Zaki. (2005) *Inside the Resistance: The Iraqi Insurgency and the Future of the Middle East*. New York: Nation Books.
Conetta, Carl. (2005) *Vicious Circle: The Dynamics of Occupation and Resistance in Iraq. Part One: Patterns of Popular Discontent*. Cambridge, MA: Project on Defense Alternatives, Commonwealth Institute.
"Convention IV Relative to the Protection of Civilian Persons in Time of War," Geneva, August 12, 1949 [full text and commentaries], at www.icrc.org.
Coppola, Paola. (2005) "The Man Beneath the Hood Speaks Out," *Guardian*, September 21.
Cover, Robert. (1986) "Violence and the Word," *Yale Law Journal* 95: 1601–29.
Danner, Mark. (2004) *Torture and Truth: America, Abu Ghraib and the War on Terror*. New York: New York Review of Books.
"Detention in Afghanistan and Guantánamo Bay: Statement of Shafiq Rasul, Asif Iqbal and Rhuhel Ahmed." (2004) Center for Constitutional Rights, New York, July 26, 2004.

Engelhardt, Tom. (2004) "Into the Shadows," at http://www.TomDispatch.com, April 5, 2004.

"European Investigator Says US 'Outsourced' Torture," *Associated Press*, January 24, 2006.

Faul, Michelle. (2005) "Gitmo Detainees Say They Were Sold," *Associated Press*, May 31.

Fay-Jones Report. (2005) "Investigation of Intelligence Activities at Abu Ghraib/Investigation of the Abu Ghraib Prison and 205th Military Intelligence Brigade," by LTG Anthony R. Jones; "Investigation of the Abu Ghraib Detention Facility and 205th Military Intelligence Brigade," by MG George Fay (2004), in Karen J. Greenberg and Joshua L. Dratel, *The Torture Papers: The Road to Abu Ghraib*, pp. 987–1131. Cambridge and New York: Cambridge University Press.

Feldman, Allen. (2004) "Securocratic Wars of Public Safety: Globalized Policing as Scopic Regime," *Interventions* 63: 330–50.

Ferrer, Ada. (1999) *Insurgent Cuba: Race, Nation and Revolution 1868–1898*. Chapel Hill: University of North Carolina Press.

Finlan, Alistair. (2005) "Trapped in the Dead Ground: US Counter-insurgency Strategy in Iraq," *Small Wars and Insurgencies* 16(1): 1–21.

Foucault, Michel. (1977) *Discipline and Punish: The Birth of the Prison*. London: Penguin.

Foucault, Michel. (1978) *The History of Sexuality: An Introduction*. London: Penguin.

Foucault, Michel. (2003) *"Society must be defended": Lectures at the Collège de France 1975–1976*. New York: Picador.

Freeman, Allan. (2005) "EU Eyes Alleged CIA Jails," *Globe and Mail*, November 4.

Golden, Tim. (2006) "Voices Baffled, Brash and Irate in Guantánamo," *New York Times*, March 6.

Golden, Tim and Dan Van Natta Jr. (2004) "US Said to Overstate Value of Guantánamo Detainees," *New York Times*, June 21.

Greenberg, Karen J. and Joshua L. Dratel, eds. (2005) *The Torture Papers: The Road to Abu Ghraib*. Cambridge: Cambridge University Press.

Gregory, Derek. (2004) *The Colonial Present: Afghanistan, Palestine, Iraq*. Oxford: Blackwell.

Grey, Stephen. (2004) "US Accused of Torture Flights," *Sunday Times*, November 14.

"Guantánamo and Beyond"; "Testimony of Guantánamo Detainee Jumah al-Dossari." (2005) Amnesty International, November 7, 2005.

Harding, Luke. (2005) "Rice Admits US Mistakes in War on Terror after Wave of Criticism across Europe," *Guardian*, December 7.

Harpham, Geoffrey Galt. (2004) "Inadmissible Evidence: Terror, Torture and the World Today," *Chronicle of Higher Education*, October 15.

Hegland, Corine. (2006a) "Who Is at Guantánamo Bay?" *National Journal*, February 3.

Hegland, Corine. (2006b) "Guantánamo Grip," *National Journal*, February 3.
Hegland, Corine. (2006c) "Empty Evidence," *National Journal*, February 3.
Hersh, Seymour. (2004) *Chain of Command: The Road from 9/11 to Abu Ghraib*. New York: HarperCollins.
Higham, Scott, Josh White, and Christian Davenport. (2004) "A Prison on the Brink," *Washington Post*, May 9.
Hirsh, Michael, Mark Hosenball, and John Barry. (2005) "Aboard Air CIA," *Newsweek*, February 28.
Human Rights Watch. (2004) *The United States' "Disappeared": the CIA's Long-Term "Ghost Detainees."* October 2004.
Human Rights Watch. (2005) *Leadership Failure: Firsthand Accounts of Torture of Iraqi Detainees by the US Army's 82nd Airborne Division*. September 2005.
Hussain, Nasser. (1999) "Towards a Jurisprudence of Emergency: Colonialism and the Rule of Law," *Law and Critique* 10: 93–115.
Hussain, Nasser. (2003) *The Jurisprudence of Emergency: Colonialism and the Rule of Law*. Ann Arbor: University of Michigan Press.
Jamieson, Ruth and Kieran McEvoy. (2005) "State Crime by Proxy and Juridical Othering," *British Journal of Criminology* 45: 504–27.
Jehl, Douglas. (2004) "US Disputed Protected Status of Iraq Inmates," *New York Times*, May 23.
Jehl, Douglas. (2005a) "Classified Report Warned on CIA's Tactics in Interrogation," *New York Times*, November 9.
Jehl, Douglas. (2005b) "Pentagon Seeks to Transfer More Detainees from Base in Cuba," *New York Times*, March 11.
Jehl, Douglas and David Johnston. (2005) "Rule Change Lets CIA Freely Send Suspects Abroad to Jails," *New York Times*, March 6.
Jehl, Douglas and Eric Schmitt. (2004) "In Abuse, a Portrait of Ill-Prepared, Overwhelmed GIs," *New York Times*, May 9.
Johns, Fleur. (2005) "Guantánamo Bay and the Annihilation of the Exception," *European Journal of International Law* 16: 613–35.
Kaplan, Amy. (2003) "Homeland Insecurities: Reflections on Language and Space," *Radical History Review* 85: 82–93.
Kaplan, Amy. (2005) "Where Is Guantánamo?" *American Quarterly* 57: 831–58, here 837.
Kennicott, Philip. (2004) "A Wretched New Picture of America," *Washington Post*, May 5.
Klemens, Oliver, Jesko Fezer, Kim Forster, and Sabine Horlitz. (2003) "Extra-territorial Spaces and Camps: Judicial and Political Spaces in the 'War on Terrorism,'" in Anselm Franke, Rafi Segal, and Eyal Weizman (eds.), *Territories: Islands, Camps and Other States of Utopia*, pp. 22–8. Berlin: KW – Institute for Contemporary Art.
Lauterpacht, Hersch. (1952) "The Problem of the Revision of the Law of War," *British Yearbook of International Law* 29: 360–82.
Levy, Adrian and Cathy Scott-Clark. (2005) "'One Huge US Jail,'" *Guardian*, March 19.

Lietzau, William K. (2002) "Combating Terrorism: Law Enforcement or War?" in *Terrorism and International Law: Challenges and Responses*, International Institute of Humanitarian Law, 75–84.

McCoy, Alfred W. (2006) *A Question of Torture: CIA Interrogation from the Cold War to the War on Terror*. New York: Metropolitan Books.

Mayer, Jane. (2005a) "Outsourcing Torture," *New Yorker*, February 14.

Mayer, Jane. (2005b) "A Deadly Interrogation," *New Yorker*, November 14.

Mayer, Jane. (2006) "The Memo," *New Yorker*, February 27.

Mills, Catherine. (2005) "Linguistic Survival and Ethicality: Biopolitics, Subjectification and Testimony in *Remnants of Auschwitz*," in Andrew Norris (ed.), *Politics, Metaphysics and Death: Essays on Giorgio Agamben's Homo Sacer*, pp. 198–221. Durham, NC: Duke University Press.

Mitchell, W. J. T. (2005) "The Unspeakable and the Unimaginable: Word and Image in a Time of Terror," *English Literary History* 72: 291–308.

Napoleoni, Loretta. (2005) *Insurgent Iraq: al Zarqawi and the New Generation*. New York: Seven Stories Press.

Norris, Andrew. (2004) "'Us' and 'Them': the Politics of American Self-assertion after 9/11," *Metaphilosophy* 32: 249–72.

Oliver, Mark. (2005) "'They Couldn't Take Away My Dignity,'" *Guardian*, November 18, 2005.

Parry, John. "The Shape of Modern Torture: Extraordinary Rendition and Ghost Detainees," *Melbourne Journal of International Law* 6: 516–33.

Paust, Jordan J. (2005) "Executive Plans and Authorizations to Violate International Law Concerning Treatment and Interrogation of Detainees," *Columbia Journal of Transnational Law* 43: 811–63.

Pérez, Louis. (1983) *Cuba between Empires, 1878–1902*. Pittsburgh: University of Pittsburgh Press.

Pérez, Louis. (1986) *Cuba under the Platt Amendment, 1902–1934*. Pittsburgh: University of Pittsburgh Press.

"President discusses year-end accomplishments in Cabinet meeting." (2003) at www.whitehouse.gov/news/releases, December 11, 2003.

Priest, Dana. (2004) "Jet Is Open Secret in Terror War," *Washington Post*, December 27.

Priest, Dana. (2005a) "CIA's Assurances on Transferred Suspects Doubted," *Washington Post*, March 17.

Priest, Dana. (2005b) "CIA Holds Terror Suspects in Secret Prisons," *Washington Post*, November 2.

Priest, Dana and Scott Higham. (2004) "At Guantánamo, a Prison within a Prison," *Washington Post*, December 17.

Priest, Dana and Joe Stephens. (2004a) "Secret World of US Interrogation," *Washington Post*, May 11.

Priest, Dana and Joe Stephens. (2004b) "Abu Ghraib Is Just the Most Notorious of a Network of Detention Centers," *Washington Post*, May 23.

Puar, Jasbir. (2005) "On Torture: Abu Ghraib," *Radical History Review* 93: 13–38.

Puar, Jasbir and Amit Rai. (2002) "Monster, Terrorist, Fag: the War on Terrorism and the Production of Docile Patriots," *Social Text* 72: 117–48.

Reid, Julian. (2005) "The Biopolitics of the War on Terror," *Third World Quarterly* 26: 237–52.

Relyea, Harold. (2005) "National Emergency Powers," Congressional Research Service, The Library of Congress, Washington DC, September 15, 2005.

"Report on Detention and Corrections Operations in Iraq" (2003) Office of the Provost Marshal General of the Army, November 5, 2003 [the Ryder Report].

Riverbend. (2004) "Baghdad Burning," at http://riverbendblog.blogspot.com, April 30, 2004.

Rodley, Nigel. (2005) "Looking-glass War," *Index on Censorship*, 54–61.

Rose, David. (2004a) *Guantánamo: America's War on Human Rights*. London: Faber and Faber.

Rose, David. (2004b) "How We Survived Jail Hell," *Observer*, March 14.

Ross, Brian and Richard Esposito. (2005) "CIA's Harsh Interrogation Tactics Described," *ABC News*, November 18.

Ross, Daniel. (2004) *Violent Democracy*. Cambridge: Cambridge University Press.

Sands, Philippe. (2005) *Lawless World: America and the Making and Breaking of Global Rules*. London: Allen Lane.

Saunders, Doug. (2004a) "US Citizen-Soldiers Terrified, Overwhelmed by Chaotic Iraqi Prison," *Globe & Mail*, May 8.

Saunders, Doug. (2004b) " 'This has disgraced America . . . ,' " *Globe & Mail*, May 7.

Savage, Charlie. (2006) "Bush Could Bypass New Torture Ban," *Boston Globe*, January 4.

Scarry, Elaine. (1987) *The Body in Pain: The Making and Unmaking of the World*. New York: Oxford University Press.

Schmitt, Eric and Carolyn Marshall. (2006) "Before and After Abu Ghraib, a US Unit Abused detainees," *New York Times*, 19 March.

Sevastopulo, Demetri, Guy Dinmore, Caroline Daniel, and Jan Cienski. (2005) "Evidence CIA Has Secret Jails in Europe," *Financial Times*, November 2.

Shane, Scott, Stephen Grey, and Margot Williams. (2005) "CIA Expanding Terror Battle under Guise of Charter Flights," *New York Times*, May 31.

Sengupta, Kim. (2006) "Voices from Guantánamo," *Independent*, March 6.

Singer, Peter. (2004a) "Beyond the Law," *Guardian*, May 3.

Singer, Peter. (2004b) "War, Profits and the Vacuum of Law: Privatized Military Firms and International Law," *Columbia Journal of Transnational Law* 42(2): 521–49.

Sontag, Susan. (2004) "Regarding the Torture of Others," *New York Times Magazine*, May 23.

"Statement for the Record: Office of General Counsel Involvement in Interrogation Issues." (2004) Memorandum from Alberto J. Mora, General Counsel of the Navy to Vice-Admiral Albert Church, Inspector General, Department of the Navy, July 7, 2004.

Steele, Jonathan. (2005) "A Global Gulag to Hide the War on Terror's Dirty Secrets," *Guardian*, January 14.

Stirk, Peter. (2004) "Carl Schmitt, the Law of Occupation and the Iraq War," *Constellations* 11(4): 527–36.

Taussig, Michael. (1987) *Shamanism, Colonialism and the Wild Man: A Study in Terror and Healing*. Chicago: University of Chicago Press.

"Translation of Statement Provided by Detainee 18470." (2005) In Karen J. Greenberg and Joshua L. Dratel (eds.), *The Torture Papers: The Road to Abu Ghraib*, p. 526. Cambridge: Cambridge University Press.

Watkins, Kenneth. (2005) "Warriors without Rights? Combatants, Unprivileged Belligerents and the Struggle over Legitimacy," Occasional Paper, Program on Humanitarian Policy and Conflict Research, Harvard University, Winter 2005.

Webster, Donovan. (2005) "The Man in the Hood," *Vanity Fair*, February.

White, Josh. (2005a) "President Relents, Backs Torture Ban," *Washington Post*, December 16.

White, Josh. (2005b) "Army, CIA agreed on "Ghost" Prisoners," *Washington Post*, March 11.

White, Josh. (2005c) "Prisoner Accounts Suggest Detention at Secret Facilities'," *Washington Post*, November 7.

White, Josh and Robin Wright. (2005) "Afghanistan Agrees to Accept Detainees," *Washington Post*, August 5.

White, Josh and Carol Leonnig. (2006) "US Cites Exception in Torture Ban," *Washington Post*, March 3.

de Zayas, Alfred. (2003) "The Status of Guantánamo and the Status of the Detainees," Douglas Mc.K. Brown Lecture, University of British Columbia, November 2003.

Zernike, Kate. (2006) "Cited as Symbol of Abu Ghraib, Man Admits He Is Not in Photo," *New York Times*, March 18.

Zoll, Rachel. (2005) "US Prisons Become Islam Battleground," Associated Press, July 14.

Chapter 3

The White Fear Factor

Vron Ware

When can we speak of "white fear" and when, if at all, can this term be used to illuminate the active forms of racism that are alive today? And how do we link this particular postcolonial legacy to the amorphous concept of terror that leeches into our contemporary fears of each other?

In 2000 I was visiting Johannesburg, famous as the crime capital of the world, and I saw a Stop sign under which someone had stenciled "Being Afraid." The effect was electrifying: in a city just liberated from one of the most brutally enforced regimes of segregation the world has ever known; in a forest of security fences, guard dog signs, and barbed wire, the sign spoke of the political choices open to New South African citizens faced with the task of learning to live together. In this context of apartheid and the struggle to end it, the links between fear and terror do not require spelling out.

In Britain we are not living in a comparable situation. The New Labour government signed us up to fight a war on terror itself, exploiting all manner of fears – including the unspecified fear of random attack by terrorists bent on destroying our collective, "British," way of life. The word "terror" has become shorthand for Islamic fundamentalism, Al-Qaeda, suicide bombers, burkas, uranium enrichment, and other threats emanating from the Muslim-majority world. The anti-war declaration, "We are not afraid," represented a refusal to behave like sheep, a recognition that militarization and war itself involves the manipulation of information as well as the deployment of armed forces.

Post-July 2005, the same slogan was more likely to be directed at the would-be bombers themselves, mingling patriotism (the Blitz spirit) with defiant pride in London's cosmopolitan reality. Today, fear and terror are still clearly linked within a discourse of securitization, but there is a danger that these terms have become increasingly disconnected from the legacies of colonial war that have shaped global geopolitics up to this point. The solipsism that locates fear and terror in the breasts of the majority population threatens to obscure the effect of the racism-as-usual that continues to poison social and political life. The phenomenon of white fear helps to identify a connection between these two currents: the reaction to perceived and imagined threats coming from outside the country, and the undertow of white supremacism that determines a predictable response to all manner of insecurity.

Anthrax Culture

As Zygmunt Bauman suggests, what we are afraid of tells us more about the epoch in which we live than the substance of the fear itself. In an essay entitled "A Catalogue of Postmodern Fears" he writes that, "Each era of history had its own fears which set it apart from other epochs; or, rather, each gave the fears known to all epochs names of its creation" (Bauman 1995: 105–6). But the threats themselves seem to have been always, stubbornly, the same. Summarizing his citation of Freud, we might agree that the fears stem from three directions: from the decay of our own bodies, from the underlying chaos of the external world, and from other human beings. And behind each of these, Bauman continues, is the mother of all threats, death itself. This is why to be human means also to experience fear.

Here I will speak about patterns of racism in the UK, but it is important to bear in mind that our insights and analytical terms are only sharpened by reference to other places to which we are connected, especially through shared experiences of fear. Ghassan Hage, writing from Australia in 2002–3, suggests that we name the political culture that emerges out of the general al-Qaeda-induced climate of fear as "anthrax culture."

> [Anthrax culture] prevails when a generalised culture of "threat" permeates the whole society. The national interior becomes subverted; the citizens begin to perceive everything and everywhere as a threat, as a

> border; a supposed Islamic threat on the border becomes an Islamic threat everywhere. Every breath of fresh air becomes imagined as a line behind which the enemy (always ready to infiltrate the nation) lurks. (Hage 2003: 45–6)

In the United States, where for months after the September 11 attacks the country was subjected to a baffling succession of color-coded alerts, local authorities busied themselves devising new emergency measures intended to secure residents, visitors, and assets from the threat of terrorist actions. In the jurisdiction where I was living, each household received a personal letter from the mayor assuring us of their efforts, and exhorting us to develop our own plans for "preparedness," a word I had not encountered before although its meaning was clear. Few would argue that this is the rational response to imminent danger, calling for a state of mind as well as a series of practical measures that anticipate disaster. Given what has already happened, people need to know what might happen in the future. But in anthrax culture, or what might be now called suicide-bomb culture, asking people to live in a state of perpetual alert has costs: it corrodes the sense of a good life, increases suspicion and distrust among citizens, and encourages them to look unquestioningly to the military for protection at home and abroad.

Corey Robin suggests that fears become political when they emanate from society or have consequences for society (Robin 2004: 2). He uses the term "political idea" to explore how fear becomes political when it refers to a collectively held emotion expressed in response to the threatened well-being of a particular group, especially where that emotion is readily mobilized by political forces. Our priority now, as we struggle with the consequences of living in suicide-bomb culture, is to analyze the source of our current fears and devise political strategies to deal with them.

Border Politics

I want to take two stories as a way of exploring this proposition. The first involves the siting of a proposed asylum dispersal center in a hotel in Sittingbourne, Kent, in January 2003. According to media reports the reaction to the proposal was immediate: "Since the news broke last week, residents have launched five petitions – one already boasting over 1,000 signatures – and demonstrated outside the hotel.

Others have thrown eggs at the building and, most disturbingly, there are widespread rumours of threats to 'burn the place down'" (Watt and Branigan 2003).

The *Guardian* reported that locals in Sittingbourne rejected the tactics of the British National Party (BNP), which had a history of organizing in the south-east around the ports connecting the UK to mainland Europe. The party immediately attempted to exploit this controversy by distributing leaflets that suggested that the "immigrants" had not been checked for diseases such as tuberculosis and AIDS and that they "could be war criminals or paedophiles."

But, the article continued, even if there is little direct support for the extremists, their messages appeared to be taking root. "We've been told [the asylum seekers] will be coming directly from airports, but we have received no assurances that they will be screened for diseases like TB," said one resident who owned a guesthouse next door to the site. "Our worst fears are that things could become intolerable if the place is badly managed and we are subjected to loud music, fighting and vandalism. We are willing to give them the benefit of the doubt, but it's the wrong choice of area. It's close to the town centre and local schools. It's a nice residential area."

His remarks were echoed by another resident who said people would be too scared to go out in case they ran into gangs of asylum seekers. "It's not a racist issue at all," she added, saying that plenty of black and Asian people lived there. "I just wonder, if there was a world war, how many of 'the asylum seekers' would go to war for Britain?"

The story requires further investigation; it is, after all, a media report. I chose to outline it here because it represents the phenomenon of border politics: strategies of inclusion and exclusion in operation at the physical, logistical borders of countries. Asylum seekers constitute a particular category of threat to those who believe that Britain is full up. Coercive controls introduced by Tony Blair in 2003 – which breached the spirit if not the letter of the Geneva Convention on refugees – cut asylum applications by almost two-thirds by 2004. But, "Thanks to the drip, drip, drip of distorted tabloid reporting, the public became so bemused that an Amnesty poll found the British believed they were taking in 24% of the world's refugees when the whole of Europe was only absorbing 3%" (Dean 2006).

This "racial situation" tells us as much about the government's handling of the situation, their embarrassment at the lack of local consultation, and their readiness to back down in the face of "scaremongering" than the predictable fears of the residents, though it is important to know exactly what people are scared of (Hartigan 1999: 280). The open expression of racist views directed against asylum seekers is muted by the rejection of fascist propaganda. But the message is repeated nonetheless: asylum seekers, refugees, and immigrants bring disease, violence, rape, and anti-social behavior. The question about whether the prospective immigrants would go to war for Britain certainly tells us more about the time we live in than the notion that their loud parties might disrupt a nice residential area.

The BNP owe their continued existence to their ability to capitalize on this type of crisis, showing how easy it is to exploit the connection between anthrax culture and routine white supremacy. In 2006 their leader Nick Griffin was acquitted on charges of using words or behavior likely to stir up racial hatred after claiming that the Qur'an incited Muslims to rape non-Muslim women. He was reported as saying:

> Their "good book" tells them that that's acceptable. If you doubt it, go and buy a copy and you will find verse after verse saying you can take any woman you want as long as they're not Muslim . . . It's part of their plan for conquering countries. They will expand into the rest of the UK as the last whites try and find their way to the sea. (Wainright 2006)

I do not want to overemphasize the importance of the BNP, but they persist in acting as a valve – first for activists psychologically or ideologically drawn to fascism, and secondly, more worryingly, for an electorate motivated by despair, resentment, and fear, and comforted by racist propaganda that appears to articulate their multiple grievances. Their limited ability to perform effectively in public office is small consolation when surveys show that a majority of British people support BNP policies on immigration, even though a significant number were prepared to disown the policies once they were informed of the association. The patchy electoral successes of the BNP requires close examination, not least because of their disinformation tactics designed to demonize asylum seekers, whether African or Albanian, and to exacerbate Islamophobia. Looking outside the UK, it is clear that these patterns are reproduced across Europe, including the former Soviet Union, and in Australia.[1]

A second aspect of this "racial situation" is the explicit connection between political discourse on asylum and issues of security, a slippage that demands attention in the light of ever-tightening immigration control in the period since 2001. The government is reliant on the way its performance is represented in a popular media that is predominantly anti-asylum, and this entails investing enormous resources in the presentation of an agenda that sounds authoritative and yet responsive to public opinion. In the House of Commons, the then Home Secretary David Blunkett distanced his own office from those responsible for not carrying out the necessary consultation with the local community, adding,

> Anyone who pretends that there is a simple answer, any more than any other country has found a simple answer, is not only deluding themselves and those around, but unnecessarily whipping up scares which can do no good in terms of our security measures and every harm to our community and race relations which are often fragile and can so easily tip over into a situation we can't control. (Allison 2006)

Blunkett's reference to other countries is clearly intended to deflect criticism of UK policies and to emphasize the intractable nature of asylum as a modern phenomenon. But it is also a reminder that this particular incident in a small town in Kent cannot be properly understood within a narrowly national framework. In her historical account of restrictive asylum policy in the UK since New Labour came to power in 1997, Vicki Squire explores the link between popular anti-asylum discourse and government policy in an international context. She points out that some analysts have argued that New Labour has responded to electoral pressures to restrict immigration, while others, such as Solomos and Schuster, have maintained that Labour have "heightened a climate of fear about refugees and asylum seekers" (Squire 2008: 254).

She suggests that there is a more complex dynamic at work than either of these theories suggests: "Election campaigns are constructed according to a political party's perception of popular opinion, yet the party political articulation of an issue also constructs it in a particular way within wider popular discourse" (p. 255). First, in the UK it is important to look at party political issues across the spectrum, as well as other "conditioning factors," both domestic and international. "At the international level," she writes, "a range of events can be interpreted as creating the conditions for the emergence for the dominance of restrictive asylum discourse: the OPEC oil crisis, the end of the Cold War, the terrorist attacks of 9/11." Add to this the momentum of economic neoliberalism, the mechanisms of European integration, and the development of internal borders within the EU (or Schengenland, as it is often known). Seen in this light, the notion that asylum policy is really about stemming an overwhelming flow of applicants or managing local "abuse" of the system appears quite unsustainable.

The politics of border control is not just about the massaging of white residents' fears of being swamped, however, or appeasing the racist mob, on the one hand, while not wanting to tarnish New Labour's vaunted commitment to the new doctrine of social cohesion, on the other. The politics of the border envisages walls, fences, and prisons (removal centers), policed by invasive screening technologies as well as ever-tightening regulations. Today, the heralded failure of multiculturalism as a doctrine that was supposed to emphasize respect for diversity is overlaid by the Powellite rhetoric of the "enemy within," coined in the 1960s, an era when the integrity of the nation-state was comparatively secure.

Five years after Blunkett's attempts to find that delicate balance between self-delusion and hysteria, Tony Blair was more direct in his attempt to address the politics of fear as part of his farewell series on "Our Nation's Future." "We like our diversity," he said. "But how do we react when that 'difference' leads to separation and alienation from the values that define what we hold in common?"

"For the first time in a generation there is an unease, an anxiety, even at points a resentment that our very openness, our willingness to welcome difference, our pride in being home to many cultures, is being used against us; abused, indeed, in order to harm us" (Blair 2006; Ware 2008).

By acknowledging the possibility that the country's hospitality was being abused, the former prime minister cemented the notion that the forced removal of unwanted asylum seekers was justified, no matter how terrified they might be of being sent back to situations from which they had escaped. Thus the routine deportations continue as a necessary evil, carried out with the help of private security personnel armed with handcuffs and leg irons, and often in secret, well away from public scrutiny.[2] Fear is used as a political tool to gain the nation's complicity, and state institutions continue to commit harsh injustices that might otherwise be challenged publicly as breaches of human rights.

Meanwhile the battlefield itself is represented as the site of the ultimate defense of Britain's integrity. In 2008 Foreign Secretary David Miliband declared that the military operation in Afghanistan was as vital to national security as the war against the Nazis. Speaking to a *Daily Mail* journalist while on tour in the Middle East, he declared:

> Why we are there is straightforward. Sixty or 70 years ago the Armed Forces defended Britain on the White Cliffs of Dover. Now to defend Britain we have got to be in the toughest areas of the world like Afghanistan. So the purpose of the mission is absolutely clear, it is to make sure Afghanistan does not become a safe haven for people who want to plot against the UK. (Brogan 2008)

The politics of the border represents one of the most important issues of our epoch, one that calls for consistent vigilance and intervention by those who are opposed to fortresses of wealth and privilege surrounded by the dispossessed, the starving, and the desperate, whose temporary services are required as labor but who have no rights as citizens. However, by focusing on the points of exclusion, the term "border politics" can distract attention from the spaces where the rich and poor, the haves, the have-nots, and the have-mores come together, and from the struggle to live with, and alongside, those marked out as racially or culturally threatening.

Colonial Paranoia

My second story explores the undercurrent of a slightly different category of fear that might tell us something more about the epoch in which we find ourselves. It emerged from the reporting of Hurricane Katrina in the British tabloids in September 2005. During the aftermath of the hurricane the following scenario appeared on the front page of the *News of the World* newspaper under the headline: "Brit Girls' Hurricane Rape Hell." "Two female Brit survivors of the hell-hole aftermath of the New Orleans hurricane told yesterday how a band of brave men saved them from being raped." Together with "other white women" they sat "huddled in the city's superdome, ringed by male tourists to protect them from rampaging mobs" (Maung 2006: 1, 8–9).

One of the young women was reported as saying: "I'd heard stories about girls getting raped inside the dome . . . The way the men protected us when we thought we were going to be attacked was so selfless and inspiring."

Inside, the story continued, under the banner: "Anarchy USA Brit Survivors tell of Horror" and in even bigger capitals: "Our Death Dome Hell". Next to a full-page color image of the body of a dead woman, clearly black, floating face down in the water, the two girls are shown smiling, relaxed, and cheerful with the quote, "Our men sat round us in a circle to keep rapists at bay."

As the British citizens who were caught up in the aftermath of the hurricane were flown home, conflicting reports of their experiences were siphoned through print, internet, radio, and TV media. The Brits who were unlucky enough to end up in the Superdome were portrayed as unlucky, exposed, abandoned, terrified, and justifiably angry that the relevant authorities took so long to come to their rescue. Some clearly expected preferential treatment: after all, they were not the same as the poorest people in New Orleans who were left to rot. They had places to go and credit cards in their pockets – but they found themselves in the wrong place at the wrong time.

Listening carefully, it was possible to hear individuals trying to explain that it was hell for everyone in the Dome, that it was the National Guard who had started frightening them with orders that the men make a circle around the women and protect them from the indigenous marauders. Some realized that there was increased tension because residents of New Orleans thought that the foreigners were getting preferential treatment. Of course, it emerged that this is exactly what happened. The timetable of events published in many newspapers showed that the Brits were removed from the Dome on the Wednesday, at least two days before the rest of the thousands were airlifted out.

The *News of the World* report implied that the European tourists were in particular danger in the Superdome because of their color. The women were in danger of being raped and sexually molested, and their brave menfolk gathered round them in a circle to protect them. The steaming fetid air of the Dome reduced everyone to near hysteria, and rumors of rape, suicide, stabbings, and other forms of violence were rife. The reporting spoke of human suffering and the failure of the authorities to protect life and property, but what made the headlines was the collapse of civil society: "Anarchy USA" in which Brits were victims. The European women were at risk from the predominantly black mob, which had also been responsible for shooting at the National Guard and hampering relief efforts by their trigger-happy lawlessness.

This scenario, so luridly described by the tabloids, was yet another example of that racist paranoia that has been such a familiar ingredient of Britain's colonial and postcolonial past. The juxtaposition of defenseless white (European) women to dark-skinned men, who, in this case, were clearly more unleashed from bounds of civilized society than ever, could not be passed up as an exercise in sensationalism. There were plenty of other reports that described the hell inside the Dome over the course of that week, including the repetition of graphic rumors flying round a panicked, starving, and furious population. As Gary Younge reported in *The Guardian*, when everyone was finally airlifted out of the Dome and the Convention centre, no one came forward to report rape or bizarre murders rumored to have taken place (Younge 2005; Usborne 2005). Later, it emerged that the inferno created in the Superdome was actually created by the authorities. As Rebecca Solnit wrote soon after: "The people within were not allowed to leave. The Convention Center and the Superdome became open prisons. Eyewitnesses reported armed authorities shooting at people who tried to walk out, including hundreds of stranded tourists who were forced back into the holding centres: That was not anarchy, nor was it civil society" (Solnit 2005: 23).

There is no doubt that the particular racist interpretation of the terror experienced by the tourists represented the frisson of colonial paranoia, evoking the deep cultural memory that white women's bodies symbolized all that was valuable and vulnerable about civilization (Ware 1992). But in this current climate of fear there was another terrifying factor: the pictures of smiling white tourists alongside the body of a drowned black woman assumed that their lives had entirely different values. This points us in one direction to take more seriously the liminal figure of the tourist: tourism is after all the largest global industry, and the freedom to travel to other people's countries is considered a key component of democratic societies. These tourists were caught off guard: they were visiting Europeans caught up in the US's internal problems, and so, according to the way this was reported, they became victims of America's racial codes. But this manner of reporting their fate obscured the real nature of the catastrophe. As many have pointed out, disasters are almost by definition about the failure of authority rather than the collapse of humanity into an anarchic free-for-all. Blinded by the dazzle of smug white supremacy mixed with opportunist anti-Americanism, the paranoid fantasy of black rape and white chivalry totally obscures the role of government and the armed forces in keeping citizens in perilous, vulnerable conditions.

This shameful outburst of colonial paranoia refers us back to that other historical legacy in which the ever-widening gap between rich and poor, white and black, becomes further naturalized by being made racialized. By chance the BBC was running E. M. Forster's luminous novel *A Passage to India* in their Book at Bedtime slot during this same period. Although this was a fictional account of what happened when a young white woman, "an English girl fresh from England" (Forster 1980: 174), claimed that she had been assaulted by an Indian man, the book draws imaginatively on the claims of the white settler community that Forster witnessed as a visitor to India in the 1920s. Within a matter of hours the news of the alleged assault flew round the town, turning apparently reasonable individuals into a demonic herd. "All over Chandrapore that day the Europeans were putting aside their normal personalities, and sinking themselves in their community. Pity, wrath, heroism, filled them, but the power of putting two and two together was annihilated" (p. 175).

Forster uses the simple device of the rumored sexual assault of a white woman to evoke the fragility of colonial order and the underlying violence that held it in place. The British elite imagined that their rule depended on mutual respect and esteem, and attributed the alleged attack to the breakdown of that compact. The "native" crowds that gathered to protest at the unjust accusation were seen as harbingers of the independence movement, an ominous sign that the old order might never be restored without force. Although they maintained the semblance of due legal process in public, in private the colonizers were able to express their passions in unrepressed manner, as the Collector demonstrated once he returned to his bungalow: "When he saw the coolies asleep in the ditches or the shopkeepers rising to salute him on their little platforms, he said to himself: 'I know what you're like at last; you shall pay for this, you shall squeal' " (p. 175).

The way that some sections of the British media reported the chaos in the New Orleans Superdome is an ominous echo of this sentiment: "we know what you are really like, and you won't get away with it." Thus, in the cause of protecting our own freedoms and rights, we can use the excuse, not just that the dispossessed of the world present a threat, a burden, a liability, but also that their sub-humanity justifies all manner of treatment in the name of protecting civilization.

Faced with the startling traffic sign in Johannesburg, few people would ask: stop being afraid of what? There, local political literacy is derived from decades of apartheid rule and the terrible legacy of structural inequality and poverty. As I write this, the Sunday papers in the UK offer two versions of a South African future that indicate stark choices: white flight and the spectacular rebirth of Johannesburg. The first, yielding to fear, is filtered through the sympathetic ears of an English journalist who has just rented out his house in Hertfordshire to a white family fleeing their gated compound in the city of their birth (Cowley 2006: 11). The second speaks more to the future, to the conquering of fears. This can be measured by factors such as the rocketing value of real estate, which has risen 35 percent in six years, and by developments such as rooftop swimming pools, helipads, luxury apartment blocks, and massive investment by international companies (Carroll 2006: 14). It is in these rapidly growing megacities that we see most clearly the spatial and racial configuration of this new global warming order: where power and capital work to create new axes of spectacular wealth and abject poverty, where privatized, securitized enclaves are surrounded by the masses, some of whose labor is required to service this economy, but the rest appears to be surplus to requirements.

In *Planet of Slums*, a terrifying assessment of the growth of slum populations in the global south, Mike Davis demonstrates that this pattern of urban development not only reflects the prevailing neoliberal economic order but inevitably perpetuates an uncompromisingly militarist response from those in power. His book concludes with the observation that the Bush regime has already decided that the "feral failed cities of the Third World" will be the "distinctive battlespace of the twenty first century" (Davis 2006: 205). He writes: "Pentagon doctrine is being reshaped accordingly to support a low intensity war of unlimited duration against criminalized segments of the urban poor. This is the true 'clash of civilizations.'"

While it is crucial to retain a sense of the global dynamics of power (and resistance), it is no less important to work close to home to dispel illusions of unbridgeable difference and to fight for social justice. Recognizing the role of white fear is an important factor in these related political tasks. As the military occupations in Iraq and Afghanistan become ever more questionable and more futile, political discourse in the UK repeatedly directs public attention to the potential disruption that "immigrants" represent to some imagined harmonious British way of life. Led from above, these successive official scoldings, warnings, and threats, combined with ever-stricter immigration controls in the name of "fairness," only serve to reinforce the borders held in place by intransigent racism and the "white fear" it feeds off. This obscures the urgency of addressing the underlying causes of social and political conflict in our streets, schools, and town halls. It also helps to divert attention from a more inclusive and open public debate about the country's role on the world stage, and the effects of a catastrophic foreign policy on domestic politics. An anti-racist politics that takes on the daunting task of unpicking the particular fears of our epoch must be able to formulate political responses that begin with, but go beyond, the cry, "We are not afraid."

Notes

1 The BNP saw unprecedented success in the local elections on May 4, 2006, winning 11 seats in one London borough, and making gains elsewhere. Their message on national media was about asylum seekers bringing disease, tribal warfare, rape – again insinuated in election material tailored to particular constituencies where they were able to exacerbate local anxieties and paranoia.

2 "Forcible Deportation of Iraqi Asylum Seekers Ended in Violence" International Federation of Iraqi Refugees-IFIR CSDIRAQ http://csdiraq.com/index.php?option=com_content&task=view&id=50&Itemid=1

References

Allison, Eric. (2006) "Second Holding Centre Hit by Hunger Strike," *Guardian*, April 17.

Bauman, Z. (1995) *Life in Fragments: Essays in Postmodern Morality*. Oxford: Blackwell.

Blair, T. (2006) "The Duty to Integrate: Shared British Values," History and Tour: No. Ten TV. http://www.number10.gov.uk/Page10563

Brogan, B. (2008) "Miliband Compares Afghanistan to 'Defending White Cliffs of Dover in WWII,'" *Daily Mail*, June 10. http://www.dailymail.co.uk/news/article-1025065/Miliband-compares-Afghanistan-defending-white-cliffs-Dover-WWII.html#

Carroll, R. (2006) "Boomtown Jo'burg Rides the New Gold Rush," *Guardian*, April 17.

Cowley, J. (2006) "Cecil Rhodes' Dream Ends Where It Began – in Bishop's Stortford," *Observer*, April 16.

Davis, M. (2006) *Planet of Slums*. London: Verso.

Dean, M. (2006) "Amnesty Offers Fresh Start on Immigration," *Guardian*, April 5.

Forster, E. M. (1980) *A Passage to India*. Harmondsworth: Penguin.

Hage, G. (2003) *Against Paranoid Nationalism: Searching for Hope in a Shrinking Society*. London: Merlin Press.

Hartigan Jr., J. (1999) *Racial Situations: Class Predicaments of Whiteness in Detroit*. Princeton: Princeton University Press.

Maung, C. A. (2006) "Brit Girls' Hurricane Rape Hell," *News of the World*, September 4.

Robin, C. (2004) *Fear: The History of a Political Idea*. Oxford: Oxford University Press.

Solnit, R. (2005) "The Uses of Disaster: Notes on Bad Weather and Good Government," *Harpers*, October.

Squire, V. (2008) "Accounting for the Dominance of Control: Inter-party Dynamics and Restrictive Asylum Policy in Contemporary Britain," *British Politics* 3: 241–61.

Usborne, D. (2005) "The Dispossessed of New Orleans Tell of Their Medieval Nightmare," *Independent*, September 4.

Wainwright, M. (2006) "BNP Leader 'Claimed Qur'an Allows Rape of Non-Muslims,'" *Guardian*, January 18.

Ware, V. (1992) *Beyond the Pale: White Women, Racism and History*. London: Verso.

Ware, V. (2008) "Towards a Sociology of Resentment," *Sociological Research Online* 13(5), September 2008.

Watt, N. and T. Branigan. (2003) "Asylum Hotel Scheme Thrown into Disarray: Tension Grows as Blunkett Charges Directorate with Incompetence," *Guardian*, January 20.

Younge, G. (2005) "Murder and Rape – Fact or Fiction?" *Guardian*, September 6.

Chapter 4

Sacrificial Militancy and the Wars around Terror

Alex Houen

In order to justify losses that seem beyond reason or reality principle, you have to rationalize them in terms of sacrifice. That, at least, was President George W. Bush's tactic as soon as the "war on terror" started taking its toll in the Iraq conflict. In a speech he delivered in October 2005, for example, Bush related al-Qaeda's militancy to Islamic insurgency in Iraq and elsewhere in order to assert that "radical Islam" had spread into a consolidated "ideology" to rival that of communism in the Cold War: "our new enemy teaches that innocent individuals can be sacrificed to serve a political vision. And this explains their cold-blooded contempt for human life."[1] By the end of this speech, though, political sacrifice is precisely what Bush himself was calling for as a response: "We don't know . . . the sacrifices that might lie ahead. But we do know . . . that the defense of freedom is worth our sacrifice."[2] And by the time of his address to US troops in Iraq in June 2006, the President's opening gambit was to thank them for "making history" by making "sacrifice[s]," and to reassure them that "Your sacrifice is noble and important."[3] Such reassurance has increasingly become routine, as any trawl for references to "sacrifice" in Bush's speeches and statements readily shows.[4]

Since their inception, the current wars around terror have been nothing if not an escalation of sacrifice on all sides. Witnessing the hijacked planes explode into the World Trade Center and the Pentagon on September 11, 2001, the Bush administration was immediately forced to consider sending unarmed fighters on suicide missions against the fourth plane because there were no armed fighters available. The subsequent mustering of forces and hi-tech weaponry by the United States and its allies for fighting terror has only exacerbated the resolve of Islamic militant groups to respond with so-called "suicide bombing," a practice that the groups prefer to view as sacrificial martyrdom (*istishad* or *shahadat*). And while the US and its allies have vehemently denounced suicide bombings as a tactic, they have also been forced to respond to such attacks with sacrifices of their own. On both sides, sacrificed lives are deemed to be immeasurably worthy because the lives are supposedly pledged for priceless, transcendent values – whether "democracy," "freedom," "God," or "the nation." And these sacrifices call for more sacrifices in turn because the lives of those remaining are held to be indebted to the boundless gift that those who died have left as a legacy. Speaking on Veterans' Day (November 11) in 2005, for example, President Bush stated that the "sacrifice" of veterans "creates a debt that America can never fully repay,"[5] for such debts cannot be settled, only accumulated.

If making sacrifices is largely how the wars around terror have been making history, is that another way of saying that we are faced with a clash of fundamentalisms? I want to argue that, no, it is not, because what is fundamental to sacrificial militancy is unclear. Just from the Bush quotations I have offered above we can see that sacrifice has not simply been a religious issue but has also been figured in secular terms. Moreover, if we consider the history of suicide bombing alone, it is evident that the practice is limited neither to radical Islamic groups nor to religious militants more generally. For example, the first suicide bombings in the early twentieth century were carried out by secular Russian anarchists, and the next major instance was that of Japanese "kamikaze" pilots in World War II.[6] Regarding modern Islamic sacrifice attacks, the "human waves" of martyrs that Ayatollah Khomeini sent into battle in the Iran–Iraq war (1980–8) are often cited as having inspired the Lebanese Shi'ite group Hezbollah to adopt suicide bombing as a tactic in the early 1980s. But Hezbollah's tactics also served as a model for militants of other religious persuasions, including Sunni Muslim groups like Hamas, and the predominantly Sikh Tamil Tigers in Sri Lanka. It even inspired secular movements like Fatah in Palestine and the Kurdistan Workers Party (PKK). Thus, as Christoph Reuter has argued, "By the late 1980s and early 1990s, suicide bombing had spread around the world in ways that could no longer be explained solely as shared religious motives or half-forgotten traditions."[7]

While there is no predominant ideology or religion underlying the tactic of suicide attacks, I want to contend that what the religious and secular groups that employ it have in common is the endeavor to use sacrifice *to institute an idealism of transcendent justifications for a community*. This does not just hold for suicide attacks; it also applies to Bush's invocation of soldiers' "sacrifices" as "mak[ing] possible" the nation's "sacred freedoms."[8] In light of this, I shall argue in this chapter that current sacrificial militancy cannot be divided up along strict lines of Middle Eastern versus Western, or religious versus the secular. Indeed, what has become clear is that on all sides the sacrifices that have been made have undermined the boundaries between politics, religion, and economics. Does this mean that there is currently only one mode of sacrificial militancy at play, or that we must develop a universal concept of it that pertains to all cultures and contexts? Not at all: to propose such a universal perspective would be to ignore the fact that the recent wars of terror have escalated largely as a conflict *about* sacrifice – about whose particular mode is justified or more powerful. At the same time, because these wars have escalated as sacrificial *exchanges* between opposed sides, this has also led to those sides mirroring each other's practices, as I shall show. The result is that particular modes of sacrificial militancy become increasingly variegated by being drawn into wider exchanges. In response to this, my contention is that we need a theory of sacrificial militancy that focuses less on its religious underpinnings and more on the complicated exchanges it establishes between disparate regions and between different realms of social life. Rather than offer a universal account, then, a revised theory of sacrificial militancy needs to offer a wider understanding of how the opposed modes of militant sacrifice are currently entangled in mutual exchanges. This will require two major reorientations. First, we need to reconsider sacrifice's *substitutive* nature. Thinkers like Sigmund Freud and René Girard have theorized ways in which sacrifice entails substitutions of the profane for the sacred, and of the victim for the sacrificers.[9] Such substitutions need to be related to particular instances in which politics, economics, and religion are variously substituted for each other through sacrificial militancy.

This substitutive function bears on the second reorientation that is required. Traditionally, sacrifice has been conceived as something that reinforces a community's *pre*-existing social relations and spiritual beliefs. If, however, sacrificial militancy is instrumental in building and modifying social exchanges, then its substitutive powers can also be *constitutive* for the community in terms of its particular social dynamic and ideals. For the rest of this chapter, I shall consider four related propositions in order to determine how the substitutive and constitutive aspects of sacrificial militancy are entwined. Again, these propositions are not intended to be universalizing summations; indeed, I will be considering how the propositions' terms are effectively being fought over by opposed sides. If the first two propositions focus largely on Islamic sacrificial attacks it is not because I want to suggest that sacrifice has greater currency for Islamist militants than any other. Rather, it is because I want to establish ways in which Islamist militancy (and that of other religious groups) reflects wider sacrificial exchanges.

Proposition I: "Neither God nor transcendence are dead; rather, they are death"

Unfortunately, in order to reverse that proposition – God is life; transcendence is alive – in order to make that reversal *work*, you have to make sacrifices. This is nothing new to the Abrahamic religions, the "religions of The Book," all of which are currently engaged in wars around terror. God's eternity, his difference from humanity, can only be envisaged with death on the horizon. Death is God's difference; thus his genesis calls for death. The principle that one's recognition and love of God ultimately requires one to value Him above all other life is reiterated throughout the Jewish Tanakh, the Christian Bible (Old and New Testaments), and the Qur'an.[10] God's continuing need for recognition from mortals necessitates a repeated call for death – whether it is Abraham's pledge to sacrifice his son, or Jesus' death on the cross. Admittedly, there are particular disagreements between these religions in figuring sacrifice: for example, the Judaeo-Christian story of Abraham's willingness to sacrifice Isaac differs from the Qur'anic version. But all three religions also uphold an intimacy around sacrifice, envisaging it as something that produces a closeness to God; thus "*korban,*" the Hebrew word for sacrificial death, denotes "proximity" and "intimacy" no less than the Qur'anic "*qurban.*"[11] And it is not just the Abrahamic God that grows around death; spirituality invariably sprouts from a corpse because the corpse's terminated thingliness, par excellence, brings home the differences between immanence and transcendence, life and afterlife. So when thinkers as diverse as Freud, Girard, and Georges Bataille have engaged with the bases of religion in general, they have each noted how sacrifice has been essential for communities wishing to give life to spirituality and gods. Once a corpse can be made to bear testament to an afterlife, dying can be *for* god. As Bataille argues: "In a sense the corpse is the most complete affirmation of the spirit."[12] To labor for transcendence thus means instituting holy spirit and lifeless matter in the same blow, which is why sacrifice – which derives etymologically from the Latin for "making holy" (*sacrum facere*) – always involves a simultaneous *reifice*; a debased "thing-making" of its own. Freud touches on this regarding the Latin term "*sacer*," which, he notes, "means not only 'sacred,' 'consecrated,' but also something that we can only translate as 'infamous,' 'detestable'"[13] – an ambivalence which, he argues, is cognate with that of the Greek "*agos*," the Hebrew "*kadesh*," and the Polynesian "*taboo*."[14] And for Girard the paradoxical nature of sacrifice means that the sacrificial victim is both "a link and barrier between the community and the sacred."[15]

This ambivalence of the sacred and sacrificial victim arises because of sacrifice's substitutive nature. As Girard avers, the victim dies "so that the entire community, threatened by the same fate, can be reborn in a new or renewed cultural order."[16] Death becomes a "source of life" for the community, at the same time as "becom[ing] part of the divine substance."[17] Freud reasons similarly, stating that sacrifice has its roots in "public ceremony" in which "religious duty was a part of social obligation"; through sacrificial killing, community, victim, and god partake "*of the same blood*" to become "*members of the one clan*."[18] For both Freud and Girard, then, the religious and the social have always been fundamentally imbricated through sacrificial exchange. And this exchangeability – involving as it does conversions of life, death, community, and transcendence into each other – clearly turns sacrifice toward the economic, as Georges Bataille points out. In *The Theory of Religion* (1973), for example, he argues that, "in sacrifice the offering is rescued from all utility."[19] Making the spiritual thus means negating a reified world in which things must have determined use-values: "Sacrifice is the antithesis of production," he writes, "which is accomplished with a view to the future; it is consumption that is concerned only with the moment."[20] But if such "making holy" is accompanied by a debased "thing-making," then it cannot simply be an "antithesis" to production or reification. Its status as pure consumption or expenditure is thus also questionable; indeed, I would argue that one of the main functions of sacrifice is to produce spirituality and transcendence as a tangible thing that a community can exchange and conserve. If that is the case, sacrifice can also become a primary means by which a community establishes its own limits (or lack of them) of both use- and exchange-values. This point clearly bears on the sacrificial militancy escalating on all sides of the wars around terror. Yet among theorists only Jean Baudrillard has repeatedly related Bataille's writings on sacrifice to terrorism, though Baudrillard leaves the central tenets of Bataille's ideas largely unquestioned. I shall come back to this issue of Baudrillard's use of Bataille later. First, let us consider some particular ways in which Islamic militancy opens to wider sacrificial exchange.

Because God needs lives to be life, life should only be given up for God. That is why suicide is taboo in the Abrahamic religions; to kill oneself for reasons other than God is to cheat him of his vital due. From God's point of view suicide is a sacrilegious waste, which is why "suicide bombing" and "suicide terrorism" are eschewed as terms by Sunni and Shi'ite Islamist militants alike. Killing oneself in killing others is usually justified only as a form of sacrificial martyrdom (*istishad* or *shahadat*) for God in a time of holy war (*jihad*). That is not to say that there is a unanimously agreed Islamic position on sacrificial militancy.[21] Indeed, the tradition of martyrdom for Shi'ites extends back to the battle of Karbala in 680 CE when the Shi'ite leader Hussein ibn Ali and his followers were slain by Sunni forces – hence the longstanding antipathy between the two communities. And while Shi'ites have emphasized martyrdom in terms of Hussein's example, Sunnis have placed greater emphasis on martyrdom being justifiable in terms of waging *jihad*. In modern times, though, martyrdom and *jihad* have become more intimate in Sunni and Shi'ite militant organizations alike, just as so-called "suicide bombing" has come to be practiced both by Shi'ite groups like Hezbollah and by Sunni groups like Hamas and al-Qaeda. For all of these groups, the "*shahid*" (sacrifice martyr) bears testament to the faith of the community. Like the Greek etymon of "martyr" (*marturos*), *shahid* also means "witness"; hence the *shahid* is viewed by her/his community as testifying to the transcendence of religious vision. Yet, as several commentators have pointed out, modern Islamic notions of martyrdom have also resulted from syncretistic exchanges between Sunni and Shi'ite Islam, as well as influences from a range of secular discourses.[22] In his *On Suicide Bombing* (2007) Talal Asad takes issue with the view that such martyrdom has traditionally been linked to Islamic notions of sacrifice, but he concedes that the link has become current for militants as "an *idea*" of modern nationalism, before he goes on to argue that "the suicide bomber belongs

. . . to a modern Western tradition of armed conflict for the defense of a free political community."[23] Such a view is too sweeping, though, for it does not account adequately for ways in which modern Islamist martyrdom has variously sought to combine some forms of Western political ideology *and* traditional Islamic notions of sacrifice, martyrdom, and holy war.[24] For example, while intellectuals like Sayyid Qutb, Hasan al-Bana, and Maulana Mawdudi were instrumental in rethinking Sunni notions of defensive *jihad,* they also used Marxist theory and theories of colonialism to posit new forms of revolutionary and nationalist Islamic ideology.[25] Similarly, the influential Iranian Shi'ite sociologist and theologian Ali Shariati rethought traditions of martyrdom with reference to Marxist and existentialist writings. In that respect, the modern *shahid* does not simply bear witness to "Middle Eastern" religious fundamentalism; rather, s/he can also be seen as testifying to the way in which boundaries of nation, politics, and religion have become porous through various exchanges.

Such exchanges are further in evidence when both religious and secular organizations invoke similar images of economy in relation to sacrificial martyrdom. Palestine provides a case in point. Whereas a commemorative martyr card of Fatah nationalists in the second Intifada typically stated: "My country is my bride, and her *mahr* [bride-price] is my martyrdom," an Islamist version was, "Blood is the [bride-price] of the precious gifts" – a reference to the delights awaiting the martyr in heaven.[26] The exchange of blood, in particular, is a trope that has flowed across a range of militant organizations that use self-sacrificial killing as a tactic. As Anne Marie Oliver and Paul F. Steinberg write in their study of Palestinian suicide bombing, "Variants of the theme of irrigation by blood were virtually infinite, crossing over factional lines . . ."[27] Ayatollah Murtada Mutahhari, who served in Iran under Khomeini, provides a clear example of how martyred blood conjoins a "sacred cause" with the sociopolitical: "at no time is the blood of a *shahid* wasted. It does not flow into the ground . . . *Shahadat* means the transfusion of blood into a society."[28] From these examples alone, it is evident that Bataille's notion of sacrifice as "anti-production" and expenditure for "the moment" does not accord with the way secular and religious groups alike view sacrifice as a way of setting up God or land as a social cause and justification that is interminable. For both these religious and secular groups, sacrificial militancy engenders transcendence *of and for* its community. In contrast to Bataille's approach to sacrificial economy, then, I would like to discuss briefly here an alternative view afforded us by Shariati.

"A *Shahid,*" argues Shariati, "is the one who negates his whole existence for the sacred ideal in which we all believe":

> It is natural then that all the sacredness of that ideal and goal transports itself to his existence. True, that his existence has suddenly become non-existent, but he has absorbed the whole value of the idea for which he has negated himself. . . . He had been an individual who sacrificed himself for "thought." Now he is "thought" itself.[29]

Thus the *shahid* effectively dies into the sacred, and in substituting himself for a figure of thought he becomes an ideological afterlife for the community: "He is always in front of us," Shariati continues, "The thought also obtains presence and permanence through him." The *shahid*'s sacrifice is thus conceived as both an absolute expenditure *and* an investment in eternal spiritual savings, and Shariati makes this economic aspect explicit when he likens the *shahid*'s martyrdom to spending money: "That amount of money was a part of me. Thus the sanctity of the cause for which the money is spent reflects on me. . . . The hundred dollars that I have paid for the cause of justice transforms itself into 'the sanctity of justice.'"[30] So not only does sacred transcendence become tangibly current through the *shahid,* it also becomes a currency to the extent that s/he becomes part of others' lives.

Such intersubjectivity raises another question: do enemy lives that are "spent" also become part of the *shahid,* part of the sacred? Shariati, for one, is adamant that an individual consists of relations to others; indeed, he turns to Martin Heidegger in order to affirm this as an existential principle:

> Heidegger says, "The sum of man's knowledge about his life's environment makes his character, that knowledge being the conscious relation of the existence of 'I' with an external 'thing,' 'person,' or 'thought.'" When I establish a mental and existential relationship with individuals, movements, phenomena . . . this relationship finds a reflection in me. . . . Thus man's character is the sum of his relations with other characters.[31]

As the lives of enemy others must clearly be added to the *shahid*'s "sums" of knowledge and character, we need to consider how these enemy deaths entail another side of sacrificial exchange. Admittedly, the martyrdom of the Iran-Iraq war that Shariati is addressing was more about dying in staged battles than killing civilians and militants alike as a lone suicide bomber, but these two modes of *shahadat* clearly overlap in terms of dying to kill others. So far, I have discussed sacrificial substitution in terms of how an individual's life is turned into transcendence and social exchanges. With the next two propositions, I want to consider how this exchange involves the deaths of enemy others.

Proposition II: "They are, therefore I sacrifice; I sacrifice, therefore we are"

How otherness bears on sacrificial attacks is an issue that various commentators and theorists have debated. In raising the issue, though, they have generally relied either explicitly or implicitly on philosophies of alterity that consider relations between a singular self and a singular Other. In a review of books on suicide bombing, for example, Jacqueline Rose ponders, "Why dying with your victim should be seen as a greater sin than saving yourself."[32] After suggesting that the "revulsion" might arise from the way a suicide bomber ultimately executes an "unbearable intimacy" with "her or his victims," Rose concludes that, "Suicide bombing is an act of passionate identification – you take the enemy with you in a deadly embrace."[33] By collocating "victim," "victims," and "the enemy," it is unclear whether that "enemy" is a singular or collective noun. Certainly, the transformation of others to a hypostasized enemy Other is, I would argue, part of the violence of sacrificial militancy in general. Farhad Khosrokhavar, for example, argues that death for a suicide bomber "becomes a way of realising both self and other."[34] In contrast to Rose, such killing for Khosrokhavar is not so much a matter of "identification" as of *differentiation*. In many instances, he argues, the sacrifice martyr perceives his enemy as denying individual and collective sovereignty to his/her people.[35] Balancing the pressure to be part of a community with expectations of individual autonomy, the "new martyrdom" is caught up in "an appeal to the self, to an individual who becomes heroic . . ."[36] In other words, sacrificial martyrdom is symptomatic of a desire to distinguish oneself from a mass of partially individuated others.

Neither Rose's nor Khosrokhavar's account is adequate, I would argue, to the complexity of exchanges at stake here. Rose does not acknowledge the extent to which self-sacrificial killing might involve differentiating one's *community* and that of the enemy. Khosrokhavar does not account for the way that martyred individualism can entail identifying with a common idealism. In both instances, what is missing is a notion of sacrifice that involves a substitution between an individual and multiple others. This is perhaps not surprising if one accepts that philosophies of alterity have repeatedly upheld relations between singular self and singular Other in order to bypass the problem of unindividuated *others*. For the rest of this section, then, I shall turn to writings by two of the most prominent philosophers of alterity, Martin Heidegger and Emmanuel Levinas, in order to delineate this exclusion of others and its ramifications. Of course, these two thinkers cannot be seen as doing justice to notions of otherness in all cultures and contexts, and in examining their work I shall point to how the issue of foreign others (and colonialism) becomes problematic for them. I shall then consider how the wars around terror largely revolve around a sacrificial economy of mass others.

Heidegger's assertion in *Being and Time* (1926) that individual existence (*Dasein*) is essentially "being-towards-death" is particularly germane to sacrificial militancy, for as far as Heidegger is concerned, "being-towards-death" is fundamental to the way an individual is differentiated from an Other.[37] Coming to terms with your own inevitable death means comprehending your life *as a whole*, argues Heidegger. Confronting your finitude thus entails grasping your "wholeness" as an individual, and so determining your identity as your own. But because your death terminates your ability to experience anything, death also denies the possibility of experiencing your "wholeness" – and that, in turn, "makes the death of Others more impressive."[38] However, just when it seems that an individual's grasp of death is given through the mortality of "Others," Heidegger reasserts death to be individually inexchangeable: "By its very essence, death is in every case mine, in so far as it 'is' at all."[39] Only you can die your death; or, in other words: *"No one can take the Other's dying away from him."*[40] For Heidegger, this means that intersubjective "representation" (*Vertretbarkeit*) "breaks down completely" when it comes to dying, because no individual's death can be substituted for someone else's. "Of course," he writes, "someone can 'go to his death for another.' But that always means to sacrifice oneself for the Other '*in some definite affair*.' Such 'dying for' can never signify that the Other has thus had his death taken away in even the slightest degree."[41] Put simply: you cannot die in place of an Other so that s/he will never die. Heidegger thus recuperates death as the possibility of determining what is one's "ownmost." And when an individual grasps death as fundamentally "mine," he argues, s/he rejects the possibility that death terminates one's individuality. People say "one dies," writes Heidegger, because "everyone . . . can talk himself into saying that 'in no case is it I myself' . . ."[42] But once death is confronted as one's own, an individual can refute the common "opinion" that "what gets reached, as it were, by death, is *the 'they.'* "[43]

Let us consider some of the implications of Heidegger's analysis. On one hand, arrogating death as one's "ownmost" means an "I" can dissociate itself from the death of others viewed as a "they." On the other hand, rooting death in "mineness" should bolster collective bonds if it means the death of someone else can be seen as that of another "I, myself." Yet this clearly risks placing the "mineness" of death into a narcissistic loop. If death is always another "me," its status as Other becomes equivocal. As history has shown all too clearly, individuals frequently stop conceiving the Other as another "me" if that Other does not share the same nationality, sexuality, or religion – if it seems *too* Other.

Re-establishing a fundamentally foreign, unassimilable aspect to alterity and death is what Levinas seeks to do. The death that kills me may happen to me and no one else, he argues, but that does not mean it is "mine." I cannot possess the death that happens to me, for death kills me and my capacity to possess. Contrary to Heidegger's thinking, being-towards-death for Levinas means being faced with what is so opposed to me that one is always, in a sense, murdered by death.[44] Death as Other thus always threatens "from beyond," he argues. Yet the otherness of this "beyond" also inflects the very character of one's being, for every instant of one's life involves a passing away toward death. For Levinas, temporal existence is thus a continual openness to death as Other such that "being-in-one's-skin" means "having-the-other-in-one's-skin."[45] Consequently, one never has identity without the Other, for being alive means "being torn up from oneself in the core of one's unity." In other words, argues Levinas, "a subject is a hostage."[46]

A hostage to who or what, though? On one hand, Levinas seems to offer an escape from Heidegger's narcissistic loop because the Other is irreducibly foreign, *not* me. There is no originary "me" prior to my subjection to otherness; instead, any sense of "me" is secondary, derived from relations with the Other. But on the other hand, because this otherness harbors the end of one's finite existence, Levinas turns it into an infinitude that is synonymous with God. As a result, his vision of alterity involves coupled substitutions between the individual and God rather than between individuals. And this subordination of interpersonal relations to metaphysics proved controversial when

Levinas addressed political issues. Israel, he argued, embodied an ethical "coincidence of the political and spiritual," and when he was asked in 1982 whether the "Other" might be "above all Palestinian," Levinas replied: "if your neighbour attacks another neighbour or treats him unjustly, what can you do? Then alterity takes on another character, in alterity we can find an enemy. . . . There are people who are wrong."[47] That is to say, there are people who are the wrong kind of Other. Like Heidegger, then, Levinas effectively asserts that one must ultimately secure *one's own* Other. For once the relation with my Other involves others more generally, where does that leave "me"? Or, as Levinas puts it: "No one can substitute himself for me who substitutes for all."[48]

In the Abrahamic religions, that is frequently God's complaint. Abraham's pledge to give the life of his son Isaac to God is only one example of a person having to renounce love for others in order to maintain a special relationship. This latter instance is taken up by Jacques Derrida in *The Gift of Death* (1996 [1992]), in which he discusses how horrifying Abraham's willingness to kill his own son now seems to us. And yet, argues Derrida, is it not the case that sacrificing others is now one of the most "banal" and "everyday" occurrences? For to commit responsibility to any other is, by necessity, always made "only by failing in my responsibilities to all the others, to the ethical or political generality."[49] Hence, my relation to an Other always involves making sacrifices of some kind: "I am sacrificing and betraying at every moment all my other obligations to the other others whom I know or don't know, the billions of my fellows (without mentioning the animals that are even more other others than my fellows), my fellows who are dying of starvation or sickness."[50]

The generality of sacrifice is no metaphor here. Commitments in responsibility always involve turning a blind eye to the plight of others, and so being tacitly complicit in their losing their lives or being put to their deaths in various ways. The result is that everyday life is bound internationally to a general sacrificial economy that is in no way limited to militant struggles between the Abrahamic religions.[51] Whether this economy implies an "ethical or political generality," as Derrida suggests, is, however, questionable. With each "I" sacrificing "others," the fraught comity that he posits means that "others" (including animals) are thought of as "fellow" individuals. Yet, as Khosrokhavar argued, one's status as an individual can be stripped or taken hostage by an enemy such that one feels less an "I" than part of a mass of partially individuated others. What drives our general sacrificial economy is the realization that one increasingly has to fight to attain individuality. Whether we are thinking of otherness in terms of metaphysics, biopolitical networks (see Proposition III), or social interpellation through language, a connection to mass sociality – an amorphous "*they*" – comes first, and individuality is something that is carved out of this sociality through acts of self-differentiation that involve negating others in some way. Contrary to what Derrida suggests, there is no fundamental comity of "fellows" in this sacrificial economy; being connected to others means being meshed with what Paolo Virno calls "a *preindividual* or *subpersonal*" social relationality.[52] This means that there is also no "ethical or political generality," for ethics and politics denote the way individuals differentiate themselves from others. Accordingly, ethics and politics are constituted on the basis of rejecting general social relations in favor of partial, separatist bonds. For that reason, asserting a general sacrificial economy of sacrifice does not amount to saying that one mode or concept of sacrificial militancy prevails universally. Instead it involves realizing that distinct modes of militant sacrifice enter into exchanges with each other on the basis of their mutual opposition. The various modes of sacrificial militancy in the wars around terror are thus rooted in the same general economy of sacrifice, but one side's mode can also involve attacking its enemy's for being ethically and politically unacceptable. On one hand, then, we must acknowledge that the cultural and political valencies accorded to sacrificial martyrdom by Islamist militants are not the same as the valencies ascribed by the Bush administration to the "sacrifices" made by American soldiers. On the other hand (as I shall argue in the next two sections), we also need to understand that these differences can become blurred in significant ways when opposed sides escalate their militancy in being caught up in mutual sacrificial exchanges.

Before turning to those issues, let us consider how the terms of the martial *cogito* that is this section's proposition – "They are, therefore I sacrifice; I sacrifice, therefore we are" – are precisely what opposed sides are currently fighting over. That is to say, the proposition is not a universal statement so much as a statement of what is being contested. In the instance of a sacrificial martyr, for example, the bomber may perceive him/herself and his community as being forced by an enemy to subsist in an unindividuated state. This sense of being part of a subpersonal "they" is seen to justify the sacrificial bombing which performs a number of substitutions simultaneously: the bomber attains a heroic "I" in her/his community by testifying to a common cause (e.g., god or land). In that respect, s/he also helps constitute a singular individuality *for* the community: "I sacrifice therefore *we* are." These transformations link simultaneously to another set of exchanges. As Khosrokhavar suggests, the bombing becomes a way of "realising self and other," but this is only on the basis of substitution: if the bomber hypostasizes the community's "they" into a singular "we," s/he simultaneously negates the enemy by blasting it indiscriminately into a subpersonal mass. A similarly complex but opposed set of substitutions can obtain in sacrifices on the other side. A soldier gives her life to defend the "sacred freedoms" of American sovereignty by killing terrorist "unlawful combatants" as a faceless, stateless mass of enemy others ("They are, therefore I sacrifice"). Gaining a heroic identity through media reportage, and buried in a coffin wrapped in the Stars and Stripes, she simultaneously helps constitute a patriotic unity (and indebtedness) for her community ("I sacrifice, therefore we are").

That is by no means an exhaustive account of sacrificial exchange in the wars around terror – there have been other permutations, some of which I will address shortly. From the two instances I have given, though, what is notable is the volatile nature of the substitutions involved. Just as Freud and Girard saw sacrifice as producing the sacred and profane in the one blow, so the hypostasized "we" that the "I" substitutes itself for invariably derives from the lives of enemy others. The work of such sacrifice is thus never done, for it modulates any attained identity with the very otherness it is supposed to negate. With so much riding on sacrificial death as underpinning the power of social exchange, it is therefore not surprising that the wars around terror have also meant fighting over the extent to which death and sacrifice actually take place in terms of one's own side versus that of the enemy.

Proposition III: "The place of death is increasingly being taken"

With globalization meaning that people's lives are increasingly connected to the natural resources and livelihood of others, the importance of a general sacrificial economy is growing. But no individual wants to think that every day s/he is somehow responsible for others being put to death or being allowed to die – others that include members of communities that are not even deemed to be an enemy Other. Such responsibility is unthinkable. And in that sense the general sacrificial economy spreads, in part, as a form of social unconscious. In order for one's own life to be bearable one must repress the fact of dying others – even if they are individualized through news reports and images. Of course, with the deaths of others taking place regardless, there are always people fighting for those deaths to be recognized. But what happens when the occurrence of others' deaths is taken hostage?

This question bears primarily on the "virtualization" of death (and killing) through media technology – a matter Baudrillard has repeatedly addressed. Regarding the 1991 Gulf War, Baudrillard's argument that the war "did not take place" made sense in so far as the majority of deaths occurring on the ground were screened out and replaced with images of surgical strikes on buildings by "smart bombs."[53] But that did not mean that deaths were not occurring, and in focusing on the war's virtualization Baudrillard's account risks being complicit with the US administration's decision to use media technology strategically so that the more visceral combat remained unseen. Waging combat is always helped by hiding it. Hence the al-Qaeda attacks of September 11 were, in part, effectively contesting the proposition that death's place is being taken. The attacks were a challenge over the right to virtualize the event of death – the attackers effectively taking the media hostage in staging the sacrifice of others and themselves for "live" television coverage. Subsequently, in its bombing of Afghanistan the Bush administration endeavored to regain some media control over death partly by instructing its Department of Defense to buy exclusive rights to all commercial images of Afghanistan taken by satellite.[54] As Derek Gregory has argued, the spaces of the war's visibility became "spaces of carefully constructed *in*visibility . . ."[55] And since then, spaces of invisibility have been precisely what the United States and its allies have spread in the shape of detention centers, which include those at Guantánamo Bay and Abu Ghraib, not to mention others that have allegedly been kept off official maps.

As I have argued elsewhere, detention camps like Guantánamo Bay's amount to the "taking place" of a new compound power that combines two forms of governance described by Michel Foucault: biopolitics and sovereignty.[56] Historically, argues Foucault, the sovereign was an individual whose exceptional power was rooted in the right to take another person's life – whether citizen or enemy. In contrast, biopolitics grew out of an increasing need for the lives and deaths of a populace as a whole to be regulated by various administrative bodies. Whereas "Sovereignty took life and let live," argues Foucault, biopolitics introduced a "regularization [that] consists in making live and letting die."[57] And while sovereignty was traditionally more focused on deciding individual cases, biopolitics involves bureaucratized networks of people regulating lives and deaths of "a multiplicity of men." Because this power provides the means for a state to manage its population as a race or nation, biopolitics is thus largely responsible for racializing and nationalizing war. "If you want to live, the other must die" – that, argues Foucault, is the sacrificial footing that underpins biopolitical conflict. It also raises the following dilemma for states: "How can one both make a biopower function and exercise the rights of war, the rights of murder and the function of death, without becoming racist?"[58] Given that the "war against terror" has involved fighting non-state militants who are predominantly Islamic, the question facing America and its allies has been: How do you function as biopower and exercise the rights of war without targeting another *religion* as other?

One answer is to reduce the enemy to the status of faceless, subpersonal others, while taking their deaths and lives hostage. The indefinite detention of "unlawful combatants" is a prime example. By legislating against unlawful combatants in its war against terrorism, the Bush administration ratified a new class of outlawed militant. Deemed to be operating outside established laws of war, unlawful combatants were denied the status of standard "prisoners of war." Unrecognizable as a normal enemy Other (a foreign "me"), the detainees were consequently placed outside the jurisdiction of international law and US federal laws and thus denied a range of human rights.[59] Stripped of sovereign control over their own lives and deaths, the "alien" detainees are thus rendered a de-individuated mass of others. And while they also face the possibility of being sentenced to death by military tribunal, the death penalty is of questionable use when indefinite detention can substitute both life and death for a state of suspended animation. Taking others' lives without killing, indefinite detention is thus *a continuation of sacrifice by other means.*

In that respect, the decision of some Guantánamo detainees in June 2006 to kill themselves presents an awful conundrum. If it was an attempt to regain sovereign control over their own lives, it also seems to take indefinite detention to its logical conclusion: my life as human is untenable because I no longer have human rights; therefore I will end it. What is the status of such suicides, though? Do they accord with the tenor of detention or are they an attack on it? The Guantánamo Camp's commander, Rear Admiral Harry Harris, opted for the attack: "They have no regard for life, neither ours nor their own. I believe that this was not an act of desperation, but an act of asymmetrical warfare waged against us."[60] As he went on to explain: "We provide safe shelter and living areas with beds, mattresses, sheets and running water toilets. . . . Even so, many detainees have taken advantage of this – crafting killing weapons from toothbrushes and garrottes from food wrappers. . . ."[61] It is tempting to speculate that Harris had been reading up on Baudrillard. In *Symbolic Exchange and Death* (1976), Baudrillard follows Bataille in arguing that death escapes utility in a modern economic order that is based on the reification of values: "death is perhaps the only thing that has no use-value, which can never be referred back to need, and so can unquestionably be turned into a weapon."[62] And that, he argues, is exactly what the September 11 attackers brought home: "they have succeeded in turning their own deaths into an absolute weapon against a system that operates on the basis of an exclusion of death, a system whose ideal is an ideal of zero deaths."[63]

In one sense, Baudrillard's comments are confirmed by the way virtual technology and indefinite detention have indeed served as means of taking the death of others hostage. Yet the opposition that he advances – Western "system" of security versus terroristic sacrificial death – is a false one to the extent that both sides, as I am arguing, are immured in a general sacrificial economy. Just as the suicides of the Guantánamo detainees can be viewed as a resistance to indefinite detention *and* its logical conclusion, so the September 11 attacks were not wholly foreign to the US. As Derrida has argued: "Immigrated, trained, prepared for their act in the United States by the United States, these *hijackers* incorporate, so to speak, two suicides in one: their own . . . but also the suicide of those who welcomed, armed, and trained them."[64] Similarly, when Islamic militants have kidnapped Western hostages and dressed them in orange jumpsuits before videoing their execution, they were both mirroring the detention of unlawful combatants *and* attacking it.[65] In this way, sacrifice in the wars around terror have escalated mimetically, and it is this substitutive doubling that is at the heart of their sacrificial exchange. So while the US administration has increasingly been forced to call for more sacrifices to fight against terror, militants using suicide bombing to oppose the US and its allies have embraced the kinds of networked media and militancy associated with the very enemies they are striking.

This point is corroborated by a number of commentators on suicide bombing. Khosrokhavar, for example, acknowledges that the new martyrdom practiced by al-Qaeda is in part a "defiance of Western superiority at the technological, economic and military. Sacrificing one's life challenges this material superiority, which has as its corollary a fear of death."[66] Yet he also accepts that al-Qaeda is itself a thoroughly modernized, global organization that draws financial networks, communications technology, and militancy together. The investment in such extra-spiritual aspects of militancy is not limited to al-Qaeda. All groups that use suicide bombing as a tactic have invariably been forced to translate death's transcendence into networked finance and reification. As Ghassan Hage argues in relation to Palestinian martyrdom, "each bombing produces a form of anti-colonial capital that in turn attracts more numbers. A higher number of bombers and of successful bombings also invites further support from those behind the financing of such operations."[67] Contrary to the sacrificial expenditure that Shariati proposed, then, not all of the *shahid*'s life is deposited with the sacred; much of it is converted back into more funds for the organization and the martyr's family. And such conversions are compounded by the fact that recruitment for suicide bombing is often nurtured through various forms of media production. Posters and cards commemorating sacrifices, final video testaments by martyrs, plus news coverage of bombing attacks, all help to give martyrs an aura of celebrity. (In the United States and other countries, advertisements for armed service recruitment together with media coverage of fallen heroes clearly has a similar effect.) As Oliver and Steinberg write, regarding Palestinian sacrifice bombers: "You will never understand anything about the lure of martyrdom . . . until you realise that someone who has decided to take that path as his own sees himself . . . as something of a movie star. . . ."[68] Attaining publicized heroism, the sacrificed person testifies to death as having an incalculable social use-value on the basis that death is the ultimate in social exchange.

Proposition IV: "Sacrifice escalates largely through necromimesis"

As I have argued (Propositions I and III), one of the major tasks of sacrifice is to establish what is beyond life (whether spirituality or secular transcendence) at the same time as turning this into a consumable *thing* for a community. If sacrifice upholds death as the apogee of social exchange, it is only because it also turns death into something it is not. And that is another reason why sacrificial labor never reaches its end. Neither the suicide bomber nor the soldier killed in action can attain or incorporate their death – it is instead what terminates any grasp of experience and capacity. Their death is thus handed over to others who can grasp it only on the basis that they themselves are not dead, and that what they incorporate as death is in fact the deposition and imitation of something that remains irreducibly other. Consequently, the substitutive nature of sacrifice is inherently *necromimetic*. Denoting the intimate exchanges that take place between death and representation, necromimesis should also be seen as complementing what Achille Mbembe has called "necropolitics" and "necropower," which work in tandem, he argues, to create "*death-worlds*, new and unique forms of social existence in which vast populations are subjected to conditions of life conferring on them the status of *living dead*."[69] Having discussed such sociopolitical dynamics more in terms of a general sacrificial economy, I shall now consider how necromimesis fuels that economy at the level of aesthetics. In particular, I want to outline the volatile nature of necromimetic productions. Involving, as they do, representations and conversions of death, they can have a distinct narcotizing effect such that they deaden death's impact. Yet because such representations are usually the only way in which death can be experienced, what is often deadened is a sense of the representations as being representations – in other words, they are experienced as all-too-real.

Joseph Conrad's *The Secret Agent* (1907), one of the first novels to feature a suicide bomber, offers an excellent introduction to necromimesis. The central terrorist plot is partly inspired by the accidental self-detonation of an anarchist, Martial Bourdin, in Greenwich, London, in 1894. In the novel, though, it is an agent provocateur, Adolf Verloc, who plots to blow up the Greenwich Observatory in order to induce a toughening of British anti-terror laws. Charging Stevie, the "simple" brother of his wife Winnie, with carrying the packaged bomb on his own, Verloc does not tell his stepson that the package is a bomb, and when Stevie trips over with it he is instantly killed. This instantaneity of death is, at least, what Inspector Heat divines when examining Stevie's gruesome remains in the hospital:

> The shattering violence of destruction which had made of that body a heap of nameless fragments affected his feelings with a sense of ruthless cruelty, though his reason told him the effect must have been as swift as a flash of lightning. . . . No physiologist, and still less of a metaphysician, Chief Inspector Heat rose by the force of sympathy, which is a form of fear, above the vulgar conception of time. Instantaneous! He remembered all he had ever read in popular publications of long and

> terrifying dreams dreamed in the instant of waking; of the whole past life lived with frightful intensity by a drowning man as his doomed head bobs up, screaming, for the last time. The inexplicable mysteries of conscious existence beset Chief Inspector Heat till he evolved a horrible notion that ages of atrocious pain and mental torture could be contained within two successive winks of an eye. And meantime the Chief Inspector went on peering at the table with a calm face and slightly anxious attention of an indigent customer bending over what may be called the by-products of a butcher's shop with a view to an inexpensive Sunday dinner.[70]

Imagining this terrible death to be *immediate*, it seems, at first, as though Heat cannot mediate it enough, for the lightning flash of violence is also the instantaneity with which the "heap of nameless fragments" affects him "with a sense of ruthless cruelty." This effect of death is thus ambivalent – not only does Heat feel cruel as death, he also feels an acute sympathy for what Stevie has undergone. Just as Levinas links death and alterity, so Stevie and his death get under Heat's skin. But as sympathy implies feeling *with* someone else, Heat can only conceive of death's approximation; namely, Stevie's last dying moments. And while Levinas sees the experience of otherness as entailing substitutions between a self and Other, Conrad emphasizes – partly by using indirect discourse – that Heat's visceral sense of what has occurred is mediated through a range of others. Heat's overpowering intuition of Stevie's death throes is thus inflected by accounts he has read in "popular publications" – the last gasps of the drowning man being just one instance. This simultaneous incorporation, approximation, and mediation of death's effects is what I am calling necromimesis. It is what gives Heat intimations of metaphysical transcendence while he absorbs the debased thingliness of Stevie's "nameless fragments." It is what enables him to sense the "ages of atrocious pain . . . contained within two . . . winks of an eye" while calmly regarding Stevie's remains as if they were meat for a cheap "Sunday dinner." As in other instances in which Conrad's characters are forced to experience what is beyond experience, the concept of the sublime is clearly at stake here. And to the extent that the heightening of Heat's critical faculties feeds off Stevie's death, this sublimity is clearly sacrificial.[71]

The intimacy of necromimesis and sacrifice has always been implicit in theories of the sublime which propose that death and terror can be substituted by a subject into feelings of autonomy and self-empowerment. In Immanuel Kant's *Critique of the Power of Judgement* (1790), for example, the sublime arises when one perceives a "boundless" object which does "violence to the imagination" and so resists being assimilated into experience.[72] Reason, through its "infinite" Ideas, is only able to comprehend the sense of the illimitable by grasping the imagination's suffering and finitude. The imagination thus acts both to mediate and incorporate the sublime experience for the individual. If death offerings can bring God's transcendence into view, so, for Kant, Reason's infinitude "might actually reveal itself only through [the imagination's] self-sacrifice [*Aufopferungen*]."[73] But just as God's continuing need for recognition requires frequent gifts of life, so Kant's rational subject must maintain the supposed transcendence of her/his agency by repeatedly imagining sacrifices for it. The dilemma finds its neatest encapsulation in a statement by one of Samuel Beckett's narrators: "Imagination dead imagine."[74]

Such sacrificial sublimity is frequently at play in the necromimesis surrounding suicide bombing. As Khosrokhavar has argued regarding Palestinian martyrs, sacrificial militancy is partly an attempt to attain "a higher unity . . . a sublime meaning" of "individuation" – one that cannot be provided by "a sovereign nation without a unified territory."[75] And media production certainly plays an important role in preparing and recruiting for this. On one hand, videos are often shown to familiarize and anaesthetize death. As a Hamas member told journalist Christoph Reuter regarding videos of martyrs: "The candidate watches his predecessor's videos over and over again, and watches his own, too, in order to rid himself of any fear . . . Then he can greet death like an old friend."[76] In many instances, an individual's pledge to become a martyr is formalized by making a video testament. As Ami Pedahzur has pointed out, as soon as the testament has been videoed the prospective bomber is referred to by some organizations as *"al shahid al-hai,"* the living martyr – that is to say, a militant form of living-dead.[77] On the other hand, videos are frequently watched by a prospective *shahid* to suscitate feelings of outrage at mortalities inflicted by the enemy. As the Hamas leader Abdul Aziz Rantisi told writer Barbara Victor: "Our martyr looks at many, many films, which show the atrocities the Israelis have done to our women and children."[78] Narcotizing *and* revivifying death's effects, the necromimetic nature of video productions is thus too much and not enough at the same time – which makes it addictively double-edged. For that reason, I disagree with Khosrokhavar when he asserts that because of mediated networkings of martyrdom, "death is experienced as a situation that has no particular affect" just as "a computer screen is emptied of its content when it is attacked by a virus."[79] Such a view ignores the fact that despite performing mediations, many necromimetic media productions represent death only to generate incendiary, militant passions.

Necromimesis does not just involve representing sacrifice, then; rather, *it continues the work of sacrifice*. Whether in the form of martyr videos or news reportage honoring a soldier killed in combat, necromimetic productions ensure that sacrificial deaths can circulate hauntingly and indefinitely as virtual afterlives while accruing indebtedness as social capital. And because self-sacrificial militancy involves exchanging one's death for others, opposed communities can be interpellated within a sacrificial economy through the same media footage. Images of the attacks on the World Trade Center, for example, have been taken by both Islamic militants and the United States and its allies as reasons for repaying debts to those who died.

From the preceding points, we can thus see that necromimesis continues the work of sacrifice along three main fronts that I have discussed under the previous three propositions, respectively: (1) it consolidates the intimacy of sacrifice and reifice for a community; (2) it facilitates aesthetically the substitutions at stake in the statement, "They are, therefore I sacrifice; I sacrifice, therefore we are"; (3) it allows death to take place collectively on the basis that it takes the place of death mimetically. Necromimesis thus helps to draw together reified transcendence, death, and social exchange into a sacrificial compound for a particular community. Yet it is also what draws that oppositional form of sacrifice into exchanges with opposing forms of sacrificial militancy. If these exchanges thereby help perpetuate a general sacrificial economy, it is tempting to ask whether we can counteract the spread of sacrifice by turning to its opposite. But what is sacrifice if not an investment in opposition *and* a negation of it in the same blow?

I would like to close, then, by considering how a novel like Yasmina Khadra's *The Attack* (2005) at least helps to establish a critical no-man's-land in relation to sacrificial militancy. The novel opens and ends with an account of Amin, the narrator, being killed in an Israeli bomb attack on the car of a radical sheikh. Like the passage in which Inspector Heat examines Stevie's remains, Amin details his final moments before dying: "I have a vague sensation of being reduced to shreds . . ."; "I hover for an eternity before plunging back to earth . . ."[80] The main body of the novel recounts events leading up to this attack. Amin, a non-religious Arab-Israeli enjoying a successful career as a surgeon in Tel Aviv, is devastated when he learns that a suicide bombing that has occurred was carried out by his own wife, Sihem. Struggling to accept her death, Amin in turn feels suicidal and numb – "I feel sickly, hallucinatory, devitalized"; "here I am . . . like a ghost"[81] – and is also full of vengeful hate toward those whom he thinks persuaded his wife to become a martyr. This potent mix of self-destructive and murderous feelings is portrayed as inclining him toward the very mindset that he cannot accept Sihem as having embraced. Indeed, the parallels between his mourning self, his eventual death, and a martyr's psychology are made explicit when a police friend explains to Amin that martyrs are able to commit their deeds because they have renounced all worldly relations: "You float. You hover. You're an extra-terrestrial. You live in a kind of limbo stalking houris and unicorns."[82] Trying to discover why Sihem became a martyr, Amin cannot help but follow in her footsteps. Only after visits to Palestine and meetings with militants does he realize that sustaining his own successful middle-class life in Israel has meant turning his back on the everyday plight of others in his homeland. Not only does this realization allow him to sympathize with his wife's decision to die for these suffering others, it also enables him to see that such a cause can blind people to the fact that the Israeli victims he operates on are also others deserving of life. At the point where one thinks of dying or killing for *one's own* others, then, there are always other others to consider. And if that consideration ultimately denies a cause some life, it is surely a sacrifice worth making.

Notes

1 "President Discusses War on Terror" (October 28, 2005) at <http://www.whitehouse.gov/news/releases/2005/10/20051028-html>.
2 Ibid. See also: "President Discusses War on Terror at FBI Academy" (July 11, 2005) at <http://www.whitehouse.gov/news/releases/2005.07/20050711-html>.
3 "President Bush Visits Troops in Iraq" (June 13, 2006) at <http://www.whitehouse.gov/news/releases/2006/06/20060613-2.html>.
4 At the time of writing, a search on the White House website for references to "sacrifice" in Bush's speeches and statements since 2001 garners 2,079 hits. See also "Fact Sheet: The Sixth Anniversary of 9/11: Remembering Lives Lost and Heroic Sacrifices Made" (September 11, 2007): <http://www.whitehouse.gov/news/releases/2007/09/20070911.html>.
5 "President Commemorates Veterans' Day," (November 11, 2005) at <http://www.whitehouse.gov/news/releases/2005/11/20051111-1.html>.
6 See Gambetta (2005: 259–99). For other general histories of suicide bombing see Juergensmeyer (2001); Pedahzur (2005); Reuter (2004).

7 Reuter (2004: 13).

8 "President's Radio Address" (May 24, 2008) at <http://www.whitehouse.gov/news/releases/2008/05/20080524.html>.

9 See Freud (2001) and Girard (2005).

10 For discussions of sacrifice relating to each of the Abrahamic religions, see, in particular, Sykes (1991).

11 For a discussion of *korban* as sacrifice see Derrida (1996: 58). For discussion of *qurban* as sacrifice see Khosrokhavar (2005: 10).

12 Bataille (1989: 40).

13 Freud (1964: 122).

14 Freud (2001: 18).

15 Girard (2005: 286).

16 Girard (2005: 270).

17 Ibid.

18 Freud (2001: 136).

19 Bataille (1989: 49).

20 Ibid.

21 For detailed discussions of these terms, see, in particular: Mehdi Abedi and Gary Legenhausen (1986); Esposito (2002: ch. 2); Strenski (2003); Khosrokhavar (2005: ch. 1).

22 See, for example, Khosrokhavar (2005: chs. 1 and 3); and Gray (2003).

23 Asad (2007: 51, 63; Asad's emphasis).

24 In her article "Theology and Power in the Middle East: Palestinian Martyrdom in a Comparative Perspective," Meir Hatina argues that modern martyrdom combines older notions of *jihad* and *shahadat* with more modern, secular concepts of *thawra* (revolution) and *fida'* (sacrifice), p. 250.

25 On this point, see, for example, Khosrokhavar (2005: ch. 1).

26 Quoted in Oliver and Steinberg (2005: 76).

27 Ibid., 92.

28 Mutahhari (1986: 136).

29 Shariati (1986: 233).

30 Ibid., 232.

31 Ibid., 231.

32 J. Rose (2004: 21).

33 Ibid.

34 Khosrokhavar (2005: 59).

35 Ibid., 135.

36 Ibid., 46.

37 Heidegger (1990: 279–311).

38 Ibid., 281.

39 Ibid., 284.

40 Ibid., Heidegger's emphasis.

41 Ibid., Heidegger's emphases.

42 Ibid., 297.

43 Ibid., my emphasis.
44 Levinas (1994: 234; Levinas's emphasis).
45 Levinas (1991: 115).
46 Ibid., 112.
47 Levinas (1989: 294).
48 Levinas (1991: 126).
49 Derrida (1996: 70).
50 Ibid., 69.
51 As Derrida argues: "Sacrificial war rages not only among the races of Abraham that expressly refer to the sacrifice of Isaac, Abraham, or Ibrahim, but even between [those] . . . who don't belong to the people of Abraham or Ibrahim, all those others to whom the names of Abraham and Ibrahim have never meant anything . . ." (ibid., 70).
52 Virno (2008: 178).
53 See Baudrillard (1995).
54 On this point, see Gregory (2004: 52–4).
55 Ibid., 53.
56 See my "Sovereignty, Biopolitics, and the Use of Literature: Michel Foucault and Kathy Acker," (2006): <http://muse.jhu.edu/journals/theory_and_event/toc/archive.html#9.1>.
57 Foucault (2003: 247).
58 Ibid., 263.
59 On this point, see Aman (2004) and D. Rose (2004).
60 Quoted in Goldberg and Muir (2006).
61 Quoted in ibid.
62 Baudrillard (1993: 176).
63 Baudrillard (2002: 16).
64 Quoted in Borradori (2003: 95).
65 See Burke (2004); also Parry (2004).
66 Khosrokhavar (2005: 161).
67 Hage (2003: 70).
68 Oliver and Steinberg (2005: 73).
69 Mbembe (2008: 176–7, Mbembe's emphasis).
70 Conrad (1990: 107).
71 For a discussion of how Conrad and late Victorian writers engage with the sublime more generally when writing on terrorism, see my *Terrorism and Modern Literature: From Joseph Conrad to Ciaran Carson*, ch. 1.
72 Kant (2000: 128, 129).
73 Ibid., 153.
74 Beckett (1997: 182–5).
75 Khosrokhavar (2005: 135).
76 Reuter (2004: 88).
77 Pedahzur (2005: 179).
78 Victor (2004: 145).

79 Khosrokhavar (2005: 61).
80 Khadra (2006: 2).
81 Ibid., 31, 67.
82 Ibid., 94.

References

Abedi, Mehdi and Gary Legenhausen, eds. (1986) *Jihad and Shahadat: Struggle and Martyrdom in Islam*. Houston: The Institute for Research and Islamic Studies.

Aman, Diane Marie. (2004) "Guantánamo," *Columbia Journal of Transnational Law* 42(2): 263–348.

Asad, Talal. (2007) *On Suicide Bombing*. New York: Columbia University Press.

Bataille, Georges. (1989) *Theory of Religion*, trans Robert Hurley. New York: Zone. First published 1973.

Baudrillard, Jean. (1993) *Symbolic Exchange and Death*, trans. Iain Hamilton Grant. London: Sage.

Baudrillard, Jean. (1995) *The Gulf War Did Not Take Place*, trans. Paul Patton. Bloomington: Indiana University Press. First published 1991.

Baudrillard, Jean. (2002) *The Spirit of Terrorism*, trans. Chris Turner. London: Verso.

Beckett, Samuel. (1997) "Imagination Dead Imagine" [1965], in Beckett, *The Complete Short Prose, 1929–89*, ed. S. E. Gontarski. New York: Grove.

Borradori, Giovanna. (2003) "Autoimmunity: Real and Symbolic Suicides; A Dialogue with Jacques Derrida," in Giovanna Borradori, *Philosophy in a Time of Terror: Dialogues with Jürgen Habermas and Jacques Derrida*. Chicago: The University of Chicago Press.

Burke, Jason. (2004) "Theatre of Terror," *Observer*, Review Section (November 21): 1–2.

Conrad, Joseph. (1990) *The Secret Agent*. London: Penguin, 1990.

Derrida, Jacques. (1996 [1992]) *The Gift of Death*, trans. David Wills. Chicago: The University of Chicago Press.

Esposito, John L. (2002) *Unholy War: Terror in the Name of Islam*. Oxford: Oxford University Press.

"Fact Sheet: The Sixth Anniversary of 9/11: Remembering Lives Lost and Heroic Sacrifices Made" (September 11, 2007): <http://www.whitehouse.gov/news/releases/2007/09/20070911.html>.

Foucault, Michel. (2003) *Society Must be Defended: Lectures at the Collège de France, 1975–6*, ed. Mauro Bertani and Alessandro Fontana, trans. David Macey. London: Allen Lane.

Freud, Sigmund. (1964) "Moses and Monotheism" [1939], in *The Standard Edition of the Complete Psychological Works of Sigmund Freud*, Vol. 23, ed. and trans. James Strachey. London: Hogarth.

Freud, Sigmund. (2001) "Totem and Taboo" [1913], in *The Standard Edition of the Complete Psychological Works of Sigmund Freud*, Vol. 13, ed. and trans. James Strachey, pp. 1–161. London: Vintage.

Gambetta, Diego. (2005) "Can We Make Sense of Suicide Missions," in Diego Gambetta (ed.), *Making Sense of Suicide Missions*, pp. 259–99. Oxford: Oxford University Press.

Girard, René. (2005) *Violence and the Sacred*, trans. Patrick Gregory. London: Continuum. First published 1972.

Goldberg, Suzanne and Hugh Muir. (2006) "'Killing Themselves Was Unnecessary. But It Certainly Is a Good PR Move,'" *Guardian* (June 12): 3.

Gray, John. (2003) *Al Qaeda and What It Means to Be Modern*. London: Faber.

Gregory, Derek. (2004) *The Colonial Present: Afghanistan, Palestine, Iraq*. Oxford: Blackwell.

Hage, Ghassan. (2003) "'Comes a Time We Are All Enthusiasm': Understanding Palestinian Suicide Bombers in Times of Exighophobia," *Public Culture* 15(1): 70.

Hatina, Meir. (2005) "Theology and Power in the Middle East: Palestinian Martyrdom in a Comparative Perspective," *Journal of Political Ideologies* 10 (October): 241–67.

Heidegger, Martin. (1990) *Being and Time*, trans. John Macquarrie and Edward Robinson. Oxford: Blackwell.

Houen, Alex. (2002) *Terrorism and Modern Literature: From Joseph Conrad to Ciaran Carson*. Oxford: Oxford University Press.

Houen, Alex. (2006) "Sovereignty, Biopolitics, and the Use of Literature: Michel Foucault and Kathy Acker," *Theory and Event* 9(1) (Spring): <http://muse.jhu.edu/journals/theory_and_event/toc/archive.html#9.1>.

Juergensmeyer, Mark. (2001) *Terror in the Mind of God: The Global Rise of Religious Violence*, 3rd ed. Berkeley: University of California Press.

Kant, Immanuel. (2000) *Critique of the Power of Judgement*, trans. Paul Guyer and Eric Matthews. Cambridge: Cambridge University Press.

Khadra, Yasmina [Mohammed Moulessehoul]. (2006) *The Attack*, trans. John Cullen. London: William Heinemann. First published 2005.

Khosrokhavar, Farhad. (2005) *Suicide Bombers: Allah's New Martyrs*, trans. David Macey. London: Pluto. First published 2002.

Levinas, Emmanuel. (1989) "Ethics and Politics", *The Levinas Reader*, ed. Sean Hand. Oxford: Blackwell.

Levinas, Emmanuel. (1991) *Otherwise than Being or Beyond Essence*, trans. Alphonso Lingis. Dordrecht: Kluwer. First published 1974.

Levinas, Emmanuel. (1994) *Totality and Infinity*, trans. Alphonso Lingis. Pittsburgh: Duquesne University Press. First published 1961.

Mbembe, Achille. (2008) "Necropolitics," in Stephen Morton and Stephen Bygrave (eds.), *Foucault in an Age of Terror*. London: Palgrave Macmillan.

Mutahhari, Murtada. (1986) "Shahid," in Mehdi Abedi and Gary Legenhausen (eds.), *Jihad and Shahadat: Struggle and Martyrdom in Islam*. Houston: The Institute for Research and Islamic Studies.

Oliver, Anne Marie and Paul F. Steinberg. (2005) *The Road to Martyrs' Square: A Journey into the World of the Suicide Bomber*. Oxford: Oxford University Press.

Parry, Richard Lloyd. (2004) "Video's Theatre of Macabre Devised by Brutal Militant," *The Times* (October 9): 1–2.

Pedahzur, Ami. (2005) *Suicide Terrorism*. Cambridge: Polity.

"President Bush Visits Troops in Iraq" (June 13, 2006) at <http://www.whitehouse.gov/news/releases/2006/06/20060613-2.html>.

"President Commemorates Veterans' Day" (November 11, 2005) at <http://www.whitehouse.gov/news/releases/2005/11/20051111-1.html>.

"President Discusses War on Terror at FBI Academy" (July 11, 2005) at <http://www.whitehouse.gov/news/releases/2005.07/20050711-html>.

"President Discusses War on Terror" (October 28, 2005) at <http://www.whitehouse.gov/news/releases/2005/10/20051028-html>.

"President's Radio Address" (May 24, 2008) at <http://www.whitehouse.gov/news/releases/2008/05/20080524.html>.

Reuter, Christoph. (2004) *My Life Is a Weapon: A Modern History of Suicide Bombing*, trans. Helena Ragg-Kirkby. Princeton: Princeton University Press.

Rose, David. (2004) *Guantánamo: America's War on Human Rights*. London: Faber & Faber.

Rose, Jacqueline. (2004) "Deadly Embrace," *London Review of Books* 26(21) (November 4): 21.

Shariati, Ali. (1986) "A Discussion of Shahid," in Mehdi Abedi and Gary Legenhausen (eds.), *Jihad and Shahadat: Struggle and Martyrdom in Islam*. Houston: The Institute for Research and Islamic Studies.

Strenski, Ivan. (2003) "Sacrifice, Gift and the Social Logic of Muslim 'Human Bombers,'" *Terrorism and Political Violence* 15(3) (Autumn): 1–34.

Sykes, S. W., ed. (1991) *Sacrifice and Redemption*. Cambridge: Cambridge University Press.

Victor, Barbara. (2004) *Army of Roses: Inside the World of Palestinian Women Suicide Bombers*. London: Robinson. First published 2003.

Virno, Paolo. (2008) *Multitude: Between Innovation and Negation*, trans. Isabella Bertoletti, James Cascaito, and Andrea Casson. New York: Semiotext(e).

Chapter 5

Postcolonial Writing and Terror

Elleke Boehmer

Let us go to another country
Not yours or mine
And start again.
To another country? Which?
One without fires, where fever
Lurks under leaves, and water
Is sold to those who thirst?
And carry dope or papers
In our shoes to save us starving?
Hope would be our passport
The rest is understood
Just say the word.
(Sorry, don't remember how it ends.)

William Plomer, "Let Us Go," quoted as epigraph in Nadine Gordimer, *The Pickup*, np and 88–9

Where will it end? Like most of our leaders, he creates a problem, then creates another problem to deal with the first one – on and on, endlessly fertile, always creatively spiralling to greater chaos . . . It was around that time that I learnt of the Rastafarian's survival.

Ben Okri, *Stars of the New Curfew*, p. 49

We live within an international situation which is, it seems, in accelerated flux, marked by convulsive periods of crisis, impasse, and conflict, now almost automatically described as "terror," "War on Terror" or in terms of some mode of terroristic response. In this situation it might be helpful to consider how the theoretical and textual approach called postcolonialism, which deals in cross-cultural contacts and transaction, as well as, importantly, with breakdowns in contact – which, in short, foregrounds a commitment to *life*, the continuation of life – confronts such crises and challenges.

In what follows I aim to bring into critical relationship these primary terms: *postcolonialism*; *terror*, that word used to denote the crises or the dark reverse of the global; and also, residually, *globalization*, the standard shorthand for describing the interconnected, deregulated state of the world today. The question I will have in front of me throughout will be whether the postcolonial, rather than merely repeating and confirming the structures of the global, is able diagnostically to explicate and interrogate, even narrativize, those resistances and reversals within the processes of empire which express as terror. Do the shaping forces of narrative and poetry provide an alternative response to situations of terror? It is with an eye to such eventual narrativization and formal organization that I include the two epigraphs from contemporary texts above.

Capitalist globalization is seen by many critics and theorists – those of the well-off north in particular (those powers that set the globalization agenda) – as the definitive condition of twenty-first-century humanity. The "borderless global economy" appears increasingly to undermine the former centrality of national structures and institutions, and to demand a refiguration of the languages of everyday life (Featherstone, Lash, and Robertson 1995: 2–3). Indeed, global interconnection has ramified to the extent that both postcolonial theory and postcolonial literatures, conventionally seen as concerned with cross-border exchange, and as privileging creolized, "deregulated," Rushdiesque writing, are now widely regarded as in some way matching that globalized world, as articulated with and within that cross-planet refiguration. Postcolonial theory in this view is associated with migrant spaces for which the colony as a situation of violent repression, and the nation as a horizon of expectation, have retreated, to be replaced with a concept of cultural exchange and contestation as primary and form-giving. Indeed, in some situations we hear "postcolonialism" used synonymously with "transnationalism," as having exclusively to do with transgressive trans-border movement and multicultural exchange. According to this view, the postcolonial text (literary, theoretical) is believed not only to reflect the contemporary world – becoming made-to-measure hybrid and predictably magic realist – but also, via transnational processes of publishing and marketing, is seen willingly to collude in its market-driven systems. As Benita Parry comments, in postcolonial discussion "the intrinsically antagonistic colonial encounter [has been] configured as one of dialogue, complicity and transculturation" (Parry 2004: 4).

At the same time, the postcolonial has also (if not equally) come to be accepted in academic circles and institutions as a critical term signifying a theoretical and writerly force field preoccupied with *resistance to empire* and its post-imperial aftermath. This is perhaps especially the case since the publication of key studies earlier this decade reminding us of the theory's historical roots in anti-colonial opposition: amongst others, Robert Young's *Postcolonialism* (2001), Nick Harrison's *Postcolonial Criticism* (2003); new work on Frantz Fanon as "post-colonial" theorist; Benita Parry's repeated reminders of precisely these forms of revolutionary provenance (2004); and Gayatri Spivak's pointed remarks in *Other Asias* (2008) that postcolonialism demands attention to idiom – the idiom of the local, the political. Postcolonialism under this heading correlates with struggle, subversion, the nation, the region, resistance to the global status quo – whether that be capitalist-driven colonialism or contemporary neo-imperial globalization (the contemporary incarnation of capitalism, according to Parry and others). From this perspective, unnervingly to some, *postcolonialism* aligns more closely with some of the theories and significations of *terror* (as in anti-colonial violence, for example), than it does with *globalization*.

So we have before us two dominant inflections of the postcolonial: a globalized and hybridizing inflection and a "resistance" inflection. The first tends to find expression in the magic realist novel; the second in form-giving national stories – "nation narration." The inflections are, however, connected in their acknowledgment, even if at times implicit, even if differently angled, of the still-lingering colonial past. Both interpretations of the postcolonial are interested in imperial after-effects which remain latent, like jiggers buried in the callus of feet, until they manifest, apparently suddenly, in a variety of economic, political, social, and religious forms: disharmonious outbreaks of poly-culturalism; unpredicted genocides (Rwanda, Darfur); multinational support for factional interests (De Beers and diamond trading in Central Africa); terroristic incidents. "Postcolonialism," as Ali Behdad, and Derek Gregory following him, compellingly suggest, "reveals the *continuing* impositions" of colonialism [emphasis added]. It does so, however, "in order to subvert them" (Gregory 2004: 9).

The shared preoccupation with belatedness aside, it is postcolonialism under the heading of resistance that is first and foremost (even definitively, I would venture to say) interested in subversion, what might also be called the practice of decentering the center or, in Dipesh Chakrabarty's phrase, provincializing Europe. This complicated practice of relentlessly interrogating and revising the global map of contemporary modernity is to be distinguished from, though it also relates to, the end-directed activity of "writing back," which Rushdie first isolated as the primary task of a postcolonial writer in English such as he. As this implies, what is often elided in discussions of globalization is that the global world is no undifferentiated neoliberal network but retains significant centers or concentrations of power and many closed borders, most of them located in or at points proximate to the West (hence, once again, belatedness). The postcolonialism that has to do with resistance is concerned to keep watch on these hegemonic centers and borders, to sabotage, subvert, and baulk them if necessary, and also to explore alternative yet co-existent locations and lineages of meaning and survival. But this is not to suggest that migrant and/or hybrid postcolonial writing is not involved in grappling with colonial aftermaths, or that such writing, as will be seen, is not equally preoccupied with a violent desire to break into the modern, metropolitan world – a world in fact that it already to some small extent inhabits and whose values it has internalized.

Let us turn now to terror, the West's current self-consolidating enemy par excellence, in an attempt to place it within the historical perspective of belated or continuing empire. At a time when terrorism is simultaneously vilified and homogenized as a common enemy, it is widely assumed that we know what terror means (we are, it is said, all implicated in this "War on Terror"). Yet, in point of fact, terror has been emptied of meaning as never before. To cite the observation of a journalist well used to defining the status quo, Simon Jenkins, in a review of David Runciman's book *The Politics of Good Intentions*, the "War on Terror" has become an ideal post-Cold War tool. It allows Western states to reinstate the condition, presumably taken from colonial times, of wielding sovereignty through war-without-end. In both situations, colonial and contemporary, terror becomes all pervasive and completely non-specific, as well as deeply contradictory (Jenkins 2006: 11). The "War on Terror" is at one and the same time unwinnable, since it has no distinct enemy and is without limit and without restraint – *and yet* it is waged, we are told, in order to be won; in order for a limit to be achieved. Interestingly, the unlocalized phrase "War on Terror" is a hostage to its own imperializing fortunes, in so far as it implies that terror is everywhere, and hence it must constitute the primary mode of sovereignty of the counter-terroristic state itself. If we are to believe Western political rhetoric, terror has become the contemporary state of being to which, for the West, there is no exception (using the word in the conventional sense), and to which there have been few exceptions for some considerable time. Its state power and the enemy's power are both terroristic – which is to say, its hegemony imposes itself through terroristic means, as does resistance to it.

The assumption that subtends these contradictory understandings is that the modern and imperialist state in fact solicits the terror through which it constitutes its authority, as several commentators in this book acknowledge. Terror according to this logic can be defined, in terms taken from Achille Mbembe's exposition of the *necropolitical*, as a politics exercised through the imposition of death and near-death. For Mbembe, whose work in this respect is interestingly informed by Frantz Fanon's concept of colonial violence, imperial and post-imperial sovereignty depends on the right to kill or, more precisely, to hold the subject in a state of continual confrontation with death: "The colony represents the site where sovereignty consists fundamentally in the exercise of a power outside the law . . . and where 'peace' is more likely to take on the face of a 'war without end' " (Mbembe 2003: 23).

Although their views on the ethics of terror differ, Mbembe cites Fanon's vivid spatialization of necropower in the colony to make his case: all is regulated by "the language of pure force" and "the principle of reciprocal exclusivity" (p. 26). In such conditions of "war without end," a public sphere, if it exists at all, can only be imposed through violent exclusion, while resistance almost inevitably takes some "terroristic" form. In his short study, *The No-Nonsense Guide to Terrorism*, Jonathan Barker, too, though in a different register, draws attention to these crucial colonial legacies of state violence, which, interestingly, many post-2001 studies tend to evade or ignore: "The colonial powers . . . [used] violence to maintain their domination, to recruit labour and soldiers . . . to seize additional territory" (Barker 2005: 61–2). By contrast with Anglo-American novelists like Don De Lillo (or indeed Martin Amis, discussed by Robert Eaglestone in this book), who regard terror as a force that cannot be incorporated within civic society, I would suggest that in the globalized world terror is a force that has been *incorporated everywhere*. As Walter Benjamin presciently observed: "The tradition of the oppressed teaches us that the 'state of emergency' in which we live is not the exception but the rule" (Benjamin 1968: 257).

Without wanting to mount a justification for terroristic modes of resistance, this essay would therefore submit that, in as much as terror has been the medium of the modern state and the modern imperium, terror has equally been the site for the critique of the modern state and imperium. To an extent it has *had to be* the site of the critique of the modern state. Under prevailing conditions of sovereignty other sites and other techniques have been rendered either unavailable or ineffective.

With its commitment to cross-border interaction and ethically inspired adjustments to the other, postcolonial writing can be said to expand and complicate, as well as to question, the shared languages and common frames of reference, legacies of a colonial history, which make globalization possible. By the same token such writing seeks to define, or redefine, home as against world, the particular and the local as distinct from, even though intricately bound up in, the global. Postcolonial writers, in other words, whether magic realist or national, find, through the medium of different modes of dialogue, ways of continuing and prolonging the lineages of life. And they see such conversation and prolongation as practices that must be continually renewed and repeated.

Intricate and deathly forms of terror and counter-terror, as I have suggested, interpenetrate the global order. Although it cannot deny its fascination with the necropolitical act (even if this is critically reflective), postcolonial writing has the power to draw attention to places outside of the terror-stricken state, to supply a fuller understanding of the painful losses as well as strategic gains of such acts. So it might, for example, explore the human inwardness that inheres to situations of extreme decimation, carnage, and grief. It might show, in the words of Kader Asmal et al., that "humanism [travels] always with . . . resistance" (Asmal, Asmal, and Roberts 1996: 50). By narrating historical division and pain, but also recovery and endurance, postcolonial writing posits futurity (whether the consummation of individual pleasures or the fulfillment of the nation) in relation to the futureless (that is: terror, necropolitics). True, "national writing" may arguably be more concerned with restitution in the future, the restoration of roots; and "migrant writing" with the hoped-for retracing and recovery of routes. Yet both tendencies within postcolonial literature direct attention to the future because of their awareness of the ongoing pressure of colonial "pasts," of the "regeneration of colonialism through other means," and of the need to remain vigilant about and survive such regeneration (Frankenberg and Mani 1996: 322–34).

Zimbabwean Yvonne Vera's 2002 novella *The Stone Virgins*, for instance, tells in disturbingly poetic terms not only of a horrifying terroristic act perpetrated upon village-dweller Nonceba and her sister during the post-independence civil war, but also of the restorative processes of mourning and healing which, for Nonceba, eventually follow. Moreover, the narrative casts a coldly penetrating eye into the frozen mind of the terroristic (and terrorized) soldier and attacker himself, representing him, by contrast with survivor Nonceba, as suspended in a place outside of history. Relatedly, Achmat Dangor's *Bitter Fruit* (2004) is concerned more with a family's attempts to come to terms with the "ordinariness" of life in the post-apartheid city and with one another, than it is with the state-inflicted act of violent rape that, years before, first distanced them from one another. In these ways postcolonial narrative maps a chronology on to the "moment of danger," the moment-in-and-out-of time, of terror, registering not only the past history but also the future consequences and repercussions of necropolitical acts for human subjects.

Then again, if we angle the concept of terror somewhat differently, through what I have called a "resistance" rather than a "global" inflection, postcolonial writing may be seen to play more of an interested than a restorative role in relation to it. This becomes especially apparent where terror is viewed not only as the manifestation of the imperial state, but also as the expression of an anti-colonial modernity. "Terror" here denotes the attempt by the colonized to *seize hold* of technical mastery and control in a situation, that of colonialism, where modernity is routinely introduced in violent forms (through land seizures, labor laws, and the like). Once again, however, this apparently alternative reading of terror allows us to examine its occurrence in the reciprocally violent historical contexts of colonialism and global neocolonialism rather than of the ahistorical "war on terror" in which terror is viewed simply as savage and irrational, an irruption of the primitive.

Terrorism is, to be sure, more often than not described as the revolutionary expression of a counter-modernity rather than of modernity. As recent studies confirm, modern terror takes many forms and the final assessment of terror's relationship to modernity may well produce a both/and rather than an either/or verdict. Allen Feldman encapsulates this as follows: "most contemporary acts of political terror have taken on both a decidedly ante-modern and post-modern shape," embracing sacrificial spectacles of pre-modernity, as in televised assassinations, as well as sophisticated postmodern technologies of mediatized warfare and surveillance (Feldman 2004: 347). In colonized contexts, however, I would add, that shape also exhibits distinctly modern dimensions. It involves the intercutting, even the collision, of different temporalities, modes of production, and frameworks of thought, in ways that are often disjointed, spasmodic, jagged, convulsive, fracturing. Understood from the position of a totalizing historicism, such violence could well appear as a throwback to the pre-modern, the pre-political. But understood in relation to plural, incommensurable genealogies of time or categories of knowledge, as in the postcolonial perspective, such violence rather expresses as points of friction or even of synapse between different spheres of activity and consciousness.

Although he is as concentrated on non-violent as on violent responses, Dipesh Chakrabarty evocatively describes this "seizing hold" of modernity by colonized nationalists as their urgent insistence on the "now" of their political demands, as against the "not yet" which they occupy on the time-line of European progress (2000: 8–9). Any number of anti-colonial resistance struggles, 1905 in Bengal, 1929 in Nigeria, Kenya in the 1950s, labeled terrorist and atavistic at the time, involved such a violent grasping of the conditions of modernity and political life by those who felt they been made its victims rather than its beneficiaries. Bursting out of "the waiting room of history," they insisted, *right now*, on a full participation in the political life of the nation, the modern society, the city. As to postcolonial writers, energetic attempts to force a way into the modern, no matter how chiasmic the break, again involve "nationalists" and "magic realists", though to different degrees, and though different aspects of the modern may draw them. It is controversial to say this at present, yet it is worth speculating whether even terrorist events such as March 11, 2004 in Madrid, usually attributed to anti-Western fundamentalism, might not be seen in a longer *durée* as attempts, from particular nationalist yet also migrant contexts, to resist the violations of *imposed* or inflicted modernity. In this respect it is worth recalling that a terrorist may be broadly defined as one who believes that their case is exceptional (they have been unconscionably denied), and that the odds stacked against them are so high that desperate action alone will suffice.

In relation to this somewhat attenuated reading of colonized "terror," the postcolonial novel, play, or poem might be understood as itself an alternative mode of seizing hold upon the now, upon the right to define *this moment*, although a seizing-hold that, importantly, does not involve a negation of the future. Novels which dramatize such attempts by the (once) colonized to propel themselves into the temporality of the modern, or forcibly to modify that temporality, include, amongst many others: Ngugi's *Petals of Blood*, Tsitsi Dangarembga's *Nervous Conditions*, Tayeb Salih's *Season of Migration to the North*, Mukul Kesavan's *Looking Through Glass*, and Caryl Phillips's *Crossing the River*. Speaking schematically, in these different novels the bourgeois native individual, excluded from the experience of moving into modernity according to need, instead projects him/herself decisively, uncompromisingly, into previously exclusive strata of temporality, so claiming agency and bringing his/her synchronous time-lines into a new configuration (where the nation's temporality is *the* modern temporality for nation narratives; and where modernity is claimed as one possible temporality amongst others for migrant writers). Rather differently from postmodern characterizations of terror in literature, evoked in terms that suggest a cancellation of temporality, the acts of projection represented in these texts are concerned to restore temporal depth, a sense of the deep layering or thickness of history. And the texts do so, it is clear, by narrating simply yet powerfully what it is to project and seize hold in these ways. Viewed from this perspective, postcolonial writing undoes the compression of time that is represented by a sudden death or bomb blast, by looking at *processes*: the slow process of successfully supplanting an elder brother, as in *Nervous Conditions*, or of subverting orientalist desire, as in *Season of Migration to the North*.

Postcolonial writing, whether defined under the heading of resistance or of hybrid cosmopolitanism, does not, however, provide justifications of terror or sidestep the pain and wrong that it is the objective of a terrorist act to inflict. This is important to acknowledge. What it can provide is an understanding of what is at stake subjectively and sequentially for the different parties involved when terrorism takes place. In this sense, I want to suggest, postcolonial writing supplies channels for thinking through and beyond terror and the shocking breaks in time it inflicts, and offers ways of developing workable political responses to its horrors.

References

Asmal, Kader, Louise Asmal, and Robert Suresh Roberts. (1996) *Reconciliation through Truth*. Cape Town: David Philip.

Barker, Jonathan. (2005) *The No-Nonsense Guide to Terrorism*. London: Verso.

Behdad, Ali. (1996) *Belated Travelers: Orientalism in the Age of Colonial Dissolution*. Durham, NC: Duke University Press.
Benjamin, Walter. (1968) "Theses on the Philosophy of History," *Illuminations*, trans. Harry Zohn. New York: Schocken.
Chakrabarty, Dipesh. (2000) *Provincializing Europe: Postcolonial Thought and Historical Difference*. Princeton: Princeton University Press.
Dangor, Achmat. (2003) *Bitter Fruit*. London: Atlantic.
De Lillo, Don. (1992) *Mao II*. London: Vintage.
Featherstone, Mike, Scott Lash, and Roland Robertson, eds. (1995) "Introduction," *Global Modernities*. Oxford: Sage.
Feldman, Allen. (2004) "Securocratic Wars of Public Safety," *Interventions* 6(3): 330–50.
Frankenberg, Ruth, and Lata Mani. (1996) "Crosscurrents, Crosstalk: Race, 'Postcoloniality', and the Politics of Location," in Padmini Mongia (ed.), *Contemporary Postcolonial Theory: A Reader*, pp. 322–34. London: Arnold.
Gordimer, Nadine. (2001) *The Pickup*. London: Bloomsbury.
Gregory, Derek. (2004) *The Colonial Present: Afghanistan, Palestine, Iraq*. Oxford: Blackwell.
Harrison, Nick. (2003) *Postcolonial Criticism: History, Theory and the Work of Criticism*. Oxford: Polity.
Jenkins, Simon. (2006) "Him and Us," *Times Literary Supplement* (February 24): 11.
Mbembe, Achille. (2003) "Necropolitics," *Public Culture* 15: 11–40.
Okri, Ben. (1988) *Stars of the New Curfew*. London: Secker and Warburg.
Parry, Benita. (2004) *Postcolonial Studies: A Materialist Critique*. London: Routledge.
Spivak, Gayatri. (2008) *Other Asias*. Oxford: Wiley Blackwell.
Vera, Yvonne. (2002) *Stone Virgins*. Harare: Weaver Press.
Young, Robert. (2001) *Postcolonialism: An Historical Introduction*. Oxford: Blackwell.

Part II

Histories of Post/colonial Terror

Chapter 6

Revolutionary Terrorism in British Bengal

Peter Heehs

There were four factors behind the success of the freedom movement in British India: (1) pressure exerted by public bodies, notably the Indian National Congress; (2) non-violent resistance campaigns; (3) violent resistance; and (4) global political and economic changes. Most histories of the freedom movement highlight the first and second factors, give an inadequate account of the third, and all but ignore the fourth. Typically, the freedom movement is shown to begin with the formation of the Indian National Congress in 1885. For the next 35 years, resolutions passed at Congress sessions define its direction. In 1920 Mohandas K. Gandhi emerges as the hero of the non-cooperation movement. The historiographical limelight is trained on his *satyagraha* campaigns; the revolutionary campaigns that precede and follow them fall into the shadow. The impact of global events becomes too obvious to ignore after 1939. From that point, attention is focused on constitutional negotiations and on the Pakistan movement.

Some accounts of the freedom movement – including many published in India – do cover violent resistance to British rule. Many such accounts make dubious linkages between eighteenth- and nineteenth-century peasant insurgencies or the Revolt of 1857 and the organized anticolonial militancy of the twentieth century. Coverage of the terrorist campaigns of 1907 to 1934 focuses largely on personalities. Until recently, the standard approach was commemorative: the verbal equivalent of statues and *shahid minars* (martyrs' monuments). Treated in isolation from political developments, violent resistance against the

British Raj ends up looking like a heroic but futile display of pyrotechnics.

In this essay, I will attempt to correct this imbalance by giving a straightforward account of the activities of revolutionary groups during the Freedom Movement. I thus confine myself mostly to the third of the four factors listed above. I mention the influence of public bodies and of non-violent resistance only to the extent that the revolutionaries took account of them. Global events, for the most part, lie beyond the scope of the essay. I look mainly at the genesis, ideology, structure, composition, and activities of the revolutionary groups, and give most of my attention to the formative period (1902–10), although I also survey developments up to the mid-1930s and after. Terrorism in British India was largely a Bengali phenomenon. I therefore concentrate on developments in undivided Bengal, although I also look at related events in other parts of the country. I offer this as a case study of a particular terroristic emergence, which occurred at a time when similar outbreaks were taking place in other parts of the colonized world. Each of these outbreaks has its own causes and development, but these often were related in one way or another to those that characterized the Bengali outbreak.

Violent Resistance before 1900

Historians have counted more than a hundred instances of peasant insurgency in British Bengal in the years before 1900 (Chakraborty 1992: 178). The better-known examples – the Sannyasi Rebellion of northern Bengal (late eighteenth century), the Bakarganj insurgency and Sylhet uprising (both 1790s), the "*pagal* rebellion" in Sherpur (1820s–1830s), the Indigo Rebellion (1859–60), and the well-organized Pabna uprising (1870s) – partook in some measure of the nature of violent revolution. But none of these incidents could rightly be considered a politically conscious attempt to throw off foreign rule. In each case the grievances were local, generally related to rent. The Indigo Rebellion, famous mostly because it caught the imagination of the Calcutta intelligentsia, was a labor movement that sometimes turned violent rather than a political rebellion. The leader of the Sylhet uprising did declare that he wanted to drive out the foreign rulers, but his motives were economic and religious, not political.

Bengal was generally quiet during the Great Revolt of 1857–8, although some people expressed sympathy for the revolting soldiers, and there were minor outbreaks in Chittagong, Dacca, and other places. By the end of the nineteenth century the government of the Raj was firmly established in all parts of the Bengal Presidency. Educated Bengalis took a large portion of available subordinate government posts not only in their home province but throughout British India. And the educated Bengali, as Lord Macaulay (1920: 562) declared, was the least warlike of all men: "feeble even to effeminacy." When the British brought the concept of "martial races" to India, they classed Bengalis among those regarded as unsuitable for military service.

This stereotyping had another side. The same educated Bengali, British observers complained, had a knack for giving speeches and forming public bodies. One of the most important bodies was the Indian Association, founded in Calcutta, the capital of Bengal, in 1876. The leader of this group, Surendranath Banerjea, became the chief spokesman of an informal constituency of middle-class gentlemen and students. In 1883 and 1885, the Indian Association sponsored meetings of the Indian National Conference, which in 1886 merged with the Indian National Congress, founded in Bombay in 1885. The political life of the country was off to a slow start.

Some of the students who attended meetings of these groups also formed themselves into so-called secret societies dedicated to the cultivation of physical strength and "national" feeling. According to Bipin Chandra Pal (1932: 247) such clubs "almost honeycombed" the Calcutta student community of the 1870s. A club to which the young Rabindranath Tagore belonged is often held up as an example of such groups, but it clearly had more to do with cloak-and-dagger romance than politics or revolution. While these nineteenth-century groups were not, as sometimes is claimed, the origin of the later revolutionary *samitis* or societies, they did mark a beginning of interest in physical improvement and the spread of proto-national spirit among young Bengalis. This spirit was intensified by the influential writings of Bankim Chandra Chatterjee, and later by the robust speeches of Swami Vivekananda. The docile Bengali had begun to take the lead in verbal opposition to the British bureaucracy.

The lead in militant opposition was taken by the men of the Bombay Presidency. In the 1870s, Wasudeo Balwant Phadke of Poona headed a poorly organized armed revolt whose aim was to free the country from the foreign enemies of Hinduism. After four years of small-scale activities, Phadke was arrested and imprisoned in 1879. Sixteen years later, Damodar and Balkrishna Chapekar, two brothers of Poona, started a physical culture club that was similar in form to the contemporaneous secret societies of Bengal, but more businesslike in the training provided and the anti-British sentiment cultivated. During the plague epidemic of 1897 the Chapekars decided that W. C. Rand, the chairman of the city's plague commission, had "made himself an enemy of our religion" by his vigorous but insensitive policies (D. Chapekar, quoted in *Source Material*, vol. 2: 1014). In June 1897 they shot and killed him and another Briton, C. E. Ayerst. This assassination, for which the brothers were executed, might be called semi-political. They were inspired, at least in part, by the writings of B. G. Tilak, a Poona-based leader of the Indian National Congress. But their primary motivations were personal resentment and religious fanaticism.

The Start of "Modern" Revolutionary Terrorism in Bengal

Richard C. Hula distinguishes two sorts of violent opposition to constituted authority: "traditional" and "modern." The first is "prepolitical," issuing from the peasantry in reaction to specific grievances. The second, organized by the urban upper classes, has an articulated political aim (Hula 1983: 420–1). The rural uprisings of eighteenth- and nineteenth-century Bengal are classic cases of traditional violence. In the Chapekars one can see the beginnings of political self-consciousness, but it is overshadowed by religious concerns and actuated by personal grievances. Organized political violence of the modern type first emerged in Bengal around the turn of the century.

Calcutta was at that time both the capital of British India and its most vocal centre of nationalist politics. But it should be remembered that "politics" then meant little more than organized public opinion. There were no legislative bodies in which non-Europeans exercised any effective power. Indians reputed to be politicians were educated men from the major cities who wrote articles in newspapers, passed resolutions at Congress sessions, and raised motions in the powerless assemblies set up by the British. One of the first voices to be raised against the inbred and inactive world of Indian politics was that of Aurobindo Ghose, a Cambridge-educated Bengali who returned to India in 1893. In August of that year he wrote in a Bombay newspaper: "the Congress, which represents not the mass of the population, but a single and very limited class, could not honestly be called national." The Congress's one victory, an enlargement of the British assemblies, was simply a "conjuring trick." "Over the rest of our political action," Aurobindo continued, "the only epitaph we can write is 'Failure'" (Ghose 2002: 14). After writing a few articles in this vein, Aurobindo was asked by an established politician to tone down his criticisms. He preferred to drop journalism altogether for a decade. He believed that India's real need was a militant revolutionary movement on the model of the American, French, and Irish movements he had read about in Cambridge and London. Around 1902 he made contact with men with similar views in Western India. He and his friends helped a young Bengali named Jatindranath Banerjee to get military training in the army of the Maharaja of Baroda, and towards the beginning of 1902 sent him to Calcutta to try to interest young men in physical training and revolutionary propaganda. Jatindranath opened a club and made a few recruits. Around the same time another young Bengali named Satish Bose started a Calcutta physical-culture group that he called the Anushilan Samiti or Cultural Society. Satish found a sponsor in Pramathanath Mitra, a High Court barrister, who brought Jatindranath and Satish together. In March 1902, Jatindranath's and Satish's groups became amalgamated under the name already chosen by Satish. Under the guidance of Aurobindo, Mitra, and other highly educated men, the Anushilan Samiti became India's first revolutionary group with a clear political aim.

For several years after its founding, the Anushilan Samiti made little impact. A small number of youths were recruited in the capital and outlying districts; they took part in some rather innocuous activities. In 1903 Aurobindo sent his brother Barindra Kumar Ghose to help Jatindranath Banerjee in the work of recruiting and organization. The two young men soon quarreled and Barindra went back to Baroda. The movement might then have died a natural death had political events not intervened. In 1905 the government announced that it would go ahead with a controversial plan, announced two years previously, to partition the province of Bengal. Unprecedented popular resistance gave birth to the *swadeshi* movement, which declared a boycott of British goods and promoted indigenous ("swadeshi") products. Protest meetings were held in every part of the province. Groups of "volunteers" were organized to enforce the boycott. These groups helped give a brief effectiveness to the movement, but they tended to alienate Muslims, who had less reason than Hindus to oppose the administrative change.

The agitation and excitement that found an outlet in the *swadeshi* movement also encouraged more radical approaches. Speakers and writers such as Bipin Chandra Pal and Brahmabandhab Upadhyaya shot to prominence as the spokesmen of the fast-growing political faction that believed that Surendranath Banerjea and his Congress allies were not aggressive enough. By the end of 1905 these men began speaking of themselves as the New Party. Their rivals, whom they called Moderates, labeled them Extremists.

From the start Extremist politicians and revolutionary samitis had a symbiotic relationship. The young men received material support and legitimization from the leaders. In return they served as the leaders' power base and strong right arm. The leaders' prestige and eloquence did much to get the samitis going. In November 1905 Bipin Chandra and Pramathanath Mitra visited Dacca and called for volunteers ready to sacrifice their all for the motherland. Among the 80 who stepped forward was Pulin Bihari Das. He was appointed head of what grew to be the most active center of the Anushilan Samiti. Under his leadership it "spread like wildfire" throughout the province. More than 500 branches were opened, linked by a "close and detailed organization" to Pulin's headquarters (*Memorandum* 1933: 4). The Dacca Anushilan Samiti "soon overshadowed its parent society" and absorbed many smaller groups, especially in East Bengal (Samanta 1995, vol. 2: 519). Within two years of its founding, the Dacca Anushilan had lost whatever interest it might have had in the swadeshi movement, and become one of Bengal's two main revolutionary organizations.

The other group, more of a federation than a centralized organization, took shape anonymously during these years. Its origins are linked with those of the newspaper that eventually gave it its name: *Jugantar*. Early in 1906 Aurobindo Ghose quit his post in Baroda and came to Calcutta. His first task was to help set up the new Bengal National College. He also helped his brother Barin and others start a newspaper that would put a frankly revolutionary program before the country. The first issue of *Jugantar* came out in March. After an initial slow period, it caught on. Young Bengalis thrilled to read its call to arms: "Would not the disappearance of fifty million men in an attempt to deliver India be a hundred times better than this impotent death under the grim shelter of peace. . . . *If you cannot be a man in life be one in death*. The foreigner has come and fixed the way in which you live, *but how you die depends entirely on yourself*" (*Jugantar* May 27, 1906, cited in Mukherjee and Mukherjee 1972: 160).

Around the same time, Barin Ghose was trying to pick up the pieces of the Calcutta Anushilan Samiti, which had broken apart as a result of his clash with Jatindranath Banerjee a year or two earlier.

The general feeling of excitement created by the swadeshi movement, augmented by the revolutionary message of the *Jugantar*, made it easier to recruit young men and instill them with revolutionary feeling. A cluster of groups that got their start at this time later became linked with others under the name Jugantar.

In the summer of 1906, Barin, tiring of his editorial duties, accepted the offer of one of the Calcutta backers of his samiti to finance an assassination attempt. The chosen target was Bampfylde Fuller, the lieutenant governor of the new province of Eastern Bengal and Assam. Fuller had made himself unpopular among Bengali Hindus by his attempts to repress the swadeshi movement and by his declared preference for Muslims. Barin and Hem Chandra Das, a recruit from Midnapore, trailed Fuller from Gauhati to Barisal to Rangpur without making an attempt. In the last place Barin planned a dacoity to get needed funds, but aborted it when he heard the police were in the neighborhood. These two planned "actions" (a translation of the Bengali terms *kaj* or *karma*) were probably the first of their kind in Bengal, the precursors of dozens of attempted or successful political assassinations and hundreds of dacoities for claimed political purposes. They thus may be said to mark the beginning of active terrorism in Bengal. Their amateurishness and failure make them typical of actions undertaken by Barin Ghose and his comrades.

In 1907 Barin and Hem Chandra attempted in different ways to become more professional. Hem went to Paris where for some time he studied revolutionary politics and bomb making with French and Russian anarchists living in that city. Barin turned a garden house his family owned in Maniktala, Calcutta, into a revolutionary school and small-time arsenal. It was from here that he organized his first serious revolutionary actions: attempts to derail the train carrying the lieutenant governor of Bengal in November and December 1907, and attempts to assassinate Douglas Kingsford, a magistrate of Calcutta and later district judge of Muzaffarpur, in January and April 1908. The Muzaffarpur action, carried out by Khudiram Bose and Prafulla Chaki, is one of the most famous events in the annals of Bengali terrorism. Like all other actions planned by Barin, it was a failure. Two innocent English women were killed instead of Kingsford. This "outrage" (as the British press called it) brought the existence of terrorism more prominently before the public than two successful attempts carried out in December 1907 by other *samitis*: a dacoity in Chingripota (24 Parganas), by a group led by Narendranath Bhattacharya, and the shooting of the district magistrate of Dacca,

B. C. Allen, by members of the Dacca Anushilan. Secretary of State John Morley claimed not to be surprised when he heard of the Allen shooting. "It has long been evident," he wrote to the Viceroy Lord Minto, "that Indian antagonism to Government would run slowly into the usual grooves, including assassination" (Morley, December 26, 1907). From this point, terrorism of the modern type was part of the political situation in Bengal.

Influences and Ideology

The remark of Morley quoted above suggests that he considered Bengali terrorism to be an almost natural result of political discontent. Minto, on the other hand, considered it entirely imitative. Writing to Morley after the Muzaffarpur attempt, Minto declared that the conspirators aimed "at the furtherance of murderous methods hitherto unknown in India which have been imported from the West, and which the imitative Bengali has childishly accepted" (Minto, May 6, 1908). Just as the members of the Congress were playing at being parliamentarians, so the terrorists were playing at being "anarchists."

There were, to be sure, some foreign influences on Bengali terrorism. We have already mentioned Aurobindo Ghose's study of the revolutionary movements of Ireland, France, and America. Members of the early "secret societies" drew some of their inspiration from Mazzini and also read books like Thomas Frost's *Secret Societies of the European Revolution* (1876). Two non-Indians influenced the Calcutta circles from which the revolutionary samitis emerged around 1902. The Japanese critic Kakuzo Okakura inspired Pramathanath Mitra and others with revolutionary and pan-Asiatic ideas just when the samiti movement was getting started. The Irishwoman Margaret Noble, known as Sister Nivedita after she became a disciple of Swami Vivekananda, had some contact with Aurobindo Ghose and with younger men like Satish Bose and *Jugantar* sub-editor Bhupendranath Bose. Nivedita was in correspondence with the non-terroristic anarchist Peter Kropotkin, and she is known to have had revolutionary beliefs. She gave the young men a collection of books that included titles on revolutionary history and spoke to them about their duty to the motherland. Apart from these somewhat shadowy influences, there is the undoubted connection of Hem Chandra Das with European revolutionaries in Paris in 1907. In his memoirs Hem explains that he was ignorant of and uninterested in the many varieties of radical politics he came in contact with. His real interest was explosive chemistry. This he learned quite well, and brought an up-to-date explosives manual with him when he came back to India. This technological debt may be said to have been the major foreign influence on Bengali terrorism.

British officials portrayed the Indian movement as imitative because they did not believe that their political grievances were legitimate. As Minto wrote in 1908: "The public at home will make a fatal mistake if they ascribe outrages such as that at Mozufferpur to the efforts of a people struggling to relieve themselves from an oppressor" (Minto, May 27, 1908). He clearly was wrong about this. The ideology of revolutionary publicists such as Bipin Chandra Pal and Aurobindo Ghose, although formed in part from a study of European history, was an indigenous and justifiable response to British imperial domination. Their ideology had three major components: political independence or *swaraj*; economic independence as promoted by the swadeshi-boycott movement; and the drive for cultural independence by means of national education. Only the first of these was of direct interest to members of terrorist groups. A circular of the Anushilan Samiti states: "This *Samiti* has no open relationship with any kind of popular and outward *Swadeshi*; that is (the boycott of) *belati* [foreign] articles, of cloths, salt, sugar, etc. To be mixed up in quarrels or disputes or implicated in the litigation about such affairs is entirely against the principles of the *Samiti*" (Ghosh 1984: 94). Members of Barin Ghose's group likewise stigmatized the swadeshi-boycott movement as *bania* (shopkeeper) politics. The one thing that mattered was political independence. The only way to get it was the use of force.

Extremist political leaders differed over the question of force: Bipin Chandra Pal was opposed; Aurobindo was in favor of its use. This was one of the reasons that Pal was ousted from the editorial board of *Bande Mataram*. Though Aurobindo's 1907 *Doctrine of Passive Resistance* was one of the first – and remains one of the best – articulations of the strategy that played a central role in the course of the freedom struggle, he "never concealed his opinion that a nation is entitled to attain its freedom by violence" (Ghose 1972: 41). But when he encouraged Jatindranath Banerjee and Barin Ghose to organize samitis, what he had in mind was a large-scale militant uprising prepared over the course of two or three decades. Impatience and the demands of financial backers pushed Barin and others toward the flashy results of terrorism. While not really in favor of assassination and dacoity, Aurobindo certainly was cognizant of his brother's attempts, and thus at least tacitly approved of them (Heehs 1998: 42–67). The question of violence versus non-violence would remain a live one throughout the history of the freedom struggle in Bengal.

There remains the problem of the place of religion in the ideology of the revolutionaries. Aurobindo, Bipin Chandra, Brahmabandhab Upadhyaya, and other so-called Hindu publicists frequently used religious imagery in their writings and sometimes spoke of the movement as a "religion." As a result, contemporary British observers and later historians of South Asia have accused them of mixing up politics and religion or even of promoting communalism. It is true that during the swadeshi movement, the old cultural divide between the Hindus and Muslims of Bengal began to become politicized. Swadeshi volunteers and Muslim activists found themselves on opposite sides and a mutual distrust was born. Pamphleteers and journalists indulged in provocative rhetoric. Serious communal riots broke out in Comilla, Mymensingh and other places in 1907. Calls for self-defense became mingled with cries for revenge.

In the midst of this degenerating situation the "religion of patriotism" that Aurobindo and Bipin Chandra proposed may have helped the movement toward polarization. It is important to note, however, that this "religion" had nothing specifically to do with Hinduism; it was a civic religion independent of the beliefs and practices of any traditional religion. Neither Aurobindo nor Bipin Chandra engaged in anti-Muslim rhetoric. They occasionally used Hindu terms and symbols in their writings and speeches, but they believed, perhaps naively, that Muslims could see through the symbolism to the nationalism that they were promoting. Both men considered Muslims as much a part of the Indian nation-in-the-making as Hindus. Both called for the increased participation of Muslims in the national movement and regretted attempts to drive the two communities apart. But both men felt that separate Muslim representation in legislative councils, introduced by the Morley–Minto reforms of 1910, would have a disastrous effect on the integrity of the movement. In this they certainly were right.

If communalist thinking had no part in the ideology of the major publicists of revolution in Bengal, it certainly entered in at the popular level. Some samiti members came to regard pro-partition Muslims as their enemies. Samiti members as well as Muslim activists took part in communal riots. Few Muslims became members of the revolutionary samitis. They were specifically barred from membership in the Dacca Anushilan, though its members were forbidden in principle "to show hostile feelings against, or to deal unjustly with the Musulmans as a nation" (Ghosh 1984: 95).

The antagonism between the two communities unquestionably weakened the revolutionary movement. For example, it prevented East Bengal samitis from gaining needed support from the Muslim peasantry. This divisiveness served the interests of the government; but the government did not create it. The worst that can be said of the British is that they may, in some cases, have exacerbated a pre-existing communal fragmentation.

Structure of the Terrorist Societies

The two main revolutionary associations of Bengal, Anushilan and Jugantar, had different sorts of structure. Jugantar was a loosely organized alliance of groups run by different leaders who occasionally acted together. Anushilan was centrally organized, with a vertical hierarchy and rigid discipline. These two approaches to structure are probably best conceived as types to which the actual structure of any given samiti approximated more or less well.

The secret society started by Barin Ghose in Maniktala in 1907 was the main precursor of the Jugantar-type organization (Heehs 1998: 14–41). In theory the Maniktala group had a complex hierarchy based on the Russian model as set forth in such books as Frost's *Secret Societies*. An organizational document shows a primary division between the two active leaders (Barin Ghose and Upendranath Bannerjee) and the rank and file. The higher leaders, including Aurobindo, were supposed to be known only to the active leaders. Each member was assigned to one or more of three circles: (1) collection of funds, (2) practical terrorist work, and (3) propaganda. In practice, the fundamental division was between "military" work (corresponding to the second circle) and "civil" work.

Members of the Maniktala and other groups often claimed that they were connected with a vast web of secret societies covering the whole of British India. In fact, links between provinces were limited to occasional contacts between individuals. Within Bengal, the various societies had links with other groups, but relations were more often competitive than co-operative. According to Leonard Gordon (1968: 204–7), in the period between 1910 and 1915 each group or *dal* in the Jugantar network was a separate unit composed of a leader, known as the *dada*, and his followers. As the name implies, the *dada* was the elder brother of the revolutionary family. He was also a *guru*, teaching his disciples practical skills, revolutionary ideology, and strategy. Gordon believes that the *dada* system developed out of pre-existing social structures of rural Bengal. He suggests that their activities – political murder and dacoity – may have grown out of a tradition of zamindar-sponsored violence in the Bengal countryside. *Dadas* both co-operated and competed with each other for men, money, and material.

It is possible to give a more detailed account of structure of the Anushilan Samiti than of Jugantar, since the leadership of the Dacca Anushilan produced many detailed organizational documents, which were reproduced or summarized in government reports after the samiti was penetrated (Ghosh 1978: 139–48). An internal circular of 1908, probably written by Pulin Behari Das, notes that "it has become particularly necessary . . . to make some good arrangements for the present by dividing the whole of Bengal into divisions and subdivisions and forming Central Samitis with a few small Samitis." The geographical structure, which largely followed British administrative divisions, required placing "the right person in charge of the right place and the right mission, in order to carry out in a thorough manner the entire work in an orderly way being bound by the tie of union" (Rowlatt et al. 1918: ch. 5, par. 88). *Dals* consisting of five or ten members led by a *dalpati* (head of circle) were grouped together in local samitis led by *adhyakshas* and other officers. These reported to district officers appointed by and responsible to the central Dacca organization. This was commanded by Pulin Das and those who stood in for him during his periods of imprisonment. Samitis were divided into four functional groups: "violence," "organization," "keepers of arms," and "householder department." Communications were by special couriers and were written in secret code. This practice and many others were borrowed from literary sources and were in part a concession to the young men's need to act out romantic drama.

Composition of the Terrorist Societies

During the period under study as well as later, the Bengali terrorist societies were composed almost entirely of young urban Hindu men of the upper classes. In the beginning there were no active woman members; indeed women were specifically excluded from the samitis, many of which required recruits to give up relations with the opposite sex. After 1924 some groups opened their doors to women, and a few female groups were formed. A handful of young women, among them Pritilata Waddedar and Bina Das, took part in important actions. But for the most part terrorism was considered a man's work.

I have already spoken of the reasons for the Hindu exclusiveness. It was not absolute. The samitis had great respect for the nationalist Maulvi Liaquat Hussain (who, however, was considered a turncoat by orthodox Muslims). Future Congress leader Abul Kalam Azad met Aurobindo Ghose "on two or three occasions" and "was attracted to revolutionary politics and joined one of the groups" (Azad 1984: 4). But Azad was an exception to the general rule that Muslims kept away from Hindu-led groups. A good number of the so-called Hindu terrorists were in practice non-religious. This was particularly true after 1920, when many young Bengalis abandoned the Hindu in favor of the Marxist world-view.

Most members of terrorist groups came from the Bengali *bhadralok* ("respectable people"). Most, in other words, belonged to the Brahmin, Baidya, or Kayasth caste. Of the 36 men on whom judgment was passed in the 1909 Alipore Bomb Case, all but two were from these castes. Of the 186 persons "convicted in Bengal of revolutionary crimes or killed in commission of such crimes during the years 1907–17," 89 percent were Brahmin, Baidya, or Kayasth and 9 percent from lower Bengali castes. The same pattern continued through the 1930s (Heehs 1992: 268–71; Samanta 1995: vol. 6). The predominance of higher classes is found in many other urban revolutionary groups, for example the Narodnaya Volya of late nineteenth-century Russia (Laqueur 1987: 82). Many attempts have been made to provide political or economic explanations for the *bhadralok* lead in Bengali revolutionary groups. The British spoke of the movement as a *bhadralok* conspiracy motivated by the class's diminishing employment opportunities. Some modern historians have suggested that the movement was in part an attempt of the *bhadralok* élite to maintain its predominance over the masses. But it is hard to see how *bhadralok* individuals furthered their interests by stepping off the educational/employment treadmill and exposing themselves to imprisonment and death.

Like revolutionaries of all periods and places, most members of the Bengali terrorist groups were young, many of them boys. The average age of the 36 Alipore convicts was 22. This sample may be divided into two groups: six leaders with an average age of 32, and 30 rank-and-file members with an average age of 20. Youth remained a constant factor throughout the terrorist movement. In Table 6.1, the

Table 6.1 Age of Bengali terrorists, 1907–8 and 1907–17

	10–15	*16–20*	*21–25*	*26–30*	*31–35*	*36–45*	*45+*	*Unrecorded*
Alipore sample	0	9	7	4	0	1	0	–
Rowlatt sample	2	48	76	29	10	9	1	11

Sources: Alipore sample: Government of Bengal, confidential political file no. 24 of 1910. Rowlatt sample: Rowlatt et al. (1918), Annexure (2). In both samples the age is that of conviction or death and not arrest. Table reproduced from Heehs (1992: 270).

21 convicts of the Alipore and/or Harrison Road Cases (1907–8) and the 186 "revolutionary criminals" of 1907–17 surveyed by the Rowlatt Report are placed in eight age categories.

Activities of the Terrorist Societies

The activities of the terrorist societies may be divided into two broad classes: (1) preliminary activities and (2) actual terrorist actions. Preliminary activities included recruitment, propaganda, training, cover activities, collection of arms, and collection of money. Most prospective members were recruited from schools and colleges. The various *dals* competed for recruits, *dadas* engaging in *chele-dhara* (boy- or disciple-snatching) when they got the chance. Many who joined the Maniktala group were students who found their way to the office of the *Jugantar* after reading that newspaper, whose influence on swadeshi-era Bengalis cannot be overemphasized. A selection of *Jugantar* articles, *Mukti Kon Pathe?* (Which Way Freedom?) was a big seller until banned by the police. Another daring publication of the group was *Bartaman Rananiti* ("Modern Military Science"), essentially a translation of portions of Ivan S. Bloch's *Modern Weapons and Modern War* (1900). In the last chapter of *Bartaman Rananiti,* the Bengali writer took up the question, "How can a weak and disarmed nation fight against armed and trained soldiers?" He answered by saying that nothing was impossible if the people were determined to attain liberty even at the cost of death. When conditions were right, native troops would desert, the hill tribes rise, and young men engage in irregular warfare. All this together with pressure from abroad would eventually wear the enemy down (quoted in Ker [1917] 1973: 50–1). The effectiveness of such propaganda led the Maniktala group to devote much of its time and resources to publication and distribution. The Dacca Anushilan seems to have relied on material published by other groups in Calcutta for its own recruiting and indoctrination.

Recruits accepted into the two organizations had to take elaborate oaths of initiation and secrecy. These were in the form of religious rituals, the religious trappings providing the vividness and solemnity that the leaders thought advisable. Physical training – exercises, lathi-play, bicycling, etc. – was a major preoccupation of new recruits. These activities helped establish the samitis' cover and taught useful skills. Trainees also spent a good amount of time studying revolutionary and religious literature. The garden-house headquarters of the Maniktala society was set up as a regular school, with a varied syllabus. According to 15-year-old Krishna Jiban Sanyal, "Barin Ghose used to read Gita to me and Upen Banerjee used to read Upanishads to me. Barin also used to read about the Russo-Japanese war. Ullas Dutt delivered lectures regarding explosives on 2 occasions" (quoted in Bose 1922: 43).

In principle, recruits were not initiated into the "military side" of the organization until they had proved themselves. In practice, they were not kept in the dark for long. Barin and the other Maniktala leaders were lax about security and the group was easily penetrated by police agents. The more disciplined Anushilan organization had a strict screening process for keeping out security risks. Citing internal documents, P. K. Ghosh stresses that Anushilan members were also vetted for "unimpeachable moral character" (Ghosh 1978: 141). Against this must be weighed persistent reports in British sources that some older Dacca Anushilan members drew younger ones into pederastic relations (Samanta 1995, vol. 2: 393–5). No doubts existed about the moral example provided by Jugantar leaders like Jatindranath Mukherjee, universally admired as a man without fear, meanness, or ambition.

Besides education, the primary ostensible aim of the samitis was social service. Following the model set by groups such as Aswini Kumar Dutt's "Little Brothers of the Poor," the Anushilan Samiti took part in organized social service, for example flood relief during the 1907 Damodar flood. It also helped manage public events, such as political rallies and *melas*. British observers were struck to see how efficiently the young Bengalis did their work, not failing to note that the uniforms and badges they wore and the lathis they sometimes carried lent a military air to the operation. As time went on, such activities became mere covers and training grounds for terrorist activities.

The Arms Act of 1878 made it illegal for most natives of British India to own guns, swords, and other weapons. The possession and handling of contraband arms became important in terrorist rites of passage and a necessary prerequisite for those who planned to carry out terrorist actions. Firearms were obtained by two methods: misuse of legal channels and theft. Chandernagore, a French enclave located about 20 miles north of Calcutta, was the principal center for the import of guns and pistols into British Bengal. Individual weapons could be obtained by means of donation or theft from persons who had the right to possess arms, such as *zamindars*, members of the nobility, civil servants, and the security forces. The most famous arms acquisition in the history of the movement was the theft of 50 Mauser automatic pistols and 46,000 rounds of ammunition from a Calcutta import house in 1914. This kept a dozen groups supplied for several years.

The use of bombs in terrorist acts was introduced to India by the Maniktala secret society. The experimental devices produced by self-trained chemists like Ullaskar Dutt were replaced in 1907 by well-made bombs manufactured by Hem Chandra Das and others. The literature on the making of explosives that Hem brought back from Europe was widely disseminated. At one point copies were sent anonymously to students of dozens of district schools. Even the passage of the Explosives Act in 1908 did not prevent terrorists from gaining sufficient knowledge of chemistry to put together sophisticated bombs.

According to the German anarchist Johann Most, "in money – even more than in dynamite – the key was to be found" (Laqueur 1987: 57–8). It costs a lot of money to purchase firearms and chemicals, and to print and distribute propaganda. It may cost even more to house and feed a few dozen adolescents. A Bengali document of 1908 lists three ways to obtain funds: (1) profit-making enterprises, (2) contributions from men of wealth, (3) "imposing taxes on rich people (with the aid of the terroristic department)," i.e., armed robbery ("General Principles": 2). The third of these methods was the most popular. The majority of terrorist actions in Bengal were dacoities, the victims almost invariably rich Indians. Needless to say, they regarded the revolutionary dacoits as dacoits, and were not amused by talk of "taxes" or by documents like the following, left behind after a Calcutta robbery: "Six honorary officers of our Calcutta Finance Department have taken a loan of Rs 9,891-1-5 from you and have deposited the amount in the office noted above on your account to fulfill our great aim." The victim doubtless took the promise of repayment with interest less seriously than the threat that if he co-operated with the police the Finance Department would "not leave any one in your family to enjoy your enormous wealth" (Rowlatt et al. 1918: par. 77).

The government claimed that once the movement got started it gave birth to a "*bhadralok* loafer criminal class and an anarchical condition of things in which, although the revolutionary idea existed, there was undoubtedly a very big element of ordinary crime" (Samanta 1995, vol. 2: 518). This is supported to some extent by statements made by Barin Ghose and Hem Chandra Das, and by the historian Leonard Gordon, who wrote that many violent acts committed by Bengali revolutionaries after 1910 "were often only vaguely related to the goals of India's independence" (Gordon 1968: 205).

Assassination attempts certainly had political significance. It is remarkable, however, that Bengali terrorists rarely succeeded in killing British officials, though they rarely failed to kill Bengalis suspected of collaborating with the enemy or failing in their duties to the samitis. The Bengali press condemned both types of murders, but public expressions of sympathy for assassins like Khudiram Bose and Kanailal Dutt showed that many if not most Bengalis did not condemn the murder of Britons or obvious traitors.

Generally speaking, Bengali terrorists were not terribly effective, particularly during the 1906–10 period. Table 6.2 presents the results of Bengal's first secret society from its inception up to the attempt that led to the imprisonment of most of its members.

In later years both the frequency and the success ratio went up. In 1915, for example, 49 "revolutionary outrages" – 39 dacoities and 10 murders – were attempted. Twenty-four of the dacoities were successful (in the sense that the dacoits escaped with some loot). The murder attempts, all of which targeted Bengalis (government employees, policemen, etc.), were successful in all but two cases (Samanta 1995, vol. 6: 341–6).

A Brief Account of the Terrorist Movement in Bengal after 1910

I have given most of my attention to the activities and structure of the samitis of Bengal during the formative period (1902–10). I will treat the events of subsequent years in more summary manner, without structural analysis. It may be observed, however, that the basic

Table 6.2 Actions undertaken by the Maniktala Secret Society

Year	*Month*	*Place*	*Target*	*Type*	*Result*
1906	?	East Bengal	Fuller	Assassination	Aborted
1906	? August	Rangpur	a widow	Dacoity	Aborted
1906	? August	Bankura	a *mahant*	Dacoity	Aborted
1907	October	Darjeeling	Fraser	Assassination	Aborted
1907	November	Mankundu	Fraser	Derailment	Failure
1907	November	Mankundu	Fraser	Derailment	Aborted
1907	December	Narayangarh	Fraser	Derailment	Failure
1908	January	Calcutta	Kingsford	Assassination	Failure
1908	April	Chandernagore	Tardivel	Assassination	Failure
1908	April	Muzaffarpur	Kingsford	Assassination	Wrong persons killed

Sources: Government of Bengal confidential political file 266 of 1908; Government of India, Home (Political) Department proceedings, series A, September 1910, 33–40: 18–21, 42; Government of India proceedings, series D, August 1911, 9: 13; Samanta (1995, vol. 2: 515–17); Bose (1922: 16). Table reproduced from Heehs (1992: 252).

patterns laid down during the formative period persisted throughout the four decades of freedom-movement-era terrorism in Bengal.

The immediate result of the first burst of revolutionary activity was a period of government repression during which the samitis were outlawed and many terrorists were imprisoned or deported. Those who were spared lay low for some time. During these years the Maniktala society was replaced by the loosely structured Jugantar organization, while the Anushilan Samiti, which had been banned in 1909, regrouped. The imperial government's rescinding of the Partition of Bengal did not have the desired result of dampening violent revolution. When the Viceroy Lord Hardinge made his ceremonial entry into the new capital of Delhi in December 1912, Bengali terrorists came close to killing him in a well-planned bomb attack.

When war broke out in Europe the revolutionary parties decided to make the best use of the opportunity. There was an increase in small-scale terrorism, while the more ambitious leaders tried to organize the sort of general insurrection that Aurobindo had looked forward to a decade earlier. In 1914 Rash Behari Bose (the mastermind of the attempt to assassinate the Viceroy), along with the Maharashtrian Vishnu Ganesh Pinglay and some Sikh militants, planned simultaneous troop risings to take place in different localities in February 1915. Unfortunately for the plotters, the plan leaked out and the only rising that took place was quickly subdued. Other groups of revolutionaries made contact with the German Foreign Office and asked for money and arms. They managed to get some funds, but the only significant attempt to smuggle weapons into the country ended in failure. A shipload of arms, purchased by a German agent in New York, was seized by United States authorities before it could leave that country for India. Jugantar leader Jatindranath Mukherjee, waiting for the shipment in Orissa, was trapped by British police and died fighting in September 1915.

Wartime terrorist and militant activity led to the passage of the Defence of India Act, which gave the government extraordinary powers to control "revolutionary crime." After the war these powers were extended by the so-called Rowlatt Acts, the passage of which was one of the goads that led to the launching of M. K. Gandhi's Non-Co-operation Movement in 1920.

During this first mass experiment in non-violent resistance, Jugantar agreed to the request of the country's other prominent political leader, the Bengali C. R. Das, to abstain from terrorist activities. Anushilan did not subscribe to the agreement but sponsored no major actions between 1920 and 1922, the year the Non-Co-operation Movement was suspended (Samanta 1995, vol. 6: 645–8). After this, Jugantar again became active. Associated groups were set up in Chittagong and in Dacca. The Chittagong group robbed the local office of the Assam-Bengal Railway in December 1923. Surya Sen, the group's leader, and two others were arrested but released. The next month Gopi Mohan Saha was arrested after killing a European whom he took to be Calcutta Police Commissioner Charles Tegart. The assassin was openly praised by the Bengali press and, to Gandhi's chagrin, proclaimed a martyr by the Bengal Provincial Congress. Around this time Jugantar became closely associated with the Calcutta Corporation, headed by C. R. Das and Subhas Chandra Bose. Bose apparently "met with active revolutionaries and knew in a general way what they planned to do" (Gordon 1990: 115). Terrorists and ex-terrorists would be factors in the Bengal local government equation from this point on.

The activity and influence of the Bengal terrorists led to the passage in 1924 of the Bengal Criminal Law Amendment Ordinance, extended the next year as an Act. This again gave the police extraordinary powers, and between 1924 and 1927 almost 200 suspects were imprisoned, among them Subhas Bose. Acts of terrorism in Bengal dropped off; but an Anushilan-linked group in the United Provinces grew to some importance. Founded in Benares in 1923 by the Bengalis Sachindranath Sanyal and Jogesh Chandra Chatterjee, the Hindustan Republican Association (as the group became known) soon had branches from Calcutta to Lahore. A series of successful dacoities in northern India culminated in an ambitious train robbery in Kakori. This resulted in two trials that crippled the organization, but several years later was reborn as the Hindustan Socialist Republican Association (Laushey 1975: 24, 27–37).

Owing to the comparative quietness of Bengal during the late 1920s, the government released most of those who had been interned under the Act of 1925. There was an attempt, ultimately unsuccessful, to forge a Jugantar-Anushilan alliance at this time. Some of the younger radicals struck out in new directions, while many, young and old, took part in the activities of the Indian National Congress, which came out in favor of complete independence from Britain in 1927. This recognition of the goal that Aurobindo, Tilak, and other Extremist politicians had put forward 20 years earlier was to some extent made possible by the pressure exerted by militant revolutionary groups since 1906.

In 1928 the national movement was revitalized by the mass agitation against the Simon Commission, which had been set up by the British government to look into the state of Indian reform but which included no Indian member. Congress leader Lala Lajpat Rai succumbed to wounds received when police broke up a Lahore protest march in October. Bhagat Singh and other members of the Hindustan Socialist Republican Association (HSRA) avenged his death in December. Later Bhagat Singh threw a bomb into the Legislative Assembly. He and other HSRA members were arrested, and three of them attracted wide attention by going on a hunger strike in jail. Bengali bomb maker Jatindra Nath Das persisted until his death in September 1929. The Calcutta Corporation passed a resolution of sorrow and condolence after his martyrdom, as did the Indian National Congress when Bhagat Singh was executed.

As the tempo of the national movement picked up during the early 1930s, some former terrorists became influential Congressmen – for example, Jugantar leader Surendra Mohan Ghose – while many Bengal Congressmen maintained links with terrorist organizations. In January 1930 Congress celebrated "Independence Day" for the first time, and in the months that followed, steps were taken to make independence a reality by proponents of the non-violent as well as the violent approach. In March Gandhi inaugurated the Civil Disobedience Movement with his famous Salt March; in April Surya Sen and his associates raided the Chittagong armory.

The four-year course of the Civil Disobedience Movement coincided with the most vehement period of revolutionary terrorism in Bengal. During 1930 alone 11 British officials were killed, notably during the Writer's Building raid of December. Three successive District Magistrates of Midnapore were assassinated, and dozens of other successful actions were carried out during the first half of the decade. But this was a last flare-up before the fire was extinguished. The terrorist movement in Bengal may be said to have ended in 1934 (Laushey 1975: 58–86, 121).

During the 1920s and 1930s, many Bengali terrorists converted to communism or other left-wing parties. Former Jugantar leader Narendranath Bhattacharya, now going by the name of M. N. Roy, became an influential member of the Communist International and helped found the Communist Party of India. Many members of Jugantar, Anushilan, and other groups were won over to the party, particularly during the mass imprisonments of the 1930s. By the end of that decade a whole menagerie of left-wing parties were competing for the youth of the province. Most of these groups were opposed in principle to terrorism, aiming instead at broad-based class warfare.

Numerous terrorists who did not join Left parties became members of Congress. When Jugantar was formally dissolved in 1938, many former members continued to work together under Surendra Mohan Ghose, who acted as a liaison between other Congress politicians and Aurobindo Ghose in Pondicherry. The ascendancy of the Congress left wing was demonstrated by Subhas Chandra Bose's election as Congress president in 1938 and again in 1939. His defeating of Gandhi's candidate in the second election angered the Congress Working Committee, who forced him to resign. In April he formed the Forward Bloc as an "organized and disciplined Left Wing Party" "to fight the Gandhi wing" (quoted in Majumdar et al. 1978: 571). Placed under house arrest in 1940, Bose escaped to Europe, met Mussolini and Hitler, and eventually became the leader of the Indian National Army (INA) in Southeast Asia. The INA's military campaign was a failure, but the trial of three of its officers in Delhi in November 1945 electrified the country at a critical moment. The remission of the officers' sentences was taken by many to mean that a revolt by a disciplined army under a provisional government was not treason. A few months later, in February 1946, the revolt of the naval ratings in

Bombay convinced the British that the loyalty of the armed forces could no longer be counted on. The next month, a three-member Cabinet Mission came to India to discuss the transfer of political power from the British Raj to the Indian people. Independence came a year and a half later, on August 15, 1947.

Throughout the Freedom Struggle, acts of violent revolt forced the government to parley more seriously with the leaders of the legitimate movement. Gandhi was aware of this. At the Round Table Conference of 1931, the apostle of non-violence declared that he held "no brief for the terrorists," but added that if the government refused to work with him, it would have the terrorists to deal with. The only way to "say good-bye to terrorism" was "to work the Congress for all it is worth" (Gandhi 1971: 358, 365). Little as they liked the Mahatma, the government followed his advice. He offered them a better way out of what had become an impossible situation than a prolonged battle with the forces of violent revolution.

Conclusions

The indirect pressure exerted by the terrorists on the public independence movement was their primary contribution to its success. Another was their public demonstration that freedom was something worth dying for. The martyrdom of such men as Khudiram Bose, Surya Sen, and Jatindra Nath Das became a powerful influence on the mentality of the generations that came of age between 1908 and 1938. Despite all of this, it would be hard to pronounce terrorists' work a success in itself. Most British targets escaped the bullets and bombs intended for them. Bengali terrorists were better at murdering other Bengalis, but many of these assassinations, as well as most dacoities, had little direct connection with the national movement. As the criminal element became stronger, more and more groups engaged in acts of gratuitous violence. Acts that were justifiable from the revolutionary point of view, such as the killing of collaborators and informers, were sometimes carried out with unnecessary brutality. The Anushilan Samiti decapitated or mutilated the bodies of some of its victims. The movement's narrow base limited its effectiveness, and may have exacerbated the divisions in Bengali society. Few Muslims and lower-caste men were members; few gave even passive support to the samitis. This, and the samitis' own divisiveness, helped the government keep terrorism from becoming a genuine threat to its rule.

In the long term, one of the most significant results of the terrorist movement was to establish violent opposition as part of the socio-political idiom of post-independence Bengal. It is no coincidence that India's most celebrated movement of communist insurgency got its start in the West Bengal subdivision of Naxalbari. The state's Left parties, their ranks swelled by former terrorists, sponsored many violent strikes and demonstrations from the late 1940s into the 1970s. Writing around the time of the Left's rise to political power in 1977 (after which the situation changed), a Western social scientist could observe: "There can be little serious doubt that violence is perceived to be an acceptable strategy to almost all political parties in West Bengal" (Hula 1983: 440). Even the violent resistance that helped create Bangladesh in 1971 may be said to descend in part from the pre-1947 revolutionary terrorist movement of undivided Bengal.

References

Azad, Abul Kalam. (1984) *India Wins Freedom*. Hyderabad: Orient Longman.

Bloch, Ivan S. (1900) *Modern Weapons and Modern War*. London: Grant Richards.

Boehmer, Elleke. (2002) *Empire, the National and the Postcolonial*. Oxford: Oxford University Press.

Bose, B. K., ed. (1922) *The Alipore Bomb Trial*. Calcutta: Butterworth.

Chakraborty, Ratan Lal. (1992) "Peasant Movements and Insurgencies," in Sirajul Islam (ed.), *History of Bangladesh 1704–1971*, 3 vols. Dhaka: Asiatic Society of Bangladesh, vol. 3, pp. 177–205.

Frost, Thomas. (1876) *The Secret Societies of the European Revolution, 1776–1876*, 2 vols. London: Tinsley Brothers.

Gandhi, M. K. (1971) "Speech at the Plenary Session of the Round Table Conference" (December 1, 1931). In *Collected Works of Mahatma Gandhi*. New Delhi: The Publications Department. 98 volumes (1958–82); vol. 48 (1971), pp. 356–70.

"General Principles of Secret Society." "Nangla Dacoity Case Exhibits," Exhibit 3g. IOR MSS Eur D 709, British Library, India Office Records.

Ghose, Aurobindo (Sri Aurobindo). (1972) *On Himself*. Pondicherry: Sri Aurobindo Ashram.

Ghose, Aurobindo (Sri Aurobindo). (2002) *Bande Mataram: Political Writings and Speeches 1890–1908*. Pondicherry: Sri Aurobindo Ashram.

Ghosh, P. K. (1978) "Organizational Structure of a Revolutionary Secret Society: Anushilan Samity, 1901–1918," *Bengal Past and Present* 97: 139–48.

Ghosh, P. K. (1984) "Ideology of a Revolutionary Secret Society: Anushilan Samiti, 1902–1918," *India Past and Present* 1: 93–7.

Gordon, Leonard A. (1968) "Portrait of a Bengal Revolutionary," *Journal of Asian Studies* 27: 197–216.

Gordon, Leonard A. (1990) *Brothers Against the Raj*. New Delhi: Viking.

Heehs, Peter. (1992) *The Bomb in Bengal*. New Delhi: Oxford University Press.

Heehs, Peter. (1998) *Nationalism, Terrorism, Communalism*. New Delhi: Oxford University Press.

Hula, Richard C. (1983) "Political Violence and Terrorism in Bengal," in Michael Stohl (ed.), *The Politics of Terrorism*, pp. 419–45. New York: Marcel Dekker.

Ker, James. (1973 [1917]) *Political Trouble in India 1907–1917*. Calcutta: Editions Indian.

Laqueur, Walter. (1987) *The Age of Terrorism*. Boston: Little, Brown.

Laushey, David M. (1975) *Bengal Terrorism and the Marxist Left*. Calcutta: Firma K. L. Mukhopadhyay.

Macaulay, Thomas B. (1920) *Critical and Historical Essays*, vol. 1. London: J. M. Dent.

Majumdar, R. C. et al. (1978) *Struggle for Freedom*. Bombay: Bharatiya Vidya Bhavan.

Memorandum on the History of Terrorism in Bengal 1905–1933. (1933) Calcutta: Bengal Government Press.

Minto, Gilbert John, 4th Earl. Letter to John Morley. May 6, 1908. Morley Papers, IOR Eur D573/15, From Minto. British Library, India Office Records.

Minto, Gilbert John, 4th Earl. Letter to John Morley, May 27, 1908. Morley Papers, IOR Eur D573/15, From Minto. British Library, India Office Records.

Morley, John. Letter to Lord Minto. December 26, 1907. Minto Papers M1005–1010, From Morley. National Library of Scotland.

Mukherjee, Uma, and Haridas Mukherjee, eds. (1972) *Bharater Svadhinata Andolane "Jugantar" Patrikar Dan*. Calcutta: Firma K. L. Mukhopadhyay.

Pal, Bipin Chandra. (1932) *Memories of My Life and Times*. Calcutta: Modern Book Agency.

Rowlatt, S. A. T. et al. (1918) *Report of the Committee Appointed to Investigate Revolutionary Conspiracies in India* ["Rowlatt Report"]. London: His Majesty's Stationery Office.

Samanta, Amiya K., ed. (1995) *Terrorism in Bengal*, 6 vols. Calcutta: Government of West Bengal.

Source Material for a History of the Freedom Movement in India. (1957–8). Bombay: Government Central Press, 2 vols.

Chapter 7

Excavating Histories of Terror: Thugs, Sovereignty, and the Colonial Sublime

Alex Tickell

> *For the holy terrorist, the primary audience is the deity [. . .] The Thugs are our most interesting and instructive case in this respect. They intend their victims to experience terror and to express it visibly for the pleasure of Kali [. . .] there is evidence that Thugs existed in the seventh century, and almost all scholars agree that they were vigorous in the thirteenth, which means the group persisted for at least six hundred years [. . .] The Thugs murdered more than any known terrorist group [. . .] if the significance of a terrorist group is to be understood by these measures, the Thugs should be reckoned the most important ever known.*
>
> David Rapoport, "Fear and Trembling: Terrorism in Three Religious Traditions," pp. 660–2

> *The connection between religion and terrorism is not new. More than two thousand years ago the first acts of what we now describe as terrorism were perpetrated by religious fanatics [. . .] The Thugs engaged in acts of ritual murder designed to serve the Hindu goddess of terror and destruction, Kali [. . .] according to some accounts the Thugs killed as many as a million persons during their twelve hundred year existence [. . .] a murder rate rarely achieved by their modern-day counterparts armed with far more efficient and destructively lethal weaponry.*
>
> Bruce Hoffman, *Inside Terrorism*, pp. 88–9

Of the many contemporary fictional works to engage with terror and the postcolonial, Michael Ondaatje's novel of the Sri Lankan conflict, *Anil's Ghost* (2000), remains one of the most enigmatic in its meditation on the relationship between truth, political violence, and personal loss. Published in 2000, just a year before terrorism was reimagined in the North as a forbidding numerical interruption or caesura in the Gregorian calendar,[1] Ondaatje's novel is a disturbing account of what it means to live in a society in which terrorist violence, of both the state and insurgent varieties, does not so much break across history as obliterate it altogether. In the Sri Lanka of the late 1980s, the period in which Ondaatje's novel is set, the nation's collective past is effectively erased by numerous casual disappearances, the result of abductions, extrajudicial killings, and bombings on every side of the conflict. In a terrible, infinitely magnified counterpart of a politicized Western anxiety about the limitless *possibility* of terrorist attack, the situation in Sri Lanka is conveyed in *Anil's Ghost* as a fearful recognition of the grim *probability* of being affected by terrorist violence, and as a kind of shared nervous condition, or, as one character in the novel describes it, terror as "a national disease" (Ondaatje 2000: 53).

The motif around which Ondaatje structures his characteristically complex evocation of loss, and the fear of loss, is excavation: *Anil's Ghost* follows the return of Anil Tissera, a forensic pathologist trained abroad and now working for a Geneva-based human rights organization, to her childhood home in Sri Lanka, and into the midst of the country's tangled network of insurgent and counter-insurgent killing. Anil's profession involves the post-mortem interpretation of the skeletal "texts" left behind in the aftermath of terror. As part of her investigation of government human rights abuses she is teamed with another latter-day augur and interpreter of bones, a Sri Lankan archaeologist, Sarath Diyasena, who can "read a bucket of soil as if it were a complex historical novel" (Ondaatje 2000: 151). Their uneasy collaboration, as they identify "Sailor," the anonymous victim of a government hit squad whose body has been buried amongst older human remains in an archaeological site, introduces yet another trope of excavation/inscription when the body is finally identified as that of a local graphite miner. The motif of excavation as a quasi-textual reading of the past acquires a further layer in the figure of Sarath's eccentric teacher, an epigraphist called Palipana, who has tarnished his professional reputation by allegedly inventing the discovery of an important sixth-century Pali rock inscription. Intriguingly, Ondaatje suggests that Palipana's "discovery" may not have been a conscious deception: "perhaps it was more than a trick, less of a falsehood in his own mind; perhaps for him it was not a false step but the step into another reality, the last stage of a long truthful dance" (p. 81).

A full discussion of the rich excavation motif in *Anil's Ghost* is beyond the scope of this chapter. Instead, by way of an introduction, I want to draw attention to just one aspect of the text's archaeological transaction with the past – its search for a historiographic mode appropriate to the aftermath of terror. As Antoinette Burton argues in her discussion of the novel's "archive of bones," this search is dramatized in the contrast between Anil, who believes in the hard empirical evidence of samples and soil types as the truth that will "set you free," and Palipana, who perceives a cultural and political relativism in all truth claims and thinks that "most of the time in our world, truth is just opinion" (p. 102):

> Ondaatje uses Palipana's story expressly to set up a dichotomy between western epistemological presumptions and practices – to which Anil is so attached – and those derived from non-western experiences and sources. In this sense, Palipana is an anti-colonialist who does [not . . .] reject history, but seeks to re-imagine it on new procedural grounds: a kind of fictional Subaltern Studies hero, albeit a fallen one [. . .] Palipana's contribution, we are told, lay not simply in a rejection of evidentiary procedures, or even in a rejection of "History per se," but rather in a more imaginative and less text-driven archive. (Burton 2003: 44–5)

The two approaches to historical truth are never fully reconciled in *Anil's Ghost* (although both analytical and creative "reconstructive" methods contribute to the ultimate discovery of Sailor's identity). However, it is clear that in the process of investigation in Sri Lanka, Anil's "Western" assumptions – her faith in the truth of forensic evidence, and her expectation that a kind of universal retributive justice will automatically follow – are gradually challenged (Burton 2003: 43).

In the insidious bloodshed of Sri Lanka's "unofficial" war, in which "murders [are] committed by all sides" (Ondaatje 2000: 17), these assumptions ring hollow because of their selectivity, their external imposition, and the constant (postcolonial) suspicion that abstract concepts of justice are the privileged discourse of a very partial Western liberalism. In its place Ondaatje suggests that a more creative response to loss, epitomized in literary evocations of the pietà and in the concluding, artistic reconstruction of a damaged Buddha statue, may be the only resource available to those scarred by violence as a form of exposure of a "primary human vulnerability" and a "touch of the worst order" (Butler 2004: 28). Writing in the midst of the earlier, but similarly uncertain, violence of the Irish civil war, W. B. Yeats's poetic "Meditations in Time of Civil War" evoke almost exactly the same sense of "factual" disorientation, and propose comparably ambiguous (creative) restitutions (honeybees building in an abandoned starling's nest): "we are closed in, and the key is turned / On our uncertainty; somewhere / A man is killed, or a house burned. / *Yet no clear fact to be discerned:* / Come build in the empty house of the stare" (Yeats 1984 [1928]: 204–5, my emphasis).

Ondaatje's ghostly novel also haunts this essay because its emphasis on excavation, as a retroactive evidential search in modern-day Sri Lanka, recalls a much earlier South Asian terror campaign with its own "archive of bones": the widespread murder and secret burial of travelers on (north) Indian roads by gangs of *phansigars* or stranglers, more commonly known as thugs, which came to the horrified attention of the British colonial authorities in the 1830s. Apart from a mutual uncertainty about how to know the post facto truth of civil violence, and a common horror at the uncanny disappearance of the victims, this distant chronological comparison may seem rather arbitrary. It is prompted, however, by an academic excavation of the activities of Indian thugs that has already occurred in the burgeoning field of Terrorism Studies, or "terrorology." Here, as in *Anil's Ghost*, "il/legible" bodies from very different eras are brought together in a search for the origins of terrorist violence and, in the process, suppositions are made about cultural difference, the truth claims of colonial archives, and the cultural-historical location of so-called "religious terrorism" that are deeply troubling, not least because they appear to be sustained by the founding assumptions and affiliations of the discipline.

Originally a field of political science, Terrorism Studies has been incorporated into sociology, international relations, and criminology in the last three decades, and now forms a significant component of graduate degrees in these subjects. Whilst often drawing on anthropological and area-studies approaches in assessments of the cultural contexts of terrorist groups, the paradigmatic mode of terrorology is empirical and instrumental, involving the compilation of statistical analyses, psychological profiling, and data gathering (Houen 2002: 9). As Houen notes, the very process of "producing a narrative or theory that outlines an aetiology of terrorism and accounts for its effects is obviously a form of counter-terror in itself," and even in studies that focus on terrorism's cultural impact, "rigid [and implicitly instrumentalist] theoretical constructions of the phenomenon also predominate" (ibid.: 11).[2] What Noam Chomsky terms the propagandist function of Terrorism Studies became fully apparent in the 1980s, when it was used (in the shape of now-discredited works such as Claire Stirling's *The Terror Network*) to lend credence to Ronald Reagan's Cold War crusade against Soviet-backed "state-sponsored" terrorism (Chomsky 1991: 13). Although my brief summary here belies the trenchantly non-partisan approach of many theorists of terrorism (see, for example, Goodin 2006), the potentially compromising relationship between Terrorism Studies, state-security/intelligence agencies and counter-terror policy making cannot be ignored, and continues in the government funding of research centers and the recurrent conceptual bias in the discipline about the actions of the USA, its allies, and its client regimes (George 1991: 76).

Amongst postcolonial commentators, Terrorism Studies has been singled out, especially after 9/11 and 7/7, for its tendency to endorse narrowly defined, often culturally and "racially" schismatic assumptions about terrorism as *anti*-state violence (in the work of Huntington 2002; Wolf 1989; Netanyahu 1986), while ignoring the manifold terrors of Western military and commercial involvement in the postcolony (Roy 2004: 92). In this bias, and in the wider discourses of terror threat that Terrorism Studies supports, postcolonial commentators perceive a reactivated "racial calculus" that "tacitly assigns differential value to lives lost according to their locations and supposed racial origins" (Gilroy 2003: 263). Thus, even as we remain open to the devastating effects of terrorism, the postcolonial, with its customary suspicion of the universal claims of liberal-humanist scholarship (Spivak 1993: 278) and its intellectual foundations in liberation movements once proscribed as "terrorist," provides an important critical foil to the politicization of difference in Terrorism Studies. As I will argue here, the postcolonial is particularly vital in instances where Terrorism Studies uses colonial history (often with impressive disregard for the political contexts of its sources) to characterize the aims of contemporary terror groups – a process which revives, very literally, an older imperial coding of the Other as a historically inert "infra-humanity," diminishing human rights and "deferring human recognition" in the process (Gilroy 2003: 263).

I am not going to attempt a full assessment of the curricular structures and political assumptions of Terrorism Studies here. Instead, I will confine my discussion to works in a previously mentioned sub-field, "religious terrorism," and to the claims of a single paper which has helped to define this area, David C. Rapoport's "Fear and Trembling: Terrorism in Three Religious Traditions" (1984). It is here that we find colonial history becoming a primary resource for theorizing contemporary forms of what Rapoport terms "holy terror":

in this case the ancient practice of *thuggee*, characterized in the first epigraph quotation above as a highly significant form of sustained pre-technological terrorism. As they appear in Rapoport's paper, the "thugs" (literally "deceivers") are described as members of a secret fraternity devoted to the terrifying Hindu goddess Kali, who targeted travelers on India's roads, ritually strangling and robbing their victims and then burying them to conceal the crime. Analyzed alongside Persian assassins and Jewish *Zealot-Sicarii*, the practices of the thugs are compared throughout with the operational modes of modern terrorists. Thus, Rapoport's essay is not only significant because of its use of colonial history within its own field; it also represents the methodological opposite of the postcolonial – finding an atavistic origin for terrorism in colonial descriptions of indigenous violence, where postcolonial theorists might interrogate the "epistemic" violence inherent in the description itself. This variance will lead us in turn to a reassessment of Rapoport's primary sources, and reflections on the very category-basis of "religious terrorism."

My second reason for a return to a colonial terror archive is to attempt to realign the terms of Rapoport's account of *thuggee* as terrorism's primeval Indian origin, and instead ask how the "discovery"/policing of *thuggee* might have supported the growth and consolidation of colonial sovereignty. This will involve moving beyond simple comparisons of colonial counter-insurgency and contemporary counter-terrorism, toward a model of British colonial power as a series of nodal encounters with terror (such as the anti-*thuggee* campaign of the 1820s–30s or the 1857 "Mutiny"), which structurally transform colonial rule, at the same time as colonial sovereignty reasserts itself as "exceptional" force (Schmitt 2005; Agamben 2005). My use of Giorgio Agamben's concept of the state of sovereign exception as "a space devoid of law, a zone of [legal] anomie" (Agamben 2005: 50) takes account here of the fact that, in establishing its rule in India, the East India Company (hereafter the EIC) operated under a makeshift "dual" sovereignty that had been dictated by North's 1773 regulating act but limited by the defeat of Fox's India bill 10 years later (see Hansen and Stepputat 2005: 19; Dirks 2006: 175). Even so, as Achille Mbembe has noted, the colony, however "dual" or provisional, was still an inherently modern political space, and may be seen as "the location par excellence where the controls [. . .] of juridical order [could] be suspended – the zone where the violence of the state of exception is deemed to operate in the service of civilisation" (Mbembe 2003: 24). Thinking about EIC rule in this way, it is necessary to qualify the absolute, extralegal terms in which Mbembe envisages the colonial sovereign right to kill (Mbembe 2003: 25), and remember that in India, British authority, whilst frequently relying on "vigorous executive action" in emergencies (Metcalf 1995: 38), developed a more complex legal relationship with the terms of its own sovereignty. This was because the abstract universal subject (theoretically) interpellated by colonial law implied an indivisible sovereignty that *replaced* electoral justification for rule, and was therefore crucial to the ethical–ideological maintenance of colonialism (Singha 1998: viii; Dirks 2006: 34).

In proposing that British sovereignty in India depended on a regulative "homeostatic" suspension of the juridical order – the exception as *iustitium* (Agamben 2005: 41) – and a linked, strategic use of terror, we are necessarily forced to revisit and supplement pre-existing studies of the colonial imaginary as inherently fearful or disturbed. The idea that British colonialism was haunted by anxieties in which Self and Other could become disconcertingly fused/reversed, revealing the instabilities of colonial authority, has already been debated in a number of ground-breaking works (Bhabha 1994; Leask 1992; Barrell 1991). However, these studies all tend to focus on the subject-effects of colonial terror, diagnosing various psychopathologies within a series of (largely metropolitan) cultural discourses, without necessarily plotting their extended "manifest" reach into colonial policy or the material operations of colonial rule. Indeed, for some critics their greatest shortcoming is their revisionist "transactional" rereading of colonialism that displaces conflict into the "in-between" spaces of negotiation (Parry 2004: 8; Hallward 2001: 26). Keeping this point in mind, and attending closely to the incorporation of an aesthetics of fear – coded as the sublime – in jurisprudence and policing, it is possible to argue that terror, as a shifting marker of unsanctioned indigenous violence, might indicate both the *limit* and the ever-collapsing *basis* of colonial sovereignty (Hussain 2003: 31). For our purposes at least, *thuggee* provides the foundation for a conceptual bridging maneuver between "complicit" psychopathological modes of colonial interaction encoded in a variety of cultural forms and the larger field of "illiberal" governmental power relations (Thomas 1991: xi, 8), in which hegemonic perceptions of threat have a direct bearing on the establishment and maintenance of repressive power.

We will start our own investigation of the thugs with an anecdotal account of a tour through the "Saugor and Nerbudda" territories by an ambitious officer of the EIC, W. H. Sleeman, the "discoverer" of *thuggee* and author of the founding text of the anti-*thuggee* campaign, *Ramseeana* (1836).[3] Prior to Sleeman, *thuggee* had been largely ignored by the EIC, and had only been characterized as a specialized, organized crime since 1815 (Bayly 1996: 175), with few contemporary sources agreeing on its exact details.[4] However, by 1829 colonial government had entered a new utilitarian, reformist phase under Lord William Bentinck's Governor-Generalship (1828–35), and was receptive to Sleeman's proposed scheme for the eradication of *thuggee*, which it saw as a moral duty equivalent to the outlawing of *sati*, or Hindu widow immolation (Chatterjee 1998: 127). A special Thuggee and Dacoity Department was set up to combat the "dreadful trade of murder" on India's roads and, while careful never to claim that it had extirpated the thug menace entirely, Sleeman's new police department succeeded in arresting numerous groups of thugs in India's central provinces through a process of "approver" testimonies, in which convicted thugs informed on others. Sleeman's celebrated anti-*thuggee* campaign not only brought a new emphasis to bear on issues of colonial policing and jurisprudence in the Bentinck government (giving rise to laws such as the "thuggee" act of 1836), it also sparked an immense popular interest in the thugs, a fascination catered for in works such as Philip Meadows Taylor's bestselling novel *Confessions of a Thug* (1839), which printed an indelible image of the murderous thug on the Victorian popular imagination (Mukherjee 2003: 102). As a trope of Indian violence, the thug would have a lengthy residual life in nineteenth-century sensation literature, merging, after the 1857 "Mutiny," into the more pointedly anti-colonial figure of the disloyal *sipahi* or soldier.

The anecdote below, taken from *Ramaseeana*, is highly significant because it reveals how a sense of terror, and an aesthetic of the sublime, are routinely evoked as part of the work of colonial policing. Here, Sleeman recounts how the famous thug leader Feringeea (who had turned "approver" and was accompanying him on his tour of the Indian countryside) directed his party to camp in a mango grove outside the village of Selohda. The next morning Sleeman and his wife found that the former "chief of thugs" had actually encouraged them to pitch their tents over the *bhil* (burial site) of some of his previous victims:

> I reached [the mango grove . . .] in the evening, and when I got up in the morning he [the thug approver] pointed out three places, in which he and his gang had deposited at different intervals the bodies of three parties of travellers. A Pundit and six attendants murdered in 1818, lay

> among the ropes of my sleeping tent, a Havildar and four sipaheas murdered in 1824, lay under my horses, and four Brahman carriers of Ganges water and a woman murdered soon after the Pundit, lay within my sleeping tent. The sward had grown over the whole, and not the slightest sign of it ever having broken was to be seen . . . my wife was still sleeping over the grave of the water-carriers . . . she has often since declared that she never had a night of such horrible dreams, and that while asleep her soul must consequently have become conscious of the dreadful crimes that had been there perpetrated. (Sleeman 1836: 30–1)

The anecdote is especially intriguing because it is so multi-accentual, playing on both the forensic and archaeological resonances of the exhumed body, but also gendering and aesthetically shading Sleeman's detection narrative as a form of gothic nightmare. In the nervous empiricism of his typology of caste, occupation, and date of burial, the epistemic weight of a whole economy of late nineteenth-century studies of Indian linguistics, religion, and law (Inden 1990; Cohn 1996) is brought to bear on Sleeman's shocked collation of the dead. However, instead of providing a sense of narrative closure, the fear that *thuggee* generates in the story seems to escape or exceed Sleeman's careful postmortem.[5] Indeed, the tropological nexus of dreaming sleep, death, and desire in this anecdote immediately invites a Freudian reading, in which *thuggee* figures as an irruption of violence in the colonial subconscious. The murders are all the more disconcerting because of the close proximity of "sleeping" bodies in the (suspiciously) overgrown mango grove; Sleeman finds he has "lain" with a murdered Indian woman in his tent, while his wife has similarly cohabited with four Brahmin water-carriers in a disturbing necrophilic intimacy. But as sleep, death, and desire become confused here (Dollimore 1998: 83) the arrangement of "sleepers" above and below the ground also serves as a parable of knowledge and power. This is because by withholding key information about the *bhil*, the thug informer Feringeea – who had previously been employed by the British resident in Malwa, and appears, with his "English blunderbuss and pistol," as a frontier version of Bhabha's mimic-man (Fhlathúin 2004a: 34; Bhabha 1994: 85) – still manages to practice a form of *thuggee* (deception) on Sleeman and his wife, misleading them just as he previously misled his victims.

The horrifying, unexpected presence of the buried dead disclosed by Feringeea poses questions about other grave-sites yet to be discovered, and, by extension, the "unknowable" breadth and range of thug activities. Indeed, earlier in *Ramaseeana*, Sleeman describes the "system of *Thuggee*" as a malignant plant-growth that had found "congenial soil" in the subcontinent, and "flourished with rank luxuriance for more than two centuries, till its roots had penetrated and spread over almost every district within the limits of our dominions" (Sleeman 1836: 13). In both instances, colonial sovereignty is dangerously undermined: firstly, in the potentially limitless sepulchral honeycombing of the landscape as a result of *thuggee* – something like the sublime infinity of sealed chambers in Forster's later description of the Marabar caves in *A Passage to India* (Forster 1965 [1924]: 125; Suleri 1992: 31) – and, secondly, in the spread of *thuggee* as a contending knowledge system: a rhizome that has proliferated and secretly rooted itself under the notice of the colonizer. On closer examination, Sleeman's anecdote stages *thuggee*, and its chief representative Feringeea, as a terrible doppelgänger of the colonial will to power, encoding an incipient information panic (Bayly 1996: 171) in the possibility of not knowing *enough*, or a fear of intelligence failure.

Sleeman's response to these inbuilt anxieties in communications with the unruly native informant, who has usurped the colonizer's "privilege of complex subjectivity" and therefore "never becomes fully naturalized as the disciplinary [. . .] knowable subject of the colonial polity" (Roy 1998: 55), is to make what seems like a formal overcompensation in the rest of his text. The compendious *Ramaseeana*, which is more a prosecution file than a monograph and includes "dialogues," tables, reports, and numerous appendices, "reads" its subject in as many ways as possible, presenting the thugs as a caste, as a devotional religious cult, as an occupational genealogy and, most importantly, as a fraternity with its own secret language – *Ramasee* – for which Sleeman provides a lexicon. And in doing so, it recycles some of the paradigmatic cultural categories (caste in particular) that had informed orientalist attempts to understand Indian society. As Parama Roy argues, taxonomized as a caste the thug could occupy discrepant subject positions: "he could simultaneously be an exceptional criminal *and* a representative Hindu, or Indian, since in the colonial imaginary the territory of Hinduism is often coextensive with that of India" (Roy 1998: 49). These "discrepant" subject positions of *thuggee*, and the fact that convictions had to be constructed around an "absence," still trouble Sleeman's account, however, generating a constant, supplemental hermeneutic.

In its cognitive struggle to contain *thuggee*, and its slide into the narrative conventions and the continually deferring plot structures of gothic fiction, Sleeman's account bears useful comparison with the sublime aesthetics elaborated by Edmund Burke in his *Philosophical Enquiry into the Sublime and Beautiful* (1757). For Burke the pleasurable pain of the sublime is associated with astonishment and an "open or latent" ruling principle of terror that "robs the mind of all its powers of acting and reasoning" (Burke 1998 [1757]: 101). Burke's catalogue of things that excite sublime feelings include immeasurable "vastness," "infinity," "darkness," and "obscurity" (ibid.: 102–3) – categories he would later evoke in describing the cognitive difficulties of colonial rule in his parliamentary speech on Fox's India bill (1783). Here, and in the impeachment trial of Warren Hastings (1786–94), Burke would use the sublime "failure of lists" (Suleri 1992: 28) to indict the EIC's financial and legal mismanagement, and its quintessentially tropical corruption in forms of despotic rule.[6] Written 50 years after the Hastings trial, and still seemingly dogged by these "sublime" anxieties of epistemic/cognitive failure, Sleeman's account of *thuggee* is crucially different, however, in that it does not admit the "economy of guilt" (Suleri 1992: 26) about EIC rule that characterized Burke's colonial sublime. By 1836 the British were more certain of the cultural legitimacy of their civilizing mission, and had bound the Company under a legal framework that ostensibly differentiated its executive powers from those of "oriental" despotism – even though some administrators, influenced by a romantic individualism, would characterize their own style of rule as "benign despotism" (Metcalf 1995: 38). As we will see below, in these circumstances the aesthetics of a colonial sublime operates on another political level, as a renewed marker of difference.

It is easy to understand the appeal of colonial descriptions of the thugs as a clandestine, caste-like terror network for contemporary Terrorism Studies theorists. And, in hindsight, the focus on "holy terror" that we encounter in Rapoport's "Fear and Trembling" essay anticipates a perceived global shift in the 1980s and 1990s (noted by the US State Department's *Patterns of Global Terrorism* report), from secular, revolutionary, and "state-sponsored" terrorism to decentralized transnational terrorist groups, motivated, more or less, by modern religious fundamentalism. My point, in focusing on Rapoport's essay, is not necessarily to deny this political change, or question the symbolic rehearsal of sacrificial violence in many religious faiths (Girard 2005; Juergensmeyer 1991), even though the category of "religious terror" tends to occlude contemporary terrorism's political objectives. Rather, I want to ask how Rapoport's historiography sustains, as unproblematic objective knowledge, the founding assumptions and procedural conjectures of Sleeman's anti-*thuggee* campaign. As we noted above, alongside the thugs Rapoport cites two other formative holy "terror" groups: the twelfth-century Muslim *Ismaili-Nizari* assassin sect, who carried out suicide attacks on officials of the Turkish Seljuk empire in Persia, and the first-century Jewish *Zealot-Sicarii*, "dagger-men" who targeted leaders of the Judean Jewish community connected with the Roman occupation.[7] Comparatively, though, it is Indian *thuggee* that Rapoport claims as the most significant proto-terrorism, both in its apparent disregard for human rather than divine witnesses, and in its relative duration (measured in centuries rather than decades). In each case, religious contexts are emphasized as a means of theorizing what Rapoport describes as the "uniqueness of [pre-technological] sacred terror," evident in the obliviousness of its proponents to personal risk, and the fact that "Holy terror never disappeared, and seems to be reviving in new forms" (Rapoport 1984: 674).

Rapoport's "Fear and Trembling" essay would be less significant had it not subsequently become a supporting pillar in Terrorism Studies readings of "religious" terrorism. Rapoport wholeheartedly accepts colonial accounts of *thuggee*, and his citation of "academic" sources such as Thomas De Quincey – who had no direct experience of South Asia and was well known for his fearful hallucinatory visions of the region as "the seat of awful images and associations" (De Quincey 1985 [1821]: 72) – is a confusing use of primary material. However, we must remember that as his 1984 essay pre-dates much subsequent historical research on *thuggee*, Rapoport cannot be blamed retrospectively for the limitations of his work. More problematic, however, is the unqualified later use of his essay by theorists of "religious terror" such as the Rand Corporation analyst Bruce Hoffman (quoted in the second epigraph above) who, in his *Inside Terrorism* (1998), describes "Fear and Trembling" as a seminal study of *thuggee* as terrorism, repeating the maximum time-span for thug activity and mortality rates stipulated by Rapoport (1200 years and a million deaths), even though Rapoport himself cautions that "this figure seems too large but half that number may be warranted" (Rapoport 1984: 661–2). For Hoffman, the facts established by Rapoport support core differentiations between secular and religious terrorism, in which the latter is described as less predictable, less dependent on a "support constituency," more alienated and more deadly than the former (Hoffman 1998: 94–5). Although some of these claims might be useful in assessing changes in some forms of terrorism (and indicating a shift in the adversarial focus of Western democracies from communist Cold War to Islamist holy war), the boundaries between religious and ethnic/political motivations in terrorist movements are more permeable than the Rand Corporation model allows, and insisting on clear secular/sacred differentiations may obscure, rather than clarify, the aims of "holy" terrorists – a category which is now too often rendered synonymous with radical Islam anyway, and rarely registers the messianic idiom of much counter-terror rhetoric (Townshend 2002: 101).

In Joseba Zulaika and William Douglass's study *Terror and Taboo* (1996), which concentrates on terrorism's discursive manifestations, "Fear and Trembling" is lauded as a "classic paper" that provides "stunning instances in which the religious traditions of Hinduism, Islam and Judaism legitimated terror" (Zulaika and Douglass 1996: 107). However, the authors are less willing to accept Rapoport's cited time-spans or mortality rates for *thuggee*, and even question, uniquely, the "allegorical" role of *thuggee* within terrorology (Zulaika and Douglass 1996: 108). Other scholars carefully contest the Rand Corporation model of religious terror while still accepting the broad assumptions of Rapoport's account (see Goodin 2006: 43). The thugs are, nevertheless, firmly reinstated as historical progenitors of terrorism in more recent textbooks for the American Terrorism Studies market, such as Gus Martin's *Understanding Terrorism* (2003), and, most clearly, Pamala Griset and Sue Mahan's *Terrorism in Perspective* (2003). Griset and Mahan reproduce Rapoport's essay in full, and provide a table comparing his three "holy terror" groups, noting the thugs' intended audience ("Kali, God of Terror"), their objectives ("Human sacrifices . . . victims' suffering pleases Kali"), and contemporary parallels ("Religious fanatics and cults that shun publicity"; Griset and Mahan 2003: 11). Griset and Mahan even cite Rapoport's essay as a model for their own "culturally-sensitive" approach: "Rapoport thus echoes the theme [*sic*] used throughout this book, that understanding the culture, religion, politics, economics and ideology of a country and its people is the best way to comprehend the phenomena of terrorism" (Griset and Mahan 2003: 11).

These seemingly laudable sentiments are diminished by the existence of so much historical scholarship on *thuggee* that implicitly contradicts Rapoport's work. Moreover, Griset and Mahan's anthropologizing gesture toward the terrorist, locating him/her beyond the boundary of immediate cultural comprehension, *anticipates* otherness, and their national–cultural mapping of terrorism misreads its contemporary political emergence within (or throughout) the "complex overlapping, disjunctive order of the new global cultural economy" (Appadurai 1996: 32). Like Rapoport's and Hoffman's works, which see terrorism as intrinsic to a particular non-European culture or belief system, Griset and Mahan's text simultaneously promises insights into motivations that are hidden from the researcher (located, implicitly, in the global north) while disavowing the historical role of the "secular" north in the development of "religious" terrorism. As one critic warns us, this approach ignores the fact that "all ideologies, secular or religious, are capable of 'fundamentalism' and [that] the resort to violence is often a response to social/political conditions rather than an inherent element of a belief-system *per se*" (Modood 2002: 208).

Was the phenomenon of *thuggee* as clear-cut as both colonial and colonially informed Terrorism Studies accounts suggest? At the very least, a sense of the difficulties of distinguishing thug-murders from other crimes is clearly evident in contemporary government correspondence. In a letter to the Court of Directors on April 6, 1830, Bentinck criticizes procedures for reporting *thuggee* killings, and his letter indicates more a sense of administrative frustration than a clear understanding of *thuggee* itself. "The reports in regard of this offence in some of the districts are very vague," complains the Governor-General. "Bodies of persons found in such a state that it could not be known whether they had been murdered or not are given as cases of murder by thugs . . . it [is . . .] suspected that in many instances persons are reported to have been murdered by thugs who have in truth died from some accident." He concludes by calling for improved policing, stating regally, "we are by no means satisfied with the proceedings of the public officers in regard to offences of this class" (Philips 1977: 425).

The official difficulty in identifying thugs, and the reliance of Sleeman's Thuggee and Dacoity Department on informer depositions, have prompted an extensive historiographic reassessment of *thuggee* in the last 15 years and, although far from consensual, this reassessment casts considerable doubt on Terrorism Studies readings of the thugs as a clandestine, ritualistic "terror organization." The first phase in this re-evaluation, and still for some the "majority opinion" (Wagner 2004), is a series of studies by "Cambridge School" historians and their associates – C. A. Bayly (1996), Radhika Singha (1993), and Sandria Freitag (1991) – all of whom argue that *thuggee* must be understood in the context of the political and social disorder caused by the decline of Mughal rule, as the EIC expanded into central India (Wagner 2004: 933). For these "social disruption theorists," whose work was foreshadowed by Stewart Gordon's (1969), the activities of thug-gangs are seen in terms of both the indigenous military economy, in which "predatory" *Pindari* soldier-mercenaries, disbanded after the colonial campaign against them in 1817–18, turned to violent highway robbery (Bayly 1996: 175), and the preoccupations of colonial law makers who sought to criminalize particular Indian ethnic groups such as nomadic *Banjara* carriers and Muslim *Wahhabi* sects (Brown 2002: 90; Bayly 1996: 172).

In the last 10 years the social disruption thesis has been joined by (and selectively incorporated into) a countervailing series of postcolonial readings of *thuggee*, influenced by Edward Said's work, that deploy broadly textual critical strategies and concentrate exclusively on *thuggee* as a colonial discursive construction, and the product of a coherent "thug archive." Amongst these commentators, Parama Roy (1996), Amal Chatterjee (1998), and Máire ní Fhlathúin (2001, 2004a, 2004b) are exemplary in their delineation of the "performative subjectivity" of the thugs, and their close reading of the colonial text of *thuggee* against the grain (an approach that I have also used here, in a limited way, to expose the epistemic anxieties and *aporia* of Sleeman's *Ramaseeana*). Differences between these two schools relate to longer-standing conflicts in the historiography of colonial India (see Lal 2003: 194) and we can only touch on them very briefly, noting that, for Cambridge historians such as Kim Wagner (to whom I am indebted for the synopsis above), the "deconstructive" postcolonial approach is flawed because it assumes no existential basis for *thuggee* beyond its discursive presence in colonial police files. Postcolonial commentators assume that the colonial construction of *thuggee* was a misrepresentation, states Wagner, without ever considering texts or discourses (drawn from Indian sources) that might prove otherwise (Wagner 2004: 937).

These criticisms will be familiar to anyone who has traced the numerous theoretical responses to Said's work in *Orientalism* (1978) (Porter 1983; Ahmad 1994; Moore-Gilbert 1997), and Wagner's objections are directed as much against the Foucauldian "archaeological" methods that inform postcolonial discourse analysis (which he regards as hermetically textual and relativist) as they are against the commentators who employ them. In Wagner's argument, "postcolonial" cultural historians are represented as naïve antagonists of the social-disruption theorists, even though they often draw on this earlier work, and routinely admit their discursive preferences (Roy 1996; Fhlathúin 2001, 2004a, 2004b). However, Wagner's criticism of the discourse focus of postcolonial readings of *thuggee* does have some theoretical bearing on my discussion of a colonial terror-politics here, since it points toward a critical approach that might recognize a "fearful" blurring in colonialism's subject–other relations but also attend closely to the (aesthetically coded) manipulation of these fears, in information panics, intelligence failures, anxieties about security, and instances of sanctioned ignorance, for particular political and legislative ends. This is not in any way to deny the psychological or discursive volatility of (neo)colonialism, but to recognize that, in analyzing exceptional violence coded as terrorism/anti-terrorism, the latter's material consequences should not be collapsed into (or substituted by) its discursive effects.

In response to the postcolonial reading of *thuggee*, Wagner proposes a reassessment of primary sources and depositions produced before Sleeman's anti-*thuggee* campaign started, since these accounts pre-dated official versions of *thuggee* and, presumably, approvers could not be "encouraged" into particular forms of confession. He accordingly examines several earlier accounts of thieves and "strangulators" in European travelogues, Mughal court proclamations and the Sikh *Janamsakhi* texts (Wagner 2004: 943), arguing, from these documents, that *thuggee*, or at least crimes involving robbery/strangulation, did exist before Sleeman's campaign. Even so, he is unwilling to accept the existence of large-scale, caste-like thug activity before the nineteenth century, and admits that Sleeman's work "obviously changed the nature of *thuggee*, both in practical terms and conceptually" (Wagner 2004: 955). Thus, Wagner both endorses the position taken by the "social-disorder" theorists, and also acknowledges Sleeman's "construction" of *thuggee*, even as he distances himself from the "folly" of discourse-based readings:

> I feel it safe to assert that travellers *were* strangled and plundered by bands of robbers in early 19th century India if not earlier . . . The men involved were part of the military labour market, sometimes joining larger armies and sometimes serving petty zemindars, and when faced with demobilization they had to find other ways of gaining a livelihood. In other words: Thuggee was the continuation of a predatory lifestyle under well-regulated circumstances by men thus deprived of the means for

> open plunder. As opposed to Sleeman's claim being a thug was not a caste-like identity, thuggee was not motivated by religious zeal and it was certainly not centrally organized. (Wagner 2004: 962–3)

Wagner's conclusion is significant because it shows that even historians unsympathetic to postcolonial readings of *thuggee* present the phenomenon in much less coherent terms than those described in Terrorism Studies. There is, in fact, scant evidence to show that the thugs operated for twelve or even six centuries, that they dispatched "eight hundred individuals every year" (Hoffman 1998: 89), or even that they were more religious or ritualistic than other social groups in nineteenth-century India. Indeed, as Singha perceptively notes, the lengthy descriptions of thug rites in texts such as *Ramaseeana* are largely indistinguishable from the popular ritual observances practiced routinely in contemporary India, and the thugs' secret language, *Ramasee* (which translates as "slang"), may simply have been a mixture of regional dialect and soldier's jargon (Singha 1993: n. 118). The thugs were not a caste organization, and the fact that colonial accounts note the prosecution of both Muslim and Hindu thugs (often in the same group) is a syncretic factor that complicates Rapoport's and Hoffman's presentation of *thuggee* as wholly defined by a fatalistic Hindu metaphysics. Even if we agree that Kali was the thugs' tutelary deity, the idea that their victims' prolonged "terror" was integral to the sacrificial act and that the thugs incorporated fear/terror into their operations is contradicted by primary accounts of the crime, where informers emphasize the importance of attacking their victims quickly, often drugging them first, to avoid detection. Even Sleeman, in the introduction to *Ramaseeana*, notes: "I have very rarely discovered any instance of what may, perhaps, be termed *wanton* cruelty; that is pain inflicted beyond what was necessary to deprive the [thugs' victim] of life" (Sleeman 1836: 8). Like the concept term "religious terror" with which *thuggee* is associated, the Terrorism Studies theorists isolate one aspect of the phenomenon – "ritualized" violence – and then transform this into an essential and unchanging badge of difference, while ignoring a nexus of other constitutive political and cultural factors.[8]

By way of a conclusion we will return to Sleeman's exhumation of the victims of *thuggee* in the mango grove at Selohda, an excavation directed by the unpredictable native informant Feringeea,[9] who was both Sleeman's "greatest adversary" and a career-making catch for his department (Fhlathúin 2004a: 34). We can now concede that, as much as it discloses an uncanny, disruptive mimicry of colonial knowledge claims, the importance of this scene lies equally in its pivotal relationship to policy and the juridical balance of norm and exception (which would be buttressed by key pieces of "exceptional" legislation, such as the "thuggee" Act XXX of 1836 and the Dacoitee Act XXIV of 1846).[10] As we have seen, Sleeman finds a threatening double in the figure of the thug leader Feringeea, whose very name, which derives from the Persian *Firingi* for "foreigners" or "Franks," reflects a *colonial* political origin: "his mother's village [was . . .] assaulted and burnt by a 'Regiment under Blake Sahib' for non-payment of taxes; 'in her flight [she] gave birth to *Feringeea*, and he got his name from the event – Feringeea, from the attack of the Feringies'" (quoted in Fhlathúin 2004a: 34). In Fhlathúin's view, Feringeea's naming makes him a spectral signifier of British complicity in *thuggee*, but I would go further and suggest that the regulative play of sovereign power as norm (oppressive revenue collection as right of conquest) and exception ("excessive" criminality and its judicially manipulated punishment) in Feringeea's story is representative of much wider rhythms of colonial violence.

If we read the East India Company in the 1830s as a governmental regime reliant, in part, on a nascent terror-politics, then it is Immanuel Kant's analytic of the sublime formulated in the *Critique of Judgment* (1790), rather than Burke's earlier definition, that approximates most clearly to its aesthetic mode. Unlike Burke's formulation, in which a cognitive inability to grasp the vastness/infinity/obscurity of India threatens to dissolve the certainties of the colonial subject, Kant's definition in the third *Critique* admits a dynamic social/political effect as intrinsic to the sublime. Indeed, for Kant the sublime operates in a restorative capacity in which the perceiving subject experiences an imaginative breakdown in the face of fearful nature, only to be renewed by surrendering to a sense of reason that transcends personal concerns (Kant 2005 [1790]: 75; Battersby 2003: 79; Burnham 2000: 88–105). As Spivak reminds us in her reading of the third *Critique*, the sublime operates here as a limit-criterion of the Western male sovereign-subject, and excludes "men in the raw" who have not been "cooked" by European culture, from the positive-pain of sublime experience (Spivak 1999: 13, 26). Kant famously includes "ordered" military warfare as a source of the sublime (Kant 2005: 76), but, in the politico-juridical structure of Company rule, warfare (as a continuous process of "wandering" counter-insurgency, annexation, and punitive violence) can only approximate to Kant's formalized terms of war. Even so, the disabling mutuality of terror-ist figures such as Feringeea is resolved if we apply Kant's version of the sublime because, as an Indian and a criminal, Sleeman's adversary is excluded from its self-affirming effects. He might play a part in situations that generate a feeling of the sublime – such as the terrifying exhumation at Selohda – but he can never be redeemed by them.

Like the current anti-terror discourses it anticipates, the colonial sublime, in Kant's terms, choreographs a response to the violence of the Other while also relocating the Other beyond the category of the human (as a type of what Gilroy has described as the "infra-human"). Integral to the political effect of Kant's sublime here is the fact that it robs us of empathy and the *sensus communis*[11] inherent in "aesthetic reflective judgement" (Kearney 2003: 43), and makes us less inclined, and less able, to approach the difficult and rewarding task of thinking through our historical connectedness (Said 1993: 408). Moreover, in these Kantian terms, colonial terror-politics not only separates and essentializes identities; it does so repeatedly. As Thomas Huhn notes: "The sublime is the realization of our dominance, our power over the supposed power of nature. But in order to feel this power of ours, in order to realize our dominance, we must insist on nature [as that which is not culture] being a fearful power – and in repeatedly staging its redoubtable character we repeatedly stage our dominance" (Huhn 1995: 272).

Here we see an all too familiar pattern emerging, in which claims about the Other's propensity for violence form the foundations of a political strategy in which subjectivity is grounded in an inverted image of threat and terror (Huhn 1995: 274).[12] In this situation – as Ondaatje's novel recognizes and Yeats's poem laments – we risk an ethical impoverishment, and a grim surrender to the imaginative consequences of fear: "We had fed the heart on fantasies / The heart's grown brutal from the fare, / More substance in our enmities / Than in our love; O honey-bees, / Come build in the empty house of the stare" (Yeats 1961[1928]: 230–1).

Notes

1 A discussion of the wider implications of designating the 9/11 attacks numerically is presented in Jacques Derrida's dialogue with Giovanna Borradori. See Borradori (2003: 85–136).

2 The contemporary role of political science in the maintenance of state power is noted somewhat satirically by Hardt and Negri when they argue

that "the paradigmatic figure of the political scientist [as terrorologist] has become the Geheimrat, the secret adviser to the sovereign" (Hardt and Negri 2005: 33).

3 The full descriptive title of W. H. Sleeman's text is *Ramaseeana: Or a Vocabulary of the Peculiar Language used by Thugs with an Introduction and Appendix descriptive of the system pursued by the fraternity and the measures which have been adopted by the supreme government of India for its suppression.*

4 A good example of this conceptual uncertainty over the operational practices of the thugs occurs in Gerald Wellesley's official correspondence. Wellesley was Resident at Holkar's court, and in a letter to the acting Resident at Gwalior in 1820 he states, "The race of thugs is more pernicious from their practice of never perpetrating a robbery without the murder also of the victims, and for this purpose they employ both the sword and the noose, and act both in gangs and individually" (British Library OIOC collection Mss F/4/774, 20927). R. Sherwood, in his article on thugs, "Of the Murderers called P'hansigars" (1820), expresses similar doubts.

5 For an interesting comparative instance of this "excessive" fear in the popular narrative of the "Black Hole" of Calcutta, see Teltscher (1995).

6 See Montesquieu (1989 [1748]) for an influential Enlightenment account of oriental despotism.

7 Given the devastating Hezbollah suicide attacks on US embassies and military barracks in Beirut the year before Rapoport published his paper, and the assassination of the Indian premier Indira Gandhi in 1984, his mapping of these groups in the eastern Mediterranean and South Asia is telling. It is also interesting that his selection of thugs and assassins as representative terror groups echoes a similar oriental configuration of terror in Frederick Holme's article "The Secret Societies of Asia: the Assassins and the Thugs," which appeared in *Blackwood's Magazine* in 1841, in which Holme represents *thuggee* as a metaphor for the corruption of Asian society as a whole.

8 In summary, the thugs (whose description as a prototypical religious terror group is highly questionable) can be interpreted both as subsidiary social and economic by-products of colonial expansion into central India and as vital self-consolidating figures in the exception-based juridical preservation of colonial sovereignty.

9 Feringeea would later appear in fictional form as the terrible king of thugs in works such as Jules Verne's *Le tour du monde en quatre-vingts jours* (1873) (*Around the World in Eighty Days*); and thugs would feature in Eugène Suë's *Le Juif errant* (1845) (*The Wandering Jew*) and René de Pont-Jest's *Procès des thugs* (1877) (*Thug Trials*). See Van Woerkens (2002: 272).

10 Kaye (1853) reproduces Act XXX in his history of the East India Company in order to emphasize its importance as an exceptional detour around the "complicated . . . formal" procedure of the courts. Before Act XXX the

thugs "throve upon the legal niceties and the judicial reserve of the English tribunals, and laughed our regulations to scorn . . . It was wisely determined, therefore . . . to make the case of *thuggee* an exceptional case, and to sanction a relaxed application of the existing laws and regulations to members of the great fraternity of thugs" (Kaye 1853: 375). Act XXX sanctioned imprisonment for life for anyone found guilty of belonging to, or having belonged to, a gang of thugs. It also made the accused liable for prosecution in courts "within or without" Company territory. The Act was retroactively applied, and unlike other laws did not require a *fatwah* from a Muslim law officer. Act XXIV applied the same exceptional ruling to cases of banditry or *dacoity*.

11 Huhn (1995) disagrees with this reading and states that the sublime is what *makes* a *sensus communis*: "The pleasure of the sublime is what binds subjectivity to itself . . . But the pleasure of the sublime is likewise the founding moment of culture, of that *sensus communis* which organises itself – but only as that which opposes nature" (Huhn 1995: 274). Huhn's version of the *sensus communis* is (consciously) riven here by the same ethnocentric assumptions about European culture that Spivak finds in Kant's third *Critique*.

12 Thuggee would soon disappear as a locus of colonial anxiety, but Sleeman's Thuggee and Dacoity Department would grow and develop in response to newer fears and fresh political terrors. By the late 1800s, in a new incarnation as the Criminal Investigation Department, it would be involved in the surveillance of nationalist activists and the policing of modern anti-colonial terrorism.

References and Further Reading

Adam, Ian and Helen Tiffin, eds. (1991) *Past the Last Post: Theorising Post-Colonialism and Post-Modernism*. Hemel Hempstead: Harvester Wheatsheaf.

Agamben, Giorgio. (2005) *State of Exception*, trans. Kevin Attell. Chicago and London: University of Chicago Press.

Ahmad, Aijaz. (1994) *In Theory: Classes, Nations, Literatures*. Delhi: Oxford University Press.

Appadurai, Arjun. (1996) *Modernity at Large: Cultural Dimensions of Globalization*. Minneapolis, London: University of Minnesota Press.

Armstrong, Meg. (1996) " 'The Effects of Blackness': Gender, Race, and the Sublime in Aesthetic Theories of Burke and Kant," *The Journal of Aesthetics and Art Criticism* 54(3): 213–36.

Barrell, John. (1991) *The Infection of Thomas De Quincey: A Psychopathology of Imperialism*. New Haven and London: Yale University Press.

Battersby, Christine. (2003) "Terror, Terrorism and the Sublime: Rethinking the Sublime after 1789 and 2001," *Postcolonial Studies* 6(1): 67–89.

Baucom, Ian. (1999) *Out of Place: Englishness, Empire and the Locations of Identity*. Princeton, NJ: Princeton University Press.

Bayly, C. A. (1993) "Knowing the Country: Empire and Information in India," *Modern Asian Studies* 27(1): 3–43.

Bayly, C. A. (1996) *Empire and Information: Intelligence Gathering and Social Communication in India, 1780–1870*. Cambridge: Cambridge University Press.

Bhabha, Homi. (1994) *The Location of Culture*. London: Routledge.

Borradori, Giovanna, ed. (2003) *Philosophy in a Time of Terror: Dialogues with Jürgen Habermas and Jacques Derrida*. Chicago: University of Chicago Press, 2003.

Brown, Mark. (2002) "Crime, Governance and the Company Raj: the Discovery of Thuggee," *British Journal of Criminology* 42: 77–95.

Burke, Edmund. (1998 [1757]) *A Philosophical Enquiry into the Sublime and Beautiful and Other Pre-Revolutionary Writings*, ed. David Womersley. London: Penguin.

Burnham, Douglas. (2000) *An Introduction to Kant's Critique of Judgement*. Edinburgh: Edinburgh University Press.

Burton, Antoinette. (2003) "Archive of Bones: *Anil's Ghost* and the Ends of History," *Journal of Commonwealth Literature* 38(1): 39–56.

Butler, Judith. (2004) *Precarious Life: The Powers of Mourning and Violence*. London: Verso.

Chatterjee, Amal. (1998) *Representations of India, 1740–1840: The Creation of India in the Colonial Imagination*. Basingstoke: Macmillan.

Chomsky, Noam. (1991) "International Terrorism: Image and Reality," in Alexander George (ed.), *Western State Terrorism*, pp. 12–38. Cambridge: Polity.

Cohn, B. S. (1996) *Colonialism and Its Forms of Knowledge: The British in India*. Princeton, NJ: Princeton University Press.

De Quincey, Thomas. (1985 [1821]) *Confessions of an English Opium Eater and Other Writings*. Oxford: Oxford University Press.

Dirks, Nicholas B. (2006) *The Scandal of Empire: India and the Creation of Imperial Britain*. Cambridge, MA: Belknap/Harvard University Press.

Dollimore, Jonathan. (1998) *Death, Desire and Loss in Western Culture*. Harmondsworth: Penguin.

Fhlathúin, Máire ní. (2001) "'That Solitary Englishman': W. H. Sleeman and the Biography of British India," *Victorian Review* 27(1): 69–85.

Fhlathúin, Máire ní. (2004a) "The Making of a Master Criminal: the Chief of Thugs in Victorian Writings on Crime," in Andrew Maunder and Grace Moore (eds.), *Victorian Crime, Madness and Sensation*, pp. 31–44. Aldershot.

Fhlathúin, Máire ní. (2004b) "The Campaign against Thugs in the Bengal Press of the 1830s," *Victorian Periodicals Review* 37(2): 124–9.

Forster, E. M. (1965 [1924]) *A Passage to India*. Harmondsworth: Penguin.

Freitag, Sandria B. (1991) "Crime in the Social Order of Colonial North India," *Modern Asian Studies* 25(2): 227–61.

George, Alexander, ed. (1991) *Western State Terrorism*. Cambridge: Polity.
Gilroy, Paul. (2003) "Where Ignorant Armies Clash by Night: Homogenous Community and the Planetary Aspect," *International Journal of Cultural Studies* 6(3): 261–76.
Girard, René. (2005) *Violence and the Sacred*, trans. Patrick Gregory. New York and London: Continuum.
Goodin, Robert E. (2006) *What's Wrong with Terrorism?* Cambridge: Polity.
Gordon, Stewart N. (1969) "Scarf and Sword: Thugs, Marauders, and State-Formation in 18th Century Malwa," *Indian Economic and Social History Review* 6: 403–29.
Griset, Pamala and Sue Mahan, eds. (2003) *Terrorism in Perspective*. Thousand Oaks, CA and London: Sage.
Hallward, Peter. (2001) *Absolutely Postcolonial: Writing Between the Singular and the Specific*. Manchester: Manchester University Press.
Hansen, Thomas Blom and Finn Stepputat, eds. (2005) *Citizens, Migrants, and States in the Postcolonial World*. Princeton, NJ: Princeton University Press.
Hardt, Michael and Antonio Negri. (2005) *Multitude: War and Democracy in the Age of Empire*. London: Penguin.
Hoffman, Bruce. (1998) *Inside Terrorism*. London: Victor Gollancz.
Holme, Frederick. (1841) "The Secret Societies of Asia: the Assassins and the Thugs," *Blackwoods Magazine* 49: 229–44.
Houen, Alex. (2002) *Terrorism and Modern Literature: From Joseph Conrad to Ciaran Carson*. Oxford: Oxford University Press.
Huhn, Thomas. (1995) "The Kantian Sublime and the Nostalgia for Violence," *The Journal of Aesthetics and Art Criticism* 53(3): 269–75.
Huntington, Samuel. (2002) *The Clash of Civilizations and the Remaking of the World Order*. London: Free Press.
Hussain, Nasser. (2003) *The Jurisprudence of Emergency: Colonialism and the Rule of Law*. Ann Arbor, MI: The University of Michigan Press.
Inden, Ronald B. (1990) *Imagining India*. Oxford: Blackwell.
Juergensmeyer, Mark, ed. (1991) *Violence and the Sacred in the Modern World* [special issue of *Terrorism and Political Violence* 3(3)].
Juergensmeyer, Mark. (2003) *Terror in the Mind of God: The Global Rise of Religious Violence*, 3rd edn. Berkeley and London: University of California Press.
Kant, Immanuel. (2005 [1790]) *Critique of Judgement*. New York: Dover.
Kaye, John William. (1853) *The Administration of the East India Company; A History of Indian Progress*. London: Richard Bentley.
Kearney, Richard. (2003) "Terror, Philosophy and the Sublime: Some Reflections on 11 September," *Philosophy and Social Criticism* 29(1): 23–51.
Lal, Vinay. (2003) *The History of History: Politics and Scholarship in Modern India*. Oxford: Oxford University Press.
Leask, Nigel. (1992) *British Romantic Writers and the East: Anxieties of Empire*. Cambridge: Cambridge University Press.

Martin, Gus. (2003) *Understanding Terrorism: Challenges, Perspectives, and Issues*. Thousand Oaks, CA and London: Sage.

Mbembe, Achille. (2003) "Necropolitics" (trans. Libby Meintjes), *Public Culture* 15(1): 11–40.

Metcalf, Thomas R. (1995) *Ideologies of the Raj: The New Cambridge History of India*, Vol. 3.4. Cambridge: Cambridge University Press.

Modood, Tariq. (2002) "Muslims and the Politics of Multiculturalism in Britain," in Eric Hershberg and Kevin W. Moore (eds.), *Critical Views of September 11th: Analyses from Around the World*, pp. 193–208. New York: The New Press.

Montesquieu, Charles-Louis. (1989 [1748]) *The Spirit of Laws*, ed. and trans. Anne M. Cohler et al. Cambridge: Cambridge University Press.

Moore-Gilbert, Bart. (1997) *Postcolonial Theory: Contexts, Practices, Politics*. London: Verso.

Mukherjee, Upamanyu Pablo. (2003) *Crime and Empire: The Colony in Nineteenth Century Fictions of Crime*. Oxford: Oxford University Press.

Netanyahu, Benjamin. (1986) *Terrorism: How the West Can Win*. London: Farrar, Straus and Giroux.

Ondaatje, Michael. (2000) *Anil's Ghost*. London: Bloomsbury.

Parry, Benita. (2004) *Postcolonial Studies: A Materialist Critique*. Abingdon and New York: Routledge.

Philips, C. H., ed. (1977) *The Correspondence of Lord William Cavendish Bentinck: Governor-General of India 1828–1835, Vol. 1: 1828–1831*. Oxford: Oxford University Press.

Porter, Dennis. (1983) "*Orientalism* and Its Problems," in Francis Barker, Peter Hulme, Margaret Iversen, and Diane Loxley (eds.), *The Politics of Theory: Proceedings of the Essex Sociology of Literature Conference*, pp. 179–82, 186–93. Colchester: University of Essex.

Rapoport, David. (1984) "Fear and Trembling: Terrorism in Three Religious Traditions," *American Political Science Review* 78(3): 658–77.

Roy, Arundhati. (2004) *The Chequebook and the Cruise-Missile: Conversations with Arundhati Roy* by David Barsamian, London: Harper Perennial.

Roy, Parama. (1996) "Discovering India, Imagining Thuggee," *The Yale Journal of Criticism* 9(1): 121–45.

Roy, Parama. (1998) *Indian Traffic: Identities in Question in Colonial and Post-colonial India*. Berkeley, Los Angeles, and London: University of California Press.

Said, Edward. (1993) *Culture and Imperialism*. London: Chatto and Windus.

Said, Edward. (2001) "The Clash of Ignorance," *The Nation*, October 22, 2001.

Schmitt, Carl. (2005) *Political Theology: Four Chapters on the Concept of Sovereignty*, trans. George Schwab. Chicago, London: University of Chicago Press.

Sherwood, R. (1820) "Of the Murderers called P'hansigars," *Asiatick Researches* 13: 250–82.

Singha, Radhika. (1993) "Providential Circumstances: the Thuggee Campaign of the 1830s and Legal Innovation," *Modern Asian Studies* 27(1): 83–146.

Singha, Radhika. (1998) *A Despotism of Law: Crime and Justice in Early Colonial India*. Oxford: Oxford University Press.

Sleeman, W. H. (1836) *Ramaseeana, or a Vocabulary of the Peculiar Language used by the Thugs with an introduction and Appendix descriptive of the system pursued by that Fraternity and the measures which have been adopted by the supreme government of India for its suppression*. Calcutta: G. H. Huttmann, Military Orphan Press.

Sleeman, W. H. (1840) *Report on the Depredations Committed by the Thug Gangs of upper and central India, from the Cold Season of 1836–7 down to their gradual Suppression under the operation of the measures adopted against them by the Supreme Government in the year 1839*. Calcutta: G. H. Huttmann, Military Orphan Press.

Spivak, Gayatri Chakravorty. (1993) *Outside in the Teaching Machine*. New York and London: Routledge.

Spivak, Gayatri Chakravorty. (1999) *A Critique of Postcolonial Reason: Towards a History of the Vanishing Present*. Cambridge, MA and London: Harvard University Press.

Suleri, Sara. (1992) *The Rhetoric of English India*. Chicago and London: University of Chicago Press.

Teltscher, Kate. (1995) "'The fearful name of the Black Hole': Fashioning an Imperial Myth," in Bart Moore-Gilbert (ed.), *Writing India 1757–1990*, pp. 30–51. Manchester: Manchester University Press.

Thomas, Nicholas. (1991) *Entangled Objects*. Cambridge, MA and London: Cambridge University Press.

Townshend, Charles. (2002) *Terrorism: A Very Short Introduction*. Oxford: Oxford University Press.

Trivedi, Harish and Meenakshi Mukherjee, eds. (1996) *Interrogating Post-colonialism: Theory, Text and Context*. Simla: Indian Institute of Advanced Study.

Van Woerkens, Martine. (2002) *The Strangled Traveler: Colonial Imaginings and the Thugs of India*, trans. Catherine Tihanyi. Chicago and London: University of Chicago Press.

Wagner, Kim A. (2004) "The Deconstructed Strangler: a Reassessment of Thuggee," *Modern Asian Studies* 38(4): 931–63.

Wolf, John B. (1989) *Antiterrorist Initiatives*. New York: Plenum.

Yeats, W. B. (1984 [1928]) "The Stare's Nest by My Window," in *W. B. Yeats: The Poems*, ed. Richard J. Finneran. London: Macmillan, pp. 204–5.

Zulaika, Joseba and William A. Douglass. (1996) *Terror and Taboo: The Follies, Fables, and Faces of Terrorism*. London: Routledge.

Chapter 8

Terrorism, Literature, and Sedition in Colonial India

Stephen Morton

In a cartoon published in the *Hindi Punch* entitled "Down with the Monster" and dated May 1908, the Indian Viceroy Lord Minto is depicted as Hercules killing the twin-headed hydra of Indian anarchism and revolution with a club, on the side of which the words "LAW & ORDER" are inscribed in capital letters. Facing this figure, on the opposite side of the cartoon, in the smoke clouds bellowing from the dying hydra's two mouths, the following words are also written in capital letters: "TERRORISM, SEDITION, LAWLESSNESS, and MOZUFFERPURE [*sic*] OUTRAGE." At first glance, what this cartoon exemplifies is the moral authority of the British government's counter-terrorism strategy in early twentieth-century colonial Bengal. For the authority of the British Empire was clearly predicated upon the strenuous suppression and consequent demonization of nationalist insurgency. By visualizing the dichotomy between law and order on the one hand and terrorism on the other, the cartoonist suggests a stable moral opposition between the rule of law in British India and the violent anarchy attributed to Bengali nationalism. The conflation of acts of terrorism with sedition may seem to parallel the introduction of draconian forms of legislation in the early twenty-first century, such as the Patriot Act in the United States or the British Anti-Terrorism Act, which vaguely define acts that glorify terrorism in an effort to control and proscribe rational debate about the historical and political determinants of so-called terrorism. The sedition legislation in British India, like more contemporary forms of anti-terrorism legislation which seek to proscribe literature that seeks to incite or glorify terrorism, suggests that there is a causal relationship between writing and so-called acts of terrorism that can be inferred from the seditious writing itself. Section 5B of the 2006 British Terrorism Act, for instance, defines the glorification of terrorism in terms of the reception of statements that glorify terrorism by persons "who could reasonably be expected to infer that what is being glorified, is being glorified" in order to encourage further acts of violence. Considered in relation to such contemporary examples of anti-terrorism legislation, the *Hindi Punch* cartoonist's juxtaposition of terrorism, sedition, and lawlessness seems strikingly prescient.

It is with such strong historical parallels in the formulation of anti-terrorism law that this chapter is in part concerned. By considering the way in which literary and journalistic writings came under scrutiny by the British colonial government in India and by the colonial office in London for evidence of sedition, the chapter examines how the sedition legislation in colonial India served to establish a connection between writing and terrorism. In British India, sedition was defined as the promotion of disaffection with the existing government via speeches, newspaper articles, and songs. And by documenting cases of sedition, terrorist outrages, and revolutionary activity in Bombay, Bengal, Punjab, Bihar, Orissa, the United Provinces, the Central Provinces, Madras, and Burma between 1897 and 1917, the 1918 Sedition Committee Report proposed a series of punitive and preventive emergency measures, under the aegis of martial law, which allowed courts to try accused subjects without juries, and granted the police special powers to confine individuals in "non-penal custody" for a year or more (*Sedition Committee Report* 1918: 205–7). It was prominently the Rowlatt Act that prompted demonstrations of civil disobedience and the subsequent massacre of at least 379 people in the Punjabi town of Amritsar in April 1919. While David Arnold has suggested that the British Raj increasingly became a kind of police state in the aftermath of India's first war of independence in 1857 (1986: 203–6), it was Lord Curzon's partition of Bengal in 1905 and the repressive measures introduced by the Governor General of India Lord Minto and the Secretary of State for India John Morley to control the press, as well as the possession of firearms and explosives, that consolidated the authoritarian powers of the British Raj. What is more, the colonial state's recourse to emergency measures posited a causal relationship between the effect of seditious writing and the cause of revolutionary terrorism. As the historian Gerald Barrier puts it in his study of proscribed literature in British India, "Aware that publications were both a symptom and a cause of unrest, the government coupled checks on extremist literature with enlarged executive and judicial powers to combat sedition in all forms" (1974: 16). The increase of political assassinations and bombings in Bengal, Maharashtra, and Punjab after 1905 prompted Morley to suggest to Minto that martial law might be required (Barrier 1974: 45). But it was not until 1915 that the police were granted wide powers "of censorship, search and arrest" under the Defence of India Act, which was designed to give the government of India special powers to deal with revolutionary and German-inspired threats during World War I, especially in the Punjab. After the end of the war in 1918, this Act was replaced by the Anarchical and Revolutionary Crimes Act of 1919, better known as the Rowlatt Act, which sought to "devise some extra-legal measure to replace the [Defence of India] Act when it lapsed, a measure which could be brought into force in any state of emergency, not necessarily one connected with war" (Tegart 1976: 131). This Act gave the colonial state the power to issue restrictive orders against a person "suspected of connection with revolutionary or anarchical movements"; and to provide for the "speedy trial" of offenses in connection with revolutionary or anarchical movements where it was deemed to be necessary for "the interests of public safety" (Muddiman 1921: 126). In British colonial India, a colonial state of emergency was produced in and through the legal prose of counter-insurgency, which partly attributed the causality of revolutionary outrages to seditious writing and its subversive aim to promote disaffection with the colonial government. Yet, as I go on to suggest, the protean character of the revolutionary terrorist and the seditionist in colonial India in different con/texts persistently subverts the claims of dominant colonial narratives of revolutionary terror to know, understand, and control the figure of the Indian revolutionary, and at the same time to foreground the violence of the colonial state. In this respect, the representation of the Indian revolutionary in literary and legal narratives of the early twentieth century provides an illuminating lens through which to understand contemporary forms of terrorism and counter-terrorism.

The emergency measures introduced and implemented during the early twentieth century in colonial India were part of a very particular series of legislative discourses that were produced in response to the figures of the Indian seditionist and the revolutionary terrorist, and the threat to British colonial sovereignty that these figures posed. By tracing the state of emergency that India's revolutionary terrorists were deemed to have created in the early twentieth-century British colonial imagination, this chapter proceeds to assess the extent to which Edmund Candler's 1912 novel *Siri Ram Revolutionist* reveals the violent foundations that underpin the liberal rhetoric of the civilizing mission in British India. For the writing of sedition and revolutionary terrorism in colonial India demonstrates the importance of subversive writing in the British colonial state's narrative of counter-insurgency, and its justification for the use of emergency measures. If the Anglo-Indian characters in British literary representations of counter-insurgency often claim to have demystified the psychological and social causes of revolutionary terrorism in colonial Bengal in order to more effectively contain it, the enigmatic revolutionary figure of the Doctor in Sarat Chandra Chatterjee's novel *Pather Dabi* eludes the gaze of the colonial authorities and refuses to be represented as a coherent subaltern insurgent. This fictional revolutionary, as I argue in the conclusion, not only provided a literary inspiration for subsequent revolutionaries, but also demonstrated that so-called seditious writing was a crucial rhetorical and political strategy in the struggle against colonialism.

"... so admirably vague" Sedition Legislation in the Indian Penal Code

In "The Doctrine of Passive Resistance," the Cambridge graduate and radical Bengali nationalist Aurobindo Ghose criticized the sedition legislation in the Indian Penal Code on the grounds that it is "so admirably vague" that there is "nothing to prevent [the Government] from using this [legal] power in any way they like, however iniquitous or tyrannical" (Ghose 1995: 108–9). For Aurobindo, the vague phrasing and unjust application of the sedition law in the case of the proscription of the *Punjabee* newspaper in 1907 exemplified the moral and political bankruptcy of British colonial rule in India in the early twentieth century, and was symptomatic of the thinly veiled oppression and violence that underpinned the liberal political rhetoric of the British colonial government in India. For this reason, the implementation of the sedition law only served to strengthen the formulation of Aurobindo's political doctrine, which was based on the premise that "the circumstances of the country and the nature of the despotism from which it seeks to escape must determine what form of resistance is best justified and most likely to be effective at the time or finally successful" (p. 119).

In Aurobindo's argument, the "means" by which "a subject nation" will use to vindicate its liberty "is best determined by the circumstances of its servitude," and the "present circumstances in India seem to point to passive resistance as our most natural and suitable weapon" (p. 98). Aurobindo did not rule out the use of violent resistance in anti-colonial insurgency, but argued instead that "it is the nature of the pressure which determines the nature of the resistance"; he cited "the denial of liberty" in Russia by "legalised murder and outrage" and "brutal coercion" in Ireland as cases where "the answer of violence to violence is justified and inevitable" (p. 98). Yet in his observation that the "penalty of sedition is at present the chief danger which the adherent or exponent of passive resistance runs under the law" (p. 109), it is clear that the sedition legislation not only delineates the illegality of the doctrine of passive resistance, but also questions the implicit premise of Aurobindo's justification for passive resistance: the liberal character of the British colonial government. Such a view is echoed in a speech that Gandhi delivered during his trial for sedition in 1922, in which he criticized the Rowlatt Act and the massacre at Jallianwala Bagh, and justified the promotion of disaffection toward the government established by law in India on moral grounds. In Gandhi's argument, Section 124A of the Indian Penal Code "is perhaps the prince among the political sections of the Indian Penal Code designed to suppress the liberty of the citizen" (Gandhi 1965: 185).

In 1867, the British Indian government passed a law proscribing the publication of seditious writing, or literature that was deemed to promote disaffection with the British colonial government. In the eyes of the British government, the literature of sedition served to establish a connection between literature and terrorism. The proscription of books, pamphlets, and newspapers in British India on the grounds that they were seditious has a history that can be traced back to the Press and Registration of Books Act in 1867. The "original impetus for the Act of 1867 came from London, where librarians in the British Museum and administrators in the India Office felt a need to keep track of the printed matter churned out by Indian presses" (Darnton 2001: 136). However, in India, the "act belonged to a general attempt to restore order in a world still shaking from the aftershocks of the Sepoy Mutiny and peasant uprisings of 1857–58" (p. 136). In this context, the documentation of Indian books in print was part of a massive process of information gathering:

> Everything was surveyed, mapped, classified, and counted, including human beings, who appeared in the first Indian census in 1872, divided neatly into castes, subcastes, and a dozen other categories determined by the columns of a printed form. The catalogues of books belonged to this effort to catalogue everything. They constituted a census of Indian literature as the imperial authorities understood it. (Darnton 2001: 138)

As the book historian Robert Darnton suggests, the British colonial surveillance of so-called vernacular literatures published in India drew attention to the political dimension of the literary: "Nothing would seem to be further from political control than an obsession with literary style, but literature under the Raj was political in itself, down to its very syntax" (Darnton 2001: 143). Yet while civil servants employed to write entries for the Bengal Library Catalogue of Printed Books in the late nineteenth century noted the political content of the literary, these books were not officially proscribed: "the government permitted the publication of books that seemed openly seditious to the men who registered them" (p. 147). This liberal policy of the late nineteenth century changed with the partition of Bengal in 1905 and the perception that literature was dangerous because it promoted nationalist sentiment and in some cases advocated the use of violent resistance.

The murder of two British women in a Calcutta railway car in 1908 by a bomb intended for Mr. Kingsford, an unpopular magistrate, and the subsequent discovery of a bomb-making factory in the Calcutta suburb of Alipur brought the political dimension of literature to the attention of the colonial authorities. For, in what subsequently became known as the Alipur Bombing Case, the terrorists were disaffected members of the elite Hindu *bhadralok* classes and the literary intelligentsia: "The leading agitators were men of letters, who drew their inspiration from literature, both Indian and Western, and gathered around newspapers and libraries" (Darnton 2001: 152). Indeed, the writings, songs, and newspaper articles of nationalist groups such as the Anushilan Samiti and Ghadr Party were felt to promote disaffection with the British colonial government.

The meaning of sedition defined in Section 124A of the Indian Penal Code of 1867 centered on the political use of language and representation, intended to bring about disaffection with the existing colonial government. For the Act declared that:

> Whoever by words, either spoken or written or by signs, or by visible representation, or otherwise, brings or attempts to bring into hatred or contempt, or excites, or attempts to excite disaffection towards Her Majesty or the Government established by law in British India, shall be punished with transportation for life or any shorter term, to which fine may be added, or with imprisonment which may extend to three years, to which fine may be added or with fine. (Swinhoe 1909: 66)

In this definition, the legal ground of sedition was predicated on a transparent model of communication, in which the intention to bring about "hatred," "contempt," or "disaffection" was self-evident in the "words," "signs," or "visible representation" of the seditious material, be it a printed text, speech, poster, or leaflet. What the government meant by disaffection was not defined until the turn of the century, with the increase of revolutionary activities in Bengal and the perception of a causal relationship between radical literature, newspaper articles, political speeches, and posters, on the one hand, and the increase of violent acts of anti-colonial insurgency, on the other.

One of the most meticulous attempts to explain and clarify the sedition legislation in the Indian Penal Code to both lawyers and laymen was that of Walter Russell Donogh, a barrister-at-law in Calcutta, in his book *The History and Law of Sedition and Cognate Offences in British India* (first published 1911). As well as explaining the history behind the formulation of the law, and distinguishing it from similar English laws, such as the Treason-Felony law and the seditious libel law, Donogh offers an account of particular cases and identifies some of the problems with the phrasing of the sedition law. One such problem is hinted at in Donogh's discussion of Sir James Fitzjames Stephen's introduction to this bill to amend the Indian Penal Code on August 2, 1870. In Donogh's account, Stephen's legal definition of disaffection or seditious intention was premised on a transparent theory of public rhetoric, in which "Every man who was going to speak, every man who was going to write ought to know perfectly well whether he intended to produce disaffection" (Donogh 1917: 8). Yet in the case of the Bangobasi sedition trial of 1891 and the Tilak sedition trial of 1897, both counsels for the defense raised questions about the clarity of the legislation, and an amendment to the phrasing of the Act was proposed in 1898 (p. 8). While the committee appointed to review the case for an amendment acknowledged that section 124A of the Indian Penal Code did not constitute "a model of clear drafting" (p. 61), what was particularly interesting about the discussion which led to the amendment was the distinction made by the Lieutenant-

Governor of Bengal, Sir Alexander Mackenzie, between the conditions of political governance in England and those in colonial India:

> It is clear that a sedition law which is adequate for a people ruled by a government of its own nationality and faith may be inadequate, or in some respects unsuited, for a country under foreign rule and inhabited by many races, with diverse customs and conflicting creeds. It is impossible in India to accept the test of direct incitement to violence, and limit the interference of the Government to such cases. (Cited in Donogh 1917: 65)

Consequently, it was decided that the Indian sedition legislation "prohibits alike the act and the attempt to excite disaffection." The reason for this, as Walter Donogh explains, "may be found in the enormous difficulty of proving that disaffection has actually resulted from the effort to produce it. This is conceivable in the case of an inflammatory speech which is followed immediately by a disturbance, or other more mistakable signs of disaffection, but in the case of seditious matter disseminated through the Press it would be next to impossible to trace a connection" (p. 77).

The revised 1909 edition of the Indian Penal Code included case notes and three explanations that were supposed to clarify the definition and appropriate circumstances in which the sedition law could be implemented. As well as asserting that "the expression 'disaffection' included disloyalty and all feelings of enmity" (Donogh 1917: 66), the section referred to cases in which a precedent had been set for the use of the sedition law. Of these, it was the sentencing of the Maratha agitator Bal Gangadhar Tilak in 1897 to 18 months' rigorous imprisonment by a court in Bombay for an article that he had published in the Marathi paper the *Kesari* on June 15, 1897 that set a precedent for subsequent cases of sedition, which were tried during the period of nationalist agitation that followed the partition of Bengal in 1905.

The *Kesari* had published an article on May 4, 1897, in which the British government's intervention in the plague epidemic in Poona was described as a deliberate attempt to oppress the people, and the Plague Commissioner, Mr. Rand, was described as "tyrannical" (*Sedition Committee Report* 1918: 2–3). While this article does not explicitly call for political resistance to British colonial rule, the authorities certainly perceived it as encouraging people to hate the existing colonial government. But it was in two subsequent articles published on June 15, 1897 that the *Kesari* was deemed by the High Court of Judicature at Bombay to promote resistance to the colonial government. These articles contained an account of the proceedings at the Shivaji coronation festival held on June 12, 1897. Shivaji was a military chief who led the Maharashtra people against the Mughal Empire in the seventeenth century. In the eyes of the colonial state, however, the *Kesari* had used the celebration of Shivaji's life as a pretext for promoting disaffection with the present British colonial government.

In an account of the *Kesari*'s seditious writing, the *Sedition Committee Report* of 1918 describes how this newspaper invoked the French revolutionaries' defense of political violence on the grounds that they were "'only removing thorns from their paths'" and suggested that the "same argument could be applied in Maharashtra"; it went on to describe how Tilak invoked the actions of Shivaji who murdered Afzal Khan for the good of others and strove to drive the foreigners away from the land of his birth (*Sedition Committee Report* 1918: 2–3). In the *Report*'s account of Tilak's speech, it is ancient Hindu stories that provide a mythological framework for resistance to British colonial rule. For just as Krishna in the *Bhagavad Gita* argued that, "No blame attaches to any person if he is doing deeds without being actuated by a desire to reap the fruits of his deeds," so Shivaji's violent actions were justified because they served the interests of the nation (*Sedition Committee Report* 1918: 2–3). In the eyes of the Sedition Committee there was a causal relationship between the publication of these two articles and the subsequent murder of two government officers, Mr. Rand and Lieutenant Ayerst, on June 22, 1897 during the celebration of the sixtieth anniversary of Queen Victoria at Government House, Ganeshkhind, Poona.

Yet the trial of Bal Gangadhar Tilak for sedition in the High Court of Judicature in Bombay from September 8 to 14, 1897 reveals a fault line both in the legal language and in the interpretation of this section of the penal code, which the *Sedition Committee Report* elides. In his concluding remarks on the case, the presiding judge, Mr. Justice Strachey, advised the jury on how best to evaluate the case for sedition against Tilak. After explaining the language of the sedition law, and the meaning of disaffection, Strachey proceeded to advise the members of the jury to read the articles using a series of phrases that recall the language of literary interpretation:

> [I]n judging of the intention of the accused, you must be guided not only by your estimate of the effect of the articles upon the minds of the readers, but also by your common sense, your knowledge of the world,

> and your understanding of the meaning of words. Read the articles, and ask yourselves as men of the world whether they impress you on the whole as a mere poem and an historical discussion without mere purpose, or as attacks on the British Government under the disguise of a poem and historical discussion. It may not be easy to express the difference in words; but the difference in tone and general drift between a writer who is trying to stir up ill will and one who is not is generally unmistakeable, whether the writing is a private letter, or a leading article, or a poem, or the report of a discussion. If the object of a publication is really seditious, it does not matter what form it takes. Disaffection may be excited in a thousand different ways. A poem, an allegory, a drama, a philosophical or historical discussion, may be used for the purpose of exciting disaffection, just as much as a direct attack upon the Government. You have to look through the form and look to the real object: you have to consider whether the form of the poem or discussion is genuine, or whether it has been adopted merely to disguise the real seditious intention of the writer. (Imperatrix versus Tilak 1897: 98)

Here, the judge highlights the connection between legal and literary judgment: the seditious intention of the writer is inferred from the tone or style of the poem or article. In order to assess the intention of the accused, the judge further directed the jury to consider both the implied readership of the *Kesari*, and the context in which the newspaper was written and disseminated: "You have not only to consider the class of persons who subscribe to the *Kesari*, but you have also got to consider the condition and the time, not in the year 1890, or 1891, or 1892, or 1893, or even 1896, but in June 1897 and also the particular state of things at the time when the articles were disseminated among them" (p. 100). In this statement, the judge alludes to the British colonial government's intervention in the plague epidemic at Poona, its segregation of individuals infected with the plague and those who were not infected with the plague, and its use of soldiers to conduct house-to-house visitations (p. 104).

Sedition and Colonial Intelligence Gathering in Edmund Candler's *Siri Ram Revolutionist*

One of the most sustained fictional treatments of the relationship between seditious literature and revolutionary terrorism in colonial India can be found in *Siri Ram Revolutionist: A Transcript from Life 1907–1910*, a novel that was written by the Anglo-Indian writer, college principal, and newspaper journalist Edmund Candler. In his letters to his sister Katherine, Candler describes the book as his "sedition book" (Corkhill 2005: 397–8). *Siri Ram Revolutionist* is certainly concerned with sedition, secret societies, and Bengali revolutionaries. Yet this is not to suggest that *Siri Ram* is a seditious novel, or a novel that actually promotes anti-colonial disaffection and advocates violent action against the colonial state. For, like many other Anglo-Indian fictions of terrorism and sedition, *Siri Ram Revolutionist* is precisely concerned with the threat of sedition and revolutionary acts of violent anti-colonial insurgency from the standpoint of the colonial state. The novel opens with an account of a seditious lecture delivered at a town hall in Punjab by Narasimha Swami, "a dangerous agitator" who "was too clever to be run down" (Candler 2005: 404). The third-person omniscient narrator compares Narasimha's influence in the north of India to that of "Arabindo [*sic*] Ghose in Bengal," and argues that the Swami's influence was "more dangerous as the material he had to work with was hardier and more robust" (p. 404). A similar historical comparison is drawn in the same chapter between Narasimha Swami and Tilak: "The Swami identified with the spiritual side of the revolutionary movement in the same way as Tilak was with the political" (p. 404).

Such comparisons with historical figures serve to locate the novel in early twentieth-century British India during a period of increasingly violent nationalist insurgency; yet they also reveal how Candler's omniscient narrator is situated at the center of colonial intelligence gathering about "sedition-mongers" and nationalist insurgents or terrorists. While the narrator often appears to claim total knowledge about the Swami's terrorist organization and its methods, this claim is undermined by the novel's status as a post-hoc response to the circulation of seditious literature and terrorist attacks in colonial Bengal. Such a response is reconstructed through a forensic approach to the detail of Siri Ram's family background and an anthropological account of the social composition, organization, and activities of secret societies in Punjab. Indeed, it was Candler's fictional construction of the profile of a young, Punjabi extremist that prompted the novelist Joseph Conrad, in a letter addressed to Candler in 1918, to compliment the "lofty impartiality of [Candler's] insight and the sincere sympathy of [his] treatment." What *Siri Ram Revolutionist* gave Conrad was a "distinct sense of enlightenment in the intricate matter of racial psychology" and "a firmer conviction of the difficulty of the problem which politicians at home are so ready to handle on mere party lines" (Conrad 2002: 303).

One of the ways in which Candler traces the psychological motivations of Siri Ram's involvement in anti-colonial insurgency is by offering a detailed account of his social background in an Indian village. At first the narrator seems to offer an ethnographic representation of Siri Ram's family home:

> You went through the gate into the *haveli*, a cramped courtyard strewn with cow fodder, save where a little mud wall divides off a square for cooking. The mud floor here is scrupulously polished; the five brass vessels, as scrupulously clean, are laid beside the chula where the pulse is being cooked for the family, or some sort of herbal concoction for the cow. The ashes of the fire under the pot are invisible for the intense glare. In the shrine-like cupboard of clay let into the wall and protruding like a peaked cowl, the boiled smoked milk is kept all day immune from the sun. From the sacred hearth you creep through a low door into a long, low, mud walled room with a roof of beams and twigs caked with clay pierced sometimes with a smoke hole to let out the smoke or let in a shaft of light. (2005: 441–2)

This ethnographic description of Siri Ram's family home is clearly marked by modifying adjectives such as "cramped" and "shrine-like." These modifiers serve to reinforce Merivale's racist characterization of Indian village life as an underdeveloped "mud world" (p. 441) that resembles "some phase of an excrescence exuded from the earth," and presents its occupants as "ants of the same hue" (p. 442). In so doing, the narrator implies that Siri Ram's motivation for carrying out acts of sedition and terror against the British colonial government is related to his cultural background rather than the British handling of the plague epidemic. Indeed, when Merivale discovers copies of English literary classics such as Alexander Pope's "The Rape of the Lock" and Robert Louis Stevenson's *An Inland Voyage*, he starts to question of what benefit an aesthetic education in English literature would be to Siri Ram, as a "child of this clay" (p. 443). Such questioning serves to construct a profile of Siri Ram as a dull, melancholy, and unimaginative young man of the elite Hindu *bhadralok* class, who is disaffected and suggestible. It also echoes the *Times* journalist Valentine Chirol's observation in *Indian Unrest* that the British colonial education system had contributed to the Indian unrest by "producing dangerous hybrids, more or less superficially imbued with Western ideas, and at the same time more or less completely divorced from the realities of Indian life" (1910: 2). This characterization is extended in the narrator's account of Siri Ram's mission to find

Narasimha Swami in the mountains: for while the narrator describes the beauty of the Indian landscape in great detail, we are told that Siri Ram marches "dully on . . . wrapped solely in his broodings" (Candler 2005: 478).

Siri Ram is not only criticized for lacking powers of observation and imagination, but is also portrayed as inept, moody, and vain. At the Bridge Club, Skene surmises that Siri Ram "has never seen a firearm" and "couldn't hit a tree" (p. 466); such an intuition is later confirmed during a target practice in the mountains when Siri Ram aims a revolver at a marmot, shoots, and misses (p. 491). Siri Ram's vanity is further exemplified by his aspiration to be a "political deportee" and by the narrator's speculation that Siri Ram would have been flattered if he had known that the CID had a copy of his passport (p. 474).

Candler's representation of Siri Ram as a moody and resentful individual – who is a passive subject of political extremism rather than an active subject of historical change – also recalls the stereotype of the effeminate Babu. This stereotype can be traced back to Lord Macaulay's description of the Bengali, who is physically "feeble even to effeminacy" and mentally "weak, even to helplessness" (Chowdhury 1998: 4). However, it was the then Viceroy, Lord Curzon's plans to partition Bengal in 1905 that prompted the rearticulation of this colonial stereotype in elite nationalist discourse during the *swadeshi* movement. As Indira Chowdury observes, Curzon's plans to partition Bengal were perceived as an affront to *bhadralok* masculinity. In response to this affront, nationalist intellectuals such as Swami Vivekananda and Aurobindo Ghose sought to awaken the inert revolutionary energy of the sons of Mother India through a program of self-discipline and spiritual education. As discussed below, Candler's account of Narasimha Swami mirrors the asceticism and nationalist spiritualism of Swami Vivekananda and Aurobindo Ghose. Before looking at that, however, the following section considers how some of the methodological insights of the subaltern studies historians could be usefully deployed to challenge the pro-imperialist thrust of Candler's novel.

Subaltern Pasts and the Limits of Colonial Intelligence

If *Siri Ram Revolutionist* presents a post-hoc response to sedition and planned terrorist activities as an a priori fiction of total omniscience about extremist organizations in British India, Candler underscores this fiction of total omniscience in a letter he wrote to his brother Henry, who was based in England, of January 8, 1913. In this letter Candler emphasizes the timeliness of his novel following an unspecified "bomb outrage" in 1913; and suggests that Constable, the publishers of the first edition of *Siri Ram Revolutionist*, should take advantage of this bomb outrage to market the book further. Such a view of the novel's timeliness, and its sensational subject matter, echoes the sensational headlines of British and Anglo-Indian newspaper reports on bomb outrages in Bengal, a connection that also recalls the relationship between late Victorian popular fiction about terrorism, such as Robert Louis Stevenson's *The Dynamitards* and Joseph Conrad's *The Secret Agent*, and the sensational reports of Fenian conspiracies and Anarchist plots contained in the London dailies, which critics such as Barbara Melchiori and Deaglan Ó Donghaile have examined in detail. Like the British newspaper reports and sensation fiction of the 1880s and 1890s, Candler's letter to his brother clearly suggests that he was concerned to capitalize on the timeliness and shock value of the violent revolutionaries depicted in *Siri Ram Revolutionist*. Yet it was Candler's attention to the detail of Indian revolutionary terrorism and his apparently intimate knowledge of the revolutionaries which many contemporary newspaper reviews praised in *Siri Ram Revolutionist*. The Anglo-Indian newspaper *The Englishman* (Calcutta), for instance, praised Candler's insider knowledge of Indian terrorism in *Siri Ram* by claiming that, "The book shows, what MR CHIROL failed to show [in his study *Indian Unrest*], the steps by which the mind of the student is debauched, the methods which are employed to make use of his simplicity and ignorance, and the subtle and ingenious arguments by which an honest idealist is deflected into the paths of Terrorism and crime" (p. 2). In a similar vein, the *Morning Post* reviewer describes *Siri Ram Revolutionist* as a "psychological study of the Revolutionary Movement in the Punjab" and praises Candler's insight into that movement: the "author, who is obviously engaged in educational work, has watched the growth of the movement in question from a position which brings him into close contact with the young 'intellectuals' of Indian nationalism."

What is crucial, however, is the way that *the novel itself* attempts to efface a crisis at the center of discourses of colonial intelligence and counter-insurgency. For if this crisis is read against the grain of Candler's narrative of colonial intelligence and counter-insurgency, it is possible to trace the articulation of what Dipesh Chakrabarty calls a subaltern past in the seditious writing of Narasimha Swami and the insurgent acts of Siri Ram. What Chakrabarty means by a subaltern past, as I explain below, is not only a history of subaltern insurgency; it is also a history that resists historicization in the rational sense of a historical event that can be attributed to a particular agent.

Since most of the early twentieth-century nationalist extremist organizations in Bengal and Punjab were composed of young, middle-class Hindu men, who had been educated in the British colonial education system, it might seem inaccurate to describe the acts of violent, anti-colonial nationalist insurgency carried out by such organizations as subaltern. Indeed, in his account of the revolutionary politics in early twentieth-century colonial Bengal, Peter Heehs suggests that the subaltern studies historical approach is inadequate to describe the participation of the elite, *bhadralok* classes in the revolutionary nationalist movement because the subaltern studies approach "champions the role of the nameless 'subaltern' classes" (Heehs 2004: ix). Such a view is echoed in Sumit Sarkar's argument that subaltern militancy during the period of the *swadeshi* movement was antagonistic toward the revolutionary activity of the elite *bhadralok* class (Sarkar 1984: 271–320).

But to invoke such arguments against such a reading of *Siri Ram Revolutionist* would be to treat Chakrabarty's theory of subaltern pasts as a positivist theory of history rather than an epistemological challenge to the positivist basis of modern historiography. For Chakrabarty, subaltern pasts "are pasts that resist historicization, just as there may be moments that resist the doing of ethnography" (Chakrabarty 2000: 101). Citing the example of the 1855 rebellion against the British in Bengal and Bihar by the Santal tribal community, Chakrabarty considers why subaltern historians have taken seriously the Santals' claim that it was the Santal god Thakur that made them rebel while at the same time conferring agency onto the subaltern (p. 103). In Chakrabarty's account, the Santals' way of knowing historical events is not merely an object of historical study and explanation for modern historians, but is also the condition of possibility for modern definitions of historicity and subjectivity: "Subaltern pasts thus act as a supplement to the historians' pasts. They are supplementary in a Derridean sense – they enable history, the discipline, to be what it is, and yet at the same time help to show what its limits are" (2000: 112). By reading the activities of Bengali revolutionaries as subaltern pasts, I am not suggesting that the Bengal revolutionaries in *Siri Ram Revolutionist* are subaltern in their class composition, but rather that the subversive activities of the revolutionaries are supplementary to colonial intelligence gathering, and therefore unintelligible within its terms. By invoking Chakrabarty's discussion of the historiographic and epistemological challenge posed by the Santal rebellion, I want to suggest that a similar resistance to historicization is evident in the ways that the insurgent acts of Siri Ram and Narasimha Swami elude the colonial intelligence gathering of the Anglo-Indian authorities in *Siri Ram Revolutionist. Siri Ram's* concern with colonial intelligence gathering is foregrounded in the narrator's account of Skene, an Anglo-Indian school principal, who observes the Swami's lecture at a town hall in the Punjab for evidence of sedition and to "discover if possible where [the Swami's] magnetism lay" (Candler 2005: 404). For Skene, the town hall "was in an atmosphere of intense excitement" (p. 404); and yet there is no positive evidence that the Swami's lecture is seditious: "There had not been a word about politics. The few allusions to Government, the British, and the Christians had been moderate and natural" (p. 405).

Candler's characterization of Siri Ram as a fanatic who is brainwashed by the spiritual nationalism of Narasimha Swami clearly works to mystify the causes of violent anti-colonial insurgency, and to deny political legitimacy to the nationalist movement. However, this characterization ignores the way in which the Swami's ascetic form of spiritualism provides a theological and rhetorical structure for the revolutionary nationalist movement. Such a history of insurgency eludes the gaze of colonial intelligence gathering in *Siri Ram Revolutionist.* At the Bridge Club, Hobbs suggests that the Swami's injunction to young Bengali men to "Go back to the Vedas" is a way of codifying and disseminating seditious messages. For the narrator and the Anglo-Indian characters in the novel, the religious ethos of revolutionary terrorism in early twentieth-century Bengal exemplifies the fanatical and irrational character of Narasimha Swami and the gullibility of Siri Ram. For Narasimha and Siri Ram, however, this religious ethos provides a structure for the political organization and militancy of the revolutionary movement. The political theology that underpins Siri Ram's revolutionary activities as a sedition monger, who willingly goes to prison for editing a seditious newspaper, and subsequently as an assassin of Merivale, a local Anglo-Indian magistrate, is not simply a sign of Siri Ram's fanaticism or irrationality. Rather, this political theology is a sign of a subaltern act of resistance that cannot be interpreted within the rational and secular framework of Candler's British colonial worldview, even though he recognizes its power. For just as Chakrabarty's subaltern past is a supplement to the historians' past, so Siri Ram's political theology is a "supplement" to Candler's post-hoc narrative of counter-terrorism.

Pather Dabi and the Bengali Revolutionaries of Burma

As if by way of riposte to Candler's so-called "sedition novel" *Siri Ram Revolutionist*, Sarat Chandra Chatterjee's novel *Pather Dabi* offers a sympathetic portrayal of a secret organization of Bengali revolutionaries who sought to renew the ethos of revolutionary terrorism in the later 1920s. *Pather Dabi* presents such anti-colonial sentiment through its evocation of the injustice committed against the protagonist Apurba and the misery of the industrial working class, as well as through the heroic rhetoric of the enigmatic character Sabyasachi (also known as the Doctor), who advocates the use of revolutionary violence in anti-colonial struggle. In so doing, *Pather Dabi* codifies the discourse of terrorism in colonial Bengal through the language of anti-colonial disaffection.

For the South Asian historian Tanika Sarkar, "the model of political work celebrated in the *Pather Dabi*" closely resembles the "cult of militant youth power" led by Subhas Chandra Bose in Bengal during the 1920s (Sarkar 1985: 451). Like Bose, the character of Sabyasachi sought to recruit members of the educated, middle-class Bengali youth to mobilize support for a nationalist struggle against the British government. Yet, despite Sabyasachi's call for a social revolution in India that would overthrow the caste system and the old order that it represents (Chatterjee 1993: 314), he ultimately believes that it is the educated, middle-class gentry alone who will deliver political independence to India.

More important, however, is the fact that the majority of the novel is located in Burma. The secret organization Pather Dabi, or "the right of way," is constituted mainly of political exiles from India, including the female characters Sumitra and Bharati, and the enigmatic figure of the Doctor. This is not to suggest that the novel is explicitly aligned with Burmese nationalism. As Tanika Sarkar observes, "*Pather Dabi* expressed no affinities with the powerful anti-imperialist struggle of the Burmese people, but portrayed a debate exclusively among Indians in Burma about alternative forms of nationalist movement" (Sarkar 1985: 453). The location of the novel is significant because it provides a clue to the historical and political context of the novel. Following the so-called terrorist outrages committed in Bengal during the first two decades of the twentieth century, the Indian government's law enforcement officials had claimed that the detention of alleged Bengali terrorists was a success, a claim that served to justify the Rowlatt Report's recommendation of emergency measures in 1918. In response to this, many leaders of the terrorist movement went underground in the 1920s and fled Bengal to other British territories, particularly Burma. In so doing, "Bengali revolutionaries were able to rely on imperial networks of trading and unemployment, while evading police detection" (Ghosh 2006: 271–2). After the release of hundreds of Bengali terrorists from detention in Indian prisons in 1919, many Bengali revolutionary terrorists fled to Burma to avoid being detained. From Burma, these individuals sought to establish new secret societies and to support the violent anti-colonial insurgency movement from outside of Bengal. This moment in the history of anti-colonial insurgency in Bengal is paralleled in *Pather Dabi* by the arrival of Sabyasachi in Rangoon after his imprisonment for three months at Poona and for three years at Singapore (Chatterjee 1993: 67) and by the suggestion that Apurba was involved in the *swadeshi* movement during his youth (pp. 21, 65–6).

The transnational movements and strategies of masquerade adopted by the Doctor in *Pather Dabi* to avoid detention by the police and government officials in Burma certainly resemble those strategies adopted by revolutionaries to smuggle arms from Singapore, Japan, and China. In her reminiscences of the Chittagong Armoury Raid of April 1930, Kalpana Dutt compares Surjiya Sen, the leader of the Chittagong Armoury Raid, to the Doctor in *Pather Dabi* (Dutt 1979: 12). In particular, Dutt describes the rumors that used to circulate about Sen or *Masterda*, as she described him: "All sorts of things used to go around about Masterda. How he slipped through a police cordon, dressed like an old mali (gardener). How he walked through village after village, in broad daylight, talking carelessly to a police officer companion – who did not know who he was talking to. There were scores of stories about Masterda" (p. 10).

Such rumors of Sen's use of masquerade to evade police detection recall the use of masquerade by the revolutionary character Sabyasachi in *Pather Dabi*. In chapter 6, for example, Nimaibabu, a senior police officer of the Bengal government, attempts to apprehend the Doctor at the port in Rangoon. In contrast to the government's claims that the revolutionary terrorists were legible to the gaze of the police, Nimaibabu asserts that "such a dangerous person has the most inconspicuous appearance, just like any common man. Hence it's difficult to recognise or catch him. There is special mention of this in our reports" (Chatterjee 1993: 68). Yet, it is the Doctor's very conspicuous appearance that enables him to pass as a hashish-smoking oil mill worker with a rather unusual taste in clothes. As Apurba observes:

> The man sported long hair in the front, but so closely was it cropped in the back and sides as to make him look practically bald. It was parted in the middle, and a liberal use of lemon oil filled the room with [an] offensive smell. He wore a colourful Japanese shirt, but had no shawl. A printed handkerchief having the imprint of a tiger's face hung out of his breast pocket. Around his waist he had wrapped a fine English mill made *sari* with a black border; a pair of green stockings were tied above his knees with red laces, and on his feet he wore shoes of shining leather, the soles studded with nails to make them durable. In his hand he carried a cane with a bundle of horn. Everything on him was dirty after the long voyage. (p. 73)

This rather comic account of the Doctor's disguise is reinforced by Apurba's outburst of laughter. Apurba assures the police chief that "he's not the man you're looking for" (p. 73). The veracity of this statement is undermined, however, by the fact that the narrator had earlier described Apurba's reverie on the political commitment of this elusive revolutionary figure. As a consequence, readers are also encouraged to recognize the ingenuity of the *bhadralok* revolutionary hero and to laugh at the ineptness of the police.

The superhuman status of the Doctor is further registered by a comparison with the character of Sabyasachi in the *Mahabharata*, a figure who could wield both hands with equal dexterity: "the intelligence reports of the government reveals that in the case of this man, each of his organs is equally dextrous. He never misses a target with gun or pistol. He can swim across the mighty river Padma; nothing can stop him" (pp. 66–7). This description has prompted Tanika Sarkar to comment on Chatterjee's superhuman characterization of the Doctor: "[T]he hero [of *Pather Dabi*], Sabyasachi, is a revolutionary who moves all over South Asia but his plans and activities are never definitely spelt out. The mystery somehow enhances his personality. Capable, literally of everything, he is the first superman in serious Bengali fiction, always a million times larger than life" (Sarkar 1987: 24). It is Sabyasachi's ability to elude the gaze of colonial intelligence that reinforces his superhuman reputation. The Doctor's precise movements and activities are never revealed to the other members of the secret society or to the reader.

By contrast to Anglo-Indian fictions of counter-insurgency, there are no specific acts of revolutionary terror carried out in the narrative of *Pather Dabi*. It is rather in the Doctor's nationalist rhetoric that he attempts to justify the recourse to violence. The Doctor freely admits to Bharati that he is "a dangerous man . . . who goes around killing people with bombs and guns" (p. 225), and declares that violence is necessary for the "true emancipation" of the industrial working class (p. 270). The doctor also vehemently rejects the strategy of non-violence as an effective means to counter the violence of colonial oppression, in his dialogue with Bharati:

> Peace! Peace! Peace! I'm fed up with this constant talk of peace! Do you know who are the people who've been preaching this falsehood for so long? They are the same people who have robbed the peace of others, who've usurped what was rightfully theirs. They are the preachers of the cult of peace! They have dinned this into the ears of the deprived, diseased and oppressed populace so that they now shudder at the very thought of unrest. (p. 271)

In this speech the Doctor's rejection of peace as an effective form of resistance could be read as a rejection of the philosophy of non-violent non-cooperation advocated by Gandhi, on the grounds that it hampers popular desire for political unrest. While the growing political support for Gandhi's non-cooperation movement in the 1920s would seem to contradict the Doctor's argument against peace, the crucial point for the Doctor is that peaceful protest does not go far enough to bring about the desired end to colonial rule. In this respect, Sabyasachi's defense of violent resistance to British colonial rule mirrors Sarat Chandra Chatterjee's own opposition to Gandhi's non-cooperation movement (see Sarkar 1987 and Chakravarti 1985). To support his argument against the reformist agenda of the advocates of peace, the Doctor invokes the revolutionary ideas of Europe, especially the French Revolution and the Russian Revolution: "Look at Europe . . . It has taken place in Russia, not once but several times. The French Revolution of June 1848 is still a landmark in the history of revolutionary movements. That day the streets of Paris were drenched with the blood of peasants and workers!" (271). In this passage, the Doctor suggests that there is a historical precedent for the use of violence in the service of India's freedom, and in so doing appropriates the political tactics of the proletarian revolutions of nineteenth- and early twentieth-century Europe, and applies them to the specific political circumstances of colonial India.

Significantly, the British colonial authorities noted the invocation of revolutionary ideas and events in modern Europe by terrorist organizations in Bengal to support terrorist activities. In the Rowlatt Report of 1918, the nationalist leader Tilak was quoted as saying the following to justify his use of violence: "'the people who took part in the French revolution denied that they had committed murder and asserted that they were only removing thorns from their side'" (*Sedition Committee Report* 1918: 2). Similarly, the violent activities of Russian anarchists such as Kropotkin were cited to justify the cause of political violence against the colonial state. The following paragraph from the Marathi journal the *Kal*, supporting the bomb attack on two English ladies in Muzzafurpur, was also translated and quoted in the Rowlatt Report:

> People are prepared to do anything for the sake of [independence] and they no longer sing the glories of British rule. They have no dread of British power. It is simply a question of sheer brute force. Bomb throwing in India is different from bomb throwing in Russia. Many of the Russians side with their government against these bomb throwers, but it is doubtful such sympathy will be found in India. . . . It is quite unjustifiable to call the bomb throwers in India anarchists. Setting aside the question whether bomb-throwing is justifiable or not, Indians are not trying to promote disorder, but to obtain [freedom]. (*Sedition Committee Report* 1918: 7–8)

It is precisely this attempt to set aside the ethical question of whether violence is justifiable or not that informs the Doctor's rhetoric in the latter part of Chatterjee's novel. For the Doctor "the independence of India is his sole aim in life, its achievements [his] only dream" (p. 274). By his own admission, the Doctor has "no love, no affection, no compassion; good and bad are both meaningless to him" (p. 274). While the Doctor may not share the philosophy of non-violence associated with Gandhi's political thought, his call for violent resistance is clearly articulated to the same political outcome: India's national independence and the end of British colonial rule. Just as Gandhi argued that the sedition law "is perhaps the prince among the political sections of the Indian Penal Code designed to suppress the liberty of the citizen" (Gandhi 1965: 185), so the Doctor argues that "Freedom is the greatest glory of mankind. But according to the laws framed by the British, it is seditious even to wish for it, leave aside striving to achieve it" (Chatterjee 1993: 280).

After the partition of Bengal in 1905 and in response to the increase in terrorist outrages in Bengal and Punjab, British fictions of counter-insurgency both rehearsed and contributed to a public anxiety around the figures of the Indian revolutionary and the Indian seditionist, which ultimately served to justify the introduction of emergency legislation in colonial India, as defined by the Rowlatt Report. Yet as I have suggested in this chapter, the instability of the stereotypical figure of the Indian revolutionary as a dangerous hybrid called into question the ethnocentric assumptions and knowledge upon which colonial intelligence was based. Moreover, the sedition legislation provided nationalist intellectuals and writers with a powerful rhetorical tool to criticize and contest the legitimacy of the British colonial government, and the violence upon which that government was based. During his trial for sedition in 1922, Gandhi asserted that he considered it a privilege to be tried under section 124A of India's penal code because "some of the most loved of India's patriots have been convicted under it" (Gandhi 1965: 187). For Gandhi, the trial provided a political platform for questioning the legitimacy of the British colonial state on moral grounds: "I hold it as a virtue to be disaffected towards a government which in its totality has done more harm to India than any previous system" (pp. 187–8). As an advocate of non-violent non-cooperation as a tactic of resistance to British colonial rule, Gandhi's approach to anti-colonial resistance may seem to differ radically from the revolutionary violence that Sabyasachi preaches in *Pather Dabi*. Yet in so far as he defends disaffection against the British colonial government in India as a virtue, Gandhi, like the Doctor in *Pather Dabi*, suggests that sedition is a crucial rhetorical and political strategy in the struggle against colonialism and the permanent state of emergency underpinning it.

Acknowledgments

I would like to express a debt of gratitude to Rachael Corkill for granting me access to Edmund Candler's papers at the British Library, and to Professor Elleke Boehmer for critical feedback on the essay.

References

Arnold, David. (1986) *Police Power and Colonial Rule: Madras 1859–1947*. Delhi: Oxford University Press.

Barrier, N. Gerald. (1974) *Banned: Controversial Literature and Political Control in British India, 1907–1947*. Columbia: University of Missouri Press.

Candler, Edmund. (2005) "Siri Ram Revolutionist," in *A Raj Collection: On the Face of the Waters, Flora Annie Steel; Siri Ram-Revolutionist, Edmund Candler; Indigo, Christine Weston; The Wild Sweet Witch, Philip Mason*, ed. Saros Cowasjee. Delhi: Oxford University Press.

Candler, Edmund. (1913) "Letter to Henry Candler," January 8, 1913. British Library Deposit 1039, Box 5.

Chakrabarty, Dipesh. (2000) *Provincializing Europe: Postcolonial Thought and Historical Difference*. Princeton: Princeton University Press.

Chakravarti, Aruna. (1985) *Sarat Chandra: Rebel and Humanist*. New Delhi: National Book Trust.

Chatterjee, Sarat Chandra. (1993) *Pather Dabi*, trans. Prasenjit Mukherjee. New Delhi: Rupa & Co.

Chirol, Valentine. (1910) *Indian Unrest*. London: Macmillan & Co.

Chowdhury, Indira. (1998) *The Frail Hero and Virile History: Gender and the Politics of Culture in Colonial Bengal*. Delhi: Oxford University Press.

Conrad, Joseph. (2002) "Letter to Edmund Candler," November 12, 1918, in *The Collected Letters of Joseph Conrad Volume VI*, ed. Laurence Davies, Frederick R. Karl, and Owen Knowles. Cambridge: Cambridge University Press.

Corkhill, Rachel. (2005) "Preface to *Siri Ram Revolutionist: A Transcript from Life*," in *A Raj Collection: On the Face of the Waters, Flora Annie Steel; Siri Ram-Revolutionist, Edmund Candler; Indigo, Christine Weston; The Wild Sweet Witch, Philip Mason*, ed. Saros Cowasjee, pp. 397–400. Delhi: Oxford University Press.

Darnton, Robert. (2001) "Literary Surveillance in the British Raj: The Contradictions of Liberal Imperialism," *Book History* 4: 133–76.

Donogh, Walter Russell. (1917) *The History and Law of Sedition and Cognate Offences in British India*, 3rd ed. Calcutta: Thacker, Spink & Co. First published 1911.

Dutt, Kalpana. (1979) *Chittagong Armoury Raiders' Reminiscences*. New Delhi: People's Publishing House. First published 1945.

Gandhi, Mohandas Karamchand. (1965) *Trial of Gandhiji*. Ahmedabad: V. R. Shah.

Ghose, Aurobindo (Sri Aurobindo). (1995) "The Doctrine of Passive Resistance," in *Sri Aurobindo, Volume One: Bande Mataram: Early Political Writings*. Pondicherry: Sri Aurobindo Ashram.

Ghosh, Durba. (2006) "Terrorism in Bengal: Political Violence in the Interwar Years," in Durba Ghosh and Dane Kennedy (eds.), *Decentring Empire: Britain, India, and the Transcolonial World*, pp. 270–92. London: Sangam.

Heehs, Peter. (2004) *The Bomb in Bengal: The Rise of Revolutionary Terrorism in India 1900–1910*, 2nd edn. Delhi: Oxford University Press.

"Imperatrix versus Bal Gangadhar Tilak and Keshav Mahadev Bal." (1897) India Office Library, L/PJ/6/462/2291.

Mehta, Uday. (1999) *Liberalism and Empire: A Study in Nineteenth-century British Liberal Thought*. Chicago: University of Chicago Press.

Muddiman, A. P. (1921) "British India," *Journal of Comparative Legislation and International Law*, third series, 3(3): 125–35.

Sarkar, Sumit. (1984) "The Conditions and Nature of Subaltern Militancy: Bengal from Swadeshi to Non-Co-operation, *c.* 1905–22," in Ranajit Guha (ed.), *Subaltern Studies III: Writings on South Asian History and Society*, pp. 271–320. New Delhi: Oxford University Press.

Sarkar, Tanika. (1985) "Bengali Middle-Class Nationalism and Literature: A Study of Saratchandra's 'Pather Dabi' and Rabindranath's 'Char Adhyay,'" in D. N. Panigrahi (ed.), *Economy, Society and Politics in Modern India*, pp. 449–62. New Delhi: Vikas.

Sarkar, Tanika. (1987) *Bengal: The Politics of Protest*. New Delhi: Oxford University Press.

Sedition Committee Report 1918. (1918) Calcutta: Superintendent Government Printing India.

Swinhoe, Charles. (1909) *The Indian Penal Code*. Calcutta: Thacker, Spink and Co.

Tegart, Lady F. (1976) *Charles Tegart: Memoir of an Indian Policeman*. British Library, MSS EUR/C235.

"The Samajist." (1912) *The Morning Post*, Thursday December 5.

"Truth About Terrorists." (1913) *The Englishman* (Calcutta), Friday, April 18, p. 2.

Chapter 9

Israel in the US Empire

Bashir Abu-Manneh

Any reader of *Israel Studies*'s recent issue on the "Americanization of Israel" would be likely to conclude that the most important aspect of United States–Israel relations was cultural and religious exchange.[1] US commodification of Israeli consumption is a key focus here, as is the impact of US religious trends on Israeli religious practices. Though politics does feature in the issue, its place is largely restricted to the influence of the United States on the Israeli party political system and to the ideological convergence between Christian fundamentalism and the Likud Party. The informing conception of the issue, then, seems to be the endeavor to pinpoint those aspects of Israel that have been "Americanized" in recent years. Contributors are thus preoccupied with determining how specific US forms and norms have migrated to and been translated into Israeli culture and society.

However valuable such an approach might be in tracing interesting connections between the United States and Israel, it is very poorly equipped to tackle a major dimension of US–Israeli relations: US state support for Israeli colonialism. The questions never raised include the following: What has US support for Israel actually meant for the Israeli state? Which state capacities have been enhanced and which were curtailed as a result of this support (importantly, force or peace)? And what impact has this had on Israeli society and its economy at large? To answer such questions would involve specifying the nature of US involvement in Israel-Palestine, spelling out the kinds of policies and objectives the US state has allowed the Israeli state to pursue. It would, in fact, involve raising the specter of Israel as a colonial and occupying power, and this is something the various contributors to *Israel Studies* seem unwilling to do. Colonialism and occupation are far from mainstream concerns in the Israeli academy. This may sound strange since both practices have defined the history of Israel since 1967 if not before. Yet it is not so strange if one considers that in this respect the Israeli academy merely reflects the attitudes of wider Israeli society: academic evasion mirrors popular denial and indifference.

One group of academics that has managed to break away from this stifling national consensus has been dubbed post-Zionist. Though by no means a unified or politically homogeneous trend, post-Zionism has come to characterize a certain critical engagement with Israeli history and society that has led to a re-examination of Israel's "founding myths" and ideology. Broadly speaking, it has been defined as follows: "In a general sense, post-Zionism is a term applied to a current set of critical positions that problematize Zionist discourse, and the historical narratives and social and cultural representations that it produced."[2] Inherited Zionist versions of Israeli history and society have thus been debunked.

In the field of history, their main contribution has been analyzing the "causes, character, and course of the Arab–Israeli conflict," where Zionist historiography has been challenged and proven fallacious.[3] Based on research conducted in newly opened Israeli archives, this revisionist history has clearly documented how, for example, Palestinians had actually been expelled in 1948, as they have always maintained (and were not asked to leave by Arab invading armies, as Israeli propaganda has it);[4] Arab armies never intended to "liberate" Palestine, and Jordan colluded with the Zionists to divide it; Israel consistently shunned peace and settlement of the "refugee problem" at every opportunity in the early years; and, finally, that Israel has always been the powerful side in the conflict and has been the party responsible for denying Palestinian rights and national restitution.[5] The picture that emerges here entirely reverses the conventional orthodoxy about victims and victimizers: Israel is seen as an ongoing perpetrator of a massive injustice against the Palestinians.[6] Edward Said has summed up the collective contribution of this revisionism in the following terms: "It is certainly true that the great political importance today of the new Israeli historians is that they have confirmed what generations of Palestinians, historians or otherwise, have been saying about what happened to us as a people at the hands of Israel."[7] And this judgment also applies to Israel's new critical sociologists.

In the field of sociology, Jewish-Israeli history and society has for the first time been examined without the blinkers of Jewish particularism and Israeli exceptionalism.[8] A crucial development here has been the analysis of Israel as a colonial-settler state and society, both in foundation and in continuing practice. Dubbed the "colonization model," this literature "depicts Israel as a settler-colonial society driven by the needs of territorial acquisition and pressures of the labor market, and it regards the Israeli–Arab conflict as the most crucial determinant in the shaping of Israeli society."[9] Spearheaded by Baruch Kimmerling and Gershon Shafir, this research has been deeply preoccupied with both charting the specific features of Jewish colonization of Palestine and comparing it to other settler-colonies like America and South Africa.[10] Jewish colonization should thus be understood as "a late instance of European overseas expansion."[11] Its unique features are the following: Jewish conquest of land and labor; pioneering and settlement; historical-biblical rights as justification; and the construction of what Avishai Ehrlich calls a "permanent war society."[12] Shafir, for example, has shown how the failure of capitalist settlement in Palestine gave impetus to the ideology and practice of Labor Zionism, in which national colonization was spearheaded by Jewish labor and supported by Jewish capital under the leadership of colonizing bureaucratic elites. The nation in Zionism thus emerges from this research as primary and determining. National primacy stifles class conflict, silences dissent and internal democracy, and sidelines social solidarity and egalitarianism, while Zionists conquer and dispossess Palestine.[13] Israel is therefore seen as a colonial-nationalist state: colonialism is constitutive to state formation and nation building, and continues to determine the allocation of power, rights, and privileges in Israel to this day.[14]

For the first time in Israeli history, then, colonialism has become a serious topic of academic research and examination. The Israeli economy, history, politics, and society can now be analyzed and studied using the colonization paradigm. What is important to note here, however, is that the academy was not the trailblazer on this front. Such analysis existed outside of the academy since at least the early 1960s in Israel.[15] As Uri Ram has noted: "The agenda of the *Matzpen* (The Israeli Socialist Organization) group exemplifies the emergence of an explicit colonization perspective in Israeli society."[16] Founded in 1962, Matzpen ("Compass," in Hebrew) was an anti-Stalinist, anti-Zionist splinter from the Israeli Communist Party, which was particularly close to radical Palestinian activists and communists inside Israel.[17]

Collectively, it launched the "Israel as colonial-settler state" analysis, and continued to develop it in its magazine *Khamsin: Journal of Revolutionary Socialists of the Middle East*, published from London, where many of its members ended up as a result of state persecution and repression.[18] A specimen of their most important contributions can be gleaned in "The Class Nature of Israeli Society," an essay they published in *New Left Review* in 1971. Here exactly the same emphases of the critical sociologists of the 1980s are clearly evident: labor colonization, class collaborationism in Zionism, and bureaucratic control:

> Israeli society is not merely a society of immigrants; it is one of settlers. This society, including its working class, was shaped through a process of colonization . . . The permanent conflict between settlers' society and the indigenous, displaced Palestinian Arabs has never stopped and it has shaped the very structure of Israeli sociology, politics, and economics.
>
> In Israel the dominant ideology was never a capitalist one; it was a blend of bourgeois elements combined with dominant themes and ideas typical of the Zionist Labor movement, ideas derived from the socialist movement in Eastern Europe but transformed to express the aims of political Zionism.[19]

There is clearly much common ground between 1980s sociologists and 1960s Matzpen, and this is an important recognition of Matzpen's critical rigor. There is also, however, one crucial divergence between them: their analysis of Western influence in the region after the establishment of Israel in 1948. For Matzpen, it takes the form of imperialism and is constitutive to the making of Israel and to shaping its role in the region. Israel's policy toward Arabs and Palestinians cannot be understood in its entirety without considering the role and interests of Western powers, Matzpen contends:

> it is clear that Israel's foreign and military policies cannot be deduced from the dynamics of the internal social conflicts alone. The entire Israeli economy is founded on the special political and military role which Zionism, and the settlers' society, fulfill in the Middle East as a whole. If Israel is viewed in isolation from the rest of the Middle East there is no explanation for the fact that 70 percent of the capital inflow is not intended for economic gain and is not subject to considerations of profitability.[20]

Imperialist subsidy, then, but for a reason: Israel's role as watchdog of US interests in the region after 1967: "*Israel is a unique case in the*

Middle East; it is financed by imperialism without being economically exploited by it. This has always been the case in the past: imperialism used Israel for its political purposes and paid for this by economic support."[21] There is no reason at all to conclude from this analysis that everything Israel does is caused by external pressure or foreign interest in order to be able to appreciate the significant connection that Matzpen makes between imperialism and Israeli settler-colonialism. This is in fact what is novel about their argument: it combines those specific exogenous and endogenous factors in the analysis of Israeli state objectives and social dynamics. Israel is thus seen as a Zionist-colonial project that is constitutively aligned with Western interests in the region: the state structure and colonizing project are sustained and consolidated by Western powers while Western objectives are fulfilled and realized. Such a consistent geopolitical configuration has provided Israel with both opportunities (to avoid reversing colonial expansion) and constraints (being ready and willing to protect vital Western interests in the region): the wars of 1956 and 1967 constitute important markers in this pattern (as I argue below).

In the shift from the 1960s to the 1980s, however, the "Western imperialism" part of the "colonization model" is dropped and forgotten. As "Israel as colonial-settler state" develops in the academy, Israel's subsidy and support by US imperialism loses its constitutive value in the analysis of the Israeli polity. In fact, a positive assessment of the US role in the region is introduced in its place.

For post-Zionists, the United States can do no wrong; it is in fact a model to emulate and a country that Israel should aspire to be. While being critical of Israel's foundation and continuing practice, post-Zionists have been exceptionally uncritical of the United States. Tom Segev's *Elvis in Jerusalem: Post-Zionism and the Americanization of Israel* is an excellent example in this regard. Segev, an independent historian who played a central role in shattering Israel's "founding myth" and documenting its abuse of the Holocaust,[22] has been completely blind to the question that US–Israel relations may have had serious negative effects on Israel or have led to the consolidation of state-sponsored colonialism in the Occupied Territories. There is a strong correlation in his work between Americanization, erosion of old forms of Zionist collectivist values, and the freeing up of the individual from constricting structures. Israel, he argues, is becoming more like the United States in political, social, and cultural norms. Israel's media has been Americanized, as has its protest movements (which he compares to American protest movements of the 1960s, no less), its multiculturalist pluralism, its new judicial civil rights activism, and its political culture. One particularly crucial connection between the United States and Israel that post-Zionists like Segev keep on repeating seems central to their world-view: the United States is good for Israel because it pushes Israel to compromise, accommodate to the region, and make peace. Segev puts it thus:

> This American [peace] spirit, which produced the Camp David agreements between Israel and Egypt, would later lead people to feel they had had enough of the occupation of the West Bank and Gaza Strip [which miraculously continues]. It also produced Israel's unilateral withdrawal from Lebanon in 2000 [not Hezbollah resistance]. The peace agreements with Egypt and Jordan and the agreements between Israel and the Palestinians were all signed under the sponsorship of the United States and due to intense personal involvement of the sitting president [not as a result of the October/Yom Kippur War of 1973, i.e., Arab readiness to use force]. All these agreements were made possible, to a large extent, because of the willingness of the American people to finance them. They also reflect Israel's dependence on the US, and the depth of American penetration of all areas of Israeli life.[23]

The portrait Segev draws here is idealist in the extreme: after the 1960s the United States developed a peace culture, which it has been busy spreading in the Middle East ever since: no strategic interests, no geopolitical considerations or wars are relevant. In Segev's world, such material factors seem to have no role to play in the US presence in the Middle East.

For post-Zionists, then, the association between the United States and peace is strong and pervasive. Peace with Egypt comes to emblematize US intervention in the region, and breeds a certain "political illusion" in Israel (as well as for the Palestinians, as I argue below) that the United States is as interested in settling the Arab–Israeli conflict as it was in exchanging the return of Sinai to Egypt for Egyptian peace with Israel. What is never appreciated here is that Camp David (forcing Israel to reverse its occupation of Sinai, i.e., to decolonize Sinai) is an exception not the rule, and has come about mainly because of Egypt's use of massive force in the 1973 war. The post-Zionists thus neglect the unique features of the Egyptian–Israeli peace settlement. They also, significantly, fail to recognize how unjust and totally rejectionist of Palestinian rights it was. Writing immediately after Camp David, Fayez Sayegh put it exceptionally well: "The Camp David Framework thus bestows *American–Egyptian* 'legitimacy' upon the continued Israeli occupation of the Palestinian areas in question for years to come." It allows Israel to maintain and expand settlements in the Occupied Territories, and it leaves the Palestinians with no right of self-determination or sovereignty: "A fraction of the Palestinian people (under one-third of the whole) may attain a fraction of its rights (not including its inalienable right to self-determination and statehood) in a fraction of its homeland (less than one-fifth of the area of the whole)."[24] No peace here, only more suffering, dispersal, and occupation.

With the signing of the Oslo Accords between Israel and the Palestine Liberation Organization (PLO) in 1993, the same correlation between the United States and peace emerges again among post-Zionists, even though the actors, powers, and circumstances are totally different here. Gershon Shafir and Yoav Peled see Oslo as a time of lasting American peace and decolonization. This structures their reading of the 1990s in Israel: economic liberalization, they argue, is inseparable from political liberalization and the ending of the occupation (a word never even mentioned in the Oslo Accords). Uncritically endorsing Bush Senior's vision of the New World Order as a time of peace and prosperity for all, Shafir and Peled contend that, "Both globalization and decolonization may, then, be viewed as sharing the goal of replacing political mechanisms and forces, identified with the nation and the nation-state, with financial and commercial ties which, on their part, are global forces."[25]

The frontier, exclusionary society that Zionism has built is thus on the decline, being slowly replaced by a liberalized nation, both economically and politically. And the Israeli business community plays a leading role in this new "neoliberal peace-and-privatization bloc": "The liberal economic values of the Israeli business community are naturally more consonant with a liberal conception of citizenship than with the ethno-republican conception of pioneering civic virtue. Thus, these business leaders have been promoting liberal reforms not only in the economy, but also in civil rights, the electoral system, health care, education, mass communications, and other areas of social life."[26] And this puts Israeli business in the position of contributing to "emancipating the non-citizen Palestinians residents of the Occupied Territories."[27]

The symbol of this triple process of economic privatization, political liberalization, and peace has been captured by Uri Ram: "A pamphlet of the Peace Now movement from the Oslo Accord period exposes explicitly the link between peace and prosperity. 'From the seed of peace your economic growth will flourish,' declares the pamphlet. The pamphlet is decorated with a figure of a flower cut from an American dollar bill. The flower symbolizes locality and life, the dollar globalization and wealth."[28] The "dollar flower" accurately captures the post-Zionist position, and it comes to obscure the fact that Oslo was neither about decolonization nor about the ending of conflict, Palestinian sovereignty, or halting the settlement drive.

Meron Benvenisti, an ex-Deputy Mayor of Jerusalem and contributor to *Haaretz*, recognized this from the beginning. Rather than reading Oslo from a post-national, globalization perspective, he stated unequivocally on reviewing the accords that: "one can hardly not recognize that Israeli victory was absolute and Palestinians *defeat* abject."[29] No dilution of Israeli nationalism here: a total victory versus a total capitulation. One nationalism is up, the other down.

The only political sociologist to contest this post-Zionist association between the United States and peace, economic stability, and political liberalization is Avishai Ehrlich. Ehrlich has updated and developed the Matzpen connection between US imperialism and Israeli colonialism and has argued that post-Zionism is "a local version of US ideological globalization."[30] He strongly contradicts all the basic premises of this approach: end of conflict, peace of the business class, more democracy and secularism and less Judeocentrism, and the diminishing role of the nation-state. Ehrlich reads a crude reductionism and economism in the post-Zionist account of the 1990s. There is no peace, stability, or liberality under US hegemony, he contends. The conflict will indeed intensify, and this is what everybody comes to recognize by the time of the outbreak of the al-Aqsa Intifada, which marks the end of post-Zionism.[31]

If Segev blames this on "Palestinian terror,"[32] Shafir and Peled are here much more cautious and recognize that it is Israeli colonialism which is to blame: "A clear indication that the colonial drive has not spent itself yet is the doubling of the Israeli settler population in the O[ccupied] T[erritories] since 1993. This was one of the main reasons for the resumption, in September 2000, of the intifada that the Oslo Accords were meant to end."[33]

Ehrlich's important reading thus holds: under US-sponsored peace Zionism-as-colonialism continues and becomes entrenched, ending both the reigns of Labor and Revisionist Zionisms and transforming Zionism into a political religion:

> Both [versions] have been replaced by religion as the source of political legitimation for the state of Israel and for its continued control and colonization of the whole of Palestine . . . political religion is the use of religion to explain the cohesion and uniqueness of the ethos, its history and ethos; it is the use of religion as an argument for the claim to territory and justification of political measures to defend the national project.[34]

The hopes of the post-Zionists for a more liberal, less colonialist Israel are thus dashed. They turn out to be based on an illusory analysis of both the US role in the region and its real impact on Israel. It is clear, then, that the categories of US peace and decolonization have to be conceptually separated and the association between globalization and political liberalization broken. US hegemony and market fundamentalism are in fact much more likely to breed religious fundamentalism than liberal values.

My aim in the following is to show why this set of developments is neither unexpected nor surprising. Since 1967, US imperialism and Israeli colonialism have, I argue, worked in tandem in order to produce both Israeli and US nationalist outcomes. This is the only reasonable conclusion one can draw from a closer look at US history in the region, which I consider below. By analyzing the roots and causes of US support for Israel, its dynamic, limitations, and major consequences, I aim to show how Washington's interests in the Middle East have become consistent with supporting the Jewish state and defending its colonialist objectives. My argument proceeds as follows: I first determine what those US vital interests in the region have historically been, and how they have evolved over time. I then go on to utilize this structure of ongoing US imperial interests in order to explain the substance of US strategy during and after the Cold War, including our contemporary moment, and show how crucial Israel has been in the realization of the US empire in the Arab world. Before concluding with a brief description of the contemporary ramifications of US empire in Israel-Palestine specifically, I trace the major impact that Israeli dependency on Washington's support has had on Israeli ideology and society.

This, I hope, will clearly show why I believe it is imperative to extend the critical analytic engagement accorded to Israel by the academic practitioners of the "colonization model" to US–Israel relations. Post-Zionism has successfully managed to integrate the Arab–Israeli conflict as a constitutive factor in the analysis of Israeli state and society, and this has been its greatest achievement. It is time to extend this theoretical framework to include relations between "actually existing US imperialism" and "actually existing Israeli colonialism" in the period after 1967. US imperialism should, then, come to be seen as an intrinsic factor in the shaping and development of both the Arab–Israeli conflict and the structure of the Israeli polity. Relevant here is a rich and growing tradition of analysis and radical critique exemplified in Israel by Matzpen and in the West by Said, Rodinson, and Chomsky.[35] Utilizing this "imperialism–colonialism" paradigm will not only make a more accurate approximation of US–Israel relations and of US interests in the Arab world. It will also actively contribute to opening up a public space for critical reflection and debate on the United States in Israel, a country that seems to be the last bastion of uncritical idealism about and identification with US global power. As Segev puts it: "The full story of the Americanization of Israel has yet to be told, even though it is central to the country's history."[36] I hope the following aids this process.

US Imperialism and Israeli Settler Colonialism

The initial point of analysis of US involvement in the region has to be oil. Nobody has made this point better and for longer than Noam Chomsky: "It has been a basic principle of international affairs since World War II that the energy reserves of the Middle East constitute an essential element in the US-dominated global system. American policy towards affairs of the region cannot be understood apart from this fundamental principle."[37] And, more recently: "In 1945, State Department officials described Saudi Arabian energy resources as 'a stupendous source of strategic power, and one of the greatest material prizes in world history'; the Gulf region generally was considered 'probably the richest economic prize in the field of foreign investment.' Eisenhower later described it as the 'most strategically important area of the world.' "[38] Gilbert Achcar has been equally forceful in making this claim, and in arguing for the decisive role that the Open Door policy over oil plays in US imperial grand strategy:

> George W. Bush's administration, like his father's administration that waged the first US war against Iraq, is as tightly linked to the oil industry as any administration in history. At the risk of annoying those who react to any explanation of US foreign policy in terms of economic

> interests, and oil interests in particular, with cries of "reductionism," the oil lobby has traditionally played a key role in formulating US foreign policy, at the very least since the Second World War.[39]

The Cold War and post-Cold War confrontation with enemies (the Soviet Union, Arab independence and fundamentalist movements, Iraq after 1991, and Bin Laden), and US relations with allies (Europe, Japan, and Israel), cannot be understood outside of this fact: control of oil is a decisive instrument of global policy.

"Regional stability" thus means a Middle East amenable to US primacy. During the Cold War, Arab regimes had to be kept away from the Soviet Union (to prevent it from gaining a strategic presence in the region) and their independent political and economic initiatives had to be stifled, if not destroyed. "Moderate" Arabs are subordinate Arabs; "extremists" are independent ones who go against US interests. Nasser became an extremist in the eyes of Washington: after 1956 he became an international symbol of Third World independence and Pan-Arabism. His Arab national project had therefore to be rolled back because it threatened US dominance in the region. Mired in Vietnam, the United States was not able to do this itself: Israel was brought in from the cold to perform this function. After having been forced by Eisenhower to return Gaza and Sinai in 1956, Israel was given the green light to attack; but this time to serve US, not British and French, interests. As former US ambassador to Israel Samuel W. Lewis has argued, the US relationship with Israel changed from being "quite cool and distant," as a result of "an acute sensitivity to America's strategic interests, clearly identified with Saudi Arabia and its oil reserves," to a strategic alliance in the period after 1967.[40] Cheryl A. Rubenberg has also emphasized this change in policy, and has described it in the following terms:

> The most important outcome of the June War was that for the majority in the policymaking elite, Israel's spectacular military performance validated the thesis that Israel could function as a strategic-asset to the United States in the Middle East. . . . The belief about Israel's strategic utility was expressed in US policy through the provision of virtually unlimited quantities of economic assistance and military equipment, a de facto alliance between Washington and Israel, and in American support for virtually every Israeli foreign policy objective.[41]

Israel thus became a tool of regional stability for the United States: "In the context of the Nixon Doctrine, Israel assumed the role of preserving a regional balance of power favorable to American interests. This meant, above all, curbing Arab radicalism and checking Soviet expansionism in the Middle East. Israel's local interest in keeping the Arabs in their place neatly converged with the Nixon administration's interest in expelling the Soviets from the Middle East."[42]

Nasser and Egyptian Pan-Arab nationalism were not the only victims of the US–Israel convergence of interests. The period when this alliance was cemented was also the period of the rise of Palestinian nationalism. The battle of al-Karamah in which both Palestinian and Jordanian troops defeated an Israeli offensive in 1968 propelled the Palestinians onto the historical stage. Palestinians became the inheritors of radical nationalism: al-Karamah ("dignity," in Arabic) turned the PLO into a mass organization. Calling for the liberation of Palestine from Zionist colonialism (backed by US imperialism), the PLO, like Nasser, had to be crushed as well. This came to be called "Black September." Here again the US–Israel alliance proved essential. Nixon and Kissinger interpreted the Jordanian civil war with the Palestinian guerrillas as a global superpower confrontation, not just a local or regional conflict, and put the US fleet in the Mediterranean on high alert.[43] Israel backed the Jordanian monarchy against the PLO and mobilized its army to protect it from a Syrian tank invasion (which failed as a result). The Iraqi contingent in eastern Jordan failed to come to the assistance of the Palestinians. Nasser was equally constrained: having accepted the Rogers Plan, which called for the return of the territories occupied by Israel in 1967, he was ready to sacrifice his anti-imperialist stance for the return of Egyptian lands. The Saudis also stood with King Hussein. The Russians, in actual fact, had no desire to destabilize the state system in the region. Even Arafat himself preferred a policy of non-interference with the Arab regimes and wanted to focus on liberating Palestine instead. Unlike the more radical Popular and Democratic Fronts, Fatah has always believed that Palestine will deliver Arab unity, not Arab unity Palestine: i.e., Palestinians should not actively seek to become social revolutionaries in the Arab world.

Fatah's position became difficult to sustain when the Popular Front for the Liberation of Palestine was hijacking planes and exploding them in Jordanian airports: Jordanian sovereignty was clearly challenged. Palestinians had, therefore, to pay the price of their radicalism: all forces converged against them. At its moment of inception, then, the Palestinian revolution was defeated by its Arab enemies and their imperialist allies. Achcar describes it in the following terms:

> The year 1970 in any case saw Arab nationalism finished off politically, so that the 1967 attack attained its political objectives with a three-year lag. This required crushing the other most advanced, most spectacular spearhead of the radicalization of the popular movement, which had temporarily counter-balanced the military victory of the US–Israel alliance. In September 1970 ("Black September") the Jordanian army drowned in blood the alternative, quasi-state power that the bloc of Palestinian armed organizations had built. . . . Thus 1970 was the year of the final rout of radical Arab nationalism.[44]

The year 1970 sounded the death knell of revolutionary transformation in the Middle East. Jean Genet, who was then with the guerrillas in Jordan, clearly understood what he was witnessing: "I'd already been told the Palestinian Revolution might be summed up in the apocryphal phrase, 'to have been dangerous for a thousandth of a second.' "[45]

The events of 1970 in Jordan should be regarded as the most illuminating in the history of the post-1967 period. The interests of global and local actors became clearly visible, and the alliance between US imperialism, Israel, and Arab reaction against revolutionary nationalism in the region was dramatically played out here. The Arab elites, it transpires, feared Arab radicalism much more than they feared the existence of Israel: the seeming contradiction between US oil interests and supporting Israel turned out to be *no contradiction at all*. Both were objectively (if not subjectively) allied and worked toward the same outcome: anti-Arab independence and democracy, and pro-Arab authoritarianism and dependence on the United States. The Arab elite understood this fundamental lesson well. The Egyptian *infitah* policy (economic and political openness) and shift toward the West was a clear indication of that. It took the 1973 war to convince the United States of Sadat's clear objectives: peace in return for Egyptian territory, while abandoning Palestinian and Arab rights and becoming a US client regime.[46] As Samir Amin concluded, after surveying these developments in his *The Arab Nation*: "the Arab bourgeoisie got what it was after: Washington was forced to take it seriously."[47]

Sadat's success in retrieving Egyptian territory by aligning with the United States in the region bred what can be described as a "political illusion" within the Palestinian camp, which would ultimately lead to Oslo. The belief was the following: national rights could only be retrieved by becoming politically "moderate" and gaining American acceptance. If Sadat could do it, why couldn't Arafat? This logic came to justify future Palestinian capitulation, which was only fully realized in Oslo (it needed the second crushing of the PLO in Beirut in 1982, the Intifada, and the alienation and weakness of the PLO after the Gulf War to create the material conditions for its actualization). But this dangerous assumption neglected the fact that there was an important difference between Egypt and the Palestinians: strategic significance. Egypt was arguably the most important state in the Arab world (in terms of size, position, and capacity) while Palestinians were the weakest and most powerless group in the region: dispossessed, stateless, and fragmented. Arafat had very little to offer the United States (other than recognizing Israel), while Sadat could offer them peace with Israel and legitimation of the status quo. The only way that Palestinians could be strategically significant was by actively threatening US–Israel domination. And that required getting organized and mobilized and gaining Arab mass support. In practice, this meant the following: lacking the objective capacity to achieve their national rights themselves the Palestinians needed the support and capacities of the Arab masses. To achieve their liberation, Palestinians had to mobilize Arabs behind their struggle and assume the position of progressives and radical nationalists in the Arab world. In short, they needed to become what they actually claimed they were: revolutionaries. As Amin put it: "the liberation struggle can only succeed if it is also a social revolution."[48]

If anything, 1970 showed how difficult it would be for the Palestinians to get their national rights with effectively the whole world against them. How to overcome this impediment was a brief topic of debate within the PLO. Its outcome, however, never led to the desired structural-organizational changes that would empower a mass movement: bureaucracy and opportunism won out. There was to be no "revolution within the revolution" as Palestinian radicals (like Husam al-Khatib) wanted.[49] In his powerful critique of Palestinian nationalism, Marxist philosopher Sadiq Jalal al-Azm blamed the PLO's defeat in 1970 on its lack of ideological preparedness for the role Palestinians were in a position to assume in the Arab world: that of social revolutionaries. For al-Azm, the PLO ironically ended up replicating exactly the same mistakes of its Arab petit-bourgeois counterparts (like Nasser). Palestinians repeated rather than transformed Arab nationalist defeats: 1970 was like 1967.[50] And, like their Arab counterparts, the Palestinian elite ultimately ends up dependent on the United States for security, support, and patronage.

What this tells us about the Israeli role in the region is, therefore, quite clear. Israeli interventions have ended up pushing the whole geopolitical alignment of the Arab elite into the American sphere. And that has been an enormous and sustained effort. Control of oil in and of itself cannot achieve that: the United States needed an activist warring state to help it perform this task. For this service, Israel has been substantially rewarded. Since 1967, the United States has been Israel's single most important strategic ally. The United States supports Israel diplomatically, politically, and economically, allowing it to continue to expand and colonize the West Bank and Gaza Strip, and to go unpunished for its countless violations of international law, including its invasion of Lebanon in 1982 (which cost 20,000 mostly civilian lives), its occupation until 2000 of a long stretch of Lebanese land (which it called its "security zone"), and its occupation and annexation of East Jerusalem and the Syrian Golan Heights. Without US support, none of this would have been possible. Israel's expansion would have been rolled back, as it had been in 1956.

Operating within the parameters and imperatives of US empire frees Israel from conforming to the international consensus which all the world shares, bar the United States (with the momentary exception of the Rogers Plan of 1970, which was sabotaged by Nixon–Kissinger): a two-state solution based on full withdrawal to the 1967 borders, the dismantling of settlements, and the creation of a Palestinian state. To complete its mission of colonizing Palestine, Zionists had therefore to fulfill Theodor Herzl's racist prophecy in *The Jewish State*: "form a portion of a rampart of Europe against Asia, an outpost of civilization as opposed to barbarism."[51] To expand, Israel has had to subordinate itself to US imperial imperatives and become dependent on the United States (which at times generates the occasional Israeli public resentment at the extent of US control). Samuel W. Lewis has described this process well:

> The 1950s and early 1960s fostered an illusion that Israel could be truly independent economically and politically, even surrounded by a sea of hostile Arab states. The 1973 War badly eroded that confidence. Since then, Israelis have come to understand that adequate modern weapons are too expensive for a small state to obtain without close allies and economic support from abroad. Their level of frustration has grown as has their realization of their inevitable dependency on Washington. That frustration periodically produces the tendency to lash out against the very American leaders whose continued support is most needed.[52]

Such moments aside (the most recent being Sharon's accusation that in the immediate aftermath of 9/11, Israel was being abandoned by the United States in the same way Czechoslovakia was abandoned by the Allies in 1938), Israel has indeed understood that there is no occupation, no expansion, and no rejection of Palestinian national rights without US support. As long as this agenda continues to be the dominant one in Israel, its reliance on the United States will continue. Chomsky describes the bind thus:

> There can be little doubt that from shortly after the 1967 conquest, Israel has been moving in the directions indicated earlier: international isolation apart from pariah states, dependence on the US with the concomitant pressure to serve US interests, militarization of society, the rise of religious-chauvinist fanaticism, the internal "feed-back" from the policies of oppression and domination, an increasing sense of the inevitability of permanent conflict and with it, the perceived need to disrupt the region and establish a form of Israeli hegemony under the US aegis.[53]

The United States has thus *allowed, encouraged,* and *aided* the continued Israeli colonization of Palestine. The expansion of 1967 is indeed a continuation of the 1948 logic of occupation and dispossession, which has defined the Zionist movement in Palestine from the beginning. What was novel about 1967 was that it went against the international consensus: Israel was seen as occupier where before it had been seen as victim. To legitimate this state of affairs, expansionism became the dominant doctrine of the Israeli elite. Colonialism was strengthened and consolidated in Israeli politics and society, breeding new political ideologies and practices of occupation and settlement. Nur Masalha has described this process well in his *Imperial Israel and the Palestinians: The Politics of Expansion*:

> The war produced a spectacular territorial expansion. This territorial expansion made messianic religious and ultra-orthodox thinking seem highly credible. The 1967 conquests also made the historical Revisionist maximalist vision highly relevant. All the ingredients of Israel's new right radicalism – militarism, ultra-nationalism, territorial expansionism, and neo-religiosity – produced political movements, including the new territorial maximalism of the Whole Land of Israel Movement and the fundamentalist settlements movement of Gush Emunim.[54]

Occupation, therefore, further fortified Israeli rejection of the Palestinian right of self-determination. Partition (albeit inequitable, leaving Palestinians 22 percent of their homeland) was actively rejected, bolstered by US rejectionism.

It is also important to emphasize that 1967 both reinforced and transformed existing Israeli "national security" patterns of militarization. Baruch Kimmerling has shown that Israeli "civilian militarism" has always been dominant in Israel: "The situation arises when the civilian leaders and the led both regard the primary military and strategic considerations as being self-evidently the only or the predominant considerations in most societal and political decisions or priority ordering." The military-political nexus rules over the Palestinians and defines the national objectives (including economic) of the Israeli collectivity.

After 1967, this prioritizing of national security was modified by the "amplification of the ideological-political sphere" of religious Zionism.[55] The Greater Israel ideology became wedded to strategic state considerations, and the former was fostered and supported by the latter:

> thus the new orientation spawned fringe variants that favored the expulsion of the entire non-Jewish population of the territories either immediately or as a result of a deliberate program that would create circumstances favorable to such dispersion (for example, war on a local-regional scale). Jewish settlements were established feverishly in regions of the occupied territories densely populated by Palestinians so as to guarantee control over the whole conquered area, and create "irreversible" *fait accompli.*[56]

Kimmerling has developed this line of analysis further in his recent *Politicide: Ariel Sharon's War Against the Palestinians.* Here he argues that occupation has already corrupted Israeli democracy to such an extent that Israel can no longer be considered a liberal democracy: it is now a *Herrenvolk* democracy: "This term, coined to describe South Africa under Apartheid [OED dates it back to the Nazis], describes a regime in which one group of its subjects (the citizens) enjoys full rights and another group (the non-citizens) enjoys none. The laws of Israel have become the laws of a master people and the morality that of lords of the land."[57]

While this reasoning is important to understanding Israeli policies in the Occupied Territories, it ignores the fact that Israel itself has always been defined by its particularist components. Post-1967 is a mere continuation of post-1948, but now in a new environment where decolonization is a powerful global ideological force (hence the UN response). The questions that Kimmerling never raises are: When was Israeli democracy ever *uncorrupted* by colonialism? When did Israel treat even its own citizens as equals? The military government of 1948–66, which only applied to Palestinian citizens of Israel, is clear evidence that Israel has never actually been a liberal democracy: its continuing exclusionary definition as "Jewish and democratic" is further evidence of that.[58] In the post-1967 period, then, Zionist exclusivism and racism have merely been extended, revitalized, and projected onto the West Bank and Gaza. For the Israeli elite, 1967 is like 1948: the similarities are more important than the differences.[59]

The dynamic of American empire/Israeli colonialism is, therefore, circular: US support reinforces Israeli colonialism and occupation, which bolsters Israeli militarization of state and society, which generates new ideological and political justifications and breeds new religious fanaticisms, leading to further indigenous resistance and to more US interventions in the region – a cycle of violence if ever there was one, ultimately determined by US imperialism. The United States thus becomes both a necessary and sufficient condition for Israel's colonial expansionism. Without it, Israel would be a pariah state. Without it, conditions of peaceful coexistence in the region are much more likely. Without it, Israeli militarism and Jewish fundamentalism in Israel would be on the defensive; and the mobilization of internal domestic forces calling for the abandonment of the "national security" ethic and the rejection of living by the sword would have a real chance of gaining political ascendancy in Israel. Siding with, serving, depending, and even subordinating itself to the imperatives of US empire in the region can only reinforce the Arab majority perception that Israel is a hostile presence. Militarized security can be no basis for peace and reconciliation. Real security can only be achieved if Israelis come to be seen as a part of the region and not as an imposition on it: in order for that coexistence to take place, the whole logic of the Jewish colonization needs to be questioned.

Which is exactly what didn't happen in Oslo. On the contrary, Oslo was about further colonization, further expansion, and further domination and control. The early critics of Oslo (most prominently, Edward Said,[60] Noam Chomsky, and Meron Benvenisti) were proven right: Oslo was a victory for Zionism and a humiliating defeat for Palestinian nationalism. The PLO aborted the Intifada (the main reason for Israel's willingness to negotiate), legalized the occupation, and became Israel's colonial enforcer. As Samih K. Farsoun has argued: "Israel achieved what it set out to do since at least the signing of the Camp David Accords with Egypt in 1978: it won limited functional civil autonomy for the Palestinians of the occupied territories and a legalized tight grip on the land, resources, economy, and security of the areas."[61] No sovereignty, no national rights, and no end of occupation: the US-sponsored peace process was as much a rejection of Palestinians' right to independence and self-determination as the post-Kissinger foreign policy consensus was.

If Israel consolidated its occupation in Oslo, the United States reaped the fruits of its victory over the Soviet Union and consolidated its hold over the Middle East. The New World Order declared by Bush Senior in 1991 set this process in motion. Iraq had to be tamed and cut back to size, and its invasion of Kuwait provided an excellent excuse for that. The end of the war with Iran had left it with a bloated army, a huge war debt, and resentment against Arab oil regimes and US double-dealing.[62] Saddam Hussein was perceived as a threat to US global strategy: oil had to be protected and regional stability (i.e., a pro-US status quo) reaffirmed. The "spectacle" of the Gulf War achieved this when Iraq was bombed back to the pre-industrial era (as one UN report put it). It is doubtful that such a diminution of state capacities, economic and political independence, and military power could ever have been realized without force. Though there was clearly an element of "demonstration effect" for both global and US domestic consumption in the projection of American military might, only war could significantly diminish Iraqi state power, consolidate American military presence, and safeguard the pre-eminence of US political and economic interests in the region. Arab oil regimes were protected, and Israeli military supremacy was assured: Iraq would never be able to pose any sort of threat to either Saudi Arabia or Israel (and, if Bush Senior had had enough support for regime change then, the United States wouldn't have had to wait for what Rice called the "opportunity" of post-9/11 to occupy Iraq). Only war, thus, could have satisfied the material and ideological requirements of US imperialism.

The end of the Cold War generated a peculiar expectation with regard to US policy toward Israel: Israel would become far less important for the United States. Because the Gulf War coalition excluded Israel (and included Syria, Saudi Arabia, and Egypt), and because Bush Senior delayed a $10 billion loan guarantee to Israel until it agreed to participate in the Madrid Peace Conference, which came on the heels of the Gulf War, Israel's role in the US empire was perceived to have been diminished. The days of the "strategic asset" thesis were over, it was claimed: the United States was now freer to create a more balanced foreign policy strategy in line with the international consensus of the impermissibility of acquiring territory by force.

The reality was quite different, however: even during the Gulf War crisis the United States forcefully rejected Saddam Hussein's (self-interested) *linkage* argument: Iraq would leave Kuwait; Israel would leave the Occupied Territories. No such universal standards were applied: double standards were the order of the day.[63] The Madrid conference ended up in near total deadlock. Bush's "peace and justice" were as elusive as ever. The 1990s would in fact prove to be the most fruitful time in US–Israel relations. The alliance became stronger than ever, intensifying and deepening. It is to Chomsky's realism that we owe this judgment: the end of the Cold War would only bring tactical modifications, not substantial changes, in US global strategy. Anti-nationalism and hostility to social radicalism would continue to define its agenda, as he predicted. And this would also apply to Israel, as the following statement from Israeli military strategist Shlomo Gazit clearly shows:

> Israel's main task has not changed at all, and it remains of crucial importance. Its location at the center of the Arab Muslim Middle East predestines Israel to be a devoted guardian of stability in all the countries surrounding it. Its [role] is to protect the existing regimes: to prevent or halt the processes of radicalization and to block the expansion of fundamentalist religious zealotry.[64]

The New World Order is, then, very much like the old world order: the United States and Israel fighting common enemies and satisfying mutual elite interests. The only difference lies in the realization of more amendable conditions of operation. US global primacy has been the main outcome of the Cold War, and after the Gulf War Israel's regional military superiority was again reconfirmed. One other slight variation is relevant here: a new enemy. If Arab nationalism was the enemy of the Cold War period, major factions of Islamic fundamentalism are the enemies of the New World Order (and this is in no way to equate the social content of each ideology). Once a Cold War ally against nationalism, Islamic fundamentalism has turned into a foe. Examples abound. Two main ones will suffice: the Mujahideen in Afghanistan (the Taliban, Bin Laden, and al-Qaeda) and radical fundamentalists in the Arab world. In the Palestinian context, the Muslim Brotherhood is an example of the latter. It went from being supported by Israel against nationalist Fatah to mutating into Hamas and becoming the main agent of anti-colonial struggle and Palestinian self-determination in the Occupied Territories. The cost of this shift is mainly paid by local societies: with the fundamentalists, regressive social agendas rule and the sphere of individual liberty (already severely curtailed by Arab secular nationalism) shrinks even more.

This is not a problem that worries Israel or the United States much, as long as the fundamentalists are suppressed or kept out of office (Algeria, Egypt, Jordan, Saudi Arabia, etc.). For the United States and Israel, the problem with democracy in the Middle East today is the problem of Islamic fundamentalism: most free elections would result in fundamentalists getting into power, as recent victories by Hamas and the United Iraqi Alliance in Iraq (and by the Front Islamique du Salut [FIS] in Algeria before that) show. Denying real democratic sovereignty remains a fundamental premise of US policy. So after the recent (January 2006) elections in Palestine (and the US hope for a Fatah win), the United States now demonizes and boycotts majority-elected Hamas and seeks to punish and "starve" Palestinians for their democratic choice (as a *New York Times* headline put it).

The "War on Terrorism" is the New World Order unleashed and unbound. It replays the Cold War dynamic, aims to reproduce its oppressive structure, and continues to satisfy longstanding US interests in the Middle East: control of oil and rejection of Arab radicalism, which have led to support for colonial Israel. And so it goes.

What this brief analysis of "imperialism–colonialism" teaches us is clear. The United States has been determining major economic and political outcomes in the Middle East since at least 1967, with Israel continuing to play a crucial role in their realization. In Israel-Palestine, this has meant that force and colonial peace have alternated as main instruments of policy, with the main objective being a constant: Jewish supremacy in Palestine – as much land as possible, as few Palestinians as possible. The United States has exploited this Zionist imperative for its own interests in the region, and has fostered a militarized and fundamentalist Israel in the process. This reality can be gauged in Israel's most recent parliamentary elections (March 2006). Gideon Levy has put it well:

> An absolute majority of the MKs [Members of Knesset] in the 17th Knesset will hold a position based on a lie; that Israel does not have a partner for peace. An absolute majority of MKs in the next Knesset do not believe in peace, nor do they even want it – just like their voters – and worse than that, don't regard Palestinians as equal human beings. Racism has never had so many supporters. It is the real hit of this election campaign.[65]

For the Palestinians, the impact of US–Israel has been much worse: collapse of the secular national project and national unity; continuing annexation of lands and resources; enclosure and "enclavization"; fragmentation, demobilization, and collective paralysis; and unending death and suffering. If, for Levy, Israelis are "One Racist Nation," for Amira Hass Palestinians have become "A Nation of Beggars": "For it is not natural disasters that have transformed the Palestinians into a nation that lives on handouts from the world; it is Israel's accelerating colonialist process."[66] This too is an outcome of the US–Israel, imperialism–colonialism relationship.

Between colonialism, looming starvation, and *sumud* (steadfastness), hope for real change seems remote, if not impossible. And this may yet prove to be imperialism's most catastrophic effect.

Acknowledgment

This essay is adapted from my essay in *After Iraq: Reframing Postcolonial Studies*, ed. Priyamvada Gopal and Neil Lazarus, special issue *new formations*, 59 (Fall 2006).

Notes

1 Abramson and Troen (2000). *Israel Studies* is one of the leading academic journals specializing in Israeli history, politics, society, and culture.
2 Silberstein (1999: 2). My interest here is not postmodern or postcolonial post-Zionism, for which see Silberstein; Shohat (2004); Matta (2003).
3 Shlaim (2001: xiii).
4 See Khalidi (1988).
5 Flapan (1987); Morris (1987); Pappe (1988); Shlaim (1988). Nur Masalha (in *Expulsion of the Palestinians* [1992]) also participated in this debate. Unlike Silberstein, however, I don't see the rationale of including Palestinians under the post-Zionist heading. The term should, I believe, also only refer to work from the late 1980s onwards, and not stretch back to inter-war figures or early Israeli nativist trends like the Canaanites.
6 Whether it is a justified injustice is a political not a historical question. What is quite unique about many of the post-Zionist historians (Pappe excluded) is that while they do acknowledge what happened in 1948 they end up justifying it nonetheless in the name of Zionism-as-refuge from anti-Semitism. Edward Said has described this as "a profound contradiction, bordering on schizophrenia" (2003: 199–202). The *New Left Review* has

been much more generous. It not only republished Benny Morris's racist interview with *Haaretz* (2004), in which he advocated ethnic cleansing of the remainder of the Palestinians, but also preceded it with much praise and adulation (even defending him against his own outrageous statements). The following is particularly troubling: "The hallmark of Morris's work has been a tough-minded realism – the inclination of a former paratrooper for the Israel Defense Force to call a spade a spade, whatever discomfort it might cause his co-nationals" (p. 37). The suggestion of course is that Morris's role in the Israeli army has provided him with a requisite dose of realism and historical clarity. But this does not square with the fact that army histories of 1948 have been as complicit with Israeli myth making as any other Israeli historical narratives before the arrival of the "new historians." Such praise diminishes Morris's own contribution in uncovering the Israeli historical record on 1948.

7 Said (2003: 201).
8 Kimmerling (1995: 41).
9 Ram (1995: 6).
10 Kimmerling (1983); Shafir (1996 [1989]).
11 Shafir (1996: 8).
12 Ehrlich (1987).
13 Sternhell (1998).
14 Shafir and Peled (2002). On Israeli culture as colonial and exclusionary, see Gover (1994).
15 This is of course not to mention early Palestinian work, such as Sabri Jiryis's *The Arabs in Israel* (1976) and Elia T. Zureik's *The Palestinians in Israel* (1979).
16 Ram (1995: 175).
17 The much neglected Palestinian Marxist Jabra Nicola (1912–74) was a foundational influence on Matzpen. His most important work is: "Theses on the Revolution in the Arab East" (1972, unpublished?). Ernest Mandel dedicated his *Revolutionary Marxism Today* (1979), to him in the following glowing terms: "Pioneer Arab Marxist & Palestinian Trotskyist, the most impressive internationalist I ever met."
18 An important film by Eran Torbiner which documents their history was released in 2003: *Matzpen: Anti-Zionist Israelis*. For a sample of their work see Khamsin (1984) and Khamsin (1989). See also Silberstein (1999: 84–7).
19 Hanegbi, Machover, and Orr (1971).
20 Ibid., 11.
21 Ibid., 7 (italics in original).
22 Segev (1998) and (2000).
23 Segev (2002: 64; my comments in parentheses).
24 Sayegh (1979).
25 Shafir and Peled (2000).

26 Peled and Shafir (1996).
27 Ibid., 409.
28 Ram, "The Promised Land of Business Opportunities," in Peled and Shafir (1996).
29 Benvenisti, "An Agreement of Surrender," quoted in Farsoun (1997: 274).
30 Ehrlich (2003: 63–97); Ehrlich (1993).
31 On what the author generously calls the "post-Zionist decade," see Pappe (2002).
32 Segev (2002: 161).
33 Shafir and Peled (2002: 336).
34 Ehrlich (2003: 93–4). See also Ehrlich (2002).
35 See the foundational works: Rodinson's *Israel* (1973); Said's *The Question of Palestine* (1992); and Chomsky's *Fateful Triangle* (1999). Recent examples include, from international relations: Fouskas and Gökay (2005) and Aruri (2003); from urban studies: Gregory (2004); from politics: Retort (2005). On Oslo and colonialism, see Tanya Reinhart's excellent *Israel/Palestine* (2002), and Bishara (2002).
36 Segev (2002: 49).
37 Chomsky (2003a: 342).
38 Chomsky (2003b: 150).
39 Achcar (2004: 36). See also Gendzier (1999).
40 Lewis (1999).
41 Rubenberg (1986: 126).
42 Shlaim (2001: 309–10).
43 Hersh (1983: 234–49).
44 Achcar (2004: 22).
45 Genet (2003: 275).
46 Sadat's recourse to war was forced by Kissinger's refusal to respond to his endless peace overtures in the early 1970s. See Chomsky (1999: 64–75) and Chomsky (2003b: 166–7).
47 Amin (1978: 72).
48 Ibid., 67.
49 Husam al-Khatib, a member of Fatah's executive committee, wrote the most important radical critique of the Palestinian Revolution, *On the Palestinian Revolutionary Experience* (1973).
50 al-Azm (1973).
51 Herzl (1988: 96).
52 Lewis (1999: 376).
53 Chomsky (1999: 462).
54 Masalha (2000: 22).
55 Kimmerling (1993).
56 Ibid., 217–18.
57 Kimmerling (2003: 39; my comments in square brackets).

58 For the contradictions between liberalism and Zionism in relation to the state, see Ahmad Sa'di's excellent "The Peculiarities of Israel's Democracy" (2002).
59 See Sternhell (1998: 335–6).
60 Said (1996); Said (2001).
61 Farsoun (1997: 270).
62 Neff (1991).
63 Finkelstein (1991).
64 Quoted in Chomsky (2002: 166).
65 Levy (2006).
66 Hass (2006).

References

Abramson, Glenda and S. Ilan Troen, eds. (2000) "The Americanization of Israel," *Israel Studies* 5(1).
Achcar, Gilbert. (2004) *Eastern Cauldron*. New York: Monthly Review Press.
Amin, Samir. (1978) *The Arab Nation*. London: Zed Books.
Aruri, Naseer H. (2003) *Dishonest Broker*. Cambridge: South End Press.
al-Azm, Sadek Jalal. (1973) *Critical Study of Palestinian Resistance Thought* [Dirasa Naqdiya li-Fiker al-Muqawama al-Falastinia]. Beirut: Dirasat il-Awda.
Benvenisti, Meron. (1997) "An Agreement of Surrender," *Haaretz*, May 12, 1994, quoted in Samih K. Farsoun, *Palestine and the Palestinians*, p. 274. Boulder: Westview Press.
Bishara, Marwan. (2002) *Palestine/Israel*. London: Zed.
Chomsky, Noam. (1999) *Fateful Triangle*. Cambridge: South End Press.
Chomsky, Noam. (2002) *Pirates and Emperors*. New York: South End Press.
Chomsky, Noam. (2003a) *Towards A New Cold War*. New York: The New Press.
Chomsky, Noam. (2003b) *Hegemony or Survival*. London: Hamish Hamilton.
Ehrlich, Avishai. (1987) "Israel: Conflict, War and Social Change," in Colin Creighton and Martin Shaw (eds.), *The Sociology of War and Peace*, pp. 121–42. New York: Sheridan House.
Ehrlich, Avishai. (1993) "The Gulf War and the New World Order," in Ralph Miliband and Leo Panitch (eds.), *New World Order? Socialist Register 1992*, pp. 227–38. New York: Monthly Review Press.
Ehrlich, Avishai. (2002) "Palestine, Global Politics, and Israeli Judaism," in Leo Panitch and Colin Leys (eds.), *Fighting Identities: Socialist Register 2003*, pp. 51–72. New York: Monthly Review Press.
Ehrlich, Avishai. (2003) "Zionism, Anti-Zionism, Post-Zionism," in Ephraim Nimni (ed.), *The Challenge of Post-Zionism*, pp. 63–97. London: Zed.
Farsoun, Samih K. (1997) *Palestine and the Palestinians*. Boulder: Westview Press.
Finkelstein, Norman. (1991) "Israel and Iraq," *Journal of Palestine Studies* 20(2): 43–56.

Flapan, Simha. (1987) *The Birth of Israel*. London: Croom Helm.
Fouskas, Vassilis K. and Bülent Gökay. (2005) *The New American Imperialism*. London: Praeger.
Gendzier, Irene L. (1999) *Notes from the Minefield*. Boulder, CO: Westview Press.
Genet, Jean. (2003) *Prisoner of Love*. New York: New York Review of Books.
Gover, Yerach. (1994) *Zionism*. Minneapolis: University of Minnesota Press.
Gregory, Derek. (2004) *The Colonial Present*. Oxford: Blackwell.
Hanegbi, Haim, Moshe Machover, and Akiva Orr. (1971) "The Class Nature of Israeli Society," *New Left Review* 65: 3–26.
Hass, Amira. (2006) "A Nation of Beggars," *Haaretz*, March 1, 2006, http://www.haaretzdaily.com.
Hersh, Seymour M. (1983) *The Price of Power*. New York: Summit Books.
Herzl, Theodor. (1988) *The Jewish State*. New York: Dover Publications.
Jiryis, Sabri. (1976) *The Arabs in Israel*. New York: Monthly Review Press.
Khalidi, Walid. (1988 [1961]) "Plan Dalet," *Journal of Palestine Studies* 18(1): 4–33.
Khamsin. (1984) *Forbidden Agendas*. London: Al Saqi Books.
Khamsin. (1989) *Palestine*. London: Zed Books.
al-Khatib, Husam. (1973) *On the Palestinian Revolutionary Experience* [fi il-tajriba al-thawria al-falastinia]. Damascus: Manshurat Wizarat il-Thaqafa.
Kimmerling, Baruch. (1983) *Zionism and Territory*. Berkeley: University of California Press.
Kimmerling, Baruch. (1993) "Patterns of Militarism in Israel," *European Journal of Sociology* 34: 196–223.
Kimmerling, Baruch. (1995) "Academic History Caught in the Cross-Fire," *History and Memory* 7(1).
Kimmerling, Baruch. (2003) *Politicide: Ariel Sharon's War Against the Palestinians*. London: Verso.
Levy, Gideon. (2006) "One Racist Nation," *Haaretz*, March 26, 2006, http://www.haaretzdaily.com.
Lewis, Samuel W. (1999) "The United States and Israel: Evolution of an Unwritten Alliance," *The Middle East Journal* 53(3): 364–6.
Mandel, Ernest. (1979) *Revolutionary Marxism Today*. London: New Left Books.
Masalha, Nur. (1992) *Expulsion of the Palestinians*. Washington, D.C.: Institute of Palestine Studies.
Masalha, Nur. (2000) *Imperial Israel and the Palestinians*. London: Pluto Press.
Matta, Nada. (2003) "Postcolonialism, Multiculturalism, and the Israeli Left," *Holy Land Studies* 2(1): 85–107.
Morris, Benny. (1987) *The Birth of the Palestinian Refugee Problem, 1947–1949*. Cambridge: Cambridge University Press.
Morris, Benny. (2004) "Ethnic Cleansing," *New Left Review* 26: 37–51.
Neff, Donald. (1991) "The US, Iraq, Israel, and Iran," *Journal of Palestine Studies* 20(4): 23–41.

Nicola, Jabra. (1972) "Theses on the Revolution in the Arab East" (unpublished?).

Nimni, Ephraim, ed. (2003) *The Challenge of Post-Zionism*. London: Zed.

Pappe, Ilan. (1988) *Britain and the Arab Israeli Conflict, 1948–51*. Basingstoke: Macmillan.

Pappe, Ilan. (2002) "The Post-Zionist Discourse in Israel, 1990–2001," *Holy Land Studies* 1(1): 9–35.

Peled, Yoav and Gershon Shafir. (1996) "The Roots of Peacemaking," *International Journal of Middle East Studies* 28: 391–413.

Ram, Uri. (1995) *The Changing Agenda of Israeli Sociology*. Albany: University of New York Press.

Ram, Uri. (1996) "'The Promised Land of Business Opportunities,'" in Yoav Peled and Gershon Shafir, "Roots of Peacemaking," *International Journal of Middle East Studies* 28: 217–40.

Reinhart, Tanya. (2002) *Israel/Palestine*. New York: Seven Stories Press.

Retort. (2005) *Afflicted Powers*. London: Verso.

Rodinson, Maxime. (1973) *Israel*. New York: Pathfinder.

Rubenberg, Cheryl A. (1986) *Israel and the American National Interest*. Urbana and Chicago: University of Illinois Press.

Sa'di, Ahmad. (2002) "The Peculiarities of Israel's Democracy," *International Journal of Intercultural Relations* 12: 119–33.

Said, Edward W. (1992) *The Question of Palestine*. New York: Vintage.

Said, Edward W. (1996) *Peace and Its Discontents*. New York: Vintage.

Said, Edward W. (2001) *The End of the Peace Process*. New York: Vintage.

Said, Edward. (2003) "New History, Old Ideas," in Ephraim Nimni (ed.), *The Challenge of Post-Zionism*, pp. 199–202. London: Zed.

Sayegh, Fayez A. (1979) "The Camp David Agreement and the Palestine Problem," *Journal of Palestine Studies* 8(2): 3–40.

Segev, Tom. (1998 [1986]) *1949*. New York: Henry Holt.

Segev, Tom. (2000 [1991]) *The Seventh Million*. New York: Henry Holt.

Segev, Tom. (2002) *Elvis in Jerusalem*. New York: Metropolitan.

Shafir, Gershon. (1996 [1989]) *Land, Labor and the Origins of the Israeli–Palestinian Conflict, 1882–1914*. Berkeley: University of California Press.

Shafir, Gershon and Yoav Peled. (2000) "Peace and Profits," in Gershon Shafir and Yoav Peled (eds.), *The New Israel*, pp. 243–64. Boulder, CO: Westview Press.

Shafir, Gershon and Yoav Peled. (2002) *Being Israeli*. Cambridge: Cambridge University Press.

Shlaim, Avi. (1988) *Collusion Across the Jordan*. New York: Columbia University Press.

Shlaim, Avi. (2001) *The Iron Wall*. New York: W. W. Norton.

Shohat, Ella. (2004) "The 'Postcolonial' in Translation: Reading Said in Hebrew," *Journal of Palestine Studies* 33(3): 55–75.

Silberstein, Laurence J. (1999) *The Postzionism Debates*. London: Routledge.

Sternhell, Zeev. (1998) *The Founding Myths of Israel.* Princeton: Princeton University Press.
Zureik, Elia T. (1979) *The Palestinians in Israel.* London: Routledge & Kegan Paul.

Chapter 10

The Poetics of State Terror in Twenty-first-century Zimbabwe

Ranka Primorac

[T]he national is a time that looks to the past and inherits a future.
Sassen, "Spatialities and Temporalities of the Global: Elements for a Theorization," p. 223

[M]emories do pile up, but the most remote ones, especially those which saw us suffer and the times when we were under bondage, under colonial rule, those can never fade away, they remain forever.
Mugabe, "We Won't go back to the Commonwealth," p. 6

A Narrative of Ordeal

In his essay in this volume, as elsewhere, Achille Mbembe outlines the main attributes of a postcolonial terrorist state. In such a state the recurrence of state-sponsored violence is predicated on the idea of salvation or redemption, and the discourse of retributive justice dominates public consciousness to an extent that knows no limits. Past suffering (in the name of which such violence is initiated) is elevated to the status of identity, and brute force is considered to be the best answer to real or imagined fear. Terrorist states seek to turn all their citizens into either soldiers or informants, and the state's fixation on identifying enemies – justified by the need to inflict on them ever-increasing amounts of retributive suffering – becomes the basis of the national ethos. Twenty-first-century Zimbabwe to date entirely fits this description.

The subject of this chapter is fiction produced under the auspices of the Zimbabwean state of the third millennium: that is to say, the discursive construct that the Zimbabwean government has adopted as the official state ideology since the beginning (in 2000) of a series of sweeping and violent interventions it has made into the sociopolitical life of the nation. Terence Ranger (2004) has written about this fiction as Zimbabwe's "patriotic history" – the nation's official historical narrative that now turns out to be an accumulation of distinct narrative segments with separate official designations. In particular, these comprise a protracted "rural" episode known as "the third *Chimurenga*" or uprising, in which white-owned farmland is "liberated" by being distributed to land-hungry indigenous Zimbabweans; and its urban supplement, operation *Murambatsvina*, "sweeping out the filth," in which the nation's crime-infested cities are restored to a state of cleanliness and order (see Kamete 2006 and Potts 2006). Because it is, as Ranger and others have pointed out, an evolving narrative project through which the state promotes and imposes on its citizens a version of the nation's history that is demonstrably untrue, the "patriotic history" is a good example of what Mbembe (1991, 2001) calls a postcolonial master code or master fiction. This chapter concerns itself with the poetics of this master fiction, which makes explicit the discursive logic underpinning the terror unleashed by the Zimbabwean state on its citizens in the third decade of its independence.[1]

In a postcolony, Mbembe writes, state power creates its own world of meanings, which it aims to make so central to everyday life that it governs the production of all the other worlds of meaning that exist in the society. The state seeks to institutionalize this master fiction as the "socio-historical world" – that is to say, turn it into reality by instilling it into the consciences of its subjects in such a way that it becomes indisputable and is turned into the "world-view" of the period or a new form of "common sense." Although clearly invented and fantastical ("given to the production of lies and double-speak" – Mbembe 2001: 118), the meanings it generates are not negotiable. Subjects are forbidden to depart from them or challenge them, and if they do they are threatened with the application of physical pain. When he writes that the rulers of an African postcolony seek to dominate their subjects through the production of "a local, coherent and codified *genre* which *strings facts and events together* in a fantastical way in order to produce the incredible" (Mbembe 1991: 173, emphasis added), Mbembe is stressing the narrative properties of master fictions, and it is with such properties of Zimbabwe's "patriotic history" that this chapter is centrally preoccupied. My key aim is to show that, in terms of fictional genre, the narrative of the "Third *Chimurenga*" is a version of what Bakhtin (1986) describes as a narrative of ordeal. Further, I aim to point out the existence of a homology between the grand narrative of the collective ordeal which Zimbabwe's rulers claim the nation to be undergoing, and the "small" ordeal narratives contained in a certain strand of Zimbabwe's popular fiction.

A broad outline of recent activities of Zimbabwe's government and ruling party, ZANU (PF), is relatively well known. Having come into power in 1980 after a bloody civil war and a protracted series of negotiations, ZANU (PF) experienced the first serious challenge to its hegemony in 2000. As a response to this challenge (mounted by a constellation of agents and alliances – see Alexander 2003 and Chan 2003), it instigated a violent take-over of Zimbabwe's privately owned agricultural land. This process, known as "the fast-track redistribution of land," led to the collapse of Zimbabwe's economy and an increase in political repression. It is, however, officially represented as the pinnacle of Zimbabwe's history as an independent nation: the final installment of a liberation war, which succeeded in redressing colonial wrongs by freeing a key material and spiritual resource from white occupiers, after decades of being sidetracked by their promises of reconciliation. A further, equally violent, state intervention was similarly described as an improvement of the national condition, even though it was aimed against the nation's poor black citizens. Starting in May 2005, the Zimbabwean army suddenly and violently destroyed the informal settlements and businesses in major Zimbabwean cities, leaving thousands homeless and without an income. This has been widely interpreted as an exercise in controlling and depopulating Zimbabwe's cities, which have for some time now been seen as the strongholds of political opposition and potential seed-beds of popular uprising (see Solidarity Peace Trust 2005 and 2006). The government, however, has insisted that it was an exercise in "restoring order" through confronting urban crime and corruption (see Charamba 2005). And so the Zimbabwean nation is officially seen as having taken yet another step toward the desired state of orderliness and freedom: "Well, our people are happy, they are very happy," Robert Mugabe has said (Mugabe 2005: 7).

Mikhail Bakhtin describes the novel of ordeal as a narrative constructed around "a series of tests of the main heroes, tests of their fidelity, valour, bravery, virtue, nobility, sanctity and so on" (Bakhtin 1986: 11). A widespread narrative type, it encompasses Christian hagiographies, chivalric novels, and other "heroic" narratives, whose key characteristic is an *absence of change*. The world of an ordeal narrative is essentially static: it is no more than an arena of struggle and testing for the heroes, whom it presents with a series of obstacles to overcome. But for the (overwhelmingly male) heroes, the process of overcoming does not amount to a *becoming*: their identities do not alter in any way. The testing merely confirms the existence of qualities (fidelity, valour, bravery, virtue, nobility, sanctity, etc.) that they possessed from the outset. Because "nothing that takes place, nothing [the heroes] see or undergo, can be utilized as life experience that alters and shapes them" (Bakhtin 1986: 12), such worlds may be said to lack "independence and historicity" (p. 15).

The Zimbabwean state fiction, with its insistence on successive phases of liberation struggle inexorably leading toward a fixed and predetermined goal, is precisely the kind of hero-centered narrative described by Bakhtin – its protagonists ZANU (PF) and Mugabe, and the value being tested, the staunchness of their patriotism. When it is regarded in this way – as a version of a commonplace genre narrative – it becomes possible to see that this particular postcolonial master fiction has been prefigured, rehearsed, and reinforced in previous nationalist narratives (Ranger 2004 and Sylvester 2003), and in fiction. Most notably it may be found in popular adventure novels of ordeal published locally in English since independence and celebrating the exploits of freedom fighters and similar figures. Such texts have, to the best of my knowledge, thus far escaped critical attention almost entirely (see Primorac 2005a). In the present historical moment, however, they deserve closer scrutiny, because they help to demonstrate that the political discourses surrounding the Zimbabwean "crisis" were not a sudden eruption. In elaborating on the various aspects of Zimbabwe's state fiction in the rest of this chapter, I will refer to a representative sample of novels alongside non-fictional texts generated by Zimbabwe's government and ruling party.

The Zimbabwean adventure novels of ordeal I will be drawing on are Garikai Mutasa's novellas "The Bridge" and "Mavhondo" (published together in *The Bridge*, 1996) and the following novels: Edmund Chipamaunga's *Chains of Freedom* (1998) and *Feeding Freedom* (2000), Claude Maredza's *When God Went on Leave* (2002) and *I Put It to You* (2004), Rodwell Machingauta's *Detective Ridgemore Riva* (1994) and Lilian Masitera's *The Trail* (2000). To the best of my knowledge, only one of these texts (Machingauta's 1994 thriller) has previously been the object of critical scrutiny (see Primorac 2005a). Four of them (Chipamaunga's 2000 novel and the texts by Maredza and Masitera) were self-published following the advent of the "Third *Chimurenga*" and may thus be read as acts of political opportunism on the part of their authors; others were published by mainstream publishers during the first two decades of independence. All appear to have been aimed at the popular literary market.

Information provided by the books' back covers identifies their authors as middle-class, urban-based Zimbabweans. Edmund Chipamaunga is a former diplomat (he has served as Zimbabwe's ambassador to the United States) who went on to become a teacher of English. His first novel, the war adventure story *A Fighter for Freedom* (1983) has attracted some critical attention (see, for example, Kaarsholm 1991), and it forms a trilogy with his two novels discussed here (*Chains of Freedom* and *Feeding Freedom*). Rodwell Machingauta and Garikai Mutasa were also high-school teachers at the time of their novels' publication; Mutasa is the author of the 1985 war novel *The Contact*, on which critics have also remarked (Kaarsholm 1991).

Claude Maredza is a chartered accountant. In 1983 he played the protagonist in the film version of Dambudzo Marechera's *The House of Hunger*; some years later, he published (through a commercial publisher) an adventure story for young readers set in pre-colonial times and written in praise of "tradition" (Maredza 1987), before embarking on a sequential self-published project (based on the condemnation of a global racial conspiracy and a personal myth of origin), part of which is represented here. The cover of her novel identifies Lilian Masitera as a mathematics teacher and the author of two previous volumes. In a 2001 interview (Primorac 2004), the internationally acclaimed Zimbabwean novelist Yvonne Vera recalled being criticized by Masitera on national radio for misrepresenting Shona culture in her work.

All the texts considered here are marked by stylistic and compositional transparency and an absence of formal experiment. Because their plots are structured by bi-polar conflict, they may be linked, on the one hand, to the macro-genre of the Zimbabwean war novel (Primorac 2006), and, on the other, to the tradition of the settler popular novel which has existed in Zimbabwe since the 1960s (see Primorac 2006 and 2005b). Furthermore, they appear to resonate with the popular/war strands of Zimbabwean fiction in indigenous languages (as described by Kahari 1990, Chiwome 1998, and Vambe 2006), itself underpinned by oral genres of pre-colonial origin, as Chiwome (1998) explains. I will attempt to show that all of these novels may be described as *axiological,* value-assigning works, that is to say, fictional texts whose primary function is to transmit dominant discourses (of the current Zimbabwean "patriotic history," or its colonial-era predecessor) and their counter-discourses (see Doležel 1990; Primorac 2006). It will be seen that these popular novels share with the "patriotic history" narrative a set of key structural traits, to do with narrative time, agency, and addressivity. The longstanding presence of a "popular" public realm, which appears to be in contact with the domain of political discourse with which it may be exchanging textual strategies, might help to explain why the implementation of the current Zimbabwean state fiction has been so successful. Mugabe does not rule (and has never ruled) by brute force and coercion alone. Indeed, a generic analysis of the fiction of the "Third *Chimurenga*" and the related smaller fictions might be of some use to those who seek to dismantle it.

Incremental Time

Researchers have noted a seeming paradox contained in the Zimbabwean government rhetoric and its attitude toward time. Although the take-over of white farmland was meant to represent a "fast-track" movement of Zimbabwean national identities into the *future,* the official discourse has often evoked a sudden return into the *past* – reviving the emphasis on the importance of liberation war veterans in the political process and using wartime methods of drawing the Zimbabwean population to its cause (see Sylvester 2003 and Ranger 2004). In so doing, it seeks to blot out the historical *present* – the national "now" in which the government inflicts pain and death on its people on a daily basis. "By looking backwards as a way of managing the unpopular present, ZANU (PF) hope[s] to write a ticket to the future, and to do so with its everyday failings as a government in full public view" (Sylvester 2003: 30).

This seeming paradox holds the key to the temporal logic that underlies Zimbabwe's state fiction. The narrative of the three successive uprisings gradually effecting a full national liberation is grounded in a notion of time that is both linear and teleological. It is, in the words of Paul Ricoeur, a "time conceived of as a series of instants succeeding one another along an abstract line oriented in a single direction" (Ricoeur 1980: 174). In fixing the origin of the national "series of instants" in the moment of colonial dispossession and its goal in an act of reversal (a complete postcolonial repossession), ZANU (PF) has claimed the ownership of national time. Moreover, in choosing to treat an inadequate present as a necessary step toward a fulfilled future, the government reveals its own master fiction to be a narrative of *sacrifice* (see, for example, Kanengoni 2003 and 2004).[2] Finally, in subdividing the "arrow of time" into discrete stages (phases of a continuing revolution separated by contiguous, dovetailing *Chimurengas*), it points at a notion of the passage of time that is *incremental.* A good illustration is a pre-election ruling party advertisement frequently reprinted in the Zimbabwean press in the run-up to the 2005 parliamentary elections, which sums up Zimbabwe's postcolonial progress as an accumulation of opportunities to vote for ZANU (PF) in elections.

Such an understanding of time (to which Ricoeur denies full historicality, since it overlooks the necessity of combining retrospection with anticipation) corresponds to the Bakhtinian concept of adventure time, in which narratives of ordeal unfold. Like Ricoeur, Bakhtin (1987) writes of an empty and mechanical time incapable of accommodating the kind of partial repetition that amounts to a change of identity or a becoming. In novels of ordeal, the passage of adventure time is punctuated by encounters with obstacles that must be overcome, if the narrative's goal is to be reached and the heroes' destiny fulfilled. In Edmund Chipamaunga's 1983 *A Fighter for Freedom,* an early war novel which may be seen as a precursor of the texts under scrutiny here, the incremental nature of progress is expressed compositionally: the titles of the novel's three parts are "Under Authority," "With Authority," and "In Authority." The testing of the novel's hero, the guerrilla Tinashe, begins at the narrative's very outset: even before he is allowed to join the freedom fighters, he is made to "engage in exploits that would leave his determination, courage and resourcefulness in no doubt" (Chipamaunga 1983: 98).

In the 2000 sequel, entitled *Feeding Freedom,* Tinashe faces the task of overcoming war-related trauma and bringing *real* independence to the black workers of a Harare factory. The idea that flag independence does not bring about true liberation is, of course, not new in African fiction. However, Chipamaunga's novel assumes that freedom can be *fed,* or augmented, in discrete stages and through decisive actions initiated by former guerrillas: "Everyone who had not fought the Ian

Smith system using a gun was an 'outsider' who must be excluded from the overall association of the ex-guerrillas. The distinction must be clear-cut otherwise the list of aspirants for the real benefits would be unending" (Chipamaunga 2000: 21–2). (The narrator's insistence here on the need carefully to distribute the "real benefits" of liberation is significant: the novel was published at a time when government-sponsored invasions of white-owned farms by "war veterans" were getting under way.) Garikai Mutasa's "The Bridge" may also serve as an illustration of the incremental nature of an ordeal narrative's timeline. In the novella, guerrillas/adventurers Torai Nyika and Shumba Yemabunhu cross the border between Rhodesia and Mozambique in order to prevent a last-minute sabotage of the Lancaster House agreement, which is about to inaugurate independence. As they struggle to stop a convoy of South African lorries from arriving at its destination inside Zimbabwe, their race against time happens in discrete stages: the novella is divided into sections named after the four weekdays on which the action takes place.

Feeding Freedom is a good example of a further temporal characteristic of Zimbabwe's master fiction: the fact that the moment of arrival of the longed-for future – the augmented and final "real" decolonization – is constantly anticipated, yet always also deferred. In "The Bridge" (written in the 1990s), the heroes somehow manage to avert a Rhodesian counter-strike in the nick of time. At the end of Chipamaunga's 2000 novel, on the other hand, black factory workers in independent Zimbabwe successfully assemble a piece of machinery which promises to free them from the need to import spare parts from apartheid-ruled South Africa. Yet the text does not celebrate this important victory: it ends, instead, on a note of ambivalence and unresolved tension: "The eyes and ears trained on the machine registered a mixture of dreadful and hopeful anticipation of a loud burst or boom" (Chipamaunga 2000: 203). The heroes of Zimbabwe's state fiction are never fully victorious: their triumph is always in danger being hijacked by hidden enemies; their ordeal is therefore never-ending, and in this lies the relentlessness of the demand upon them and the greatness of their sacrifice for the good of the nation.

In distinct parallel, a recently published ZANU (PF) propaganda booklet formulates the entire history of the region as an accumulation of distinct historical phases, during which individuals must choose between supporting and betraying their (nascent) nation. The booklet is made up of chapters entitled "Background and First Phase of Traitors

(Slavery)," "First *Chimurenga* Phase of Sellouts," "Second *Chimurenga* Phase of Traitors," "The Post Independence Phase of Traitors," and "Other Forms of Traitor." And yet – having thus established both the teleological and incremental nature of historical time – the booklet does not deem it contradictory to warn its readers: "The nation and the party ZANU PF needs to be constantly reminded that *the enemy cannot be fully defeated*. It [*sic*] will keep returning back disguised in various forms even as one of us" (n.a. [2005]: 26, emphasis added).

Mbembe suggests this constant and violent deferral of what is nevertheless declared as inevitable is linked to the postcolonial autocrat's fear of death: the "autocrat seeks to render his own mortality of no effect by deferring for as long as possible the inevitable violence of death" (Mbembe 1997: 161). Indeed, the ageing Mugabe has repeatedly brushed aside thoughts of stepping down and of possible succession (see for example Mugabe 2005: 9). Bakhtin, too, points out that in ordeal narratives "history *and biography*" are taken out of adventure time (Bakhtin 1986: 15, emphasis added). In this way, as the self-declared heroes of a never-ending national rite of passage, ZANU (PF) and its leader have appointed themselves owners of the future and controllers of death.

Polarized Agency

Mbembe has been widely criticized for disallowing the possibility of "outright" resistance in a postcolony. In the context of Zimbabwe such criticism is valid; the current state fiction has had to take into account the existence of an active and resilient political opposition and civil society. Unlike in Cameroon, where "the postcolonial system of domination was, until recently, keen to maintain a fiction of a society without conflict" (Mbembe 1991: 167), Zimbabwe's rulers seek artificially to maintain an image of a society permanently engulfed by a certain kind of conflict; that is to say, a society constantly threatened by hostile outsiders and their internal allies, so that its very identity as an independent entity is at stake. The master fiction therefore firmly specifies the kinds of agents that it allows to function as its subjects. It is structured around the distinction between "patriots" and "sellouts" or traitors. Patriots are "authentic" Zimbabweans, who drive the national narrative forward. "Sellouts" (outsiders to Zimbabwe and Africa) attempt to sway it away from its goal, in effect threatening to reverse the arrow of time and re-channel the national temporal flow *backwards* and into a ghostly reverse arrow, until they achieve national regression or degeneration. In contrast to the implied foresight of ZANU (PF), the opposition is on occasion represented as emphatically backward-looking. Government apologist Tafataona Mahoso has written: "The MDC [Zimbabwe's main opposition party] was born already weighed down by dog-tired ideas, trying to repackage for Zimbabwe *some 1920s cliches in the twenty-first century*" (Mahoso 2004, emphasis added).

The "Third *Chimurenga*" narrative is "nativist" in that it links "sell-outs" to Western identities. Although sellouts are typically white, they may also be black Zimbabweans whose blackness functions as a disguise. Speaking of the political opposition, Mugabe has said: "They should think African, and not think white" (Mugabe 2005: 9). In a similar vein, *Traitors Do Much Damage to National Goals* uses quasi-Fanonian language to warn readers that traitors are "simply the manifestation of a phantom that is trying to rise again after having been slain by the heroic children of the Zimbabwean Revolution. The only thing that camouflages [it] and confuses many is that in this attempt to rise, the phantom has now adopted a new face, the face of a Blackman" (n.a. 2005: 22). In theory, this allows for the possibility of white persons who "think African" – and indeed, government representatives have recently referred to "progressive" white farmers, to whom the repossessed farmland may in the future be leased (see Meldrum 2005). In practice, however, it has been much easier to be added to the historical scrapheap of enemies than to be rehabilitated – as the *Traitors* series of listings demonstrates (in one memorable instance condemning an entire clan to historical damnation).

New ranks of traitors may at any time "emerge from deep within us; from university colleges, the clergy, captains of industry, students, academics, professionals, workers as well as trade union leaders, to name but a few" (n.a. 2005: 21) – and this explains the need for constantly extending the boundaries of incremental time. The list of potential suspects makes it clear that the state fiction associates sellouts with cities, which are thus excluded from the "organic" unity of the "authentic" national space. This is so because they are in contact with the hostile Western spaces beyond the national boundaries. Chipamaunga's second novel, *Chains of Freedom*, anticipates such a stance: in it, a former guerrilla is sidetracked by both rich overseas enemies-posing-as-friends *and* the corrupting influence of Zimbabwe's capital city, which acquires a life of its own by refusing to be decolonized: "The newly independent city was undergoing agonizing birth into existence as the colonial city *stubbornly resisted to slide into mere recorded history* (Chipamaunga 1998: 97, emphasis added).

The patriots' staunchness, on the other hand, comes from their adherence to "traditional" – that is to say, rural and pre-colonial – identities and values. In a 2005 post-election speech, Mugabe praised "our rural people" for being "the vanguard in the sweet defence of [Zimbabwe's] sovereignty. The rural communities remain the most consistent, reliable and decisive pillar support for the party – a formidable defence for our revolution" (Herald Reporter 2005). Patriots conform to Bakhtin's description of heroes undergoing ordeal by possessing a fixed set of characteristics, so that, indeed, nothing they see or undergo can alter or shape them. They are routinely represented as disciplined, vigilant, and resourceful; importantly, all of these traits are radically gendered as masculine, and they are opposed to the softness and corruption of women and "sellouts." Claude Maredza's *I Put It to You* is both a story about the life of a government lawyer-cum-detective, and a protracted invective against the conspiracy of white men, various foreign agents, and black women against long-suffering black, male Zimbabweans. The novel's "traditionalist" narrator rails against the fickleness of women coupled with the "pseudo sophistication" of city life, which, he says, "produced more prostitutes, more alcoholics, more murderers, more promiscuity . . . and all that went with it than all the rural areas of Zimbabwe combined could produce" (Maredza 2004: 37). This statement accurately prefigures the official government line on operation *Murambatsvina*.

Rodwell Machingauta's 1994 thriller *Detective Ridgemore Riva* foreshadows Maredza's interest in global justice and the law. This novel is remarkable in that it anticipates the contemporary attribution of the role of "sellout" to the process of law, which is, in the various versions of the state fiction, often constructed as a Western imposition. Riva is a government detective investigating the loss of important secret documents from the Ministry of Foreign Affairs, which he sees as part of an effort to destabilize his country. Working with a team of helpers, "patriotic" Riva (who models himself on freedom fighters and listens to local *Chimurenga* music) conducts the entire investigation almost speechlessly: he is able to spot foreign enemies and internal traitors simply by applying his expert, scout-like gaze to his surroundings. When the South African spies who were responsible for stealing the documents are finally caught, Riva and his aides torture them. They know that this is against the law, but consider the law itself to be an outcome of external interference in the affairs of the nation. One of them says: "At times I wonder whether some of our laws were not imposed on us to please certain organisations or outside countries" (Machingauta 1994: 156). In a different context, Renate Lachmann has written of how "[w]ithin his own state, Ivan the Terrible erected a counterstate that suspended the prevailing laws through its own set of counterlaws" (Lachmann 1997: 140). As part of the project of turning its state fiction into reality, Zimbabwe has, since 2000, done something comparable (see Crisis in Zimbabwe Coalition 2003).[3] As this suggests, its current attitude to democracy and the rule of law was rehearsed and disseminated by popular texts such as *I Put It to You* and *Riva*.

The prototype of a patriot is a liberation-war participant, embodied (paradoxically) in a representation of Mugabe himself as the eternally young and ever-consistent leader of "the people's party" (Mugabe 2001: 69). Sorrowani, the hero of Claude Maredza's *When God Went on Leave*, is also a "man of the people." A Zimbabwean Everyman – a talented but poor university graduate trying to raise the money he needs to start a business venture – Sorrowani is certain that the obstacles in his path are the result of racism. This is confirmed when he is swindled by the text's "sellout" – a local white man called Dave. Only when Sorrowani finally takes the law into his own hands, hijacks Dave's mother and daughter and forces them to live in a village, like black Africans, does he begin to feel liberated and socially appreciated. A condition of the women's release is a "three million donation to the war vets" (Maredza 2002: 56). An extended reference to the events of the "Third *Chimurenga*" illustrates the confluence of gender, agency, and (urban or rural) space characteristic of Zimbabwe's state fiction, as well as its tendency to defer the moment of final fulfillment. The defiant tone of the passage highlights a final characteristic of the Zimbabwean state fiction: its constant engagement in a one-dimensional mock-dialogue with its imaginary opponents:

> And the message I give the brothers who are liberating the land from the crackers, the most noble piece of politico-socioeconomic action to happen in Zimbabwe since 1980, is to go all the way and liberate everything once and for all. We might as well be called a rogue state wholesomely than to be called a rogue state in a piecemeal fashion. So the brothers must open another front and that is liberating banks, factories, the financial sector and all these cracker places that frustrate black endeavours. . . . We might as well liberate everything now. (Maredza 2004: 19)

A Ghostly Polemic

Zimbabwe's master fiction is by its very nature polemical, and its articulations are often marked by a tone of shrill defiance. "Some countries, particularly in the developed West, provide safe havens for fugitive economic saboteurs from our country," said Robert Mugabe (2004) in a public speech, adding yet another category to the official list of "sellouts." Because it envisages progress as a gradual overcoming of obstacles – that is to say, a constantly anticipated hard-fought victory over internal and external enemies – the master fiction must remain locked in a perpetual, polemical quasi-exchange with precisely those enemies. Because its self-reproduction involves a continuous fabrication of mock-threats and opponents, the "Third *Chimurenga*" narrative comes across as parasitical. Because "patriotic history" is a narrative of victimization and reaction, rather than of initiative and invention, it is only the constant re/production of various kinds of obstacles that keeps the master fiction alive.

The plots of Garikai Mutasa's "The Bridge" and its companion novella, "Mavhondo," are built entirely on the principle of obstacle proliferation. This is obvious in particular in the short yet fast-paced "Mavhondo," which in a narrative composed of 40 breathless segments tells the story of an unsuccessful siege mounted by the Rhodesian army around a Zimbabwean freedom fighters' base located on the Mozambican border. The text stresses the Mavhondo-based guerrillas' oneness with nature and skill in detecting the hidden maneuvers of enemies. *However,* the story's real protagonist is the base itself, which is explicitly identified with the Zimbabwean nation and ruling party: "[Mavhondo] was the nerve centre of ZANU and if it was destroyed, the struggle would be set back five to ten years. All the weapons belonging to the party were here. . . . This was the future of Zimbabwe" (Mutasa 1996: 112). In the officially sanctioned version of the Zimbabwean postcolonial world of today, the very identities of "patriots" depend on the existence of "sellouts," who thus endow the entire historical process with purpose and a meaning.

And yet the constant exchange within which the state fiction purports to engage with its opponents is a parody of a dialogue, because their voices are never allowed to be heard in their own right. They are always only ventriloquized – as in the references to "rogue state" in the citation from Maredza above (see Ranger 2004). The national enemies and "sellouts" are thus made to resemble ghosts, in that they are always represented as other-worldly and inaccessible, but also dangerous and real (because they embody unrealized alternatives to the current master fiction). The ordeal that the heroes of Zimbabwe's master fiction claim to be undergoing on behalf of the nation always represents itself as both a vanguard action and a counter-measure.

A particularly *literary* version of such ghostly polemic is Lilian Masitera's 2000 novel *The Trail*. Lindiwe, its young female narrator, dreams of a transformed identity in the elite boarding school which she aspires to attend. She longs to learn to speak English fluently, and learn "city" habits such as using a knife and fork. Just like the heroine of Tsitsi Dangarembga's canonical *Nervous Conditions* (which has been widely interpreted as feminizing Fanon's findings on the pitfalls of nationalist consciousness), Lindiwe has a rebellious aunt and a penchant for reading forbidden books, as well as a relative called Nyasha, to whom she looks up, and who guides her. In what can only be understood as a riposte to Dangarembga, however, Masitera's "Nyasha" is the heroine's older brother, who also happens to be a member of the Zimbabwe National Army's elite Presidential Guard. In contrast to Dangarembga's, Masitera's story takes place after independence, and her heroine's rebellion is not directed at a proto-nationalist patriarchy. Instead, it turns itself against the foreign white nuns who run Lindiwe's school without understanding the Zimbabwean students' desire for "freedom and justice" (Masitera 2000: 62). Couched in the flat monotone characteristic of much "patriotic" discourse, Masitera's polemic with *Nervous Conditions* excludes the pluri-vocality and subversive laughter of Dangarembga's famous text, and thereby reduces it to a ghostly echo.[4]

And yet it is true that by its very nature, a narrative of ordeal cannot openly disallow the possibility that ghosts can be laid to rest, patriots can be magnanimous, and "sellouts" may be made to see the light. Despite his declared animosity to "non-African" discourses and values, Mugabe has allowed for the possibility of renewing reciprocal exchanges with the West (see Mugabe 2005: 11). There have also been Western voices encouraging the possibility of re-establishing such an exchange (Dowden 2005). But even if this were to happen, Zimbabwe's master fiction seems unlikely to be able to find an easy way of doubling back on itself. Because the hard-won identities it constructs are grounded in temporal and narrative structures that are unidirectional and cumulative, Mugabe's government's fiction of ordeal can give up on its goal of "total liberation" no more easily than the colonial government could renege on the concept of "civilizing mission." The officially sanctioned, oft-paraphrased statement that "capitulation is not an option" (Gono 2005) keeps the master fiction true to the conventions of its genre.

Post-script: On the Perils of Adventurism

In a 1911 essay on the implications of time and form entitled "The Adventure," Georg Simmel anticipates both Ricoeur and Bakhtin and provides additional insight into the implications of the formal properties of Zimbabwe's master fiction. When he stresses the conspicuous temporal boundedness of adventure time (which has a clearly defined beginning and ending, and therefore an aura of dream-like unreality about it), Simmel is in alignment with Bakhtin's thoughts on the absence of change in the narrative of ordeal, and he foreshadows Ricoeur's wording when he writes that "the adventurer is . . . the extreme example of the ahistorical individual, the man who lives in the present" (Simmel 1959: 245). But it is when he refers to adventurism as a form of experiencing life that Simmel provides an uncannily accurate perspective on the tensions that inhabit Zimbabwe's officially sanctioned culture.

In describing the interplay between chance and necessity in the formal makeup of an adventure, Simmel stresses the analogy between an adventurer and a gambler, who "abandon[s] himself to the meaninglessness of chance" (Simmel 1959: 246) and treats contingency as if it were fate: "the professional adventurer makes a system of life out of his life's lack of system" (ibid.). Commentators have noticed that, in initializing the 2000 land appropriations which led to the emergence of the current version of the Zimbabwean nationalist narrative, ZANU (PF) has behaved in a manner which may be described as recklessly adventurous, and it has continued to do so ever since. In the context of discussing Zimbabwe's monetary policy, for example, Stephen Chan writes that "repaying an overdue portion of its IMF debt by printing Zim$ 21 trillion . . . was an act of *such reckless bravado* that it seems the government still feels it can deny and swagger its way towards recovery" (Chan 2006, emphasis added). Simmel would have pointed out that, like all true adventurers, Zimbabwe's rulers treat the incalculable elements in life as if they were calculable. His line of thought is in keeping with Achille Mbembe's remark that a postcolony is distinguished by "a distinctive style of political improvisation" (Mbembe 2001: 102), and he could have had the Zimbabwean master fiction in mind when he wrote that "[a]dventure has the gesture of *the conqueror*, the quick seizure of opportunity" (Simmel 1959: 248, emphasis added).

But in the second half of his essay, Simmel adds a caveat to his thoughts on adventure by stressing that only the young are truly at home with this never-ending burning of bridges: "adventure does not belong to the lifestyle of old age" (Simmel 1959: 253). The ruthlessness and violence of Zimbabwe's state terror designates the anxiety of an adventurer divested of youth and faced with death. Constantly haunted by a ghostly parallel world of their own making, Zimbabwe's ageing rulers have emptied the narrative figure of *arrival* of its usual meanings. Instead of celebrating officially proclaimed acts of closure, the image of anxious eyes and ears anticipating the burst of an overheated machine encapsulates well the expectant silence and enforced stillness implicit in the Zimbabwean fictions of today.

Notes

1 My understanding of "poetics" here goes beyond a mere study of the confluence of generic and semantic properties of a quasi literary discourse, as outlined in Todorov (1977). I am guided by the views of Doležel (1990), for whom poetics involves incorporating generic and other knowledge about literature into broader frameworks of knowledge acquired by the human and social sciences. The fictional texts considered by this article are not regarded, in the first instance, as aesthetic constructs, but as what Mieke Bal (2003) calls *theoretical objects* – that is to say, triggers, if not containers, of theoretical ideas which would, without their presence, be difficult or impossible to articulate.

2 An important type of ordeal narrative is the Christian hagiography, where the hero's holiness is tested through suffering and temptation.

3 At the time of writing, Zimbabwe's raft of repressive legislation includes the Public Order and Security Act (POSA), the Access to Information and Protection of Privacy Act (AIPPA), the Broadcasting Services Act (BSA), and the Miscellaneous Offences Act. The Suppression of Foreign and International Terrorism Bill has been gazetted.

4 Paradoxically and disconcertingly, the plot of *The Book of Not* – Dangarembga's own 2006 sequel to *Nervous Conditions* – is a narrative of ordeal, which bears an uncanny resemblance to the plot of *The Trial*.

References

Alexander, J. (2003) "'Squatters,' Veterans and the State in Zimbabwe," in A. Hammar, B. Raftopoulos, and S. Jensen (eds.), *Zimbabwe's Unfinished Business*, pp. 83–117. Harare: Weaver Press.

Bakhtin, M. M. (1986) "The *Bildungsroman* and Its Significance in the History of Realism (Toward a Historical Typology of the Novel)," in C. Emerson and M. Holquist (eds.), *M. M. Bakhtin: Speech Genres and Other Late Essays*, pp. 10–59. Austin: University of Texas Press.

Bakhtin, M. M. (1987) "Forms of Time and the Chronotope in the Novel," in M. Holquist (ed.), *The Dialogic Imagination: Four Essays by M. M. Bakhtin*, pp. 84–158. Austin: University of Texas Press.

Bal, M. (2003) "Meanwhile: Literature in an Expanded Field," in I. Hoving, F. Korsten, and E. van Alphen (eds.), *Africa and Its Significant Others: Forty Years of Intercultural Entanglement*, pp. 183–97. Amsterdam: Rodopi.

Chan, S. (2003) *Robert Mugabe: A Life of Power and Violence*. Ann Arbor: The University of Michigan Press.

Chan, S. (2006) "Mugabe's Last Gasp," *Prospect*, June.

Charamba, G. (2005) "Zimbabwe Operation Restores Order," *New African* 442 (July).

Chipamaunga, E. (1983) *A Fighter for Freedom*. Gweru: Mambo Press.

Chipamaunga, E. O. Z. (1998) *Chains of Freedom*. Harare: Zimbabwe Publishing House.

Chipamaunga, E. O. Z. (2000) *Feeding Freedom*. Harare: Mercury Press.

Chiwome, E. (1998) "The Interface of Orality and Literacy in the Zimbabwean Novel," *Research in African Literatures* 29(2): 1–22.

Crisis in Zimbabwe Coalition. (2003) "Constitutional and Legal Issues," in *Dialogue and Transition Conference Report*, pp. 33–5. Harare: Crisis in Zimbabwe Coalition.

Dangarembga, T. (2006) *The Book of Not*. Banbury, UK: Ayebia Clarke Publishing.

Doležel, L. (1990) *Occidental Poetics: Tradition and Progress*. Lincoln: University of Nebraska Press.

Dowden, R. (2005) "We've Got to Talk to Mugabe," *The Times*, May 16.

Dowden, R. (2006) "Engaging with Mugabe," *Round Table* 95(384): 283–6.

Gono, G. (2005) "Capitulation Is Not an Option," *New African* 441 (June).

Herald Reporter. (2005) "Rural Voters Hailed," *The Zimbabwe Herald*, April 11.

Kaarsholm, P. (1991) "From Decadence to Authenticity and Beyond: Fantasies and Mythologies of War in Rhodesia and Zimbabwe, 1965–1985," in P. Kaarsholm (ed.), *Cultural Struggle and Development in Southern Africa*, pp. 33–60. Harare: Baobab Books.

Kahari, G. (1990) *The Rise of the Shona Novel*. Gweru: Mambo Press.

Kamete, A. Y. (2006) "The Return of the Jettisoned: ZANU-PF's Crack at 'Re-Urbanising' in Harare," *Journal of Southern African Studies* 32(2): 255–71.

Kanengoni, A. (2003) "One Hundred Days with Robert Mugabe," *The Daily News*, Harare, April 12.

Kanengoni, A. (2004) "The Long Way Home: One Man's Story," in D. Harold-Barry (ed.), *Zimbabwe: The Past Is the Future*, pp. 47–51. Harare: Weaver Press.

Lachmann, R. (1997) *Memory and Literature: Intertextuality in Russian Modernism*, trans. R. Sellars and A. Wall. Minneapolis: University of Minnesota Press.

Machingauta, R. M. (1994) *Detective Ridgemore Riva*. Harare: Zimbabwe Publishing House.

Mahoso, T. (2004) "MDC Born Senile, Living in Denial," *The Sunday Mail*, Harare, April 4.

Marechera, D. (1978) *The House of Hunger*. London: Heinemann.

Maredza, C. (1987) *Harurwa*. Harare: Longman Zimbabwe.

Maredza, C. (2002) *When God Went on Leave*. Harare: Norumedzo Enterprises.

Maredza, C. (2004) *I Put It to You*. Harare: Norumedzo Enterprises.

Masitera, L. (2000) *The Trail*. Harare: Now I Can Play Publications.

Mbembe, A. (1991) "Power and Obscenity in the Post-colonial Period: The Case of Cameroon," in J. Manor (ed.), *Rethinking Third World Politics*, pp. 166–82. London: Longman.

Mbembe, A. (1997) "The 'Thing' and Its Double in Cameroonian Cartoons," in K. Barber (ed.), *Readings in African Popular Culture*, pp. 151–63. Oxford: James Currey.

Mbembe, A. (2001) "The Aesthetics of Vulgarity," in *On the Postcolony*, pp. 102–41. Berkeley: University of California Press.

Meldrum, A. (2005) "As Country Heads for Disaster, Zimbabwe Calls for Return of White Farmers," *Guardian* (UK), May 21.

Mugabe, R. G. (2001) *Inside the Third Chimurenga*. Harare: The Department of Information and Publicity, Office of the President & Cabinet.

Mugabe, R. (2004) "Zim Emerges from Difficult Phase: Address on the Occasion of the 59th Session of the United Nations General Assembly, New York, on Wednesday," *The Herald*, September 24.

Mugabe, R. (2005) "We Won't Go Back to the Commonwealth," *New African* 441 (June).

Mutasa, G. (1996) *The Bridge (Two Novellas)*. London: Macmillan.

n.a. (2005) *Traitors Do Much Damage to National Goals*. Harare: The Department of Information and Publicity, ZANU PF HQ.

Potts, D. (2006) "'Restoring Order'? Operation Murambatsvina and the Urban Crisis in Zimbabwe," *Journal of Southern African Studies* 32(2): 273–91.

Primorac, R. (2004) "'The Place of the Woman Is the Place of the Imagination': Yvonne Vera Interviewed by Ranka Primorac," *The Journal of Commonwealth Literature* 39(3): 157–71.

Primorac, R. (2005a) "The Eye of the Nation: Reading Ideology and Genre in a Zimbabwean Thriller," in R. Muponde and R. Primorac (eds.), *Versions of Zimbabwe: New Approaches to Literature and Culture*, pp. 161–76. Harare: Weaver Press.

Primorac, R. (2005b) "Rhodesians Never Die? The Zimbabwean Crisis and the Revival of the Rhodesian Discourse." Unpublished paper presented at the "Cultural Nationalism and Social Critique" Cadbury Conference, Centre of West African Studies, University of Birmingham, May 13–14.

Primorac, R. (2006) *The Place of Tears: The Novel and Politics in Modern Zimbabwe*. London: I. B. Tauris.

Ranger, T. (2004) "Nationalist Historiography, Patriotic History and the History of the Nation: the Struggle over the Past in Zimbabwe," *Journal of Southern African Studies* 30(2): 213–33.

Ricoeur, P. (1980) "Narrative Time," *Critical Inquiry* 7(1): 169–90.

Sassen, S. (2000) "Spatialities and Temporalities of the Global: Elements for a Theorization," *Public Culture* 12(1): 215–32.

Simmel, G. (1959 [1911]) "The Adventure," in K. H. Wolff (ed.), *Georg Simmel 1858–1918*, pp. 243–58. Columbus: Ohio State University Press.

Solidarity Peace Trust. (2005) "Interim Report on the Zimbabwean Government's 'Urban Cleansing' and Forced Eviction Campaign," <http://www.solidaritypeacetrust.org.za/> Accessed June 27, 2005.

Solidarity Peace Trust. (2006) "'Meltdown' – Murambatsvina One Year On," <http://www.solidaritypeacdetrust.org/reports/meltdown.pdf> Accessed August 30, 2006.

Sylvester, C. (2003) "Remembering and Forgetting 'Zimbabwe': Towards a Third Transition," in Paul Gready (ed.), *Political Transition: Politics and Cultures*, pp. 29–52. London: Pluto Press.

Todorov, T. (1977) *The Poetics of Prose*, trans. Richard Howard. Oxford: Basil Blackwell.

Vambe, M. (2006) "The Struggle for Land in the Shona Novel: Allegory, Seizure and Betrayal," *The Round Table* 95(384): 255–72.

Chapter 11

The Mediation of "Terror": Authority, Journalism, and the Stockwell Shooting

Stuart Price

Migrants, caught up in and driven by
the globalized sweep of late capitalism,
seek to become members of risk society . . .
but . . . pay the price of such risk with the currency
most available to them ...
that of their bodies and even their lives
Parvati Nair, "Voicing Risk," p. 67

Introduction

This chapter examines the thematic content of material generated by the British press in the immediate aftermath of the Stockwell shooting (July 22, 2005), in which the Brazilian electrician Jean Charles de Menezes was killed by armed assailants officially identified as Metropolitan police officers.[1] In the course of the analysis, a number of themes, or categories of meaning, have been identified as particularly significant: the perennial question of the "balance" between security and civil liberty; the subjective positioning of readers/spectators as moral participants in the "dilemma" faced by armed officers;[2] the production of mediated conceptions of identity and citizenship; the conflation of terrorism, immigration, and asylum; and, finally, the characterization of an individual death as a tragedy[3] within the discourse of guilt and innocence.[4]

Based upon these observations of press performance, broader political issues are brought into focus; in particular, armed police intervention is examined within the context of other authoritarian measures ostensibly designed to reinforce public security. The position outlined in this chapter is thus fairly simple: that current "anti-terror" policy does not emerge solely from the conviction that new tactics are required to meet an enhanced threat. My contention here is that contemporary procedures like Operation Kratos[5] (which includes the authorization to shoot "suspected suicide bombers"),[6] have clear historical precedents in counter-insurgency operations, and also provide evidence of a more ambitious agenda. This is the determination, amongst some elements of the "security state," to secure a much greater paramilitary capability than currently exists. This power may then be deployed in circumstances that may well fall short of the "crisis paradigm" disseminated by official sources but, in an attempt to justify the extension of coercive force, the narrative of public emergency can nonetheless be repeated within media forms. In propagating a "worst case" scenario, Britain's political executive has refined (through trial and error), a number of techniques which represent not so much an open "war" against its own citizens (Bull 2006), but rather the secretive *over-production* of repressive capacity. When this power is applied to real situations, the result is the kind of overkill characteristic of the Stockwell shooting.

In tracing the appearance in the press of "defensive" themes (where a theme is a substantial and familiar aggregation of subject matter), I would suggest that much of the mediated narrative material generated in the press served only to obscure the essential question that the killing of Jean Charles de Menezes should have raised: the degree to which it represented both a dangerous concentration of lethal force, and the *strategic* diffusion of responsibility. In its first acknowledged appearance, at least, the procedures mobilized under the aegis of Kratos were characterized by breakdowns in communication; yet this very confusion may have allowed senior commanders, surveillance personnel, and firearms officers to act with impunity. They were in effect protected by the "catalogue of errors" referred to in the IPCC (Independent Police Complaints Commission) report, so that no single individual could be charged with a crime.[7] The operatives on the ground were further protected by anonymity, a condition which remained in place during the Inquest held in 2008.

Press confusion and docility during the initial period of confusion may be attributed to the existence of a number of structural factors.

These include media reliance on authoritative sources, the use of pre-existing frames of reference in an attempt to categorize unfolding events, and the nature of crisis communications during a period of *mediated* vigilance. The difficulty faced by senior journalists and editors was how to modify their initial perspectives, which expressed no substantial reservations about the shooting, while maintaining their broad support for both the police and a "shoot to kill" policy.[8] This challenge, I would argue, was met (at least in discursive terms) by drawing attention to the "exceptional" nature of the event. The reports that emerged in the days following the death represented, therefore, an uncomfortable reformulation of the earliest media responses.

Framing the Event: Authority and Utterance

Just after 3.45 p.m. on the day of the Stockwell shooting, Sir Ian Blair, the Metropolitan Police Commissioner, announced that the death of a suspect had been directly linked to the "on-going and expanding anti-terrorist operation," and provided a brief rationale for the use of fire-arms. The incident was indeed related to the hunt for the failed bombers of July 21, in the sense that it was one by-product of the investigation, but the suggestion seemed to be that the dead man was implicated in the attempt to detonate explosive devices. Press reports, however, did not examine this issue; instead, they carried excerpts from the official announcement, and appeared to give a reasonably faithful account of the terms used.

If, however, journalists had examined the police version of the original source, they would have discovered a strange discrepancy between the account given by the Commissioner, and their own stories. So, for example, *The Financial Times* online of July 22, 2005, BBC News online of July 22, the *Sun* of July 23, and *The Sunday Times* of July 24, all reproduced Blair's explanation for the killing. According to these sources, the Commissioner had declared that the suspect had "refused to obey police," "refused to obey instructions," or, more fully, "refused to obey police instructions." Yet, according to the police website (www.police.uk/content), Blair had said no more than that the victim had been "challenged and refused to obey."[9]

This seemingly trivial difference between the terms used raises an important question: had police excised the last one or two words because they wished to play down their own responsibility, and had they done so in order to obscure the fact that no "police instructions" had been issued before the shots were fired? Even in the case of the truncated version, it seemed clear that an individual had been shot dead because he had failed to comply with an order, not necessarily because he was about to carry out a violent act.[10] This interpretation was not, however, suggested within the newspaper reports that followed.[11] Yet the answer to this puzzle may lie in material that was not initially accessible. The minutes of the Metropolitan Police Authority of March 21, 2002[12] reveal that officers had two options for stopping suspected suicide bombers, described as follows: "if 100% sure head Shot," and "if not sure, challenge from a position of safety." There is the possibility here that the first option does not require the officer to issue any challenge. It is this kind of information that suggests that the use of the Kratos "technique" should not be regarded as a "mistake." In 2002, the police emphasized that a resort to extreme measures was unlikely, while describing the "very positive action" that might be needed to stop a suicide bomber (Metropolitan Police Authority minutes, March 21, 2002). They also noted that "any officer involved in the implementation of these tactics will be subject to full and proper scrutiny and investigation" and finished the paragraph by stating that "we [the police] are not above the law" (ibid.). Evidence from Tube passengers who witnessed the shooting, given at the 2008 Inquest, ran counter to official claims that a challenge had been issued: they had heard no shout of "armed police" before officers opened fire.[13] Such an utterance, it is worth noting, does not actually represent an order, the neglect of which could justify firing a weapon. In fact, one officer revealed that he had only shouted "armed police" once he had decided to shoot de Menezes.[14]

During the initial phase of media coverage, however, the dependence on available police sources was hardly surprising, since the credibility of any public remark is not based simply on content, but depends to a large extent on its source,[15] the status of the speakers, and the setting in which it appears.[16] The inability of journalists to contest Blair's utterance lay partly in their predetermined role as subordinate elements in a hierarchical structure, so that the overall relationship between news media and authoritative sources can be characterized as one of press dependence. In other words, the role of journalists was to act as conduits for information. It is also clear that, in ordinary circumstances, journalists already rely on the police as "primary definers" for many of the "crime news stories" they receive (Franklin et al. 2005: 248, after Harcup 2004).[17] In addition, media workers are forced to recognize the dual character of the authority invested in the police, where authority is both the place of origin for a particular policy or enterprise, and the "right" of an established power to expect or enforce compliance (Watt 1982: 11).

The Metropolitan Police may be acknowledged, therefore, not only as a repository of certain forms of legal knowledge, but also as an essential element of the state's "preponderance of force" (Gill 2003: 5). Its personnel make up one part of the state's "administrative staff," which is trained to uphold "the claims to the *monopoly* of the legitimate use of physical force in the enforcement of its order" (Weber, cited in Pierson 1996: 7). The police appear therefore as both administrators and enforcers of the social order.[18] It is this concentration of powers that helps to explain, for example, the existence of the Independent Police Complaints Commission, and which reflects the anxiety of the IPCC to "increase confidence in the police complaints system."[19] The authoritative institutional position of the police also calls for other forms of accountability. So, for example, the Metropolitan Police Authority (MPA) is designed to provide a bureaucratic overview of police work, though it is clear from the Authority's minutes that the members were kept in the dark about certain developments.[20]

From an official perspective, however, *public* statements like the one issued by Blair are not meant to be definitive or even entirely truthful. They are conceived instead as holding operations, intended to fulfill formal requirements, offering no more than is strictly necessary. The "safest" declaration, considering its inevitable reproduction within larger mediated narratives, is one that avoids complexity. The earliest police announcement, following the principle of simplicity, was indeed relatively straightforward,[21] but the tendency to produce forms of explanation was already in evidence, providing the first indication that official sources were attempting to justify the actions of armed police and their commanders.

In many of the early reports, therefore, critical perspectives were subsumed in the rush to produce formulaic observations, based on the reanimation of *established* themes.[22] Harris, in the *Daily Mail* of July 23, is a good example: he reproduced the misleading perspective that the *victim* was "linked to last Thursday's London bombings" (Harris 2005). Even in the simplest of processes, it is therefore possible to observe the use of "framing" devices in the presentation of experience, where framing is the process of selecting "some aspects of a perceived reality" which are then made "more salient in a communicative text" in order to promote a particular point of view or perspective (Simons 2006: 2, after Entman 1993: 52). The *Daily Mail* journalist had not, of course, invented the rather subtle distinction suggested in Blair's remarks, but had simply made it explicit.

It appears that the initial statement had encouraged the assumption that the link between the shooting and the investigation was substantial and legitimate. Ian Blair had achieved this outcome through the power of *implicature*, the practice of creating meanings through suggestion or implication rather than literal forms of description (Grice 1989: 44). His statement may be seen therefore as the generation of an appropriate *alibi* for timely purposes.[23] This cover story addressed the general conception of "terrorist"[24] activity, and played on assumptions about the conduct expected from a police officer. Reinforcing these notions was not, however, ultimately helpful to the authorities, because they include the expectation that a suspect is supposed to be made aware that he or she is facing *armed* officers. The claims made by the Commissioner were only plausible because his listeners remained in ignorance of two essential factors: (1) a change in police tactics which had already moved to a "shoot to kill" policy under Operation Kratos (see below); and (2) the actual circumstances of the shooting, in which no challenge was given and no disobedience offered.[25]

Surveillance and "Shoot to Kill"

When Mann expressed the conviction that the executive leaderships of the "capitalist democracies" may suffer from dishonesty and corruption, but do not "brazenly expropriate or kill [their] enemies" or "dare to overturn legal traditions" (Mann 2003: 55), it was probably difficult to anticipate the exact extent of current practice, which includes "extraordinary rendition" (Rejali 2007: 504) and the growth of the philosophy of military "pre-emption." In the wake of the attacks carried out on September 11, 2001, the demand for a tougher attitude to terrorist conspiracy was not entirely new, but did revive a number of dormant or hidden practices.

Although "9/11" is cited as the origin of much "anti-terror" activity, precedents may be found in the growth of "low intensity" conflicts, fought by colonial powers after World War II.[26] The nascence of post-World War II coercive authority, therefore, together with the increasing predominance of the secret state, may be traced back to British and American plans to control the development of European nations after the defeat of Nazism (Ganser 2005). The CIA and MI6 were the "executive agents" behind the creation of clandestine networks of armed groups that eventually "fought a secret war against the forces of the left" (Ganser 2005: 2). In some cases, the construction of a "national security state" would lead to the imprisonment and maltreatment of a generation of radicals, socialists, and trade union cadres, in which the existence of armed conflict and "terrorism" was used as an excuse for outright repression of all internal opposition.[27]

In Britain, increasing preference for a "shoot to kill" policy was supposedly based on the simple perception that "significant gaps" existed in the state's mobilization against "suicide bombing delivered by a person" (*Panorama*, "Stockwell: Countdown to Killing," 2006). In examining this rationale, my point is not that such a conviction was completely unfounded but that, in common with all forms of structural change, a particular aspect of existing circumstance is selected as the justification for a more general transformation in policy.[28] The adoption of the "suicide" rationale, we are told, led to the creation of Operation Kratos. Yet, as with other "responses" to specific threats, precedents had already been established.[29]

The reality of such encounters does not, however, correspond to the conditions set out by security chiefs and military planners. So, when evidence has emerged at enquiries and inquests that particular killings have been unorthodox (such as the execution of wounded suspects), then the narratives composed *after the fact* by operatives are adjusted to match the range of activity which might be deemed reasonable in the circumstances. This often includes descriptions of suspects making movements that led the operatives to believe that the insurgents were about to fire guns or detonate bombs (Urban 1992: 183). A similar example of this tendency was revealed during the 2008 Inquest, when one of the officers said he had been convinced that de Menezes was a suicide bomber because the suspect had walked toward him.[30]

In the case of Operation Kratos, Barbara Wilding, currently Chief Constable of the South Wales police, was chosen to lead the "Suicide Bomber Working Party," and was part of a group which traveled to Israel to learn how the Israeli Defense Force and police dealt with individuals engaged in "spontaneous suicide attacks" (*Panorama* 2006). The application of Israeli methods to the British context may appear surprising, but was presented as a necessary adjustment made in order to meet a special and extraordinary circumstance. The point, however, is that the British security state was in the process of refining techniques already established in armed confrontation with nationalist opponents in "colonial" territories. Yet, in adopting the behaviors of a client power which is "internally" *mobilized for war* and which is prepared to make aggressive incursions into the territory of deliberately subordinated enemies, the possibility of occasional episodes of armed "response" being directed against certain ethnic minorities within the British population cannot be entirely discounted.

A sense of unease with this extraordinary condition emerges in even the right-wing press. The *Daily Mail* journalist Paul Harris began his story, for example, by noting that "it [Stockwell tube station] might seem an unlikely front line in Britain's war against terror," with people caught up in "the kind of drama more normally seen in the Middle East" (Harris 2005). Here, the "drama" of terrorism, supposedly belonging to a distant sphere of conflict, is brought into the realm of current realities "in full view of terrified passengers" (ibid.). The emphasis placed on the visual corroboration of the shooting through the testimony of eyewitnesses confirms the relocation of the event within an urban and *British* setting. The vague invocation of the "appropriate" location for terrorism (a generalized "Middle East") may remind the reader, though perhaps it does so unintentionally, that the root causes of violent dissent lie in unresolved social, political, and religious conditions, exacerbated by the "West's" inability to mediate in an unequal struggle between opposing powers. Harris's remarks represent the shadowy existence of important historical issues, questions that should be made more explicit if they are to produce an understanding of "anti-terrorist" actions undertaken by the state.

Although the actual confrontation with suicide bombers in the UK and Israel may appear identical, the different political conditions that exist within the two nations suggest that the implementation of Kratos may entail the growth of paramilitary capability.[31] The immediate consequence of the new policy was that pre-emptive killing became a *general principle*; and once this was established, the *interpretation* of circumstances could itself produce the emergency leading to the application of "shoot to kill."[32] In this sense, the Stockwell incident represented the inevitable execution of policy in a real-life scenario, a "dry run" which could be interpreted as a demonstration of its power. The situation envisaged in planning exercises – the instant incapacitation of a bomber by delivering shots to the head – set up the possibility of an application of force in similar conditions. Once the rules of engagement had been set, the initiation of the action proved difficult to control. Officers were given operational autonomy, and were protected by the diffusion of responsibility (see above) that meant neither those directing the operation nor those firing the shots could be held accountable.

Suicide bombing had, therefore, provided the rationale for the creation of a structure that favored a *pre-emptive* act: based on the discretion of an individual acting in an "emergency," this created the opportunity to execute suspects if enough of the necessary conditions could be argued *in retrospect* to have existed at the time of the incident, just as alibis were assembled in Northern Ireland (Urban 1992). The fact that the Stockwell killing was shown subsequently not to have fulfilled the required criteria could not have compelled the security state to reconsider the use of a "shoot to kill" policy. In fact, calling the incident "a mistake," was in effect to argue that the procedure itself was justified, and simply needed a more suitable target to fulfill its true potential.

Surveillance and Mediation

The genesis of the whole process was the *identification* by police of four men thought responsible for a series of attempts to detonate explosive devices on the London transport system on July 21, 2005. This helped establish the immediate circumstances in which Jean Charles de Menezes was killed.[33] The circulation of the suspects' images within print and electronic media, accompanied by the production of official posters appealing for information, was based on CCTV pictures[34] released by the Metropolitan police on July 22, 2005. The perception that their targets could be assigned to a particular ethnic group was one of the reasons why some, though not all, officers classified de Menezes as a possible terrorist.[35]

The provision of the CCTV images allowed newspapers to carry their own reproductions, which in some cases included additional captions giving details of suspects' clothing and subsequent movements. This represents a clear move from the use of image as mere illustration to the use of image as a form of generic representation; this, in turn, suggested a general consensus that the press should help apprehend the individuals concerned. The *Guardian* of July 23, for example, printed such information on its front page, under the headline "Faces of the Suspects," while the *Independent* of the same date devoted its cover to a declaration that identified "THE FOUR MOST WANTED."[36]

Such forms of publicity conform to the precepts held by state agencies, in which all channels of public communication are expected to help disseminate appeals in times of crisis. Yet the compliance of media organizations in obeying authoritarian norms, expressed through their readiness to assume a particular *generic* appearance, is bound to focus attention on their ability to maintain a broader *discursive* autonomy.[37] The fabrication of front pages resembling "wanted" posters does not necessarily suggest complete submission to a state agenda (since alternative perspectives may appear in other reports within the same publication), but it is nonetheless evidence of an alignment with a disciplinary edict.[38]

Any discussion of editorial procedures in this case should ask (1) why CCTV material was presented in the format described above, (2) if the reproduction of photographs and information in this way was a serious attempt to help identify the individuals concerned, and (3) whether or not the strategic prominence assigned to this representation was decided in consultation with the police.[39] The front page of the *Daily Mirror* on July 22 provides an instructive contrast in this respect, posing a question ("IS THIS HOW WE MUST NOW LIVE?"), which, unlike the dominant practice followed in the other papers, is at least open to multiple interpretations.

Although it might seem absurd for a newspaper to depart entirely from convention and use the CCTV evidence of these particular activities to illustrate a discussion of, for example, civil liberties, it is *exactly* the circulation of closed-circuit images under "incontestable" circumstances which reinforces the wider and largely unreflective reproduction of public surveillance *as a principle*. Lyon describes this trend as one that moves toward "pre-emptive surveillance and 'categorical suspicion'" (2003: 168). McGrath, examining these forms of electronic scrutiny, depicts the predominant frame of debate (engineered through discourses of privacy and crime), as ideological because they hide as much as they reveal about surveillance society (McGrath 2004: 2).

Surveillance alone is not much use in the general reproduction of a culture, unless it can become an accepted *generic* form through which people can recognize their own activities. In other words, it cannot remain a private condition, viewed only by police, secret agents, and private security firms. Surveillance comes to exemplify the trajectory of a public culture only when it is publicized. Television, for example, reproduces CCTV footage and hidden camera work in news reports, undercover investigations, and entertainment. The cinema, in addition, has only to mimic on screen the appearance of surveillance to demonstrate the relationship between the public and authority.

Where terrorism is concerned, CCTV and other forms of recorded observation provide an important part of the "validation" of the state's role as overseer. This, of course, makes the original failure to produce CCTV footage of Jean Charles' movements (when a good half dozen cameras may have tracked his progress) into an expression of the coercive state's inconsistency and untrustworthiness. It also gives rise to the plethora of conspiracy theories that allow for an easy dismissal of current policies as a cover for illegal activity.

The creation of a convincing sense of heightened national security ultimately depends, however, not on the state's rhetoric about terrorism, but on the ability of media forms to present the "terrorist threat" as an autonomous sphere of activity. In other words, violent conspiracy must be presented first and foremost as a genuine *discovery*, rather than the partial or fanciful creation of informants, intelligence agencies, politicians, or indeed the media. Media institutions, for their part, present their own activities as a response to, rather than an enlargement of, existing material conditions; in plain terms, they retain the notion of objectivity as an important component of their claim to even-handedness. Notions which threaten to destabilize our supposed faith in the authenticity of representation, such as Boorstin's theory of "pseudo-events" (1961), which argues that manufactured phenomena like news conferences replace democratic exchange, are not accepted by journalists *as a critique of their own practices*; rather, media organizations retain allegiance to "objective" standards, and assign the exercise of dubious strategies to a separate political arena of spin and manipulation.

The animation of such issues can be interpreted as part of a general reflection on the effects of hierarchy and structure, in which a social order or formation composed of established, durable institutions produces standardized practices, forms of exchange, and behavior. Any analysis of media coverage is therefore bound to animate discussions about news values, agenda setting, journalistic practices, and ultimately the exercise of power in a neoliberal democracy.

Where news media follow the ideal of objective reporting, they can generate highly principled journalism; where objectivity is designed to reinforce formal oppositions between "the truth claims of the antagonists in conflicting situations" (Altschull 1995: 64), it becomes no more than "a strategic ritual" (Tuchman 1972). In the early days of the de Menezes case, corroboration of one set of claims actually delayed the revelation of the truth. The use of eyewitness accounts was used as the basis for a "factual" insight into events, but the persistent reproduction of errors proved difficult to escape once these reports had been circulated.

The *Independent*, for example, based part of its July 22 report on the testimony of the eyewitness Mark Whitby. It noted that "he had been sitting on the train reading his paper as it was stationary with its doors open in Stockwell station . . . he said that an Asian man ran on to the train pursued by three plainclothes police officers" (Press Association 2005). In this case, the journalist is careful to attribute statements to the witness; the misidentification of de Menezes as Asian revealed the assumptions made by Whitby, but these are not the responsibility of the newspaper. The notion that the suspect was "Asian" forms part of a recently disseminated conception: the threat of "home grown" terrorism in which "alienated" British citizens (described in the press nonetheless by ethnicity rather than simply by nationality) turn against their "own country." The eventual appearance of a debate over the dead man's innocence crucially turned on the fact that he was not a disaffected national but the citizen of another state motivated by the apparently laudable project of self-improvement.

Many reports at this stage, however, despite some attempts at qualification, helped to circulate a series of entirely bogus details, dramatic touches that took on a life of their own, directing the story's development. The *Guardian* of July 23 described "bewildered eyewitnesses" who "told how they had witnessed the moment . . . when the suspect was repeatedly shot" (Cobain, Cowan, and Norton-Taylor 2005). This, which may be regarded as uncontroversial, is followed by the assertion that "all described the man as wearing a bulky, winter coat, despite the warm weather, and at least one said he thought he spotted a belt with wires running from it" (ibid.). The "bulky coat" and the phrase "despite the warm weather" appeared in numerous stories, while the reference to the belt and wires was attributed to one Anthony Larkin, who in fact claimed that "I saw this guy who appeared to have a bomb belt and wires coming out" (ibid.).

A day later, the *Daily Express* had turned these assumptions into a coherent narrative: "The Asian man, who was wearing a heavy padded jacket despite the warm temperature, was originally thought to have been wearing a bomb belt" (Willey and Flanagan 2005).[40] Perhaps the most remarkable replication of the "bomb belt" myth appeared in a drawing on page 5 of the *Daily Mail*'s July 23 edition, which carried a large cartoon drawing of plainclothes police, about to shoot a man wearing a belt with wires protruding. No belt with wires attached and no bulky jacket had ever existed beyond the imagination of eyewitnesses, newspaper cartoonists, and "graphic artists." The police did not intervene to correct these impressions. No retraction of, or apology for, a series of misleading reports was ever produced; the "state of emergency"[41] and the "disposable" nature of print seemed to provide its own justification.

It is worth observing that the material character of the press has been shaped, at least until the advent of on-line journalism,[42] by its appearance as an "ephemeral" physical product. Free of certain temporal constraints, to the extent that it can be consumed at any point within and beyond the day of publication, print is nonetheless limited by its apparent transformation into "stale news" the day after publication. Unlike television reportage, which is able to "clear the space" for more open-ended coverage of the unexpected (especially in the case of "rolling news"), the press is unable to *simulate co-presence* with its audience, or provide the spatial/temporal anchorage which audiences are offered during "live" broadcasts.[43]

In the case of Stockwell, the fact that no news organization had direct access to the immediate site ensured dependence on official statements and first-hand accounts; these consisted of police conferences and press releases, together with eyewitness reports. Crucially, the symbolic production of meaning was limited by the inability of the public to "view" the scene through electronic media[44] (unlike, for example, the destruction of the Twin Towers on September 11, 2001). This circumstance generated alternative forms of visual narration.

Until photographs from the shooting were leaked to the press, a number of representational phenomena, based on verbal accounts, supplied the deficit and were used to dramatize the course of events. Diagrammatic "narratives," cartoons, and photographs all contributed to mistaken accounts of the shooting. Jean Charles de Menezes was portrayed refusing to stop, vaulting barriers, running down escalators, and finally being shot by his pursuers. Press coverage of the Stockwell shooting then evolved from its initial phase, which repeated official assertions about the death of a terrorist suspect linked to the events of July 21, to a confused recognition that the victim was not connected with the police enquiry.

Entering the Domain of Risk: "Tragedy," Guilt, and Innocence

If the news media "partly function to disseminate appropriate values and reinforce moral boundaries" (Manning 2001: 27), then this role may be emphasized during those events which most clearly seem to offer an aberration from the norm. In the case of "terrorist" activity, journalists composing news stories may give prominence to malevolent acts from this *implicitly judgmental position*. Sub-editors, columnists, and leader writers, however, take up certain details of the established narrative in order to emphasize those aspects that seem to confirm the *explicitly* "political" perspectives they espouse. In sum, material is inflected in order to resonate with the perceived prejudices of the readership. So, for example, the *Daily Express* produced a front page that traded on an established theme: the supposed correlation between seeking asylum, reliance on benefit, and antipathy toward the host nation. Here, a dominant agenda is pursued by fitting new material into an existing perspective. In a similar vein, the *Daily Mail* of the same date produced a front page that discussed the question of asylum. Alternative themes that might have been animated remained in embryonic form.[45]

While the tendency to pass on fashions of speech and arresting narrative episodes is a common feature of everyday conversation, in the context of journalistic practice the repetition of particular incidents and images can establish them as unassailable *points of reference*. It is this process – the circulation of clichés and sometimes quite prosaic forms of explanation – which provides the basic elements of a burgeoning *ideological folklore*.[46]

So, to take an example of this discursive process, the discovery that the police had been operating a shoot-to-kill policy could be discussed in the press as a pragmatic response to an extraordinary threat, and may therefore be used to circumvent the issue of civil liberties. An instance of this may be found in Melanie Phillips's comments on the same development, which showed that she could mimic the propositional content[47] of an account that police and security sources had presented as a justification for their actions.[48] Once such a position had been established, it could be developed without needing further direction from source (in this case, the police and other authorities). A close identity in political outlook between social actors in the media and representatives of established authority is enough to guarantee the generation of particular themes.

A condition of "emergency" provides the alibi for such collaboration, allowing many commentators to reproduce official explanations despite the clear and widely shared perception that provisional utterances should be treated with caution. Another related question is the commonsense expectation of a significant difference between editorial or personal opinion on the one hand, and standard reportage on the other. This belief disguises the fact that the latter is equally capable of reproducing not only *uncritical* versions of official briefings, but also politically conformist positions within news accounts.

In the *Guardian*'s July 23 report, for example (see above), the shooting was described in a simple manner ("a man was chased by officers and shot around five times in the head at point-blank range as he lay on the floor of a train"), but framed through an almost obsequious narrative introduction which read, "the urgency of the operation – and the determination of police to prevent any further suicide attacks – were demonstrated dramatically at an underground station in Stockwell, south London, yesterday."[49] Factors which might explain the readiness of journalists to maintain such positions range from the assertion that the institutions they serve are "agencies of social control" (Altschull 1995: xix), through perspectives which emphasize simple market calculation, to the belief that both news and other established practices such as the law are "disciplinary and normalizing discourses . . . fundamentally concerned with *policing*" (Ericson, Baranek, and Chan 1991: 7), where policing is defined as a mechanism for maintaining "moral" perspectives.

Although journalists across media forms co-operate with authority in emphasizing the "performative significance" of an important event (Blondheim and Liebes 2003: 186), newspaper stories rely on a variety of techniques to attract the interest of their readers. Acting essentially through the power of *display*, newspapers, certainly at times of crisis, offer readers an emotional connection with the events they describe. They also present a form of continuity in which certain occurrences are aligned with the imagined horizons of their readers. The treatment of the Stockwell incident, for example, bore a close resemblance to mediation of the Forest Gate assault in 2006, in which Abul Koyair was shot and injured by police: both events were set, in their initial phases at least, within the framework of terrorist rather than purely criminal discourses,[50] and both had to accommodate the eventual intrusion of a "counter-narrative" based on the (nonetheless contested) innocence of the victims.[51]

Yet the particular circumstances of the Stockwell shooting reveal *a crisis of the state's own making*, a rupture in the perceived character of democratic procedures; the attempted resolution was to attribute the ultimate cause of de Menezes' death to terrorist activity and to exculpate the police. The attempt to repair the disruption can be found in those forms of explanation that employ the concept of a "tragedy." Once again, the origins of this idea appear in the announcement made by the authorities on July 23: "Scotland Yard admitted Mr Menezes had been shot by mistake and apologized to his family for the "tragedy" (BBC News online, Wednesday, August 17, 2005). The theme was then circulated by commentators like Tony Parsons, whose reaction appeared under the title "A TRAGEDY – BUT POLICE STILL DESERVE OUR SUPPORT," and began with the rhetorical assertion that the "last thing in the world we needed right now was screaming front-page headlines with the words POLICE and BLUNDER in the same sentence" (*Daily Mirror*, July 25, 2005).

Parsons clearly reveals his understanding of the mechanism of cohesive association between terms and the production of simple themes. The idea of police error is, however, a notion he is anxious to dismiss, even as his remark calls it into view. Where the discourse of tragedy and innocence failed to prevent critical attacks upon the police handling of the event, other themes were rapidly deployed, casting some doubt on the sincerity of journalistic accounts that appeared more liberal. For example, broadly sympathetic but vaguely patronizing positions which turned on the notion of de Menezes' attempts at betterment (such as this in *The Times*: "The Hard-working Son Who Moved to London in Search of a Better Life," by Bird, Rajeev, and Hennigan 2005), and that might have animated discussion of "multicultural citizenship" (Isin 2000) and globalization, were curtailed by a countervailing process in which the victim's entitlement to reside in Britain was questioned.

The *Daily Mirror* of July 29, 2005, for instance, declared in a headline over a page 10 article "BRAZILIAN'S VISA 2 YEARS OUT OF DATE." The most questionable tactic used to discredit the dead man was finally dismissed when the *Independent* revealed on April 26, 2006, that police had dropped an allegation of rape against de Menezes after his DNA was found not to match a sample taken from the victim of an attack. The circulation of this allegation had, nonetheless, helped to throw de Menezes' innocence into doubt. In effect, calls for unity with police during this period could be understood as an attempt to reinforce social solidarity and demonstrate defiance against terrorism. Such claims may also have entailed, however, an unquestioning support for the principle of pre-emptive execution. Other individuals, as blameless as de Menezes but identified as a threat, may quite unwittingly have entered the domain of risk.[52]

Conclusion

All academic studies of mediated incidents, whatever their particular theoretical provenance, recognize that the structure of any public occurrence is partly determined by the act of representation; most also admit that events have a separate existence from their "dominant" mode of signification.[53] Media forms, therefore, constitute the primary location for the production and *circulation* of meaning, basing their habitual narrative practices upon a potent amalgam of accurate information and mistaken assumptions. The generic conventions applied to the "core" material gathered by the press (official statements, eyewitness accounts, visual material produced at the scene, etc.) are largely automatic, and often unreflective practices. As Bruck observes, the media may well employ "their own codes and conventions" (Bruck 1992: 142) when composing narratives, but rely on perspectives generated elsewhere. In effect, "the discursive material they work with . . . is not their own" (ibid.).

My contention here is that established symbolic practices seen in newspaper reports may be understood as the mobilization of pre-existing themes,[54] which are then consolidated by columnists into explicit positions.[55] Reports of the shooting, therefore, typify the *dramatization*[56] of public events produced during periods of crisis. Gerbner, following Knight and Dean (1982), makes a similar point when he argues that crime and punishment are transformed into a "selectively choreographed" event (Gerbner 1992: 96). There are important comparisons to be made between the example Gerbner mentions (the Iranian embassy siege in London, 1980), and the Stockwell incident. Considered as responses to terrorist activity, both reveal the existence of violent practices that could be classified as executions.[57] An important difference, however, was the difficulty of turning the death of de Menezes into a "morally coherent" scenario of "violence and terror" (Gerbner 1992).[58] In other words, the concurrence of reports in establishing the clear innocence of de Menezes, despite the uncertainty about his status as a "legal" migrant, made it difficult to use the event to justify a "shoot to kill" policy. Instead, one newspaper, the *Daily Mail,* attempted to present de Menezes as a "victim of the terrorists" (Comment, *Daily Mail,* July 25, 2005).

This would seem to be an extremely precarious strategy. If de Menezes is to be portrayed as a victim of *terrorism,* it would be reasonable to assign direct guilt to the actual perpetrator of the assault; in other words, it would be necessary to identify the terrorist. This, in turn, might lead to the conclusion that the officer who fired the shots must assume this role. The writer of the *Mail*'s piece seemed aware of this interpretation, arguing that the family of the dead man might "perhaps in time come to accept that although he was killed by a police officer," he was "as much a victim of terrorism as the 52 innocent people killed on July 7" (ibid.). According to this line of thinking, the death can be attributed not to the specialist firearms officers of S019, but to the July 7 bombers who are supposed to have provoked the urgent implementation of Operation Kratos.

Arguments that the Stockwell killing represents a "paradigmatic" shift toward armed repression within the British state have been opposed by the excuse that the event was no more than a tragic accident, or the unique product of exceptional circumstances. Though unusual, the death of Jean Charles de Menezes can be understood more readily if its rhetorical composition within news media is set aside. The shooting can be analyzed with reference to a number of other events and procedures; these include past counter-insurgency operations, contemporary developments in "anti-terror" techniques, and armed interventions made by police against civilians.

Although a full analysis of all these factors is beyond the scope of this chapter, it would be useful at this point to turn briefly to the "ordinary" shooting of civilians, precisely because they provide an example of individuals who were not placed in the category of "terrorists," yet whose actions nonetheless provoked extreme measures. One feature seems to predominate: this is the fact that no police officer was convicted for the death of any member of the public. In 2005, the *Independent* ran a front-page article which analyzed 30 fatal shootings caused by armed police; in none of these cases had any officer been convicted of an offense (Verkaik and Bennetto 2005). This is not to say that police had not been faced with some kind of threat on at least half of these occasions and, according to the *Independent*, weapons had been discharged by civilians during four of the incidents.[59]

Although details of the circumstances are not provided for 11 of the dead, four of those killed had been completely unarmed.[60] While the increase in the use of firearms officers (Waldren 2007) can explain in part the general toll of casualties in recent years, the situation in which de Menezes was placed was nonetheless atypical: although a civilian, the circumstances of his death did not resemble the ways in which many ordinary individuals had been shot. These events usually occur when some public disturbance has been in progress or where police have intercepted, or lain in wait, for armed criminals. Jean Charles de Menezes, another civilian victim, exhibited no sign of carrying, or having access to, a weapon. All the negative attributes that supposedly justified or at least explained his death were assigned to him by eyewitnesses or police.

This reflects a psychological collusion between these groups, produced because they resisted the logical conclusion: that the police had in effect terrorized the public.[61] Such a notion could not be translated into a viable public discourse because, at least within the mainstream political parties and press, the political and communicative resources were not available; these were monopolized by established forces. More critical perspectives appeared within new media forms, where speculation about the growth of paramilitary action was more common; this, however, lies outside the current field of enquiry. Ultimately, no police officers were charged with an offense. Instead, the Metropolitan Police as an institution was found guilty of endangering the public.

The apparent proliferation of armed police cannot in itself explain the events of July 22, 2005. It is only in the context of the British state's long involvement in counter-insurgency and "anti-terror" policy that de Menezes' death can be understood. Even then, the emphasis on *minimum force* that once characterized military policy (whatever the actual reality "on the ground") cannot provide a fully comprehensive account of the turn to "pre-emption." Kratos must be studied in conjunction with other developments, such as the application of anti-terror legislation to public dissent, in order to appreciate the full implications of the Stockwell debacle. When demonstrations, acts of civil disobedience, and even everyday public activities (Hewitt 2008: 113) seem to attract the use of repressive surveillance, and sometimes violent arrest, then it is possible to appreciate Malcolm Bull's argument that, under the guise of the "war on terror," the state is actually engaged in another kind of war, one directed against civil society itself (Bull 2006).

If this is the case, then certain qualifications should be made. First, that this "war" is not fought through the seamless efforts of a "unitary" state. The state is best understood as a *composite* structure or, in Jessop's words, "an ensemble of power centres" (Jessop 2008: 37). These centers offer *unequal* chances to "different forces within and outside the state to act for different political purposes" (ibid.). Jessop continues by arguing that "it is not the state that acts; it is rather specific sets of politicians and state officials" located within various parts of the state system (ibid.). This leads to the uneven development of bureaucracy, as various factions, embedded in particular functional environments or agencies (different strata of the law, armed forces, police, and political executives), defend and attempt to enlarge their own interests and social vision.

Clearly, in the case of paramilitary developments, these are advanced by the combined powers of different elements within the security state, whose operatives are given relative autonomy by the political executive. As a consequence of divided responsibilities and devolved power, it is possible for organizations like the Association of Chief Police Officers to set an agenda which "liberal" elements of the state may find difficult to contain, largely because they operate in a different field of activity. The political direction of coercive authority may therefore be dictated by hidden agreements between an executive and selected agencies, without close scrutiny from elected officialdom, informal civil networks, or liberal elements within the law and judiciary. Kratos avoids careful dissection because it is both a policy and an amorphous set of procedures; the type of response it envisages is not made explicit in public documents like the Terrorism Act 2006, and in this sense at least it stands outside the law itself.

The second qualification that should be applied to Bull's concept of a war against civil society is that only a small part of this assault is directly physical; just as "the war on terror" is economic and rhetorical, so too is the internal organization of the neoliberal project. With regard to the "repressive apparatus," my argument can be summarized as follows. The state has accrued great powers and a well-equipped "counter-insurgency" capability, but this has not been brought into being by the growth of any generalized challenge from the left or working class: there is no mass industrial unrest, because employment has been reconfigured and the unions are relatively weak; the extra-parliamentary political left exists but is divided and can mount no widespread challenge; and the "terrorist" organizations that have been identified are isolated, amateurish, and poorly organized so that, despite their ability to inflict serious harm on civilians, they have nothing like the support, capacity, or sophistication once possessed by the IRA in Northern Ireland. For these reasons, the present conflict does not resemble the paradigm of "total war," in which every resource is concentrated on the obliteration of an (internal) enemy.

In sum, therefore, the threat to the core of the British *state* is negligible. The security establishment has therefore *overproduced* the coercive capital needed to prosecute a "counter-insurgency" against domestic opposition. As a consequence, it has attempted to justify its expansion by trying to erode the distinction between terrorist activity and legitimate public protest, using stop and search powers under terror legislation to disrupt the organization of environmentalist and anti-war events; even so, this action has still not provided enough live bodies to repress. Although the security establishment does not have universal power to develop all its aims, because it is structurally constrained by other social forces, procedures like Kratos will not be reversed. Without effective public access to, or control over, police activity, a repetition of "the Stockwell syndrome," even where no shots are fired, may increasingly become the norm.

The application of lethal force is described by those in authority as selective, to be used against only the most unpredictable or implacable of foes, but the truth of the matter is that such explanations are designed to encompass a much wider range of eventualities; the consequence is that the demonstrable power of armed intervention is increased. When this power is discharged it may, like an electric current, run in unexpected directions, but this does not affect the structure that produced it. The "armed demonstration" (Price 2008), whether active or passive, remains a useful tactic within the extensive repertoire of coercive authority.

Notes

1 Sir Ian Blair, Chief Constable of the Metropolitan Police, declared at the press conference of July 22, 2005 that "*Met police officers* have shot a man inside Stockwell Underground Station at approximately 10 a.m. this morning." Newspapers repeated this attribution and reproduced it in various forms; the *Guardian*, for example, reported that "a man was chased

by *officers* and shot around five times in the head at point-blank range" (Cobain, Cowan, and Norton-Taylor 2005). Some commentators had attributed the action to military personnel.

2 See for example Dodd (2005).

3 *Daily Express*, "IT WAS JUST A TRAGIC MISTAKE," August 18, 2005; see also *Daily Mail*, "Tragic Victim Who Loved London," July 25, 2005, pp. 2–3.

4 See "Innocent Died in Hail of Bullets," *Sunday Express*, July 24, 2005, p. 2.

5 The Metropolitan Police have issued a document emphasizing that Kratos is based on "a range of tactics" including "an unarmed uniformed police officer stopping someone" (www.met.police.uk/communities_together/docs/v_05-11-08_srb_anna_de_vries_1_.pdf). Accessed August 28, 2008.

6 See Metropolitan Police Authority minutes, August 8, 2005 (www.mpa.gov.uk/downloads/about/foi/log/kratos-attach.pdf). Accessed August 28, 2008. Other tactics associated with a "shoot to kill" policy include "a second separate strategy for dealing with a suspected suicide bomber targeting a major public event . . . [when] a commander has the authority to order a sniper to fire without warning from a hidden position" Casciani (2007). (http://news.bbc.co.uk/1/hi/uk/7085244.stm). Accessed August 29, 2008.

7 See http://www.ipcc.gov.uk for details of the two IPCC reports into the Stockwell shooting.

8 "'Shoot to kill' is a vernacular term which the police themselves prefer not to use," Metropolitan Police Authority minutes, August 8, 2005 (www.mpa.gov.uk/downloads/about/foi/log/kratos-attach.pdf). Accessed August 28, 2008.

9 In the *Sun* of July 23 this appeared as "any death is deeply regrettable. *But as I understand it* the man was challenged and refused to obey instructions." The passage on the UK Police Service website reads: "The information I have available is that this shooting is directly linked to the ongoing and expanding anti-terrorist operation. Any death is deeply regrettable. I understand the man was challenged and refused to obey."

10 The death could at this stage have been reported in a variety of ways – including murder, manslaughter, and illegal killing. Verdicts of illegal killing were passed in two cases of police shootings, in 1997 and 2005, though these were overturned at, respectively, retrial and judicial review. (See Inquest, at http://inquest.gn.apc.org/data_unlawful_killing.html).

11 Instead, attention was devoted to the dramatic character of the incident, supported by the extensive use of eyewitness evidence, accounts which themselves produced misleading impressions of de Menezes' movements and behavior.

12 These are contained within Metropolitan Police Authority minutes, August 8, 2005 (www.mpa.gov.uk/downloads/about/foi/log/kratos-attach.pdf). Accessed August 28, 2008.

13 See "Menezes Police 'Gave No Warning,'" BBC News online, October 30, 2008 (http://news.bbc.co.uk/go/pr/fr/-/1/hi/uk/7699657.stm). Accessed October 30, 2008.

14 See "Menezes Identification 'Definite,'" BBC News online, October 28, 2008 (http://news.bbc.co.uk/go/pr/fr/-/1/hi/uk/7695088.stm). Accessed October 28, 2008.

15 The speaker in this particular instance possessed not only privileged information, but also the authority to disseminate it.

16 *Setting* is a concept used by the linguist Hymes to describe the context in which a speech event takes place. It refers not only to the physical arena provided for formal utterance, but also to the psychological conditions encountered by participants (Price 1998: 96).

17 The representatives of formal authority are also seen, following Wheeler (2005), as "actors." They are treated, in everyday practice, as the first focus of enquiry for the press, and their opinions are actively sought through "calls" or "ring-arounds," unlike less exalted bodies, which are not usually asked to "generate their own proactive copy" (Wheeler 2005: 57).

18 In the days that followed the Stockwell shooting, the public were to learn a little more about the extent of the coercive powers which the police, armed forces, and intelligence services had begun to develop.

19 See IPCC at http://statguidance.ipcc.gov.uk/index.php?id=4.

20 The following excerpt may demonstrate the reluctance of some in authority to keep the MPA fully informed: "After that meeting in March 2002 a critical incident exercise weekend was conducted, called Operation Tavistock, at which Sir John Quinton represented the Authority. Unfortunately I can find no records of Sir John subsequently briefing the Authority in any formal way on the outcome of that weekend but it is clear that the MPS felt that through his attendance the Authority was being kept in touch with this policy as it was being developed." (Metropolitan Police Authority minutes, August 8, 2005).

21 "Man shot at Stockwell tube station: We can confirm that at just after 10 a.m. this morning, Friday 22 July, armed officers from the Metropolitan Police entered Stockwell tube station in south London. A man was challenged by officers and was subsequently shot . . . the man was pronounced dead at the scene. Stockwell tube station is closed and cordons of 200 metres are in place. As is routine, officers from the Met's Directorate of Professional Standards have been informed."

Bulletin 0000000232 cms.met.police.uk/news/major_operational_announcements

This appeared in the *Daily Mail* on July 22 as, "We can confirm that just after 10 a.m. armed officers entered Stockwell Tube station. A man was challenged by officers and subsequently shot. London Ambulance Service attended the scene. He was pronounced dead at the scene."

22 Press management of the transition between themes might be expected to include some recognition that the original police statement was a falsehood; the actual process of adjustment, however, tended to concentrate on the novelty of the new situation, rather than the misrepresentations already offered.

23 "Political interventions depend upon 'timeliness.' In other words, the actual function of rhetoric is to provide *alibis* to cover decisions made in advance of public revelation, provisional interventions which, if necessary, can later be qualified. They are therefore . . . required formalities within a hierarchical system which is *known* as democratic" (Price 2006).

24 The ubiquitous appearance of "terrorism" as a catch-all description of a condition requiring a systemic response is described by Makdisi, who considers that the label constitutes a "politico-juridical foundation for a universal campaign" (Makdisi 2002: 267). The "war on terror," therefore, represents "the proposal for a new system of governance and control whose declared enemies are indefinite and spectral" (ibid.).

25 This marks an interesting revision of Althusser's conception of the police officer calling the citizen to account (Althusser 1971), and the individual immediately recognizing their place within the symbolic order. In the Stockwell case, the officers made no "call to order," but executed an individual who turned out to be the citizen of another state.

26 So, for example, the Prevention of Terrorism Act of 1989 was introduced in Britain as temporary legislation requiring annual renewal and was used to proscribe organizations such as the IRA and INLA, armed nationalist groups that used, amongst other methods, bombings and assassinations to disrupt British occupation of the Six Counties.

27 The Italian state, for example, had by 1981 incarcerated some 3,500 individuals without trial, in some cases under a law ("insurrection against the powers of the state") that had remained on the statute books since the fascist era (Red Notes 1981: 42).

28 For example, the whole narrative concerning "weapons of mass destruction" may be seen as a rationale designed to unite competing agencies in the pursuit of an "imperial" aim which could not be fully delineated in public. As Wolfowitz explained, "the truth is that for reasons that have a lot to do with the US government bureaucracy we settled on the one issue that everyone could agree on which was weapons of mass destruction as the core reason" (interview with Sam Tannenhaus, 2003).

29 The use of the ambush or "hard arrest" in Northern Ireland, dating from the deployment of the SAS in 1976, provides one example (Urban 1992). On the mainland, other instances can be found in the fairly regular calls to update public order tactics to deal with "enhanced" threats. So, for example, the *Sunday Times* of April 8, 1990 carried an article on the Poll Tax riot of the previous weekend, in which the group of reporters that formed the "Insight" team speculated on the possible use of "marksmen"

to shoot armed assailants hiding in crowds. As with all such plans, the establishment of a convincing *scenario* is an important initial step. This particular narrative involved imagining a situation in which terrorists or criminals were ready to discharge weapons, using crowds of demonstrators as cover. The headline read, "Police Plan a 'Shoot to Kill' Policy in Riots" (Insight 1990).

30 See "Menezes Identification 'Definite,'" BBC News online, October 28, 2008 (http://news.bbc.co.uk/go/pr/fr/-/1/hi/uk/7695088.stm). Accessed October 28, 2008.

31 This is not to say that either society lacks democratic institutions which oppose these developments, but rather that most elements of civil society seem relatively powerless under the terms of conflict set by each nation's security apparatus, at least at the specific place and time in which fatal coercive force is applied.

32 Ian Blair attempted to turn this phrase into "shoot-to-kill-to-protect" (see Twomey and Dixon, "Police: We Will Shoot to Kill Again," *Daily Express*, July 25, 2005).

33 The shooting was attributed to a case of mistaken identity, in which the appearance and location of one suspect was supposedly confused with that of de Menezes. The *Panorama* report of March 8, 2006 revealed that one of the surveillance team was part of a specialist unit, the origins of which lay in Army operations in Northern Ireland. This was most probably the Special Reconnaissance Regiment, which absorbed 14 Intelligence Company (see Urban 1992).

34 It is worth noting that police forces often publish requests for assistance featuring ordinary demonstrators whose supposed misdemeanors are unspecified and who, unlike at least three of the London suspects, were not photographed "after the fact." One example, which appeared on the website of the "Post G8 Investigation Team, Lothian and Borders Police" gives no information about the offense which might have been committed. On April 26, 2006, the *Guardian* carried three pictures of demonstrators being pursued by Scotland Yard, on the basis of their participation in protests outside the Danish embassy on February 3, 2006. The photographs were supposedly issued to the press because police had not been able to trace them by other means.

35 An undercover soldier, who was part of the team monitoring de Menezes' residence, revealed that he believed the suspect to be an "IC1 male," meaning he thought he was a white European (*Panorama* 2006).

36 The caption at the top of page 5 inside the paper reads "CCTV images of the four suspects."

37 Nonetheless, the "wanted" genre can produce alternative and oppositional views; take for example the *Daily Mirror*'s front-page treatment of George W. Bush during the build-up to the Iraq war.

38 An edict in which the imagined members of a collective are presented with a common perspective and the urgency of recognizing a "duty" they should be willing to fulfill.

39 These points were framed as questions in an email enquiry to a *Guardian* journalist on December 9, 2005, which received no response. The *Guardian*'s Editorial Code was published in January 2002.

40 The *Express* headline, in keeping with its overall attitude, read "SHOOT ALL BOMBERS." This declaration, which appeared without quotation marks, originated in remarks made by the Mayor of London and the Conservative "Homeland Security" spokesman.

41 For sources on press and media behavior in emergencies, wars, and crises, see Raboy and Dagenais (1992); Taylor (1992); Zelizer and Allan (2002); Noll (2003); Allan (2005); and McNair (2006). For specific incidences of police or military interventions in public order or security situations, see Gilbert (1975); National Council for Civil Liberties (1980); Cramer and Harris (1982); and Gray (2006).

42 See Allan (2005: 67–81).

43 Tolson regards "liveness," even where simulated, as "indispensable" to television (Tolson 2006: 12).

44 States of emergency can also be manufactured through the attempted control of spatial circumstances, and as a consequence the wider semiotic/discursive environment.

45 The caption to a photograph of Muktar Saed Ibrahim, which noted that he "Turned to extremism during jail term" (*Daily Mail*, July 27, 2005), does not then prompt a study of social and political conditions in Britain's jails.

46 This, however, is not intended to support the conception of "common sense" perpetuated in many academic critiques of news and agenda setting. Fairclough attacks what he sees as "common sense" assumptions, calling them "the conventions according to which people interact linguistically, and of which people are generally not consciously aware" (Fairclough 1989: 2).

47 Propositional content is the essential meaning of a statement or utterance, and can therefore be expressed in a number of different guises.

48 In a column of July 25, Phillips explained that new rules meant that armed police were directed to shoot suspected suicide bombers "in the brain," adding that "this is because even if a suicide bomber is shot in the chest, he could still detonate himself by a twitch of the finger" (Phillips 2005).

49 Cobain, Cowan, and Norton-Taylor (2005).

50 In both cases, the discourse of criminality was deployed when the "terrorist" device proved difficult to sustain.

51 Neither of these events provides unique examples of the "legitimate" use of armed coercion or force, in which civilians have been killed in

political, criminal, or public order situations. Obvious examples of fatalities caused during political protests include the deaths of Kevin Gately at an anti-fascist demonstration in 1974 (see Gilbert 1975) and Blair Peach at a similar mobilization in 1979 (see National Council for Civil Liberties 1980); neither, however, involved the discharge by police of firearms. Instances of fatal shootings carried out by police marksmen include the killing of Harry Stanley in 1999, Derek Bennett in 2001, and Keith Larkins in 2003.

52 One such incident, also based on "mistaken identity," occurred on July 8, 2008, when armed police arrested a 21-year-old male commuter, ordering him to lie on the platform of Bournemouth station as they aimed their weapons (see "A Chilling Echo of de Menezes," *Metro*, July 8, 2008). Another well-known parallel was the shooting by police of Abul Koyair during the Forest Gate incident in 2006 (Goodchild and Elliott, "Tip-off by Police Informer Led to Forest Gate Raid," Goodchild and Elliott 2006).

53 For a fuller explanation of the realist position, see Archer (2000) and Price (2007).

54 Preference for a thematic approach derives from dissatisfaction with the vague modes of enquiry marshaled beneath the category of "discourse."

55 A political point of view or perspective, which uses themes in order to achieve communication aims.

56 See for example Price (2008) on "armed demonstrations" as a form of mediated public spectacle.

57 In the final moments of the embassy siege, witnesses recounted how members of the SAS assault group shot dead a number of hostage takers who had, by this time, thrown down their own weapons (Cramer and Harris 1982).

58 The preference for descriptions of the shooting as a "tragedy" is analyzed above.

59 Between "1990 and March 2003" four officers had been killed and 135 injured by the "criminal use of firearms" (Waldren 2007: 222).

60 Analyzing the brief details provided on the 30 deaths, the number of individuals who were said to be armed with, or in possession of, real weapons was 12; of these, two carried swords only, two carried air rifles, one carried a sword and a gun, and the remaining seven had guns of some description, of which four were discharged. Three individuals carried replicas. In 11 cases, it is not clear from the information if the victims were armed are not. In four cases, the dead were entirely unarmed.

61 On July 22, an armed officer chased the driver of the Stockwell Tube train into the tunnel, see BBC News online, October 1, 2007. (http://news.bbc.co.uk/1/hi/uk/7021401.stm). Accessed August 29, 2008. See also "Menezes police 'out of control,'" BBC News online, November 3, 2008. (http://news.bbc.co.uk/1/hi/uk/7706033.stm). Accessed November 3, 2008.

References and Further Reading

Allan, Stuart. (2005) *Journalism: Critical Issues*. Buckingham: Open University Press.

Althusser, Louis. (1971) *Lenin and Philosophy*, trans. Ben Brewster. London: New Left Books.

Altschull, J. Herbert. (1995) *Agents of Power*. White Plains: Longman.

Archer, Margaret. (2000) *Being Human: The Problem of Agency*. Cambridge: Cambridge University Press.

Barker, Martin. (1989) *Comics*. Manchester: Manchester University Press.

Bird, Steve, Syal Rajeev, and Tom Hennigan. (2005) "The Hard-working Son Who Moved to London in Search of a Better Life," *The Times*, July 25.

Blair, Ian. Press Conference on the Stockwell shooting, July 22, 2005. (www.police.uk/content)

Blondheim, Menahem and Tamar Liebes. (2003) "From Disaster Marathon to Media Event," in A. M. Noll (ed.), *Crisis Communications*, pp. 185–98. Maryland: Rowan and Littlefield.

Boorstin, D. J. (1961) *The Image: A Guide to Pseudo-Events in America*. New York: Vintage.

Bruck, P. A. (1992) "Discursive Movements and Social Movements," in J. Wasko and V. Mosco, *Democratic Communications in the Information Age*, pp. 138–58. New Jersey: Garamond/Ablex Publishing Co.

Bull, Malcolm. (2006) "States of Failure," *New Left Review* 40 (July–August): 5–25.

Campbell, Duncan. (2006) "The Moment of Decision: When Do You Pull the Trigger?" *Guardian*, July 26.

Casciani, Dominic. (2007) "Shoot to-Kill-Policy under Debate," BBC News online (http://news.bbc.co.uk/1/hi/uk/7085244.stm). Accessed August 29, 2008.

Cobain, Ian, Rosie Cowan, and Richard Norton-Taylor. (2005) "They Held the Pistol to Him and Unloaded Five Shots," *Guardian*, July 23.

Cramer, Chris and Sim Harris. (1982) *Hostage*. London: John Clare Books.

Dodd, Vikram. (2005) "Seconds to Decide if Suspect Is Suicide Threat," *Guardian*, July 23.

Entman, R. M. (1993) "Framing: Towards the Clarification of a Fractured Paradigm," *Journal of Communication* 43(4): 51–8. Hoboken, NJ: Wiley/Blackwell.

Ericson, Richard V., Patricia M. Baranek, and Janet B. L. Chan. (1991) *Representing Order*. Milton Keynes: Open University Press.

Fairclough, Norman. (1989) *Language and Power*. London: Longman.

Franklin, Bob, Martin Hamer, Mark Hanna, Marie Kinsey, and John Richardson. (2005) *Key Concepts in Journalism Studies*. Thousand Oaks, London, New Delhi: SAGE.

Ganser, Danielle. (2005) *NATO's Secret Armies*. London, New York: Frank Cass.

Gerbner, George. (1992) "Violence and Terror in and by the Media," in Marc Raboy and Bernard Dagenais, *Media, Crisis and Democracy*, pp. 94–107. Thousand Oaks, London, New Delhi: SAGE.

Gilbert, Tony. (1975) *Only One Died*. London: Kay Beauchamp.

Gill, Graeme. (2003) *The Nature and Development of the Modern State*. Basingstoke, New York: Palgrave Macmillan.

Goodchild, Sophie and Francis Elliott. (2006) "Tip-off by Police Informer Led to Forest Gate Raid," *Independent*, June 11.

Gray, Roger. (2006) *Armed Response*. Virgin Books: London.

Grice, Paul. (1989) *Studies in the Ways of Words*. Cambridge, MA, London: Harvard University Press.

Harris, Paul. (2005) "One Suspect, Five Shots in the Head," *Daily Mail*, July 23: 4–5.

Hewitt, Steve. (2008) *The British War on Terror*. London, New York: Continuum.

Insight. (1990) "Police Plan a 'Shoot to Kill' Policy in Riots," *Sunday Times*, April 8.

Isin, Engin F. (2000) *Democracy, Citizenship and the Global City*. London, New York: Routledge.

Jessop, Bob. (2008) *State Power: A Structural-Relational Approach*. Cambridge, Malden, MA: Polity.

Knight, G. and Dean, A. (1982) *Journal of Communication* 32(2): 144–61. Hoboken, NJ: Wiley/Blackwell.

Leiss, William, Stephen Kline, and Sut Jhally. (1990) *Social Communication in Advertising*. London and New York: Routledge.

Lyon, David. (2003) "Surveillance Technology and Surveillance Society," in Thomas J. Misa, Philip Brey, and Andrew Feenberg, *Modernity and Technology*, pp. 161–84. Cambridge, MA: MIT Press.

McGrath, John E. (2004) *Loving Big Brother*. London, New York: Routledge.

McNair, Brian. (2006) *Cultural Chaos: Journalism, News and Power in a Globalised World*. London, New York: Routledge.

Makdisi, Saree. (2002) "Spectres of 'Terrorism,'" *interventions* 4(2): 265–78.

Mann, Michael. (2003) "The Autonomous Power of the State: Its Origins, Mechanisms and Results" (1988), in Neil Brenner, Bob Jessop, Martin Jones, and Gordon MacLeod (eds.), *State/Space: A Reader*, pp. 53–64. Malden, MA, Oxford: Blackwell.

Manning, Paul. (2001) *News and News Sources*. Thousand Oaks, CA, London, New Delhi: SAGE.

Metropolitan Police Authority. (2002) *Minutes*, August 8, 2005, including minutes of March 21, 2002.

Metropolitan Police. (2005) *Bulletin 0000000232*, July 22, 2005. (cms.met.police.uk/news/major_operational_announcements)

Misa, Thomas J., Philip Brey, and Andrew Feenberg. (2003) *Modernity and Technology*. Cambridge, MA: MIT Press.

Nair, Parvati. (2006) "Voicing Risk: Migration, Transgression and Relocation in Spanish/Moroccan Rai," *interventions* 8(1): 67–82.

National Council for Civil Liberties. (1980) *Southall 23 April 1979*. Nottingham: NCCL.

Noll, Michael A. (2003) *Crisis Communications: Lessons from September 11*. Oxford: Rowman & Littlefield.

Panorama. (2006) "Stockwell: Countdown to Killing," March 8, 2006. BBC.

Parsons, Tony. (2005) "A Tragedy – but Police Still Deserve Our Support," *Daily Mirror*, July 25.

Phillips, M. (2005) "A Terrible Tragedy – but This Is No Time for Weakness," *Daily Mail*, July 25.

Pierson, Christopher. (1996) *The Modern State*. London, New York: Routledge.

Press Association. (2005) "Police Shoot Suspect Dead after Tube Chase," *Independent*, July 22.

Price, Stuart. (1998) *Media Studies*. London: Longman.

Price, Stuart. (2006) "Brute Reality: Television, War and Timeliness," in Anthony Barker (ed.), *Television, Aesthetics and Reality*, pp. 50–72. Newcastle: Cambridge Scholars Press.

Price, Stuart. (2007) *Discourse Power Address*. Aldershot, Burlington: Ashgate.

Price, Stuart. (2008) "Missiles in Athens and Tanks at Heathrow: Urban Security and the Materialisation of 'Global' Threat," *Social Semiotics* 18(1): 1–16. Taylor and Francis: Routledge.

Raboy, Marc and Bernard Dagenais, eds. (1992) *Media, Crisis and Democracy*. Thousand Oaks, CA, London, New Delhi: SAGE.

Red Notes. (1981) *After Marx, Jail*. London: Red Notes.

Rejali, Darius. (2007) *Torture and Democracy*. Princeton, Woodstock: Princeton University Press.

Simons, Herbert W. (2006) "What's In a News Frame?" Paper for ATINER conference, Athens, May 22–24, 2006.

Tannenhaus, S. (2003) "Interview with Paul Wolfowitz," *Vanity Fair*, May 9.

Taylor, Philip M. (1992) *War and the Media: Propaganda and Persuasion in the Gulf War*. Manchester: Manchester University Press.

Tolson, Andrew. (2006) *Media Talk*. Edinburgh: Edinburgh University Press.

Tuchman, Gaye. (1972) "Objectivity as Strategic Ritual," *American Journal of Sociology* 77(4): 660–79.

Twomey, John, and Cyril Dixon. (2005) "Police: We Will Shoot to Kill Again," *Daily Express*, July 25.

Urban, Mark. (1992) *Big Boys' Rules*. London: Faber and Faber.

Verkaik, Robert and Jason Bennetto. (2005) "Shot Dead by Police, 30. Officers Convicted, 0," *Independent*, October 21.

Waldren, Michael J. (2007) *Armed Police*. Stroud: Sutton Publishing.

Watt, E. D. (1982) *Authority*. London: Croom Helm.

Wheeler, Sharon. (2005) "Get Me a Great Quote," in Richard Keeble, *Print Journalism*. London, New York: Routledge.

Willey, Jo and Padraic Flanagan. (2005) "Policeman Pumped 5 Bullets into Head and Body of Terrorist," *Daily Express* July 23.

Zelizer, Barbie and Stuart Allan, eds. (2002) *Journalism after September 11th*. London, New York: Routledge.

Part III

Genres of Terror

Chapter 12

Terror Effects

Robert J. C. Young

> *We are occupied by gods. The mistake is to identify with the god occupying you.*
>
> Michael Ondaatje, *Anil's Ghost*, p. 230

Terror as Affect

"Terror" effects terror effects spontaneously, for terror comprises nothing but its effects. Terror effects are self-generating, uncontrollable, proliferating. Totally random. Terror messes up and violates the smooth transition between causes and effects. It seems to come from outside but it manifests itself inside, sliding between the visible and the invisible. Terror is a kind of militarized aura, erupting indeterminately from the object or event and in the viewer almost at the same time. The propaganda of the deed is more powerful because no one can be sure what its meaning may be. Terror is nothing if it does not produce effects: it's designed to create them.

What is the effect of terror? It works as both an individual and a collective emotion, subjecting all to a charged state of fear, an overpowering sense of imminent danger – extreme anxiety, danger so near that it overwhelms and paralyzes you. The "war on terror" is paradoxical not just because, as has been remarked, it is odd to make war on an abstract noun, but because it must mean that you are also making war on a state of fear – in yourself. To declare war on terror therefore is, strictly speaking, to declare war on – yourself. Or on something within yourself, that you feel sure somehow is not you, produced by someone or something else.

Terror repulses: discussions of terror move quickly away from terror to its cause. "Terror" gets conflated with "acts of terrorism," which produce the effect of terror or fear, or with "terrorists" who carry out acts of terrorism.[1] This leaves terror itself unchallenged and unexamined. The subject of terror is not the terrorist, but those who fear the terrorist and live in fear of him or her, in a state of terror. Like history, terror is known only by its effects, its aftermath, on the people subjected to terror. Terror brings error, a perpetual confusion of subject and object, in which the one folds in to the other. Is this how terror works, is this what inspires the fear, the anticipation? Imperceptibly crossing the border between inside and outside? It's uncanny.

To live in terror is to live in fear. Of what? You don't know. Something. What's scary is that terrorists threaten to act randomly. If it's a kind of war, it's a performative war that seeks no military advantage. Terrorism involves the staging of an act, an event – not an attempt to capture land or the apparatus of the state. It is not like a military campaign, where you might be surprised, but you expect to be able to react, to resist, to counter-attack. With terrorism it seems that there is no space for reaction – other than the move into the state of affect, of terror. Or to try to take out the agents of terror. If they've already blown themselves up, then the focus turns to prospective agents of terror's feared return in the future.

So what terror generates, in effect, is an affect, "the conscious subjective aspect of an emotion considered apart from bodily changes" (Merriam-Webster dictionary). The terror effect is affect?

> The confusion of the verbs *affect* and *effect* not only is quite common but has a long history. The verb *effect* was used in place of *affect* (1) [to make a display of liking or using] as early as 1494 and in place of *affect* (2) [feign] as early as 1652. If you think you want to use the verb *effect* but are not certain, check the definitions here. The noun *affect* is sometimes mistakenly used for the noun *effect*. Except when your topic is psychology, you will seldom need the noun *affect*.[2]

Dangerous homophones. They dissolve boundaries. Things seem alike and different at once. You really don't know where you are, or what's what. To say that the terror effect is an affect, means that strictly speaking it belongs to the realm of the aesthetic, in its earliest sense, "Of or pertaining to sensuous perception, received by the senses" (*Oxford English Dictionary*), as first proposed by Alexander Baumgarten in 1735: "a science of perception, the science of things perceived, or *aistheta*."[3] Since Burke's day, the state of affect in the subject who perceives the sensuous world outside has found its deepest double in the ways that the subject perceives the world of art, now the primary meaning of the word "aesthetic." Aesthetics leads a doubled life, and what marks terror is that it knows no distinction between the two.

Terror moves you into a state of producing fiction: it makes you live imaginatively on the borderlines of the real. It has reference to the real, but is essentially a fictional anticipation of how the real might become, how it might turn out. For while terror is produced as an effect of an event that has already passed, the after-effect of this shock is riddled with the anticipation that the originating traumatic event will be repeated once more in the real. Terror therefore is intimately entangled with a logic of an anticipated repetition, in which how it was will turn out to be repeated once more in the future. Terror looks forward, fueled by the explosion of history, its imagination grasping the future. The anticipation, proleptic fiction, of ominous things to come merges with the memory of the real from the past, the reimagined real, so that it becomes impossible to distinguish them. Fiction and the real alike produce a series of effects – going off like inventive and spectacular fireworks that dazzle, come too close, and sometimes turn lethal.

While terror works through a structure of anticipated repetition, the strategies have remained remarkably consistent through the centuries. On October 30, 1883, Irish Fenians effected two explosions on the London Underground between Charing Cross and Westminster stations, an act mimicked over 100 years later in the 7/7 Tube bombings.[4] The Clerkenwell bombing of 1867, when Fenians detonated a wheelbarrow packed with gunpowder against the wall of Clerkenwell Gaol in an attempt to free the American Fenian Richard O'Sullivan Burke, also found its echo 140 years later when a Taliban bomber parked a fuel tanker outside Kandahar prison.[5] Detonated by a rocket-propelled grenade, the explosion made a breach in the prison walls large enough for 900 Taliban prisoners to escape. For the last two centuries at least, "terror" has been transhistorical. It could be said to constitute the distinctive mark of modernity itself: the age of terror.[6] As the object of terror moved from the aristocracy to the bourgeoisie, the curve of terror has followed a parallel course to the rise of the novel, and it is there that we find its secret and subversive staging.

Within fiction, terror belongs to the discourse of the gothic, which has been aptly named "the literature of terror."[7] This does not just represent the terrible – it actually works by making you scared. Like terror itself, the gothic novel operates by effect, affect, not by content. Terror is therefore the form of the gothic experience. The war on terror is in some sense about trying to counter a thoroughly gothic fear, repeated in countless dreams, of finding yourself out of control. It is a performative, a staging, a drama that works for just as long as you are reading. The content rarely has significance in itself, for content is merely the vehicle for producing terror – a random explosion that works only through its effect on the reader who is undergoing the reading experience. Just as with the gothic novel, there is no meaning to terror in the real.

To understand the gothic aspect of terror means that we have to peer into its psychic space. Which is why, in this essay on terror, it is necessary to submit to the friction of fiction. True fictions. Literature is, unexpectedly, one of the best places to learn about the war on terror. It has been anticipating the condition of the twenty-first century for centuries: ever since, indeed, the French invented Terror in 1793. Fiction has the unique ability not only to represent terror, to mediate it through narration, but also to produce it. The question to be asked is whether it can also effect a counter-discourse of resistance.[8] Can fiction also show us how to move out of terror, how to refuse its effects? Which is as much as to say: can literature tell us how to escape its own effects?[9]

Terror as Gothic

My first literary example comes, as one would expect from the context of the war on terror, from Jane Austen, in a memorable passage when she describes news of a terrorist attack. Despite her reputation for erasing contemporary history and politics, Jane Austen was in fact the first English novelist not only to mention the game of baseball but also, in the same novel, *Northanger Abbey* (1818), to describe a terror attack:

> The general pause which succeeded his short disquisition on the state of the nation, was put an end to by Catherine, who, in rather a solemn tone of voice, uttered these words, "I have heard that something very shocking indeed, will soon come out in London."
>
> Miss Tilney, to whom this was chiefly addressed, was startled, and hastily replied, "Indeed! – and of what nature?"

> "That I do not know, nor who is the author. I have only heard that it is to be more horrible than anything we have met with yet."
>
> "Good heaven! – Where could you hear of such a thing?"
>
> "A particular friend of mine had an account of it in a letter from London yesterday. It is to be uncommonly dreadful. I shall expect murder and every thing of the kind."
>
> "You speak with astonishing composure! But I hope your friend's accounts have been exaggerated; – and if such a design is known beforehand, proper measures will undoubtedly be taken by government to prevent its coming to effect."
>
> "Government," said Henry, endeavouring not to smile, "neither desires nor dares to interfere in such matters. There must be murder; and government cares not how much."
>
> The ladies stared. . . .
>
> "Miss Morland, do not mind what he says; – but have the goodness to satisfy me as to this dreadful riot."
>
> "Riot! – what riot?"
>
> "My dear Eleanor, the riot is only in your own brain. The confusion there is scandalous. Miss Morland has been talking of nothing more dreadful than a new publication which is shortly to come out, in three duodecimo volumes, two hundred and seventy-six pages in each . . . – do you understand? And you, Miss Morland – my stupid sister has mistaken all your clearest expressions. You talked of expected horrors in London – and instead of instantly conceiving, as any rational creature would have done, that such words could relate only to a circulating library, she immediately pictured to herself a mob of three thousand men assembling in St. George's Fields, the Bank attacked, the Tower threatened, the streets of London flowing with blood, a detachment of the Twelfth Light Dragoons, (the hopes of the nation) called up from Northampton to quell the insurgents, and the gallant Capt. Frederick Tilney, in the moment of charging at the head of his troop, knocked off his horse by a brickbat from an upper window. Forgive her stupidity."[10]

Government should take steps to prevent terror "coming to effect." Jane Austen was writing here in the context of the original Terror – the Terror of the French Revolution, in which Terror was the effect of the state, the first instance in which the state itself became the instrument of terror on its subjects, who lived in fear of execution, imprisonment, and torture. Just as the meaning of terror moves from cause to effect, and from the effect on the public to the terrorist, so terror as a term migrated quickly from being a description of practices of the state, the violence of the state perpetrated against its own citizens, as originally in the French Revolution, to practices aimed against the state from below. Terror as a practice of the state is now described in other terms – the "axis of evil," rogue states, state terrorism, states that sponsor terrorism. Either way, the citizens remain the victims of terror, of its effects.

"Proper measures will undoubtedly be taken by government to prevent its coming to effect," remarks Miss Tilney, showing that for Austen terror, not yet here named as such but rather as the alarming prospect of something "shocking," "horrible," and "dreadful," had already moved from state terror to an event that it becomes the state's duty to prevent. Austen may here be remembering and alluding to the Gordon Riots in London of 1780, when 400 or so rioters were killed by the defending military or subsequently executed.[11] After 1789, in the absence of revolution, the terror of the state abroad quickly produced its own mimesis, a counter-terror from the threatening populace below, the fear of the vengeful mob. State terror and anti-state terror have been inextricably locked within an intense economy, mimicking the master-slave dialectic, ever since. The logic of their fractious union underpins the sense of outrage when innocent bystanders are killed, or worse, targeted – an improper way of attacking the state even if it was state terror that first practiced a targeted vendetta on its coerced and cowering citizens. What the "proper measures" to prevent terrorism were, and how proper the measures taken, such as the suspension of habeus corpus in England, were considered to be, was in Austen's day, as now, a fiercely contested subject of debate.

Austen's interleaving of political terror and fiction also introduces a new issue – of gender. Here the terror effect is something that irrational women feel, while men laugh at it. At this stage in the novel, Tilney is confident that he can demarcate the boundary lines between fiction and the real. To live in terror, in the gothic novel, is to live in a female, not a male discourse. This is because the effect of terror operates at the level of affect: "the riot is only in your own brain. The confusion there is scandalous." As a man, Henry can afford to smile at Miss Tilney's disgraceful confusion between the fictional and the real – but only because terror in this case exists in the realm of fiction, and men in Jane Austen generally disdain to read fiction, especially gothic novels. To live terror in the real is when fiction becomes overpowering, and makes everyone feel its effects, subjecting men to a form of their own law of the feminine – when you find yourself getting caught up in a process which you originally sought to comprehend, which subjects you to feelings of "astonishment, suspense, uncertainty, ambivalence."[12] Confused and overwhelmed with surprise and fear. Macho or not, maybe Henry Tilney had a point. The way to resist terror may be to move away from the terror effect of fiction. But is it possible to move out of the orbit of the terror effect itself?

Terror as Sublime

Fiction lives dangerously on the borderlands of the aesthetics of sense perception. To live in terror is painful, but to live in terror vicariously gives you a certain kind of pleasure: masculine vs. feminine, pain vs. pleasure. It was Burke who, in the *Philosophical Enquiry into the Origin of Our Ideas of the Sublime and Beautiful* (1757), first analyzed this curious phenomenon of what Freud would call the pleasure thermometer, and worried at the way in which the border between the two is perpetually dissolving, so that you constantly find yourself on the other side of the line between pleasure and pain, so much so that finally you find yourself in a state of confusion between the two, no longer able to tell which is which. Burke argued that terror as a performative has a dynamic cascading structure; terror as an effect produces a further effect – the sublime:

> Whatever is fitted in any sort to excite the ideas of pain, and danger, that is to say, whatever is in any sort terrible, or is conversant about terrible objects, or operates in a manner analogous to terror, is a source of the *sublime*; that is, it is productive of the strongest emotion which the mind is capable of feeling. I say the strongest emotion because I am satisfied the ideas of pain are much more powerful than those which enter on the part of pleasure. . . . But as pain is stronger in its operation than pleasure, so death is in general a much more affecting idea than pain; because there are very few pains, however exquisite, which are not preferred to death; nay, what generally makes pain itself, if I may say so, more painful, is, that it is considered as an emissary of this king of terrors. When pleasure or pain press too nearly, they are incapable of giving any delight, and are simply terrible; but at certain distances, and with certain modifications, they may be, and they are delightful, as we every day experience.[13]

Terror and the body in pain, according to Burke, produce the most intense form of aesthetic experience. Terror is "the ruling principle of the sublime" (Burke 1990: 54), and the sublime is the effect of terror, its spectral psychic foundation, most of all when pain comes as the emissary of the king of terrors, Death. Terror supervenes with the anticipation of death, the rupture of all signification, a self-reflective consciousness of our own immanent obliteration, the threat to annihilate the self. The sublime is terror's aestheticized translation, the shock of transumption from lowly *terra* to rapturous *caelum*. So in Milton's description of death: "all is dark, uncertain, confused, terrible, and sublime to the last degree." There is, however, a beyond to death, for the highest form of the sublime comes as the effect of the power and presence of the Deity himself. Divine "power" with "its inseparable companion" terror, adds Burke, "is undoubtedly a capital source of the sublime" (pp. 64–5).

Burke's text, which would itself provide the foundations for the Irish gothic, invokes the sublime specifically as a form of compounded colonial experience: his examples of the "noxious things" that produce terror are drawn from the social institutions of the state, "capital punishment, despotic heads of state, Kings, military chiefs, heads of families," from state executions and from war, famine, and social violence.[14] The colonial sublime is the means through which a society is kept within a state of consent, the overarching external power of its visible apparatus and symbolic objects internalized by colonial subjects into a state of fear, disempowerment, and subjugation. The recognition of the mode and means of state power in Ireland was the experience that allowed Burke to anticipate with such apparently mysterious prescience the state terror that would emerge in France during the Revolution. He could anticipate state terror in France because he had already seen it at work in Ireland. Colonial terror, like terror itself, worked proleptically, anticipating the corruption of state terror, just as Burke would argue during the impeachment of Warren Hastings that the colonial sublime of an India ruled by the East India Company would eventually come home to corrupt the British state itself.

Burke's *Enquiry*, as Sara Suleri observes, operates "as a study of the psychic proximity of aesthetic discourse with the concomitant intimacy of cultural terror."[15] Colonial terror is simply another version of state terror, depoliticizing politics by turning it into the form of the aesthetic. For colonial terror, producing an effect whose effect is an affect, translates politics into aesthetics, the strategy that would be later pursued, as Benjamin pointed out, by the fascist state. The only way to counter the effects of state or colonial terror would then, according to Benjamin, be to politicize art, to turn the aesthetic into something other than itself, to turn effect into significance, to retrieve meaning. But what if the terror was so extreme as to disable language and logic themselves?

Aimé Césaire too would argue that the state terror of fascism worked identically to that of the colonial sublime, mimicking the power of God himself, designed to produce shock and awe. According to Burke, the sublime operates as a form of mimicry throughout, for when distanced through art, the terror of the sublime is transformed into the pleasure of art. Terror is real, but what is uncanny is that the effect can be mimicked, reproduced:

> HOW THE SUBLIME IS PRODUCED.
>
> Having considered terror as producing an unnatural tension and certain violent emotions of the nerves; it easily follows, from what we have just said, that whatever is fitted to produce such a tension must be productive of a passion similar to terror, and consequently must be a source of the sublime, though it should have no idea of danger connected with it. (p. 121)

At such moments, when terror is imagined, those violent emotions of the nerves can easily become sources of pleasure. The sublime is doubled, so that its experience in the real is reproduced through the shadowy simulacrum of art. The copy works by impersonating the original: so long as you remain aware that art is riffing off the real, it offers to turn pain into pleasure, to anaesthetize its effect. Yet in so far as you experience the terror, this rollercoaster ride also threatens to break down the difference between the authentic and the inauthentic, splicing the split between life and art in order to make itself most effective. The risks do not stop there, for when we move away from the overwhelming power of the exterior sublime, a new danger arises. As Freud perceived, an even greater terror can emerge when the source of danger is not some overpowering strange external force, but something familiar coming to light in the wrong place, displaced and alien, illegitimate. Imagination – immigration. The terror of the sublime re-emerges as affect when something from the outside slides through your defenses and begins to inhabit your body and possess your haunted dreams.

God and the sublime; fiction and terror: each dwells in the borderlands of the other, fiction being the form in which terror mimics the invasion of the psyche, the transitions of effective terror from outside to inside. You cannot stop its porosity as it slides inside you and takes you over. The self finds itself checked, brought short; terror apes terror; confusion reigns.

Terror as Suspense

If the eighteenth century invented terror, the nineteenth was the great age of terror novels. The gothic sublime re-emerges at the time of the renewed political ferment toward the end of the nineteenth century with the first terrorist novels. In England these began in the mid-1880s when, following the logic of the economy of terror, the Irish brought to the mainland the gothic terror that had been visited on them by the English since Cromwell's day, returning it with interest. The state Terror of the French Revolution had reversed decisively into anti-state terrorism with the invention of dynamite by Alfred Nobel in 1863. Dynamite could be easily carried on the person, virtually undetectable, and the "infernal machine" or "peccant engine" then detonated at will by the ruthless dynamitard. While revolutionary nihilist and anarchist groups in Russia inspired novels such as Dostoevsky's *The Possessed* (1872), in England the Fenian "outrages" produced a new genre of novels about terrorism from authors as various as G. K. Chesterton, Henry James, George Moore, R. L. Stevenson, and, most famously, Joseph Conrad. Typically, the villains in these novels are vaguely defined East European anarchists rather than Irish Fenians, conjuring the fear of an international conspiracy of foreigners bent on some version of bringing down the British state.[16]

Edgar Wallace's *The Four Just Men* of 1905 marks an exception to this rule. Wallace's remarkable book concerns a group of terrorists who perform acts of justice on those who elude the institutional processes of justice of the state. They issue a threat on the life of the British Foreign Secretary, Sir Philip Ramon, who is steering an Aliens Extradition Bill through the House of Commons. Should the Bill become law, then Manuel Garcia, exiled leader of the Carlist movement fighting against the government of Spain, would be delivered into the Spanish government's hands and the corrupt regime would be saved. Though many today would question the claim that the Carlists were fighting to oust an oppressive and corrupt secular regime, the novel is sympathetic to the ideals, even the methods, of the Four Just Men:

> "It is monstrous," said the colonial secretary hotly; "it is inconceivable that such a state of affairs can last. Why, it strikes at the root of everything, it unbalances every adjustment of civilization."
>
> "It is a poetical idea," said the phlegmatic premier, "and the standpoint of the Four is quite a logical one. Think of the enormous power for good or evil often vested in one man: a capitalist controlling the markets of the world, a speculator cornering cotton or wheat whilst mills stand idle and people starve, tyrants and despots with the destinies of nations between their thumb and finger – and then think of the four men, known to none; vague, shadowy figures stalking tragically through the world, condemning and executing the capitalist, the corner-maker, the tyrant – evil forces all, and all beyond the reach of the law. We have said of these people, such of us as are touched with mysticism, that God would judge them. Here are men arrogating to themselves the divine right of judgement."[17]

Other crimes of justice committed by the Four Just Men include killing a sweatshop factory owner who abused his women employees, an embezzling French government official, an American gangland mass killer who had repeatedly eluded justice by bribing the jurors, and a New York City treasurer who was a notorious grafter. What marks out the Four Just Men is the international conception and reach of their justice, which means that they are particularly at home in a cosmopolitan city such as London. As scary as their threats and eventual assassination are the Four Just Men's uncanny ability to move about London at will, to penetrate effortlessly its most guarded buildings, to outwit all Scotland Yard's efforts against them, to execute the one man, Marks, who can recognize them . . . together with their unshakable confidence in their ability to carry out their predicted execution.

The novel, in which Wallace for the first time in fiction used the spare prose style he had learnt as a *Daily Mail* reporter, is particularly striking because of the ingenious form of the terrorism: the Four Just Men issue a series of threats to kill the Foreign Secretary at a particular time on a particular day. As time proceeds and Ramon ignores the threats, which are regularly repeated, the tension mounts for the police, the public, and for the reader. Though there is a high security alert and the Foreign Secretary is locked for his own safety in a room in a house filled with police, at the appointed hour the Four Just Men successfully carry out their threat of execution.

The difference in this scenario from random bombings is that such terrorism is directed not against innocent members of the public but against a government minister: this reflects the fact that much early terrorism was generally directed directly against political targets –

the Phoenix Park murders in Dublin, for example, carried out by the Invincibles, or the rash of political assassinations culminating in the assassination of the Archduke Franz Ferdinand in 1914, which initiated the chain of events that started World War I. This kind of terrorism still occurs today, witness the assassinations of Mahatma, Indira, and Rajeev Gandhi, or Israel's Minister of Tourism, Rechavam Ze'evi, in 2001, or the threats in 2006 to behead the Canadian Prime Minister, Stephen Harper. However, security is so efficient these days that terrorists rarely attempt to kill major public figures and instead attack them and their governments by proxy, by picking on innocent members of the public, who are easy targets and whose random execution prompts a general climate of fear.

Although the range of cases pursued by the Four Just Men are concerned with both high and low, the Four Just Men themselves are self-appointed rather than popular or elected. This is the political weakness of all terrorism. David Glover observes:

> If there is a certain aloofness about [Sir Philip Ramon], then this is not so far removed from the distant, rather magisterial demeanour of the Four Just Men themselves, whose high principles appear to lift them above any ordinary human community. However noble or humanitarian their motives may ultimately be, they are too morally fastidious and too independent simply to pass as men of the people.[18]

Terror, precisely, is never of the people. It's always a minority sport. The very "spontaneity" of terror was what worried Leon Trotsky, Vladimir Lenin, and Frantz Fanon, still regarded by some today in France as a terrorist, alike:

> the terrorists bow to the spontaneity of the passionate indignation of intellectuals, who lack the ability or opportunity to connect the revolutionary struggle and the working-class movement into an integral whole. It is difficult indeed for those who have lost their belief, or who have never believed, that this is possible, to find some outlet for their indignation and revolutionary energy other than terror.[19]

To create terror, paradoxically, is an admission of your political weakness, your lack of mass support.

The protagonists' politics of terror in *The Four Just Men* is as focused as it is elitist: their terrorist threat is issued in response to the government's proposed legislation on immigration, the Aliens Extradition Bill. The threat of terrorism in the face of a parliamentary bill was in fact not a fictional one: in February 1885, the Dynamite Revolutionary Section of the Irish Revolutionary Party had threatened to use "the resources of civilization" if the British parliament renewed the Crimes Act.[20] Wallace's novel of 1905 connects terrorism with immigration, an issue that can be linked to the invasion scare genre of novels popularized by William le Queux, Bram Stoker, E. Phillips Oppenheim, H. G. Wells, and others. The Aliens Extradition Bill in *The Four Just Men* represents a fictional version of the 1905 Aliens Act, which was the first immigration legislation in Britain and marked the beginning of the end of Britain's long history of being an open place of refuge for refugees and political exiles from Europe. In fact, the Aliens Act was primarily directed not against terrorists but the large numbers of Russian and East European Jews who had been settling in great numbers in the East End of London. The popular campaigns for immigration restriction at the time combined the language of race, in this case anti-Semitism, with the fear of anarchists and other foreign revolutionaries. "A recurrent theme in speeches and editorials was the spectre of East End anarchism, projected as a secret conspiracy of foreign revolutionaries ready to strike at the heart of the nation. This fear could take a variety of forms and the meaning of a phrase like 'foreign undesirables' could slide imperceptibly from the destitute to the degenerate to the politically dissident."[21] "Foreign undesirables" had been an issue from the end of the nineteenth century: its insistent repetition marks the course of the twentieth.

Terror as Farce

While *Northanger Abbey* stages the effect of terror on one of its characters, showing how fiction and revolutionary politics can equally produce the same effects, *The Four Just Men* follows the format of most nineteenth-century novels of terror, such as Donald MacKay's *The Dynamite Ship* (1888) or George Moore's *A Drama in Muslin* (1886), in representing the historical narrative of terrorist activity.[22] These novels are themselves only mildly performative: the reader senses fear and apprehension from the safety of her fictional distance; only the characters within the novel experience terror as such. Its production within a formal aesthetic genre, the novel, offers the novel as a para-site for and of terror where everything happens at a safe remove. For the reader, such novels produce suspense more than terror, as in André Brink's more recent *An Act of Terror* (1991), reversing into the reassurance and security of the detective story, a form which turns unknown terror inside out so as to track down and articulate the causes of its conjured fears by means of the power of the rational mind.[23] "In times of terror," writes Walter Benjamin, "everybody will be in the position of having to play detective."[24] Paradoxically, suspense novels about terror do not produce the "pure" terror effect of gothic fiction, of the kind that Benjamin himself experienced with the tales of E. A. Hoffmann. Forbidden to read Hoffmann by his parents, he could only read him on the sly in the evenings when his parents were away from home:

> And I can remember a particular evening, when I was sitting alone under the lamp at the giant dining-room table . . . and there was not a sound to be heard in the entire house. And as I sat there reading "The Mines of Falun," all the horrors gradually gathered around me at the table edge in the surrounding gloom, like fish with blank expressions, so that my eyes remained fixed on the pages of the book from which all this horror emerged, as if redemption might come from them. Another time, earlier in the day – I can still remember – I was standing right by the bookcase that was open just a crack, ready to throw the book into the case at the first noise. I stood there reading "The Entail," with hair on end, and so frozen with the twofold horror of the terrors of the book and the risk of being caught that I failed to grasp a single word of what I was reading.[25]

Gothic fiction forces Benjamin the reader to submit to apprehension and horror, the shudder of dread breaking down the barrier between interior and exterior, between fiction and the real, so that the very room in which the story is being read takes on the poetry of terror that pervades Hoffman's tale: "The bourgeois interior . . . fittingly houses only the corpse."[26] Benjamin himself would later transform the dynamic experience of gothic terror into an aesthetics of shock. In alluding to contemporary terrorism, the novel about terrorism by contrast feeds off the terror of the real that pervades the public sphere, reduplicating it for reading pleasure, and in that way offering an aesthetic anesthetic for the everyday fears that the reader feels. The novel of terror, it turns out, in fact offers a way of resisting terror.

While *The Four Just Men* is very different in tone from the most famous English novel about terrorists, written just two years later – Conrad's *The Secret Agent* – Conrad's novel is also concerned with issues of terror and immigration. The basis of the plot, in fact, is exactly the same: the need to stop the British giving Continental political undesirables asylum – a situation that makes one feel positively nostalgic for certain aspects of the days when the British could put their own liberal principles and beliefs before international political pressure:

> "What we want is to administer a tonic to the Conference in Milan," [Mr. Vladimir] said airily. "Its deliberations upon international action for the suppression of political crime don't seem to get anywhere. England lags. This country is absurd with its sentimental regard for individual liberty. It's intolerable to think that all your friends have got only to come over to –"
>
> "In that way I have them all under my eye," Mr. Verloc interrupted huskily.
>
> "It would be much more to the point to have them all under lock and key. England must be brought into line. The imbecile bourgeoisie of this country make themselves the accomplices of the very people whose aim is to drive them out of their houses to starve in ditches. And they have the political power still, if they only had the sense to use it for their preservation. . . . What [the middle classes] want just now is a jolly good scare. This is the psychological moment to set your friends to work. I have had you called here to develop to you my idea."
>
> And Mr. Vladimir developed his idea from on high, with scorn and condescension, displaying at the same time an amount of ignorance as to the real aims, thoughts, and methods of the revolutionary world which filled the silent Mr. Verloc with inward consternation. He confounded causes with effects more than was excusable; the most distinguished propagandists with impulsive bomb throwers . . .
>
> "A series of outrages," Mr Vladimir continued calmly, "executed here in this country; not only *planned* here – that would not do – they would not mind. Your friends could set half the Continent on fire without influencing the public opinion here in favour of a universal repressive legislation. They will not look outside their backyard here."
>
> . . . "These outrages need not be especially sanguinary," Mr Vladimir went on, as if delivering a scientific lecture, "but they must be sufficiently startling – effective."[27]

Terror must be "effective." Because Vladimir's plan mimics a terrorist act, and is not really the real thing, this particular outrage must carry a meaning – to be achieved by destroying a building whose symbolic meaning is dear to the bourgeoisie. Vladimir's strategy to shake the bourgeoisie out of their liberal complacency is to force Verloc to blow up the bourgeoisie's most respected icon, the Greenwich Observatory, which offers a symbolic target to anarchists and revolutionists in its role as preserver of global, imperial time. As so often, the leader of the group gets someone else to do the dangerous work for him. So Mr. Verloc contrives to make Stevie, his wife's half-witted brother, plant the bomb for him. But it goes wrong: climbing up the hill, Stevie trips and blows himself up:

> "Stumbled," [the constable] announced positively. "I stumbled once myself, and pitched on my head too, while running up. Them roots do stick out all about the place. Stumbled against the root of a tree and fell, and that thing he was carrying must have gone off right under his chest, I expect."

Stevie tripping was just a random, spontaneous act, which caught Verloc short. Today, Stevie would be characterized a suicide bomber. His "suicide" was the spontaneous trusting act of a trusting boy, which in itself is enough perhaps to make him a typical suicide bomber. What began as farce turns into tragedy, and it is the human tragedy of the ending that gives the novel its particular power. This belated swerve of the narrative also serves to reduce further the stature of the characters who have already been presented as self-interested individuals wallowing within an ineffective, comfortable fantasmatics of terror and revolution. Conrad's novel annuls the terrorist in two ways: first, by reducing his politics to domestic farce; and second, by contrasting his self-serving selfishness with the altruistic love of Winnie for Stevie. Once again the novel of terrorism serves to reduce the power of the aesthetic of terror in the public sphere.

Terror as Trauma

While the gothic novel released the horrors of terror, the novel of terrorism as exemplified in *The Secret Agent* thus typically contains it through the downgrading of the characters of individual terrorists, or the reduction of terrorism to a farcical travesty of itself. Later examples working within this genre would include Doris Lessing's *The Good Terrorist* (1985) or Hari Kunzru's novel *Transmission* (2004).[28] The fear of terror represented in such novels is typically compounded for character and reader alike by the fear of immigration or the foreign. As Wallace, Conrad, Lessing, and Kunzru suggest, terror, migration, and globalization are not randomly linked: fear of migrants and illegal immigration has turned out to be one of the most consistent terror effects of all. But if the fear of immigrants and the imagined threat that they embody fabricates a dominant relation between Western states and terror, this is very different from the ways in which terror operates in the postcolonial world itself. The war on terror is often projected as if it were Americans and Europeans who are the main victims of terror. In many cases they are, but I want to end by switching my geographical focus and suggesting that there are in fact different forms of terror that operate very differently elsewhere. What if the terror in which you are living is too ubiquitous to allow its dismissal by the distancing literary effects of belittlement or comedy?

Terror, in the ways that I have been describing it, is essentially a First World form of terror. You fear it, you fear its psychic, somatic, and potentially bodily effects, but for most people it remains, thankfully, always at a Burkean remove. Compare this with the experience of people who actually live terror, suffer terror, in one form or another, on a day-to-day basis. We can see this marked by a linguistic survival: the verb "apprehend" is still used in South Asian English today as it was in Shakespeare's day – "Oh let my Lady apprehend no feare" (*Troilus and Cressida* III. ii. 80) – meaning "To anticipate with fear or dread; to be fearful concerning; to fear" (*OED*). This meaning, elsewhere lost in modern English, corresponds to the existence of more immediate forms of fear, to the state of living in apprehension.

To get a sense of this, you have only to think of contemporary Sri Lanka. The explosion of fiction from Sri Lanka in the past 20 years is in itself remarkable, but no less remarkable is the way in which almost all that fiction, whether obliquely, as in Romesh Gunesekera's masterpiece *Reef* (1994), or directly, as in his more disturbing hallucinatory novel *Heaven's Edge* (2002), makes you realize the difference between terror effects to which the subjects of terror are submitted in the West, and the incomparably more traumatic experiences of the civil war in Sri Lanka.[29] This terror works very differently from that of a particular traumatic event, such as the Partition of India in 1947. Indeed, can this civil war even be called a form of terror, when society has broken down and the government itself has become simply another ruthless and morally indifferent agent of revenge and mass slaughter?

Powerful and extraordinary though Gunesekera's novels are, it is in Michael Ondaatje's *Anil's Ghost* that we vicariously experience the full extent of a terrorism that has descended into a civil war in which the different sides (one technically legitimate, the violence of the state, the others not) have become indistinguishable: train killings, massacres, beheadings, crucifixions, night visitations, kidnapping, murders in broad daylight, a man being cycled off to his death holding on to the handlebars of a bike. "Everyone's scared, Anil. It's a national disease."[30] Is this state of affairs, apparently unending, still "terrorism"?

Such violence, as the novel shows, spreads into the violence of relationships, of people sealed within themselves. "We are full of anarchy," one of the characters comments accurately enough. There seems to be no closure: "This was the scarring psychosis in the country. Death, loss, was 'unfinished' so you could not walk through it" (Ondaatje 2000: 56). And lest we think this kind of terrorism does not continue to effect an affect, then recall the fact that Sri Lanka has the highest suicide rate in the world. The lesson of *Anil's Ghost* is that in this situation, when terror moves from being the actions of a specific group against a state, to the form of a civil war in which the government and military themselves engage in methods that are as arbitrary, illegal, and violent as the terrorist groups, then you have a very different kind of terror. Here terror has moved from the dialectics of traditional terrorism into a porous landscape in which terror has leaked into unreadable forms of arbitrary violence beyond the realm of all political and social institutions of power: in short, into trauma. "She used to believe that meaning allowed a person a door to escape grief and fear. But she saw that those who were slammed and stained by violence lost the power of language and logic. It was the way to abandon emotion, a last protection for the self" (pp. 55–6).

Anil's Ghost critiques the assumption that people in the West know how to respond to such terror, in particular the assumption that international human rights discourse is the best way to help those who are living through it. The novel portrays a series of characters who respond to the context of terror, its violent erasure of meaning, by locking down into a state in which emotion itself is abandoned. Anil's co-worker Sarath, and his brother the emergency doctor Gamini, both survive by operating within this enervated psychic sphere, abandoning emotion and retreating into the self. Some individuals are eventually able to move beyond this state of traumatized self-protection by making imaginative and creative choices through which at a psychic level they refuse terror's debilitating affect. At this point, Ondaatje suggests, the only way to respond to the trauma of terror has to be about controlling yourself, detaching yourself, rebuilding yourself, changing yourself from being reactive to proactive, reconstructing in the face of deconstruction, finding forms of protection for the self against terror beyond the abandonment of emotion, and moving out of the normative realm of the social to establish a different relation with the temporality of the world beyond the human.

> The noise of the hammering stopped and there was just the wind around them, its tugs and gusts and whistles. He handed the tools to his nephew. Then he drew from a satchel the colours for the eye. He looked past the vertical line of cheek into the landscape. Pale greens, dark greens, bird movement and their nearby sounds. It was the figure of the world the statue would see forever, in rainlight and sunlight, a combustible world of weather even without the human element. (p. 306)

The terrorist's power can be exorcised individually and communally by a resistance, a self-control, placing the human into a new relation with the environment that may not change the political chaos but at least allows you to free yourself from its negativity and sense of helplessness and fear and refuse its effect. When asked to reconstruct the face of the skull of the victim known as Sailor, Ananda the sculptor instead creates an image of his wife who had earlier been abducted and killed, and then recreates the face of the Buddha statue that has been destroyed. Palipana the famous archaeologist eliminates borders and categories and begins to read half-perceived interlinear texts into an imagined rewriting of the past that reassembles and reorganizes its fragments: "this is the basis of the incomparable aura [*halo*] that surrounds the storyteller. . . . If one keeps silent, it is not only to listen to him, but also in some measure because it is there."[31] This constructive quality of some of the local responses told in *Anil's Ghost* gradually earns Anil's respect as her Western assumptions peel off her, though not soon enough for her not to be responsible for effecting the death of her co-worker Sarath. The novel attempts to find ways to refuse the gothic discourse of social terror, and shows how in the context of an unimaginable horror that continues without respite, the characters retrieve a sense of the dignity and creativity of being human within an extended sense of the universe around them – the very qualities that terrorists themselves had abandoned in Conrad's portrait.

What does terror want? Terror makes us reactive rather than proactive and creative. It prevents us from telling stories. To live in terror is to acknowledge a state of submission to it. The fear has to be overcome: here ordinary people in their unhistorical lives show the way by moving spontaneously into a world that offers a richness and generosity of response, refusing the random and its state of fear, resisting its aestheticized politics, refusing to submit to the terms, the discourse and demands of terrorism, and refusing too the macho political response which only responds with further destruction. Some people let their ghosts die, some don't, observes Ondaatje. In *Anil's Ghost* he shows how some people have learnt how to stop the cascading demons of the terror effect. Rather than trying to anesthetize terror by denigrating the terrorists, *Anil's Ghost* shows how individuals subjected to terror learn how to resist the terror effect, challenging its affect through a radically reimagined voyage into the ethical, psychic, and political space of androgyny, non-violence, and the post-human.

Notes

1 For one exception in the huge literature on terrorism, see Gearty (1991).
2 Purdue University Online Writing lab, Spelling: Affect / Effect http://owl.english.purdue.edu/handouts/grammar/g_spelprob.html
3 Gasché (1987: 143).
4 Melchiori (1985: 12).
5 Newsinger (1994: 64); *New York Times*, August 27, 2008.
6 Cf. Foucault (1984: 32–50).
7 Punter (1996).
8 Taussig (1987: 3).
9 Attridge (2000).
10 Jane Austen, *Northanger Abbey* (2006: 113–15). The mention of baseball comes in Chapter 1, p. 7.
11 Ibid., 332–3.
12 Brown (1987).
13 Burke (1990: 36–7). Further references will be cited in the text.
14 Michel Fuchs, cited in Gibbons (2003: 7).
15 Suleri (1992: 36).
16 Melchiori (1985: 23).
17 Wallace (1995: 66).
18 Ibid., xvii.
19 Lenin (1970, 1: 179); cf. Leon Trotsky: "By its very essence terrorist work demands such concentrated energy for 'the great moment', such an overestimation of the significance of individual heroism, and finally, such a 'hermetic' conspiracy, that – if not logically, then psychologically – it totally excludes agitational and organisational work among the masses" (Trotsky 1909).
20 Wallace (1995: 46).
21 Ibid.
22 MacKay (1888); Moore (1886).

23 Brink (1991).
24 Benjamin, *Gesammelte Schriften* (1989, 1: 542–3); "The Paris of the Second Empire in Baudelaire", *Selected Writings* (1996–2003, 4: 21).
25 Benjamin, *Gesammelte Schriften* (1989, 7: 88); "Demonic Berlin," *Selected Writings* (1996–2003, 2: 323–4).
26 Benjamin, *Gesammelte Schriften* (1989, 4: 89); "One-Way Street," *Selected Writings* (1996–2003, 1: 447).
27 Conrad (1990: 27–9).
28 Lessing (1985); Kunzru (2004).
29 Gunesekera (1994); (2002).
30 Ondaatje (2000: 53). Further page references will be cited in the text.
31 Benjamin, *Gesammelte Schriften* (1989, 2: 1309); "The Storyteller," *Selected Writings* (1996–2003, 3: 162, 166).

References

Attridge, Derek. (2000) *Joyce Effects: On Language, Theory and History*. Cambridge: Cambridge University Press.

Austen, Jane. (2006) *Northanger Abbey*, ed. Barbara M. Benedict and Deirdre Le Faye. Cambridge: Cambridge University Press.

Benjamin, Walter. (1989) *Gesammelte Schriften*, ed. Rolf Tiedemann and Hermann Schweppenhäuser, 7 vols. Frankfurt: Suhrkamp.

Benjamin, Walter. (1996–2003) *Selected Writings*, eds. Marcus Bullock and Michael W. Jennings, 4 vols. Cambridge, Mass.: Belknap Press of Harvard University Press.

Brink, André. (1991) *An Act of Terror*. New York: Summit Books.

Brown, Marshall. (1987) "A Philosophical View of the Gothic Novel," *Studies in Romanticism* 26 (Summer): 275–304.

Burke, Edmund. (1990 [1757]) *A Philosophical Enquiry into the Origin of Our Ideas of the Sublime and Beautiful*, ed. Adam Phillips. Oxford: Oxford University Press.

Conrad, Joseph. (1990) *The Secret Agent: A Simple Tale*, ed. Bruce Harkness and S. W. Reid. Cambridge: Cambridge University Press.

Foucault, Michel. (1984) "What Is Enlightenment?," in Paul Rabinow (ed.), *The Foucault Reader*. New York: Pantheon Books.

Gasché, Rodolphe. (1987) "On Aesthetic and Historical Determination," in Derek Attridge, Geoffrey Bennington, and Robert J. C. Young (eds.), *Poststructuralism and the Question of History*. Cambridge: Cambridge University Press.

Gearty, C. A. (1991) *Terror*. London: Faber and Faber.

Gibbons, Luke. (2003) *Edmund Burke and Ireland*. Cambridge: Cambridge University Press.

Gunesekera, Romesh. (1994) *Reef*. London: Granta.

Gunesekera, Romesh. (2002) *Heaven's Edge*. London: Bloomsbury.

Kunzru, Hari. (2004) *Transmission*. New York: Dutton.
Lenin, V. I. (1970 [1901]) *What Is to Be Done? Burning Questions of Our Movement*, in *Selected Works*, 3 vols. Moscow: Progress Publishers.
Lessing, Doris. (1985) *The Good Terrorist*. London: Jonathan Cape.
MacKay, Donald. (1888) *The Dynamite Ship*. London: Page, Pratt & Turner.
Melchiori, Barbara Arnett. (1985) *Terrorism in the Late Victorian Novel*. London: Croom Helm.
Moore, George. (1886) *A Drama in Muslin*. London: Vizetelly.
Newsinger, John. (1994) *Fenianism in Mid-Victorian Britain*. London: Pluto Press.
Ondaatje, Michael. (2000) *Anil's Ghost*. London: Bloomsbury.
Punter, David. (1996) *The Literature of Terror: A History of Gothic Fictions from 1765 to the Present Day*, 2nd ed., 2 vols. London: Longman.
Suleri, Sara. (1992) *The Rhetoric of English India*. Chicago: Chicago University Press.
Taussig, Michael. (1987) *Shamanism, Colonialism, and the Wild Man. A Study in Healing*. Chicago: Chicago University Press.
Trotsky, Leon. (1909) "Why Marxists Oppose Individual Terrorism," http://www.geocities.com/CapitolHill/Congress/1602/textosmarxistas/trottext/terror.html
Wallace, Edgar. (1995 [1905]) *The Four Just Men*, ed. David Glover. Oxford: Oxford University Press.

Chapter 13

"Gendering" Terror: Representations of the Female "Freedom Fighter" in Contemporary Sri Lankan Literature and Cultural Production

Neluka Silva

The Female Militant: Critical Readings

When I was about seven months pregnant, and dressed in a *salwar khamees*, I was stopped at an Army security checkpoint in Colombo. After my national identity card was checked and I was "cleared," I jokingly said to the soldiers, "Do I look like a suicide bomber?" They laughed, but then seriously replied, "Nowadays, most of the suicide bombers are women, and they strap the bombs to their stomach and wear a salwar and pretend to be pregnant."

This incident enacts a phenomenon that was/is a part of everyday reality in Sri Lanka, that is, where the exigencies of the ethnic war have enabled women to enter the realms of armed conflict as active participants. The Liberation Tigers of Tamil Eelam (LTTE) and the Sri Lankan Army have recruited women into its military force since the mid-1980s, though almost all the Tamil militant groups emphasized women's participation in the liberation struggle and made appeals for them to enlist. The change in policy toward women's participation appears to have been the result of several factors: a strategic need for more fighters in the face of an insufficiency of men as the young male population was increasingly decimated through combat and the refugee flow out of the conflict areas; the ideological need to demonstrate that these separatist forces were also an all-encompassing mass social movement; and the pressure from young Tamil women themselves to actively participate in armed conflict (Talbot 2001).

The entry of women into the realms of conflict has provoked intense debate and created a deep-seated unease in the public consciousness for several reasons. As Dorit Naaman argues, "When women opt to fight alongside men, they challenge the dichotomy of woman as victim/man as defender" (2007: 935). The thought that women fighters are "active" and willing to kill is clearly unpalatable, and certainly troubles conventional gendered stereotypes. For both the figure of the female soldier and the female martyr challenge the traditional patriarchal binary opposition that postulates women as physically and emotionally weak and incapable of determining and defending the course of their own lives (Naaman 2007: 935).

In order to rationalize this phenomenon, the image of women fighters is inscribed by the rhetoric of military organizations such as the LTTE or the Sri Lankan Army with particular attributes that are counterposed with prescribed forms of femininity, and the discourse pivots around the denial or suppression of woman's delicacy and fragility but also her generosity, caring nature, motherliness (Naaman 2007: 935). It becomes necessary to efface traditional notions that "women have been associated with biological life and denied access to the biographical; they have been associated with procreation as the survival of the species and not as the creation of new values and new meaning for life" (Oliver 2008: 10). These roles so drastically deviate from the "typical" female roles circulated in news and entertainment media that they "enhance the sense of perplexity, fear, and aversion to the perpetrators of the acts" (Naaman 2007: 935).

The ascendancy of the female suicide bomber in conflicts all over the world has generated a wide range of debates, and "the distinction between suicide and martyrdom is crucial" to many of the debates (Rose 2004). Jacqueline Rose has argued that although religious discourses proscribe suicide, "Martyrdom, however, is something else. 'If a martyr wants to kill himself because he's sick of being alive, that's suicide. But if he wants to sacrifice his soul in order to defeat the enemy and for God's sake – well, then he's a martyr,' the late

Abdel Aziz al-Rantissi explained in 2001" (Rose 2004). The concept of martyrdom in general and female martyrdom in particular has also been pivotal in the LTTE's discourses in Sri Lanka, as I will now suggest.

In her article about the women LTTE cadres in the Tamil nationalist movement in Sri Lanka, Radhika Coomaraswamy presents a persuasive analysis of the privileged female stereotypes – of the militant mother and the armed virgin – that pervade the LTTE discourses (1996: 9). Although neither of these ideals conforms to the "traditional" Tamil wife image, both are paradigmatic of patriarchal underpinnings. Female sexuality is brought into the arena of nationalist struggle and is trammeled and contained. Coomaraswamy notes that the single woman's agency is contingent on the denial of sexuality. Even the realm of revolutionary practice is governed by the notion that *shakthi* (the Hindu concept of female energy) has to be curbed. The anxiety to maintain the ideal of virginity is part of a social construction that stems from the fear that the single, *sexual* woman liberally allows her body to be abused – translated in larger terms as the metaphor for prostituting the nation to the foreign investor/colonizer, outsider, or enemy within.

The "armed virgin," in particular the suicide bomber, has conspicuously prefigured as a weapon for the LTTE, and has become both a source of intrigue as well as a disconcerting presence in the public consciousness. This character has shored up many questions relating to the motivation to give up her life for a political cause, ranging from whether she is brainwashed by the (male) commanders of the movement or is fully aware of the action she is to undertake. Bloom's interrogation of the underlying causes for enlisting in the case of Sri Lanka is restrictive, as she attributes their participation almost entirely to sexual abuse, either of the female militant herself or a close family member (2005: 159–60).

The overarching concern among recent commentators on the female suicide bomber, such as Mia Bloom, Kelly Oliver, and Jacqueline Rose, is how to read the *act* of suicide, and whether this moment is a sign of female emancipation or patriarchal suppression, victimhood or agency. What is compelling are the *responses* to this phenomenon. Whether it is in the media or political and public discourses, what is apparent is the anxiety (almost reaching the proportion of paranoia) to represent the female suicide bomber in ways that abstract the act of martyrdom from the specific political context of territorial conflicts and international power relations. Typically, such public discourse tends to frame the actions of women suicide bombers in ways that seek to contain the challenge to predominant patriarchal constructs of femininity instantiated by the women's own narratives and actions. As I will demonstrate through an analysis of cultural texts, there is a heavy reliance on convenient stereotypes which are attendant upon conventional images that deny women agency and instead represent them as monsters or brides in a hegemonic framework that preserves intact conventional gender categories (Naaman 2007: 952).

Aggressor to Victim: The Female Militant in Contemporary Sri Lankan Cultural Texts

Many of the anxieties outlined above are played out in contemporary literary works and cultural production in Sri Lanka where suicide bombers, especially female suicide bombers, have become a visible and dominant part of the ensuing conflict. Through an analysis of two works – a play, Visakesa Chandrasekeram's *Thahanam Adaviya* (1998, later translated into English as *The Forbidden Area*) and a popular soap opera (referred to as "teledrama" in Sri Lanka), *Vishwa Gamana* – this essay explores some of the issues discussed above through the specific geopolitical context of Sri Lanka, and the location of the woman militant (in this case suicide bomber) within the discursive frame of socio-political spheres. The texts will be interpreted as typifying the media and popular responses to the mobilization of women into the role of suicide bomber.

Although cultural works in contemporary Sri Lanka are replete with images of women in conflict situations, their roles are largely confined to that of victim, drawing upon existing notions of, for example, the suffering mother/daughter etc. either waiting for protection from the "patriotic" soldier or violated by the "malevolent" antagonist. Scant attention is paid to the spectrum of other female roles such as women heads of households, sex workers, factory workers, or professional women that have existed and been the mainstay of the Sri Lankan economy for several decades.

Likewise, the female militant has rarely figured in Sri Lankan literature and popular culture. The two works I have selected, therefore, stand out as deviating from the norm by assigning the protagonist the role of the female militant.

To begin with brief plot outlines, in *Thahanam Adaviya*, the central character, Urmila, on the eve of acting as a "live target" encounters

Raman, another member of the group. During their meeting she reveals her reasons for joining the movement. Her narrative, with its undertones of idealism and romanticism, sharply contrasts with Raman's more pragmatic, if not cynical, approach to what he perceives to be "revolutionary" praxis. As they are isolated in a room waiting to embark on their mission, Urmila finds herself attracted to Raman, and then seduces him. After their sexual liaison, she changes her mind about giving up her life for the "cause." When their leader, Supremo, arrives she tries to plead with him to abort this mission. He refuses to do so, and compels her to fulfill her mission.

In *Vishwa Gamana*, a popular teledrama, a Sinhala Buddhist CID officer, Banuka, meets a Tamil woman, Ishwari. Initially, her role as a suicide bomber is implicitly cast. She poses as a professional photographer, which enables her to scrutinize the targets and take photographs of strategic locations. After she meets Banuka they become romantically involved and she decides to abandon the organization. The CID pressure Banuka to hand over Ishwari to them but he resists. They later flee together to Banuka's ancestral home, which is situated outside Colombo, and are pursued by both the members of the "organization" and the CID. They are discovered by two leaders of the organization and when Banuka tries to shoot them he is killed. The CID and police then arrive, shoot the two men and take Ishwari into custody. At the denouement she is alone in a prison cell.

In both works, the configuration of the female character converges in certain respects: both women single-mindedly pursue their political objectives until they become romantically involved. At this point, the tensions between individual aspirations and the collective aims of the group become apparent. This tension is symptomatic of the patriarchal transactions that occur in relation to women's roles within the nation-state. The responsibility conferred upon the woman/mother by the nation is summarized by Floya Anthias and Nira Yuval Davis: "it is to [re]produce its citizens, to ensure that cultural codes are transmitted, to maintain the sanctity of one's ethnic/national group and to act as signifiers of ethnic/national differences" (1994: 314–16). Though the woman militant superficially presents a shift in the paradigm, she too appears to be controlled by authoritarian male-dominated power hierarchies. Thus the casting of the woman militant in the two texts converges with some popular perceptions attached to the role of woman in the nationalist frame. Both Urmila and Ishwari conform to these perceptions which identify the female militant as (a) ruthless; (b) only acting in a supporting role within terrorist organizations; and

(c) unfeminine in some way (Talbot 2001). Their roles also conform to what Gus Martin has noted of women in military organizations: "More commonly, women serve as combatants rather than leaders for women are recruited to participate as support functionaries such as finding safe houses or engaging in surveillance" (2006: 99).

However, both works also go beyond the conventional by attempting to offer feminized and empowering alternatives for the protagonist (at least at the beginning of the narrative). Despite conforming to the propaganda (though *Thahanam Adaviya* is a more complex and sensitive rendering of the female militant than *Vishwa Gamana*), the characters' psychobiography and personal history are detailed in the course of the narrative. Though the personal narratives provide for a more "individualized" perspective of the female militant, attention to the personal needs to be contextualized within the politics of representation. Naaman observes that the representation of the female militant contrasts sharply with that of the male militant. In the case of the former, "their names are publicly emphasized and the videos aired; furthermore, they are contrasted with photos of the women from their previous lives, photos that emphasize the fact that they were young women engaged in traditional teenage habits and activities" (2007: 942).

The emphasis on the "traditional" occurs in both *Thahanam Adaviya* and *Vishwa Gamana* and are deployed to stress that though militant organizations appeal to women by providing a mechanism for rejecting "traditional" conventions, this is illusive, as the organizations are governed by and operate within "traditional" frameworks.

In order to gain a more precise purchase on Chandrasekeram's perceptions of the politics of gender within the patriarchal framework of the "movement," it is useful to compare Urmila's story of her recruitment and political commitment with research on the LTTE women cadres in Sri Lanka. In her conversations with Raman, Urmila reveals that her membership constitutes a radical gesture, a mechanism for flouting social and religious conventions. The patriarchal structures that constrained her are forcefully mapped out. Three reasons impel her to give up her family and undertake the ultimate sacrifice of giving up her life. Firstly, she sees the "movement" as destabilizing a rigid caste system. Caste differences are most prominently coded in the serving of food and drink to those who belong to the "lower" castes. Her narrative of her mother's position as a domestic help in an upper caste doctor's house foregrounds the controls imposed by this system. As a child, Urmila was denied entry into the house, and on one occasion when she visits her mother, she says: "I was given a cup of tea in a cup with a broken handle" because they did not want someone from a lower caste drinking from one of their cups (Chandrasekeram 1998: 24). She comments: "I could not bear these injustices. I looked for the answer to these problems on my own, and finally I found them" (ibid.). After this incident she decides to ". . . find the answer to such injustices," which becomes a determinant in committing herself to the movement. According to her, the "movement" presented her with the opportunity to destroy these structures, since the propaganda professed that everyone in the "movement" was treated with equality. What is ironically rendered here is the way in which, while trying to eschew the limitations of one system, she becomes further entrapped in another, and is not able to recognize it.

Secondly, after her father is brutally killed by the Indian Peacekeeping Force (who acted as peacekeepers in the Jaffna Peninsula in from 1987 to 1989) she realizes that the state does not offer any recourse to alleviate the suffering of the masses, but the "movement" in contrast, offered a possible redress to the injustices perpetrated on the common person, by allowing people to fight for their rights. Finally, she argues that the "movement" promised to overturn structures of gender discrimination. For her, the most potent of these patriarchal manacles is the dowry system. As a poor woman, her family could not afford a dowry for her, and without a dowry she was divested of the possibility of marriage. In addition, she regards herself as "unattractive," a personal flaw which in her eyes fails to compensate for her lack of monetary value. What Urmila's autobiography suggests here is that the system of marriage is tantamount to bribery (Chandrasekeram 2000: 25).

Her view that the lack of traditional norms of beauty precludes her from romantic involvement taps into the dominant assumptions of beauty that determine gender and social relations: the internalization of the ideal woman, and the inbuilt sexism operating within marriage. This revelation points to notions of the ideal woman, referred to as a *Pancha Kalyani*, who is imaged as fair-skinned, youthful, with long black hair and beautiful teeth and is a benchmark for assessing "beauty" in Sri Lanka.[1] On the issue of female beauty, Inderpal Grewal has made some invaluable observations, especially its class configurations. As she argues, working women, or underclass women, worn out by hard work, childbearing, and undernourishment, "could not possess the kind of beauty that the more comfortable life of the upper-class allowed. . . . Thus beauty as a normative concept seemed to transcend class even while it did not do so" (1996: 39). Urmila is psychologically governed by these notions of beauty and the playwright enacts the psychological impact of these attributes.

The rationale that is worked out through Urmila resonates with the variety of interconnected motivations for enlisting in the LTTE that Miranda Alison demonstrates in her research on LTTE women. Their perceptions of the societal insecurities of their ethno-national community, their own individual insecurity and, for some, the gender-specific insecurities associated with being a Sri Lankan Tamil woman in the context of the war are all interwoven in the play. In addition, nationalist commitment; the death of a loved one and/or other experiences or perceptions of suffering and oppression at the hands of the state (including experiences of displacement); educational disruption and restrictions; poverty; sexual violence against women; and ideas of women's emancipation are mitigating factors (Alison 1994).

In his portrayal of Urmila, Chandrasekeram eschews romanticizing her status within the "movement," and he does not ignore the gender and class inequalities that circumscribe her (1998: 49). For instance, she is initially made to believe that she is going to blow up the President (a greater honor in her eyes), but when Supremo arrives, he abruptly changes the target to the Chief Minister, a lower-ranking politician, and then refuses to entertain any questions or protests from her. This act of patriarchal dominance is underscored by the patriarchal rhetoric of revolutionary praxis that is presented throughout the text, and the act of being able to join the movement does not efface its existence. Urmila's role, albeit active, is a problematic one, because we witness how she is entirely dependent upon and dictated by a strong male-dominated power base. By referring repeatedly to male voices, leadership, and commands, the playwright reinforces the patriarchal undertones that are masked by the rhetoric of "equality" in the movement's revolutionary narrative. For instance, although Urmila pleads with the Supremo to grant her freedom from this mission, it is denied, and his polemic of her "martyrdom" is portrayed as an act of male dominance (Chandrasekeram 1998: 48). In their final conversation, the Supremo's insistence on her service to the "motherland" reveals how patriarchal politics intersect with nationalism, which governs female subjectivity. The relationship between them is inscribed within a dominant discourse wherein the "deviation from traditional womanly roles is [justified] by adopting a thesis that female suicide bombers are victims of patriarchy" (Naaman 2007: 943).

Her suicide, ultimately undertaken reluctantly and under duress, therefore, fails to offer a mode of resistance. Here, notions of male superiority and expectations of female subservience are prevalent and undercut the discourse of "feminism" espoused by the LTTE leadership. For instance, Adele Balasingham, wife of Anton Balasingham, described the entry of women into the movement in the following terms:

> Tamil women guerrillas' articulated a tremendous determination to fight the Sri Lankan army who they firmly feel have no place in their homeland. It is the strength of this conviction that allows these young women to fight . . . it is the conviction that sustains them emotionally when their colleagues die in battle; and make supreme sacrifices. (Balasingham 1990)

This statement presupposes the commitment of women toward armed conflict, but it discounts the individual emotional and psychological complexities and the cost of their entry into such organizations.

Even as revolutionary politics enables Urmila to dislodge the traditional political boundaries, controls on female sexuality are stringently enforced. In the prelude to her sexual liaison with Raman, Urmila unmasks the blatant erasure of womanhood demanded by the "movement." Discipline and chastity become the basis of female containment, so much so that they function as desexualized repositories of terror. As is evident in the play, the sexual experience dilutes her resolve. Urmila's anxieties and fears about death, which lie beneath her bravado, are brought to the surface after this moment. Sexual intimacy becomes an extension, then, of the experience of awaiting death, and to her is an affirmation of life. Radhika Coomaraswamy's analysis of the overemphasis placed upon the armed virgin in the LTTE is germane to the way in which Urmila is circumscribed in her role as armed combatant. As Coomaraswamy argues, "Sexuality is seen as an evil, debilitating force . . . self-sacrifice, austerity and androgyny are put forwards as ideals" (1996: 10). Whether empowered by a gun or acting as a live target, the ideal woman remains a virgin. This containment is underpinned by the fear of female sexuality/energy, *shakthi*, that has to be trammeled, whether it is the revolutionary or the more socially acceptable subject position of wife/mother.

Urmila derives *shakthi* from the goddess Kali, whose notoriety is linked to her ferocity. After Urmila joins the "movement" she becomes a Kali devotee, erects a shrine to her, and visits a Kali temple on the eve of her mission. This is a significant act, demonstrating the strength she derives from this figure. Her enraptured tone in rendering this account to Raman calls attention to the correspondence between nationalist politics and religion. Religion is designed or, to use Gananath Obeyesekere's term, "transformed" (1989) to accommodate the needs of the nationalist agenda and make militancy permissible. The motif of ruthlessness associated with Kali seems to empower Urmila, and the mission she prepares for is situated within the politics of religion. Historically, *shakthi* has been marshaled for a "political" purpose: to mobilize women into armed struggle or resistance, implicit in, for instance, Gandhi's rallying cry to women during the anti-colonial struggle, invoking the attributes of Kali, of the capacity for exceptional heroism. The mythologizing of such acts of heroism is problematic, because even as Urmila internalizes these myths, her certainty in their heroic potential and so-called "liberation," while constituting subversion, at another level is illusory, as we find that, ultimately, they exert an ideological and psychological hold on her.

Chandrasekeram's achievement in the portrayal of this character lies in bestowing Urmila with a humanity that counterbalances her militancy, of unveiling the slippages between life and death, humanity and ruthlessness, so that she becomes a figure who throws into crisis the certitudes transmitted through the media of the brutality of the female militant. The final act of suicide therefore becomes a tragic moment revealing how the enactment of suicide cannot be glossed over or explained simplistically.

The complexity of character evident in Urmila is entirely lacking in the teledrama *Vishwa Gamana*. Though innovative, in terms of storyline, it underscores stereotypical notions of the female militant, thereby forestalling the prospect of transforming popular perceptions attached to such a character. The initial stages of the narrative rely heavily on the media representations of the female suicide bomber. Ishwari enacts crude and popular images such as the actress Damitha Abeyrathne's view of the LTTE women that "they act like men." These qualities are rendered in her assertiveness, aggression, and dominance of her male colleagues in the "organization," inscribing the masculinity and ruthlessness that is associated with the female militant. Concomitant to this image is her "respectable" and well-groomed demeanor, depicted as a strategy to provide access to her targets.

The externalization of the "respectable" female body plays upon received notions of Victorian middle-class values – of the bourgeois body as compliant and passive, rather than anarchic or rebellious, thereby deflecting any suspicion from her. She inhabits a classed position that is replete with the trappings of the middle class in Sri Lanka. The furniture in her small apartment, the electronic gadgets and conveniences, as well as her Western dress (mostly trousers or jeans and T-shirt or blouses), modern hairstyle and accessories contribute to this construction of bourgeois femininity. Although the dress suppresses a distinct ethnic identity and is largely a device to serve her political objective, this image of a respectable, middle-class, female militant alienated audiences, and their responses revealed that such a persona was unacceptable within the terms of reference for what is deemed as "appropriate" for a Tamil woman.[2] It was argued that "she did not dress or act properly for a Tamil," suggesting how external facets govern perceptions of identity, and even the female militant (not regarded as "conventional") is expected to conform to the markers of identity.

The Western dress, coupled with her independent pose, also served as the mechanism for arousing sexual desire. Historically, ideologues of Sinhala and Tamil nationalism associated Western cultural practices with the corrupting effects of colonialism. Such practices included dancing, mingling with the opposite sex in public, and sexual licentiousness. This nexus is subliminally invoked through the allusions to the impact of Ishwari's Western dress and behavior and her "familiarity" with men at the early stages of the narrative. Negative audience reactions were also determined by the fact that her independent pose "misleads" the "virtuous" Sinhala man (Banuka). I use the word "pose" deliberately here because this independence is merely cosmetic. The image of the "independent," aggressive woman cadre that is initially constructed in *Vishwa Gamana* is, as in *Thahanam Adaviya*, deceptive. In actuality, though Ishwari seems to be able to forcefully argue with her colleagues, she is entirely compliant with the dictates of the (male) leadership of the "organization," and we find that even her donning of Western dress is a military tactic that she follows. And while the fact that she lives alone and entertains a young single man may seem to connote the "liberation" of the female militant, these signifiers also preclude the audience's sympathy for this character.

The "liberal" face of the female militant is subsumed by the dictates of tradition as her relationship with Banuka develops, and her entire persona, finally, is drastically altered. Her anxieties about her dress and profession, and her doubts about the "organization," are foregrounded in her conversations with her best friend Apsara, a Sinhala girl. After she decides to leave the organization of her own volition, she adopts the dress code of a conservative Tamil woman wearing sari and *pottu*, jasmines in her hair. She also becomes more demure. Not coincidentally, these are perceived as the markers of the "traditional" Tamil woman.

Ishwari claims that this transformation makes her feel more "real." The patriarchal male in Banuka (though Sinhalese) soon asserts itself in his endorsement of her ethnic dress. Even though he is from a different ethnic group, he is better disposed toward her new image because it is more conformist. Banuka then replaces the leaders of the organization as her authority figure, and at the culmination of the narrative, Ishwari's submission to the Sinhala man (predicated on his terms) is complete. It is through scenes like this that the teledrama highlights how both patriarchy and ethnic dominance are complicit in asserting dominance over the minority, especially the minority woman.

In addition, throughout the rest of the teledrama she vehemently articulates the transgressions of the "organization." Embodying the "authentic" Tamil voice, she validates the ethno-nationalist perceptions of Tamil militancy as ruthless and inhumane. Their brutality, which is reinforced earlier – in the episode where Ishwari's older brother is murdered for no apparent reason, allegedly by the "organization" – is persistently pitted against the "humanness" of the Sinhalese, even when Ishwari is taken into custody in the final sequence. In this sequence, close-up shots of the troubled face and sighs of Banuka's boss clearly establish his compassion as he brings Iswari to prison to meet Apsara.

The trajectory of Ishwari's character can be interpreted as the desire on the part of the Sinhalese scriptwriters and producers who voice the views of their mammoth audiences, to regulate the female militant, because of the widespread reputation of the LTTE women as being more violent than their male counterparts. It also marks societal insecurity, where the behavior of the female militant is seen as threatening the cultural and political security of their social group since their behavior deviates from the patriarchal norms established by that group. Such representations are problematic because of the effect they have on public consciousness. Since teledrama in Sri Lanka is deemed to represent "real life," the portrayal of Ishwari provoked concerns about the impact of such constructions on the public imagination, which have been reaffirmed by the viewers' antipathy toward her.

These two works reveal that for the female militant the contestation between individual aspirations and the collective objective impinges vehemently on their lives. Paradoxically, even while fighting against the societal insecurity engendered by the state, the female militant is instrumental in contributing toward the societal insecurity *within* the ethno-national groups (Alison 2004). Even as she transcends the bounds of traditional ethnic identity, she is, nevertheless, uneasy about the transformative aspects of the new role she embraces, glimpsed in the discursive contradictions or hesitancy emerging in her dialogues with male counterparts in the narratives. Urmila and Ishwari, as female militants, though outwardly ruthless and masculinized, are pitted against their male peers and leaders and emerge as stringently policed by them. This illustrates that the female figure has the potential to become a threat not only to the state but also to the male hierarchy within the movement. For the state, she constitutes a real, physical security threat in terms of her military actions, but she also poses an ideological threat to the security of the political and social status quo, made evident in the final scenes of *Vishwa Gamana* where Ishwari needs to be placed in solitary confinement so as not to "corrupt" the other women prisoners.

For the "organization," it is imperative that the female militant is contained within strictly defined ideological boundaries to avoid a situation where she renounces commitment to it (as evident in *Thahanam Adaviya*). Renouncing her position in the organization has to be proscribed not only to safeguard numbers, but also to preclude the outflow of vital information to the "other side." Though gender equality is avowed, Urmila's predicament reveals that there is in-built reliance on the male leader, affirmed by a forceful male discourse, so that any form of "equality" is attributed solely to him and rendered visible on his terms. Moreover, within this framework, the female militant's agency seems to be located within the concept of sacrifice. By primarily acting out the commands of her male leader, she functions within the normative, prescribed role of woman.

Conclusion

In this essay, I have engaged with the way in which the radical shift from "masculinised virgin warrior" (to use Coomaraswamy's term), to the "feminine lover" occurs in dominant cultural production, and, after this transition is made, the certitudes hitherto embraced by the female militant and faith in their roles are challenged. Ishwari abandons her position in the organization, while Urmila desperately seeks a way out of her mission after a romantic involvement with a man. This provokes the question: is the erasure of sexuality and the construction of those who successfully accomplish their mission as "asexual" (divested of familial or social relationships, denied a personal history), propagated in the media, the only way to reconcile ourselves to the phenomenon of the female militant? In reinforcing this discourse, the interests of the hegemonic structures of the state in demonizing the "organization/movement" are served. Furthermore, pity and sympathy are evoked for the women who are denied the possibility of sexual gratification and what is enacted as a "normal life." By casting their position as "involuntary," as intimated in both texts, the political cause of the movement and of the female militant is subordinated to the monstrous image of the suicide bomber, and there is a tacit suggestion that women ultimately succumb to their "feminine" desires to nurture human life rather than destroy it.

The configuration of "femininity" in the texts suggests that it precludes or disrupts militant action. Ishwari abandons her position in the "organization" in order to fulfill her desire for a romantic relationship, while Urmila has to be coerced into fulfilling her mission, a coercion that necessitates that she relinquish her desires. This representation, underscored in both texts, seeks to contain the anxiety generated by the specter of the female militant and may indirectly bolster the legitimacy of restricting women in other spheres – for instance, the Sri Lankan state military – to operating in more conventional gender roles. Yet, scholarship on the LTTE and the figure of the female suicide bomber (for example, the work of Coomaraswamy, Miranda Alison, and Rhiannon Talbot), and popular culture, demonstrate that while the expectation of "heroic masculinity" is placed upon the female militant, the *perpetration* of terror by the female militant is attendant upon strategically deploying the very "markers" of female/feminine that women are expected to suppress. The female militant is thus placed within an irreducible double bind in which the performance of a feminine masquerade is predicated on the subordination of female desire and subjectivity to the deadly *telos* of military strategy.

Acknowledgments

This essay draws upon the research carried out from 2003 onward as part of a Research Fellowship from the Social Science Research Council (SSRC). I am grateful to SSRC for the grant that enabled the research. I am also indebted to Stephen Morton and Elleke Boehmer for their support in terms of providing secondary material, discussions on framing the material and for editing.

Notes

1 Kumari Jayawardena and Mala de Alwis describe how constructions of the "ideal woman" in South Asia are central in the recreation of community because she is the symbol of cultural purity in religio-nationalist discourses (1996: xi).

2 My previous research on teledramas, which included audience surveys, demonstrated these attitudes.

References and Further Reading

Alison, M. (2004) "Women as Agents of Political Violence: Gendering Security," *Security Dialogue* 35(4): 447–63.

Anthias, Floya and Nira Yuval Davis. (1994) [1989]. "Women and the Nation-State," in J. Hutchinson and A. D. Smith (eds.), *Nationalism*. Oxford: Oxford University Press.

Balasingham, A. (1990) *Women Fighters of Liberation Tigers*. Jaffna: Tasan Printers, Publication Section of the LTTE.

Balasingham, A. (2001) *The Will to Freedom: An Inside View of Tamil Resistance*. Mitcham: Fairmax Publishing Ltd.

Bloom, Mia. (2005) *Dying to Kill: The Allure of Suicide Terror*. New York: Columbia University Press.

Brunner, Claudia. (2007) "Occidentalism Meets the Female Suicide Bomber: A Critical Reflection on Recent Terrorism Debates," Review Essay in *Signs: Journal of Women and Culture in Society* 32(4): 957–71.

Chandrasekeram, V. (1998) *Forbidden Area*. Colombo: Sarasavi Press.

Coomaraswamy, R. (1996) "Tiger Women and the Question of Women's Emancipation," *Pravada* 4(9): 8–10.

De Mel, N. (2004) "Agent or Victim? The Sri Lankan Woman Militant in the Interregnum," in W. Giles, M. De Alwis, E. Klein, and N. Silva, *Feminists Under Fire: Exchanges Across Warzones*. Toronto: Between the Lines.

Grewal, I. (1988) "Salman Rushdie: Marginality, Women and Shame," *Genders* 3: 24–42.

Grewal, I. (1996) *Home and Harem, Nation, Gender, Empire and the Cultures of Travel*. London: Leicester University Press.

Jayawardena, K. and and M. De Alwis, eds. (1996) "Introduction," in *Embodied Violence: Communalising Women's Sexuality in South Asia*. New Delhi: Kali for Women.

Martin, G. (2006) *Understanding Terrorism: Challenges, Perspectives, and Issues*, 2nd edn. London and New York: Sage.

Naaman, Dorit. (2007) "Brides of Palestine/Angels of Death: Media, Gender, and Performance in the Case of the Palestinian Female Suicide Bombers," *Signs: Journal of Women and Culture in Society* 32(4): 933–55.

Obeyesekere, G. (1989) *Buddhism Transformed*. Princeton, NJ: Princeton University Press.

Oliver, Kelly. (2008) "Women: The Secret Weapon of Modern Warfare?" *Hypatia* 23(2) (April–June): 1–13.

Rose, Jacqueline. (2004) *Deadly Embrace*. http://www.lrb.co.uk/v26/n21/rose01.html

Talbot, R. (2001) "Myths in the Representation of Women Terrorists," *Eire-Ireland* 35(3 & 4): 165–86.

White, Aaronette. (2007) "All the Men are Fighting for Freedom, All the Women are Mourning Their Men, but Some of us Carried Guns: A Race-Gendered Analysis of Fanon's Psychological Perspectives on War," *Signs: Journal of Women and Culture in Society* 32(4): 857–84.

Chapter 14

Terror, Spectacle, and the Secular State in Bombay Cinema

Sujala Singh

If the prevalent rhetoric in the West perpetuates the notion that migrants from the Third World are desperate to arrive in its precincts in search of money, liberty, and civilization, in contemporary Bombay cinema, characters are often desperate to return to India: from the diasporic Indian (inevitably privileged, usually upper-class Hindu) who returns to a nostalgic spiritual homeland, to the terrorist who arrives from the peripheries of Kashmir and the north-east (sometimes trained in Pakistan) to disrupt the central core of Indian civic life. The core shifts depending on the context for arrival into India: whilst the diasporic Indian in *Dilwale Dulhaniya Le Jayenge* (*I Will Take Away the Bride of My Choice*, dir. Aditya Chopra, 1995) prefers the swaying mustard fields of Punjab to the pigeons in Trafalgar Square, the terrorist aims to destroy identifiably Indian iconic religious monuments such as the Hazratbal mosque and Shankaracharya temple in Kashmir (in *Mission Kashmir*, dir. Vidhu Vinod Chopra, 2000), or the celebrations of independent India as displayed in the pomp of the Republic Day parade (in *Dil Se*, dir. Mani Ratnam, 1998). Both the NRI (non-resident Indian), who can afford nostalgia and the economic means of return, and the disaffected terrorist who is willing to lose his/her own life are obsessed with the idea of India, with the abstraction of what the nation-state stands for or represents.

Bombay cinema's imaging and producing of citizen-subjects who are contained and containable in the nation-state of India has been addressed in diverse ways by film theorists such as Ravi Vasudevan,

Sumita Chakravarty, Madhava Prasad, Vijay Mishra, and Aashish Rajadhayksha. According to Ravi Vasudevan, one consequence of Bombay cinema's constructing of a "certain abstraction of national identity" has been the positioning of "other national/ethnic/socio-religious identities in stereotypical ways under an over-arching north Indian, majoritarian Hindu identity."[1] The prevalent model for discussing the relationship between the citizen-subject and the nation-state in Bombay cinema has been through the trope of the family. Commenting on domestic dramas which are located in the diaspora, Patricia Uberoi writes of "the phenomenon of the internationalisation of the middle-class family" (1999: 165). According to her, "the assertion and endorsement of Indian 'family values' in an uncertain and globalising world has become a conspicuous and insistent theme in popular culture in the 1990s" (p. 169). For Ashish Rajadhyaksha, the feel-good films that are targeted toward diasporic audiences display what he terms a "techno-nationalism": the hybrid Indian thus mobilized can be a heady mixture of secular and Hindu, capitalist and feudal, modern and devout (2004: 125).

The period from the 1990s onwards has also seen the release of a number of films on terrorism which are concerned with documenting the threat to the nation-state from across the border (primarily Pakistan) as well as internally, in Kashmir and the north-east, for example. The destruction of the Babri Masjid in 1992 and the Bombay riots of 1992–3 led to the killings of both Hindus and Muslims but the leading opposition party (the BJP in the case of the Babri Masjid) and the state government (under Shiv Sena's Bal Thackeray in Bombay) were implicated in the specific and active targeting of the Muslim population. In this essay, I will discuss two films, *Dil Se* (1998) and *Mission Kashmir* (2000), which were made in the aftermath of these events: they are set in the border zones of the nation-state (in the unspecified "north-east" and Kashmir) and are ambivalent in their representation of terrorism. City films such as *Bombay* (1995) and *Fiza* (2000), which are located in urban spaces, also share this ambivalence as they show the impact of city riots (usually the Bombay riots of 1993) on families of civilians. The excesses of Hindu fundamentalism were so visible and disturbing during this period, the partisan role of agents and representatives of the nation-state such as politicians and police in colluding with the violence so obvious, that these films, I contend, are caught up in the bind of guilt and responsibility. Even as they attempt to imagine a secular, all-embracing India, they also depict state violence and torture. Problematic though the erasure of specific histories, the infantilism of terrorist figures or the inclusion of token "good" minority characters may be (as I show later), these films attempt to humanize "othered" identities. A significant shift in nuance takes place in the blatant jingoism and representation of the menacing Muslim after the Kargil skirmish in 1999 and the attack on the Twin Towers in New York in 2001. Both these events took place beyond the boundaries of the nation-state. The Kargil battle was fought in mountainous terrain over the "line of control" (or LOC) after months of escalating tension between India and Pakistan and the alarming testing of nuclear weapons in 1998. The representation of Muslim terrorists becomes more overtly virulent in films such as *Gadar* (2001), *Hero* (2002), *LOC Kargil* (2003), and the differently styled *Dev* (2004), made by the well-known "art" director Govind Nihalini. These films promote barely disguised aggressive Hindu ideologies and rally a call to arms for the protection of the motherland. They mobilize the idea of terrorism as a global infection and legitimize the paranoia of the menacing Muslim who can strike at any time. A comparative analysis of the films that fall in different categories is inevitably beyond the scope of a short essay and so here I will focus primarily on two films, *Dil Se* (dir. Mani Ratnam, 1998), and *Mission Kashmir* (dir. Vidhu Vinod Chopra, 2000) from the earlier period.

Since the 1990s, the marked shift in the definition of the state has been the change from a post-independence socialist, secular Nehruvian apparatus to one that has sought to "globalize" economically whilst becoming increasingly communal as manifested in the rise of Hindu nationalism. Of the compensatory agenda within *hindutva*'s seamless narrative of globalization and Hindu chauvinism, Arvind Rajagopal writes:

> Liberalization positioned itself as a conversation about the economy, qua economy, whereas in fact it sought at the same time to address the failures of politics and to bypass its impediments. Arguments advancing liberalization appealed to criteria of productivity and market success as a way of compensating for the deterioration of political legitimacy and the waning of Nehruvian understandings of the collective good. (1999: 144)

Liberalization and the opening of markets has thus gone hand in hand with the increasing delegitimation of political and civil rights. It has also been an era which has seen instances of political terror multiply: in the secessionist movements in Kashmir and the north-east *as well as* those organized and staged by right-wing political parties and state and national governments. Besides the examples already mentioned, one of the most horrific instances of fascistic state terror took place in Gujarat in 2002 where the state government of Gujarat (with Narendra Modi as Chief Minister) in effect sanctioned the massacre and rape of Muslims, with the blessing of the BJP coalition at the center. Achin Vanaik refers to the "regularised routine" with which states unleash violence in the name of national security as "state terrorism." Making a distinction between the capability and intent of state terror and what he terms "combat terror," Vanaik writes, "state terrorism remains the single biggest component of the problem of global terrorism":

> A struggle for national liberation to which combat group terrorism is often harnessed, is certainly a grand ultimate objective but each particular act of terrorism has much more limited and specific objectives even as it is part of the larger pursuit of a final grand goal. It is states alone that can most convincingly claim to be pursuing such supposedly grandiose objectives as a matter of *regularised routine.* (2002: 178)

The return of the NRI and terrorist figures in Bombay cinema with which I began this paper is no coincidence but a manifestation of the debates surrounding the relationship between state and civil society, territorial borders and "free" markets, and the religious and the secular. Crucial to the Indian nation-state's self-image as a liberalized, global player has been the mobility of transnational capital. The return that is permissible and made legal is that of wealthy non-resident Indians. This doesn't have to be a physical return; what the "liberal" economy has facilitated, legitimized, and provided incentives for is the return of diasporic capital. The other kind of return – that of the terrorist, the illegal alien, the monster from the outside – though abject and threatening, has been equally crucial for the maintenance and justification of state power in what Giorgio Agamben has theorized as a "state of exception," whereby the exceptional, extra-juridical powers that a state grants itself in moments of emergency is embedded within and integral to its constituted constitutional character at all times (2005).

This essay will examine how the tension between the abstraction that is India and the conflicted encounters of "becoming Indian" are played out in two films that represent terrorism in the 1990s. Whilst domestic dramas celebrated transnational mobility (of people and capital), films dealing with terrorism appeared different because they highlighted the dangers and threats to middle-class values by marginalized, often subaltern characters and communities, and because they could also depict the Indian state as corrupt and violent. Visually and ideologically, these films provisionally question the ideals of a normative Hindu/Indian identity only to reinstate them at the end. Both kinds of films are seeped in the spectacle of capital and in reconciling the dichotomies between tradition and modernity. Cinematically, Madhava Prasad calls the mode of reconciling the traditional and the modern, the feudal and the bourgeois, the "feudal family romance." This, according to him, is hardly new, and he traces the trend whereby potentially threatening modern forces are reconciled and neutralized within the crucible of the feudal as a recurring feature of Bombay films from the 1940s to the 1960s. Of films such as *An Evening in Paris* (1967) and *Love in Tokyo* (1966), which are set in exotic foreign locales, he writes:

> even though the action unfolds against an international setting, the essential features of the feudal family structure remain firmly in place. From the organic space of the north Indian village to the high-tech tourist spots of the world, the feudal structure displays a mobility that demonstrates how powerful its ideology was and to an extent still is. This structure could incorporate consumerism and other "modern" features without damage as long as it did not slide into a position of affirmation of new sexual and social relations based on individualism. (1998: 67)

The issue then is not merely of combining seemingly disparate elements but of reconciling them so they can provide an apparently coherent mapping of a private discourse of the individual and the family on to the public arena of the nation and the world. These strategies of containment may still be in place, but their ideological underpinnings and visual iconography have changed as the relationship between the state and citizen has itself undergone major transformations.

The primary question I wish to address in relation to *Dil Se* and *Mission Kashmir* is this: how do these films, with their mix of romance, politics, tourism, and terrorism, deliver an account of contemporary terror through a vision of national unity at a time when the very foundations of a secular polity in India has been under threat? Both films share the following traits: they are set in border zones; show state terror; portray well-known stars as sympathetic terrorist figures; and propound an inclusive, secular vision of the nation-state.

My analysis of the two films will focus on four key issues. As with the domestic dramas that Uberoi refers to, critics writing about films on terror tend to highlight the sustaining presence of the family unit within the larger symbolic order of the nation-state. In particular, since films on terror provide more disturbing accounts of the nation-state and depict estranged, dysfunctional characters, the language of re-patriation within the family unit is used to account for the place of terrorists within the family/nation. While recognizing the relevance of these accounts, I point to an important omission, which is the crucial role of the child within the family unit. The terrorist protagonists in both *Dil Se* and *Mission Kashmir* figure unsurprisingly as aberrations, estranged from normal social structures and existing outside of normative filmic codes of heterosexual romance and family values. But in both films, children are converted to terrorism because they have been victimized by security officials who are representatives of the state. In *Dil Se,* twelve-year-old Meghna is raped and in *Mission Kashmir,* eleven-year-old Altaaf witnesses the extermination of his entire family unit. In what ways does the trauma of children's experience stand in for historical causality in these films? And what are the effects of this substitution both visually and ideologically? Secondly, I consider the depiction of state terror in both films and explore how the films balance the state's contradictory roles as agent of violence and protector, as both cause and solution to the disaffection that leads to terrorism. Thirdly, I show how both romance and terror are staged as phantasmic spectacles in both films and examine the implications of such stagings. Finally, I contend that the idea of national unity/secularism circulates either as a ubiquitous political cliché (in *Dil Se*) or as a melodramatically performed event (as in *Mission Kashmir*).

Dil Se (*From the Heart,* dir. Mani Ratnam, 1998)

Dil Se is a film structured through deferment and unfulfilled teasing promises. Amarkant Varma (played by mega-star Shah Rukh Khan) is an investigative journalist who travels to the north-east of India to report on militant terrorists who are fighting for a separate homeland. In the liminal zone of the train station, as he waits for a train to travel from Bengal to an unnamed region in the north-east, he encounters a mysterious, beautiful woman (Meghna played by Manisha Koirala) on a stormy night. For the rest of the film, through some chance, some deliberate encounters, he follows her and declares his love for her "from the heart" ("dil se"). She is elusive and keeps disappearing. Amar repeatedly declares his identity as government employee and legitimate Indian citizen by thrusting his name and badge, "Amarkant Varma, All India Radio," to all and sundry (to Meghna; to the police; to security guards who man border controls). Amar is interpellated by the identifiable codes of the contemporary "hero" of Bombay cinema: he is an urban, middle-class Hindu male, full of his own charm and as confident in his bluster and patriotic idealism as he is in his ability to stalk a woman in the name of romance. Rather than validating this identity position, the film seems to undermine the certainties of such heroics. So enchanted is Amar with Meghna's eroticized mystery that even though on assignment to report on terrorism in the north-east, he remains oblivious to obvious clues regarding her terrorist identity. Amar's unshakeable belief in his own legitimacy is also undermined by Meghna's refusal to comply with expected rituals of romantic coyness and banter. At the level of plot and storyline, then, Amar the journalist and Meghna the terrorist seem to unsettle expected social and gender norms.

Indeed, the title song of the film *Dil Se*, shown from Amar's point of view, situates Amar's self-image of double-daring as brave patriot and rescuer of innocent damsel within the space of fantasy. The song renders both terror and romance as spectacle as Amar protects Meghna and enacts the risk of romantic love against the background of thudding boots of army personnel. As the idealized hero as savior protects the vulnerable heroine from the potential violence of state terror (terrorists are strangely absent here), the song sequence self-consciously provides a montage of clichés of Bombay cinematic conventions. The fantasy of the declared secular journalist is of sensuous erotic play enacted under the threat of terror. The obvious level of irony that unfolds is that it is Meghna who is the terrorist while Amar, the complacent, middle-class journalist, is the one under threat and is beaten up by her "comrades" later in the film. It is tempting to think that Ratnam is deliberately highlighting the naivety and arrogance of the journalist for whom war and explosions become a mere background for the enactment of erotic games. This is complicated, however, by the replaying of similar visual images at another, more disturbing, moment in the film: in Meghna's memory of childhood rape by army personnel. When Amar finally discovers her terrorist identity and confronts her, she accuses him of a complacent, secularist ignorance: "You sit in Delhi playing songs on AIR." "We've been oppressed for fifty years." Her flashback then replays images from the song: explosions, gunshots, fire on snow. The striking difference is that while in the song sequence, death and destruction are continually thwarted through

Amar's narcissistic presence, Meghna's flashback shows the effects of state terror: her parents are killed and she stumbles upon a room where her sister is being raped by soldiers. The camera then moves towards a 12-year-old Meghna, positioning the audience in the same space as the rapist, zooming in to trap her until there is only her face letting out a voiceless scream. The adult Meghna asks Amar, "Do you know what the smell of death is like?"

This mode of juxtaposition gestures that "reality" is elsewhere and Amar's unshakeable authority and belief in his identity as a government worker is questioned. One could read this kind of meta-coding as Ratnam's attempt at resisting the conventional codes of Bombay cinema. Referring to these conventions, Ananya Kabir reads *Dil Se* as more radical than Mani Ratnam's first two films, *Roja* and *Bombay*, which were successful because they "endorse the affirmative patterns of Bombay cinema, thus sublimating politics through the triumph of love and the couple's reintegration into the family and the nation" (2003: 144). Rather than heterosexual fulfillment and/or reclamation within the family fold, at the end of the film, Meghna, strapped up with bombs, en route to disrupt the proceedings of Republic Day in the capital, is intercepted by Amar, finally accepts his embrace, and the film ends with an explosion. Kabir commends this ending for its "narrative irresolution" and reads the film as "an alternative discourse on minority subjectivities" of the north-east (p. 145). She claims that the film is subversive not only in its focus on the dilemmas of minorities within India but also in the way in which the minority subjectivities of the film's crew erupt at various points to dislodge the normative certainties of majoritarian subjectivities. Thus, according to Kabir, the South Indian origins of the film's director, music director, and cinematographer, as well as Shah Rukh Khan's Muslim identity, challenge the North Indian, Hindu hegemony that informs the majority of Bombay films.

Kabir's thesis is an interesting one and she provides a detailed reading of the film but she tends to read the "narrative irresolution" of the film as too easily subversive. For the end of the film, which seems to provide a critique of sentimental heroism in the song "Dil Se," also provides a reaffirmation of those values. Amar rescues the country at the cost of his own life. The suicide bomber ends up hurting no one other than herself and her suitor. The destruction of the capital city during its national parade of honor, which has been imaginatively played out earlier, is averted in the final scene of the film. What is reinstated is the unsullied, incorruptible image of the urban Hindu male (the son of an Army officer) who saves his country and dies for his lady love in one stroke. Even Meghna, who has mocked Amar's naivety through most of the film, sees it as a virtue and protectively tells one of her "cell" members, "Woh bahut bhola hai. Usme koi shak nahin" (He is very naive/innocent. He is not suspicious of anyone). Thus, the fantasy motifs of the song, far from being questioned, are doubly reinforced and validated.

Not just "Dil Se," but all songs in the film are located in zones of fantasy and imagination; there is a remarkable lack of clarity about point of view as songs erupt within the narrative without specifying point of view and perspective. Through the playing out of heterosexual romance in exotic settings, song sequences *resolve* the seemingly impossible reconciliation between a female terrorist and an upright government servant. Even though she resists him in "real" story time, within the frame of not one but two songs, Meghna complies not just with gendered desire codes of Ratnam's heroines in his earlier films (who are child-like, innocent, and eroticized), she also fits in within the frame of the visualized spectacle of romance in exotic settings that is such a staple of contemporary Bombay cinema. The different spaces of terror in the film are sutured through Meghna's presence: in the north-east, in Ladakh and Delhi. These are also locations in which she is present during or after scenes of terrorist violence, but Amar refuses to make the connection. Implicit in Meghna's move from the north-east to Ladakh is the training and networking of terrorists in two disparate regions, but the focus of the Ladakh section is on the erotically charged encounter in the vast expanse of snowscape between Meghna and Amar. The terrorist woman cannot participate in heterosexual desire, so the songs enact and fulfill compensatory desire through their sumptuousness and exotic locales. Sumita Chakrabarty calls this phenomenon the "liminal space of dreaming" (2000: 233):

> It is here, I contend, rather than in the traditional visual paraphernalia of flags, maps or buildings, that the films do their ideological work of re-affirming the nation. Moreover, the appeal of the new India is not constituted on moral or ideological grounds but on the level of the experiential and sensuous. Song and dance sequences powerfully evoke the pleasures of an essentially fluid, joyful and globalised world in which viewers are invited to participate, while the world to which the terrorists belong is essentially closed and claustrophobic, rule-governed and predictable. Terrorism or separatism in these films is essentially atavistic, out of sync with a multiethnic, multicultural ethos shaped by transnational influences. (2000: 233–4)

Chakrabarty sets apart the "atavistic" worlds of terror and a "joyful and globalised world": once the terrorists travel into Delhi, there is a marked visual contrast to the vast spaces (despite the barbed wire and the presence of the army) of the north-east and Ladakh and the crowded, starkly lit, cramped and claustrophobic rendering of the streets of old Delhi where the cell members meet and attempt to retain their anonymity. However, as I have suggested, the visualization and imagining of terror in the film is *also* portrayed as phantasmic. Chakrabarty is right in pointing out that "the world to which the terrorists belong is essentially closed and claustrophobic, rule-governed and predictable," but the imagined playing out of the plan to bomb the President during the Republic Day (January 26) celebrations by Meghna and her cell-members, as they stare at the vacant streets surrounding India Gate in New Delhi, is located in the visual imagery of fantasy, of dramatic explosions as army bands march to the tune of the patriotic song, "Saare Jahan Se Achcha, Hindustan Hamara" (Better than all in the nations in the world is our India).

While terrorist conflagrations and bombings and deferred romance are visualized as spectacular, the secularist ideal itself circulates as an endless political cliché. As with the song above, it is mouthed by schoolchildren and sung on national days. In the early part of the film, with his fearless questions and loud voice, Amar, the liberal investigative journalist, articulates his own position as normal. When he travels into the heart of the jungle to question the terrorist chief on his networks and motives, he wonders at how a terrorist can look so normal; like "one of us." The silent Meghna likewise appears as a "normal" woman to Amar; in the rare moment when she reveals anything of herself, she speaks of children and the things she finds precious: her mother's hands, the pigeons in the temple courtyard, and poetry. So comfortable is Amar with the common-sense notion of what it means to be a secular Indian that he can joke about terror: as the taxi approaches a checkpoint at the border, he asks the taxi driver, "I hope you don't have a bomb/'shomb' in the boot of your car." When Meghna's friends threaten him with a beating, he says, "I have terrorist friends, you know." Later, to security officials who consider him a "suspect" as they are attempting to bust the terrorist plot, he announces, "I am the son of an Army officer." If terrorism functions as an infection that spreads among traumatized children such as Meghna, secularism/nationalism becomes a genetic inheritance, biologically and indelibly passed on. In *Dil Se*, the photograph and the memory of a dead father are invoked to proclaim the sacrifice and martyrdom of army officers. In *Mission Kashmir*, the role of the "fouj"/ army as conscientious and trusted protectors of the motherland is repeated as a mantra: echoed in speeches and songs and exhibited in military paraphernalia such as trophies, uniforms, and badges. What does it mean to position the army as an agent of deliverance of national unity and secular ideals even as these films depict the trauma of children haunted by the memory of abuse by army officials?

Mission Kashmir (dir. Vidhu Vinod Chopra, 2000)

As in *Dil Se*, in *Mission Kashmir* the subjectivity of the terrorist is constructed through personal, individualized trauma. In *Mission Kashmir*, 11-year-old Altaaf becomes vulnerable to terrorism after witnessing the shooting of his family members by a police officer. In *Dil Se*, Meghna's trauma is manifest through the bulk of the film in her refusal to speak to Amar about her rape and the killing of her family members ("You won't understand"). It is visualized once as flashback when she is confronted by Amar, who accuses her of using his respectability to further her terrorist cause. In *Mission Kashmir*, on the other hand, Altaaf's trauma is replayed and relived over and over again by the adult Altaaf as flashback and nightmare. I will now provide a brief synopsis of the film before I proceed with a discussion of how the child figure is positioned in relation to the trauma of terror.

At the beginning of the film, Kashmiri militants issue a fatwa against doctors who treat injured patients. Inayat Khan, a Muslim police official, loses his son because of the fatwa. Wearing a balaclava, and acting on intelligence information received, Inayat Khan shoots Malik-ul-Khan, the head terrorist responsible for issuing the fatwa, along with an entire family attending a wedding party. The young son of the family, Altaaf, is witness to this and traumatized. On Khan's Hindu wife Neelima's suggestion, they adopt Altaaf as a compensation for the loss of their son. Just as Altaaf seems to be settling into home pleasures of food and cricket, he stumbles upon and recognizes the black balaclava, tries to shoot his foster father, and flees. He is brought up by an Afghani Muslim Pathan, a monstrous, stooping, distorted caricature. *Mission Kashmir* is a film full of good Muslims: Inayat Khan, Altaaf's childhood love, the journalist Sufiya Parvez, and even the terrorist Altaaf who is eventually redeemed. The caricature of a Muslim is of an Afghani Pathan: of a Muslim from elsewhere, from across the border; one who is willing to infect the liberal Indian edifice with his mercenary fundamentalism and to expose vulnerable children like Altaaf to the dictums of a fundamentalist jihad. Ten years later, Altaaf, played by Hrihtik Roshan, has evolved into a terrorist who is trapped in the nightmares of the loss of his original family and obsessed with killing Khan. He makes various attempts at killing his foster father; during one such attempt, the bomb in the briefcase targeted at the father accidentally kills his mother. He becomes an unwitting accomplice in a grand plan (hatched by unnamed Muslims in a foreign land) to fire missiles at two iconic religious monuments in Kashmir, the Hazratbal mosque (which is meant to house a strand of the Prophet's hair) and the Shankaracharya temple, an ancient Hindu temple. As in the imagined replaying of the spectacle of Republic Day in *Dil Se*, the camera dramatically pans over the two religious institutions as crowds kneel for prayers under the panoptical gaze of the terrorists. Finally, the foster father, the good Muslim police official, intervenes, lectures Altaaf on nation and nationalism, temple and mosque, and the terrorist son sees sense. All ends in overdetermined excess with explosions and drownings and the death of the Afghani Muslim. The repetition and circularity of trauma through hallucinatory flashbacks is brought to a closure by suturing the terrorist into the family of the honorable police officer.

This suture into family life takes place through an imaginary return to childhood. As Inayat Khan and Sufiya sit by his bedside, Altaaf is shown smiling as he dreams of playing cricket with his foster family. The dream sequence intertextually weaves with his early drawings as a child and his early life with his foster family. Not only is he repatriated to the womb of the family, he is also returned to a state of innocence. His rebirth brings to a closure the opening frames of the film, which begins with dead children. Even prior to the young Altaaf's witnessing of the shooting of his sister by Inayat Khan – as she runs with doll in hand, unsuspecting and diagonally off-angle from the camera, in slow motion – two children die in the film.

The first is the young daughter of the doctor who had defied the fatwa and treated the injured Inayat Khan and the second is Khan's son who jumps off a balcony and has to be moved to several hospitals because doctors refuse to treat him. Sufiya Parvez and Altaaf himself mention at several points in the film that the gentle, art-loving Altaaf himself had died a symbolic death the day he witnessed the shooting of his family.

The imagined utopia of Altaaf's final dream is rendered in stark contrast to the repeated hallucinatory flashbacks that he is subjected to throughout the film. The repeated fetishization of nightmares and trauma is featured as what Ravi Vasudevan calls a staple of melodrama, "the hyperbolising of interiority" (2002). Maureen Turim argues that the subjective focalization of flashback narrations sets up an inevitable causality, a philosophical and psychoanalytical fatalism in films, which

> presents a cynical view of history as cyclical, guaranteed to repeat that which we have already seen; the release from the repetitions inherent in history is then forged in a singular solution that serves a prevailing ideology, such as patriotic identification or a retreat into the "personal" as a microcosmic, idealized world. Further, the history narrated in flashbacks is often a didactic history, containing moral lessons . . . (Turim 1989)

The specific histories of disaffection, political resistance, militancy, and fundamentalism in Kashmir are erased as the horror of the traumatized child's experience is revisited cyclically. The paradigmatic narrative of separated and reunited families has been read by critics such as Vijay Mishra as Bombay cinema's re-enactment of the repressed historical trauma of the Partition of 1947. Amit Rai in "Patriotism and the Muslim Citizen in Hindi Films," where he discusses *Mission Kashmir*, writes, "the traumatic history of partition is imaginarily resolved through a romanticized notion of the national family" (2003). Instead, however, I wish to contend that the use of the child figure displaces questions of historical accountability and responsibility. In *Mission Kashmir*, the adult Altaaf is depicted as so paralyzed by his past that he is released from present and future responsibility. Indeed, Altaaf remains an infantilized figure throughout the film. In an exchange with his foster mother, he begs for sympathy for the deaths he has seen and the nightmares that are a consequence of it:

> For ten years that face has not allowed me to sleep. Whenever I try to sleep, those eyes start staring at me and for ten years, all the burning villages that I have seen, all start burning in my brain. For ten years, all the screams I have heard all start crawling in my ears; in the ten years, all the corpses I have seen all hide behind that face and laugh at me. Unless I wipe out that face, I won't be free; I won't be able to sleep. Ammi [mother], what shall I do?

Foregrounded here is the language of passive witnessing rather than active agency: "I have seen," "I have heard," rather than "I have committed" or "I have killed." Even though he has been a terrorist for 10 years, he exempts himself from the responsibility of committing terrorist acts. The "I" is strangely displaced in this exchange as moral and narrative responsibility is abnegated. In *Dil Se*, after listening to Meghna's account, when Amar tells her that he understands that injustice has been done to "your people," but that this doesn't justify the wreaking of vengeance on the nation, she says, "you don't understand . . . the rape of a twelve year old . . ." The history of terror (of the state or terrorists) is thus replaced by the ontogeny of terror.

As in *Dil Se*, in *Mission Kashmir* the phantasm of terror is played out in visual imagery: from the turbulent orange fireballs shattering the calm of an idyllic Dal Lake at the beginning of the film, to the explosion of a TV tower with the silhouette of the Shankaracharya temple in the background and to the imagined horror of what may happen to teeming masses of Hindu and Muslim pilgrims who kneel down for prayer. The scale of the imagining is far more colossal than in *Dil Se*: at the end, Inayat Khan and Altaaf rescue not only Kashmir but India itself. Inayat Khan mentions the demolition of the Babri Masjid in 1992 as a reminder to Altaaf of the devastation that could follow if two religious monuments were destroyed. As the missiles pointing toward temple and mosque are defused in the nick of time, a crescendo of patriotic music bursts through and the iconic symbols of various religions ("Allah," "Om," and the figures of Christ and Guru Nanak) appear from an aerial point of view in a dramatic display of an all-inclusive "unity in diversity" version of secularism.

If this dénouement seems overly melodramatic, at other points, Vidhu Vinod Chopra, the film's director, self-consciously deploys the conventions of melodrama as quotation. In a song sequence choreographed by the journalist Sufi, Hindu–Muslim harmony and love are staged as a cultural event. As she watches the song with Altaaf, she imagines him dancing and leading a song on national unity and a compassionate India. In a parallel frame, and simultaneous to her imagining, his terrorist mates are on their way to bomb the TV tower, executing a plan that has been organized by Altaaf. A further layer of meta-commentary operates in that Kashmir as it appears in the film itself had to be filmed on a studio set. The overblown dramatic climax of *Mission Kashmir*, with burnt-out houseboats at the edge of Dal Lake, was filmed at the studios of Film City in Bombay. Prior to the "troubles," Kashmir had functioned as a site for romance in Bombay cinema. The safety of shooting of films in the idealized landscape of Kashmir has been lost to film directors. The film opens with an idyllic view of Dal Lake, with a long shot of an eerily quiet and isolated houseboat set against misty mountains. There is a sudden explosion that disrupts the peace.[2] The song on Hindu–Muslim harmony is staged on a television set because it is the only safe space for its enactment.

In *Mission Kashmir,* national unity becomes a performed event, staged and enacted as melodrama. In *Dil Se,* secular ideals float as "always-already" clichés. As both films strive to imagine the nation-as-family, they also point to its dysfunction, epitomized in the universalized trauma of the orphaned child. It would be too simple to assert that in the figuration of the terrorist as child, the role of the nation as family remains unquestioned. I have tried to show that the reclamation into the family/national fold that critics have addressed is never complete. The cracks in the imagining of national unity is not merely a comment on the ideological limitations of these films: I want to conclude by suggesting that they point to an unrealizable aporia, to an unfulfilled promise in the Indian nation-state's imagining of itself as secular. As such the representation of the terrorist and her/his goals may be circumscribed within the imaginative resources that generate the popular appeal of Bombay cinema, but it is still circulated in spectacular imagery with the power to manipulate and pervert the site of the imaginary – in particular, the imagined cohesive ideals of a secular nation.

Notes

1 Vasudevan has also written about the hybrid genre of Bombay cinema with its varied influences ranging from Hollywood continuity narrative, Parsi theater, Hindu mythologicals, darsanic framing (as in the act of worshipping the divine), and tableau art. Influenced by Hindu mythologicals, social-national agendas (the position of women for example), and the trauma of partition, both the content and aesthetic of Bombay cinema are caught in the negotiation of tradition and modernity.

2 Mani Ratnam's film on Kashmiri militants, *Roja* (1992), was also filmed against the mountains of Himachal Pradesh rather than Kashmir.

References

Agamben, Giorgio. (2005) *State of Exception*, trans. Kevin Attwell. Chicago: University of Chicago Press.

Chakrabarty, Sumita S. (2000) "Fragmenting the Nation: Images of Terrorism in Indian Popular Cinema," in Mette Hjort and Scott Mackenzie (eds.), *Cinema and Nation*, pp. 222–37. Routledge.

Kabir, Ananya Jahanara. (2003) "Allegories of Alienation and Politics of Bargaining: Minority Subjectivities in Mani Ratnam's *Dil Se*," *South Asian Popular Culture* October: 141–59.

Mishra, Vijay. (2002) *Bollywood Cinema: Temples of Desire*. Routledge.

Prasad, Madhava. (1998) *Ideology of the Hindi Film: A Historical Construction*. Delhi: Oxford University Press.

Rai, Amit. (2003) "Patriotism and the Muslim Citizen in Hindi Films," *Harvard Asia Quarterly* VII(3) Summer. http://www.asiaquarterly.com/content/view/136/5

Rajadhyaksha, Ashish. (2004) "The 'Bollywoodization' of the Indian Cinema: Cultural Nationalism in a Global Arena," in Preben Kaarsholm (ed.), *City Flicks: Indian Cinema and the Urban Experience*, pp. 113–39. Kolkata: Seagull Books.

Rajagopal, Arvind. (1999) "Thinking through Emerging Markets: Brand Logics and the Cultural Forms of Political Society in India," *Social Text* 60 (Autumn): 131–49.

Turim, Maureen. (1989) *Flashbacks in Film: Memory and History*. Routledge.

Uberoi, Patricia. (1999) "The Diaspora Comes Home: Disciplining Desire in *DDLJ*," in Veena Das, Dipankar Gupta, and Patricia Uberoi (eds.), *Tradition, Pluralism and Identity*, pp. 163–94. Delhi: Sage Publications.

Vanaik, Achin. (2002) "Nuclear Terrorism: A New Threshold," *Economic and Political Weekly* January 26–February 1: 277–9.

Vasudevan, Ravi. (2002) "Another History Rises to the Surface: Melodrama Theory and Digital Simulation in *Hey Ram*." http://www.sarai.net/research/media-city/resouces/film-city-essays/ravi_vasudevan02.pdf

Chapter 15

"The age of reason was over . . . an age of fury was dawning": Contemporary Fiction and Terror

Robert Eaglestone

How have leading contemporary Anglophone writers to date reflected on the "War on Terror"? Each of the four texts I am going to look at – Ian McEwan's *Saturday*, Salman Rushdie's *Shalimar the Clown*, Jonathan Safran Foer's *Extremely Loud and Incredibly Close*, and, as a coda, Martin Amis's short story "The Last Days of Muhammad Atta" – clearly engages with the melange of anxiety and anger that make up the West's fuzzy understanding of the current multiple and interlinked crises (the "War on Terror," 9/11, and the wars in Iraq and Afghanistan, bombings across the globe, and so on). I am going to suggest, influenced by work done in the sort of postcolonial thought that is central in addressing our inextricably interwoven contemporary world, that these novels, despite their merits, fail to address precisely the concerns with terrorism that they set out to claim. Yet this failure does not mean that we should ignore them: indeed, it is exactly their failure that draws us up and makes us aware of the limits of current Western understandings of these crises, and perhaps, also, of the contemporary limits of the novel's form itself.

Each of these writers believes that the world has changed: Rushdie, at his most prophetic, wrote in *Fury*, published in the United States on September 4, 2001:

> The whole world was burning on a shorter fuse . . . Human life was now lived in the moment before the fury, when the anger grew, or the moment during -- the fury's hour, the time of the beast set free – or in the ruined aftermath of a great violence, when the fury ebbed and chaos abated . . . craters – in cities, in deserts, in nations, in the heart – had become commonplace. (p. 129)

And earlier in that novel: "America, because of its omnipotence, is full of fear; it fears the fury of the world and renames it envy" (p. 114). This theme, the end of one age (of happily mixed chutneys) and the start of another (of fury and terror) recurs throughout his 2005 *Shalimar the Clown* like a chorus: "the time of demons had begun" (p. 89); "The age of reason was over, he was telling her, as was the age of love. The irrational was coming into its own. Strategies of survival might be required" (p. 226); "An age of fury was dawning and only the enraged could shape it" (p. 272). Foer and McEwan also deal with the unease and uncertainty that stem from the ending of one established order and the beginning of a new: *Extremely Loud and Incredibly Close* directly concerns 9/11, and *Saturday* the disruption of both the world and domestic order by terror and the war in Iraq. Of course, this sense of a global political shift is ever present in the Western mediasphere and novelists feel the need to address it. That the "War on Terror," whatever its newness as a paradigm, has its political antecedents in imperial and colonial histories is clear: from the global issues of Islamist terror to the colonial histories of extrajuridical "sites of exclusion," as Paul Gilroy argues in his 2005 *After Empire*, many threads of the current crisis are not new.

These novels, which concern the break-up of the world order, all feature a significant break-in to a home. *Shalimar the Clown* begins and ends with the forced entry of the assassin Shalimar into his daughter's LA apartment, and the crux of *Saturday* is the violent break-in by the thug Baxter and his accomplice. *Extremely Loud and Incredibly Close* is consistently structured around attempts to get in or break in: these include the protagonist's entry into people's homes, including his grandmother's apartment, and (more metaphorically perhaps) his illegal exhumation of his father's empty coffin. As in Coetzee's *Disgrace*, it is hard not to see these as an allegory of how world history cannot be excluded from the domestic. Foer's novel especially, which is both moving and kitsch-ily exploitive, uses a child narrator, whose father was killed on 9/11, as a cipher for a search for a pre-9/11 security. It is also hard not to see these moments as symbolic for the forced entry of terror into the sphere of the contemporary Anglophone novel itself.

How does each novel engage with this "forced entry"? Not well: indeed, each reacts by drawing up the limits of what the novel can, in fact, do. Each enacts, perhaps, its own failure. In *Shalimar the Clown*, this is most clearly seen in responses to the various horrors. Language and narrative are not competent to describe the events: Nazarébaddoor's last prophecy is that "what's coming is so terrible that no prophet will have the words to foretell it" (p. 247). And when it comes, it is clear that "stories were stories and real life was real life, naked, ugly and finally impossible to cosmeticise in the greasepaint of a tale" (p. 204). The terrible destruction of the village of Pachigam is summed up three times. While it "still exists" on official maps, this is the only memorial: what

> happened that day . . . need not be set down here in full detail, because brutality is brutality and excess is excess and that's all there is to it. There are things that must be looked at indirectly because they would blind you if you looked them in the face, like the fire of the sun. So to repeat: there was no Pachigam any more. Pachigam was destroyed. Imagine it for yourself.
>
> Second attempt: the village of Pachigam still existed on maps of Kashmir, but that day it ceased to exist anywhere else, except in memory.
>
> Third and final attempt: the beautiful village of Pachigam still exists. (p. 309)

The very rhetoric of attempts, and the final collapse of Pachigam into an existence that is solely textual, marked only in a map and in a guidebook, reveals simply the inability of the text to enunciate the terror. This inability of the text to resolve or clarify or finalize events is echoed in the novel's lack of closure.

In *Saturday*, too, art is constantly shown as ineffective, especially in comparison to the neurosurgical ability of the protagonist. Perowne cannot seem to get on with the novels that his poet daughter insist he read, and in her poem based on watching him work, "he caught . . . art's essential but – he had to suppose – forgivable dishonesty" (p. 139). Confronted by Baxter on Saturday morning, it is not art but his medical skill that saves him. And in the evening, as Baxter terrorizes Perowne's family, he is distracted from his purposes by Daisy's recitation of "Dover Beach" in place of one of her own poems. In one reading this moment might mark the high point of literature as literature:

"It's beautiful. You know that, don't you. It's beautiful. And you wrote it" (p. 223). However, apart from the fact that it had been learnt by rote for money as part of the "obvious stuff" (p. 134) and so already marked in the text as a counter in a restricted economic exchange, and is framed in a lie (Arnold, not Daisy), it is also simply a ruse. It works not as a piece of literature, as it were, but rather as a piece of propaganda: mere *techne*, like a good squash stroke or deft surgical cut with nothing irreplaceable and uniquely literary about it – a dog rushing in or a shout in the street would have done just as well as a distraction. Even its emotional impact on the easily distractible Baxter could have been replicated by something else (his admiration for a dog, for example). Far from any transformative power, or (McEwan's scare-quoted phrase) "secular transcendence" (p. 138), the poem is simply one trick in the process that allows the family to throw the invader down the stairs. In attempting to praise literature as a salvation from a sticky place, in part clearly an allegory, the novel reduces it to a simple transaction: just the sort of view Perowne himself might adopt (one can imagine him saying that "patients recover more quickly if they keep their brains active: doing crosswords, playing push pin, reading great books et cetera").

Foer's novel, too, marks the failure of the novel to get to the issues. Various innovations with the materiality of the text (which build on his use of this strategy in his previous novel, *Everything Is Illuminated*) and Sebald-esque photographs both illuminate and illustrate the end point of communication. Three examples: at a crucial revelatory moment in the text the lines get closer and closer together, and then overlap, so in the end one is left only with an inky illegible mess. The revelation is literally lost in or under the text. Later, the protagonist encodes the "sum of his life" (p. 269) into three pages of text messaging numbers (which – try decoding it – become indeterminate pretty soon). Finally, the book ends wordlessly with the last pages given over to the famous shots of a man falling or jumping from the World Trade Center. These are presented like a child's flipbook: as you have to flip them you discover that (ta dah!, happy ending) the man falls upwards. The closing passage, just before the pictures, does a similar *Time's Arrow* trick, unfalling Oscar's father, ungetting him to work in the Twin Towers, unwaking him up and so on. The conclusion? "We would have been safe" (*Extremely Loud*, p. 326). (Other approaches are possible: for example, this self-conscious childishness contrasts poorly with the poem "Photographs from September 11" on the falling people by the Polish Nobel Laureate Wisława

Szymborska).[1] All these textual tricks serve to delimit the text, to mark what it cannot do.

But more than marking their inability to grasp the trauma-like effects of terrorism and the war on terror, each of these three novels is, perhaps, dishonest, in a way that seems almost to betray the novel as a form in a grand sense. Rosalind Morris argues that the language-less pictures of terrorist acts, shown in the media, fetishize a lack of communication and understanding of events and their context; similar critiques have been made of images from the Holocaust or from wars and global disasters. Founded on the "belief that the need for translation has itself been surpassed by the fact of the image," the "Empire of Images" – the US – "displays rather than explains itself" and "demands imitation not understanding" based not through "reference . . . to the image as sign but to the image as trace of the real" (Morris 2004: 406). She writes that to reclaim the "possibility of peace" will "require an understanding of language in which foreignness is not conflated with noise, and communication is not reduced to the conveyance of commandments" (p. 422). It seems these language-full novels repeat this conflation of foreignness and noise.

In *Extremely Loud . . .* it is the lack of understanding of the child protagonist that licenses the misleading simplicity of the novel. "Mohammed Atta was evil," he declares (p. 159), and in an extended day dream he reimagines 9/11:

> I imagined the last second, when I would see the pilot's face, who would be a terrorist. I imagined us looking at each other in the eyes when the nose of the plane was one millimetre from the building
>
> I hate you, my eyes would tell him.
>
> I hate you, his eyes would tell me. (p. 244)

This is hardly the "communication" that Morris feels is vital for peace. Indeed, the child narrator authorizes a repetition of the "Axis of Evil" rhetoric. Contrast this with, for example, the view of complexity offered by another Oscar child narrator (invoked by Foer's choice of name), Oscar Matzerath from Grass's *The Tin Drum*. This Oscar does not explain away the evil of the Nazis, but engages with it in its difficulty. By focalizing the novel through his Oscar, however, Foer avoids complex issues and reiterates a simplistic position.

Likewise, in *Saturday*, Baxter – a metonym for illness, Saddam Hussein, Osama Bin Laden, the anti-war demonstration, terrorism, the war on terrorism: in short anything that disrupts Henry Perowne's organized life – is a pantomime villain, an image not the locus of an act of communication. In their morning clash, Perowne saves himself from being beaten up by Baxter by diagnosing Huntingtons's syndrome (a genetic disease but also, of course, a sly reference to the Huntington of *The Clash of Civilisations*). Perowne changes – medicalizes, in fact – Baxter the person into Baxter the series of symptoms (an inability to move his eyes, "poor self-control . . . explosive temper"), which recaptures the pure disruption of Baxter back into the ordered, safe world of Perowne. And even, in the evening, as he is thrown down the stairs, Baxter's "sorrowful accusation of betrayal" (p. 227) reflects Perowne's own anxieties over his happy marriage, successful children, and material wealth. Here again, no communication takes place, only an event which allows Perowne a neurosurgical strike to resolve the illness, forgive the villain, and quell the disruption by bringing it and delimiting it within his field of knowledge: another fantasy of safety.

Rushdie's novel offers the most complex elisions. One brief snapshot: Shalimar ascends to a Forward Camp 22, a terrorist training camp. His goals are "personal as well as national" (p. 258): not a terroristic religious ideology but a personal one of revenge and honor. Here, encountering pantomime villain straight from central casting, the Iron Mullah, he pretends to be converted to the Islamist "truth" and tears his clothes in a performance of such acting skill that he convinces the Mullah and almost himself. There are at least two odd things here: the bearded Mullah and his teaching is an incongruous un-Rushdie-like figure, lacking in complexity or difficulty. The second is the strangely hopeful idea that this terrorist assassin is motivated by personal not religious motives: motives, that is, that might be satiated fairly easily. What is missing is precisely a sense of the world of the Islamist. Where, before, Rushdie's novels offer complexity, detail, difficulty, here it offers only a cipher of evil, lacking a real sense of motivation.

What can we conclude from these brief comparisons? Apart from applauding the attempts of these novelists to engage with the issues of our times, and sensing that something profound has changed, it might be said that the novels can do what they want. However, part of the kudos given to the novel form stems from its ability to encounter and to think through, in singular and irreplaceable ways, "how we are" and "how the world is for us" (I use these vague phrases intentionally). As this is the case, these interesting failures serve to illuminate the limits in Western responses to the "age of fury." Despite their attempts, they show an inability to address the terror that is their proclaimed subject, and indeed perform their own failure and collapse of voice. And at the same time, as the other side of the coin, their refusal to come to terms with it leads to a simplistic refusal to engage with the otherness of the terrorists and their ideas. Instead, they use an array of techniques to recapture this within a pre-established framework of understanding: terror is simply evil (Foer), an illness (McEwan), or stems from universally comprehensible personal motives (Rushdie). There is little sense that there is, in the current crisis, a very different set of discourses that demand engagement, and that cannot simply be recapitulated (retranslated into, as it were) within a Western intellectual framework. This movement itself is characteristic of Western thinking, in its attempt to bring all "otherness" inside its own hegemonic discourse. To argue this is not to evade ethical issues over terrorism, nor to pretend that judgments cannot be made, but rather to illustrate the inability of at least these writers in at least these books to get to grips with what is outside their world-view.

These characteristics are highlighted again in Martin Amis's short story, "The Last Days of Muhammad Atta," published in the UK to coincide with the fifth anniversary of 9/11. It is the latest of Amis's engagements with the "big issues" of our times and in it he imagines the early morning of September 11 from Muhammad Atta's point of view in order to offer an insight into him. For Amis, Atta hates his body, which is characterized by sickness and decay, bought on by fasting; hates women; feels Islam abandoned by God ("for centuries God has forsaken the believers, and rewarded the infidels," p. 25). Though his mind seems calm, his body is having a hostile reaction to his intentions (the "core reason was good enough for the mind. But it couldn't carry the body," p. 26) even though for Amis's Atta "mind and his body were not separable" (p. 19). Amis follows the historical sources in relation to some details – the four-page booklet that Atta and the other terrorists had, Atta's personal friendships and enmities – but does not at all portray Atta as the more complex "charismatic, intelligent, and persuasive, albeit intolerant of dissent" character discussed by the US *National Commission on Terrorist Attacks upon the United States* (2006: para 5.3).

Amis shies away from a complex explanation involving Islamism. While Atta is "doing what he was doing for the core reason . . . for the core reason only" (p. 19), there is little sense in the story of what the core reason actually is. It would seem to be bodily disgust and a death drive:

> Muhammad Atta was not religious; he was not even especially political. He had allied himself with the militants because jihad was, by many magnitudes, the most charismatic idea of his generations. To unite ferocity and rectitude in a single word: nothing could compete with that . . . If you took away all the rubbish about faith, then fundamentalism suited his character, and with an almost sinister precision. (p. 19)

Fundamentalism in the abstract (with no "rubbish about faith") does not exist: one has to be fundamentalist about something. Amis's explanation boils down to a sense that Atta had an innate type of "fundamentalist streak" to which the Islamist movement pandered. Indeed, with a trick borrowed from Julian Barnes's *The History of the World in 10½ Chapters*, it is also clear Amis has condemned Atta, as evil, to hell ("He didn't expect paradise. What he expected was oblivion. And, strange to say, he would find neither," p. 21). The last days (plural) are the infinite infernal repetition of Atta's last day ("And eternity never ends, Ziad – it never even begins" (p. 26), he says to a companion). Amis's version of Atta, then, is comprehended, judged, and made safe, as it were, by a Western discourse that brands him as evil, and as psychologically (and so bodily) sick.

Martin Amis maintains that a "novel asserts nothing: it provides a framework for thinking about things".[2] The terrorists under discussion attack not only their victims, but also the framework of Western thought: these fictions, in response, seek to "recapture" these events, intentions, and actions within these Western frameworks, rather than to attempt to understand them in their own right. I have suggested that these fictions mark the limits of the current understanding of terror from the Western point of view. From, as it were, within the work of these novelists (rather than, say, contrasting them to non-Western accounts of terrorism), I have attempted to show how quickly they run up against the limits of their understanding of contemporary terrorism. Not only do the narratives performatively enact this inability; at the same time, to mask it, they seek to recapture or rephrase terror in distinctly Western terms – blaming it on evil, illness, or on universal desires.

This is absolutely not to argue for some cultural relativism, nor, of course, to excuse the acts of violence. Quite the opposite. My suggestion is that the West has not yet begun to understand fully what this current crisis is about, and that these texts, for all their intellectual courage, illustrate this. I would argue that to understand better the sources of terrorism in its own terms is to begin to think about better ways of defeating it. Whether this understanding itself would be a form of orientalist control (in the classic Saidian sense) or the start of some sort of dialogue is beyond the scope of this essay; but to redescribe the terror by understanding it solely within a Western discourse is explore neither of these options, but is instead a blindness, of a sort well known to postcolonial theory.

Notes

1 Wisława Szymborska, *Moment,* trans. Clare Cavanagh and Stanisław Barańczak (Kraków: Wydawnictwo Znak, 2002) p. 67. I thank Renate Zdziebtowska for bringing these remarkable poems to my attention.
2 Cooke (2006: 8).

References

Amis, Martin. (2006) "The Last Days of Muhammad Atta," *Observer*, September 3, 2006, Magazine, 16–28.

Cooke, Rachel. (2006) "Martin Amis: the Interview," *Observer*, October 1, review 8–9.

Foer, Jonathan Safran. (2005) *Extremely Loud and Incredibly Close*. London: Hamish Hamilton.

Gilroy, Paul. (2005) *After Empire*. London: Routledge.

McEwan, Ian. (2005) *Saturday*. London: Jonathan Cape.

Morris, Rosalind C. (2004) "Images of Untranslatability in the US war on Terror," *Interventions* 6: 401–23.

The National Commission on Terrorist Attacks Upon the United States. (2006) September 26, 2006. http://www.9-11commission.gov/

Rushdie, Salman. (2001) *Fury*. London: Jonathan Cape.

Rushdie, Salman. (2005) *Shalimar the Clown*. London: Jonathan Cape.

Chapter 16

Bodies of Terror: Performer and Witness

Emma Brodzinski

Bodies of Terror

In *Stages of Terror* Anthony Kubiak posits theatrical activity as a primal force; a pre-condition of sociopolitical power which can articulate sociopsychical operations. Kubiak perceives theater as a space where the Lacanian Real of the psyche – i.e., unincorporated material which troubles the individual – may be articulated. Kubiak suggests that theater's affinity with the Imaginary order and that which cannot be represented (and here he addresses Freud's characterization of basic psychical operations as theatrical productions) makes it a powerful and effective forum for exploring the experience of terror. Dealing with terrorism theatrically is always problematic as there is a limit to what can be represented on stage. Kubiak sees this dynamic as a benefit in that, rather than entering into a mediatized circulation of images, theater gestures toward the terror which is at the heart of terrorist activity. Walter Reich describes terrorism as "a strategy of violence designed to promote desired outcomes by instilling fear in the public at large" and, rather than focusing on the spectacle of violence, theater may work to explore the psychical effects of acts of violence (quoted in Whittaker 2003: 1). In addition, rather than presenting a mediated image, the theatrical event presents a real body in front of an audience and invites a direct response to that encounter.

In this chapter I am going to explore two contemporary pieces. *Happiness*, by American performance artist Laurie Anderson, and *My*

Neck Is Thinner Than a Hair: A History of the Car Bomb in the 1975–1991 Lebanese Wars Volume 1: January 21, 1986, by the Atlas Group, represent personal performance-based responses to terrorist activity. In examining these works I shall consider how the artists employ the resources of the theatrical medium in the presentation of their material. In particular I will explore how they make use of personal trauma to shape the work; how the performance pieces gesture toward that which cannot be represented; and the significance of the relationship between the body of the performer and the bodies of the audience. I will consider how these performance actions can be understood as interventions in the circulation of the discourses of terror and terrorism. Rather than responding to the spectacle of violence with a counter-attack, these pieces appear to encourage reflection through an aesthetic encounter that considers the effect on the senses. Through analysis of the performances, I will examine how the multifaceted interactions they engender challenge mainstream rhetoric and question a causal relationship between terror and counter-terrorism through encouraging a complex readership of the process of representation and a reflection on the unrepresentable.

Happiness

Schlesinger, Murdock, and Elliott argue that, in cultural products about terrorism, "it is always the terrorists who initiate the plot with a violent attack on the existing order" (1983: 84). The trigger for Laurie Anderson's work *Happiness* (premiered in London in January 2002) was the terrorist attack on the Twin Towers in New York on September 11, 2001. However, the work differs from the media representation described by Schlesinger in that, rather than focusing on displaying the brutal action and trying to recreate the spectacle, the piece seeks to explore the psychological ramifications of the events. As Kubiak suggests, the focus of this theatrical presentation is the re-presentation of the unarticulated rather than the circulation of violent imagery.

Anderson states that "the shock of terrorism propelled me into a different place . . ." (2003a). *Happiness* is an intimate account of the personal journey that Anderson undertook in response to that shock. Happiness is a quality enshrined in the American Declaration of Independence and Anderson's piece traces the exercising of her political right to pursue happiness in the face of events that undermine a sense of personal and public security. Thus the work grew directly out of her own experience and Anderson describes the piece as her "most autobiographical to date" (2003a). As in her other work, there was no sense of the presentation of a character on stage; instead Laurie Anderson appeared as herself, or – perhaps more correctly – her selves. Anderson was presented as a small figure behind a mixing desk. Unlike her larger-scale productions, the desk did not swamp her and she stepped out in front of it at moments. Anderson's storytelling relied on subtle modulations of her voice. She describes herself as not acting but engaging in different "talking styles" (in Howell 1999: 407), as happens in everyday life. So, in telling the episodic stories that made up the piece, she adopted different tones but essentially remained herself. For *Happiness* Anderson wore no overt costume that might suggest character but formal clothing – black trousers and jacket with a white shirt – and related directly to the audience in the first person.

Anderson's starting point for the piece was the witnessing of troubling events which upset a sense of personal and public safety, and this sense of the loss of security permeated the work. Anderson's studio is in the Tribeca district in downtown Manhattan, only a few blocks away from the Twin Towers, and the events of 9/11 had a particular impact on her. In her piece she worked around the after-shock of such an incident and sought to articulate the psychic processes that might be at work. Within *Happiness* Anderson comments that "when things disappear they leave a void" (2003b). There did appear to be a void at the heart of the piece, which was symbolized by the large, dark, empty space that surrounded Anderson throughout the performance. Although light was thrown upon that space at key moments it remained empty and devoid of representation in a manner which served to heighten the awareness of what was not being shown. Orr argues: "This is not to say that theatre should ignore terror as spectacle – it always needs to embody it in some form – but that it should find jarring ways of estranging us from it in an age of dramatic self-consciousness where performance is often regarded as an aggressive thrusting of spectacle in the faces of spectators" (Orr and Klaic 1990: 55).

September 11 was primarily a visual event with particular images being endlessly circulated throughout the media. In presenting her personal response to events, however, Anderson chose to employ a limited range of visual stimuli – some colored lighting and a small number of abstract projections – and, as a result, the focus remained on her and her stories rather than library images relating to the terrorist attack. Anderson's work avoided an ossifying fetishization of images of terrorism and allowed her audience to step back from the spectacle of the event and observe the (psychical) space around it with an emphasis on the human encounter of the storytelling. Anderson noted that what was important for her as an artist was to stay in the moment and be truthful to the mood that might arise – thus some of the music was improvised as part of the performance and Anderson regularly paused to mark responses from the audience. Anderson's performance piece was not "in your face" in terms of shocking action, but moved lightly from moment to moment, taking up and dropping threads relating to the key theme as it went. This also gave an opportunity for audience members to project their own memories and imaginings into the darkness and may have served to engage to the Lacanian "Real" of the psyche, and, in turn, allowed space for people to acknowledge and process their own doubts and fears with the context of the safe space of a well-crafted theatrical event, mediated by a professional performer.

The act of witnessing is central to the reception of autobiographical pieces such as *Happiness*. Rather than being passive spectators, the audience are acknowledged as active listeners and the authentic nature of the material often draws the audience into a relationship with the performer. In a review of Anderson's piece, Betancourt notes: "Her stories leave us with the feeling that we have no answer to what we witness, and that simply bearing witness to these horrors through stories is a way of diminishing them through repetition until the meaning goes away" (2002).

The reality of the material that Anderson presents within the work – as she tells stories about her visit to an Amish farm and her stay at a Buddhist retreat – as well as the intimate, first-person manner in which she presents it, can be seen to command an active mode of readership, which Betancourt identifies as witnessing. Theater is fundamentally predicated on the presence of an audience but witnessing suggests a different level of engagement. In examining the process of witnessing within performance, scholars have drawn on work within the field of trauma studies that is concerned with the analysis of emotional trauma/wounding, memory, and the relationship between the two within its sociopolitical context. As in trauma studies, performance scholars acknowledge the efficacy of personal narratives and recognize the impulse within witnesses to bear testament to the story that has been presented to them. What was central to Anderson's work was the "in-the-same-roomness" element of the theatrical encounter where the audience's affective response – both in terms of peals of recognitory laughter and in reverential silence – functioned as an essential element of the piece.

Although the audience's presence was acknowledged by the performer in her direct address to them, she did not lead them through a clear-cut journey to a polemical message at the climax. Clements describes the end of *Happiness* as "insubstantial," indicating a dissatisfaction at the open nature of Anderson's text (2003). Anderson stated that she promised her audience a "beginning, a middle and an end – although not necessarily in that order" (2003a). It appears that she wanted to encourage the audience to explore and interpret the material in a manner that might differ from the reception of the carefully edited media news that offers a particular perspective on terrorist activity. Anderson presented her experience as a mediating factor between sociopolitical events and the response of the public and through the sharing of her personal stories she allowed her audience to witness trauma at second hand or once removed, thus offering them the freedom to explore possible responses to the material which were not caught up in the spectacle of terror. Anderson's closing question to the audience, "Now what – what happens next?" served to foreground the significance of the audience's role and communicated a desire for spectators to reflect and act upon what they had been witness to in the world outside the theater (2003b).

My Neck Is Thinner Than a Hair

My Neck Is Thinner Than a Hair: A History of the Car Bomb in the 1975–1991 Lebanese Wars Volume 1: January 21, 1986 has been performed internationally. It takes the form of a presentation by Walid Raad in a lecture format followed by a question and answer session. The style of the work is very similar to Anderson's piece in that Raad presents as himself in front of the audience in a formal suit with only key staging equipment – a desk, a glass of water, a lap-top – serving as aids to his presentation. The core areas of inquiry for the lecture are the "public and private discourses surrounding the 3614 car bombs that were detonated during the period outlined in the title" (Raad 2004). Raad explains the choice of the car bomb as subject material in the following terms: "I am finding that the history of the car bomb is also a history of the way that wars were physically and psychologically experienced" (quoted in Eller 2004). For Raad, like Anderson, there is a commitment to an artistic exploration of the socio-emotional effects of terrorist activity. For *My Neck Is Thinner Than a Hair* an actual car bombing which took place on January 21, 1986 was taken as a starting point for an inquiry into the psychic terrain.

As in Anderson's work, the personal experience of shock and fear at the witnessing of real events appears to be central to the creative process. Raad notes that the work is a "Chirascuro reflection on how I moved through the city [of Beruit] – awareness of how I moved from one side of the pavement to another on the street" (The Atlas Group Discussion 2004, London, June 10). He notes his awareness of different brands of cars because of newspaper reports of car bombs which focused on the make and model of the vehicles used in attacks, and the efforts he took to avoid the danger he perceived. Raad posits that the cars made the psychological processes of fear visible and easier to discuss through their status as fetishized objects. This link between factual objects and the unconscious desires they represent/relate to is at the heart of Raad's work. Raad also appears aware of the way that the notion of Beirut may itself be fetishized by a Western audience. Bonami notes: "I feel that (Beirut) is one of those places that can stir a kind of lay fantasy in the Western art world" (quoted in Wilson-Goldie 2003). Raad states that he views the context of the audience as being very important and constructs a caricature of audience when he is creating work so that he is not writing in a void. Like Anderson's work, *My Neck Is Thinner Than a Hair* relates directly to the audience in its lecture format, and Raad is seeking immediate communication with audience members with an awareness of their particular sociopolitical positioning. For example, in the performance at the ICA in London, Raad announced: "the faces I am showing you are very familiar to the Lebanese," thereby constructing the audience as outsiders to the reported events (2004). Like Anderson, Raad places himself as a mediator of information around the issues of terrorism and stands in the gap of information between spectacular images of horror and the ineffable experience of fear.

Like Anderson's, Raad's work approaches the subject of terrorism from an oblique angle. He defends this methodology by claiming that the experience of violence is itself indefinable: even when things are shown something remains undefined and this interest in the unpresentable appears to marry with the theatrical format he has chosen to work with. Like Anderson, he is interested in the effects of the violence and the experience of trauma that he sees as inhabiting the space in between the binary of that which is shown and that which is hidden in a manner which cannot be represented but only gestured toward. A key component of *My Neck Is Thinner Than a Hair* examines this in an aesthetic manner. The film *We Can Make Rain but No-one Came to Ask*, which is screened as part of the lecture presentation, includes sequences where cars appear and disappear and city streets that are empty in the middle of the day. In the question and answer session Raad commented that The Atlas Group found it puzzling that, although people were present when the film was shot, when it was developed they had disappeared. He asked: "what is the universe where people appear/disappear on film?" (2004). This commentary highlights an underlying anxiety about the movement of cars and people through the landscape of Beirut. Like Anderson, Raad is not working in a mimetic way – that might echo media representations of terrorism – but in an indirect way that might circumvent those hegemonic structures of representation and point to that which is beyond, and his physical presence draws attention to that which is absent and encourages the audience to reflect upon that which is unpresentable.

Like Anderson, Raad works with silence and absence to gesture toward the ineffable and, like Anderson, this is marked in the performance. At one point in *Happiness* Anderson commented: "in the real world something like this happens" (2003b). This was followed by silence. After a few uncomfortable moments, she stated: "if this happens on TV it is a disaster" (2003b). This section highlighted the significance of the live encounter and the different discourse that the performer was inviting the audience to engage with within the theater. Silence also played an important role in Raad's piece. The delivery of the stories of the people caught up and killed in the terrorist attacks – the mother and daughter crossing the street and the local shopkeeper – were interrupted as Raad fell into an abrupt silence. In this way the performers resisted a narrativization of terrorism which echoes a conventional media product. Indeed, part of *My Neck Is Thinner Than a Hair* took the work of a photo-journalist and restructured it in a manner which highlighted the construction of spectacle within media accounts. Through destabilizing the representation of terrorism and highlighting the manufacture of media spectacles, such theatrical work points to the principles of fear and anxiety that underpin cultural products. It also serves to reassert the human encounter that is at the heart of the performance event and the moment where the performer simply looks at the audience and meets their gaze.

Like Anderson, Raad directly addresses the audience as himself in lecturer mode. Indeed, in Raad's work the relationship between performer and spectator is more explicit since it ends with a question and answer session. There is a true sense within the work of a place being opened up for discussion and permission being given to speak. Raad states: "Lots of people come to see the work, not because we are experts but because the work makes a space where politics is possible" (The Atlas Group Discussion, 2004, London, June 10). This discussion space can be seen to be opened up by the aesthetic approach of the artist who does not seek to deliver spectacle but to unsettle discourses of spectacular representation. At the center of the Atlas Group project is the supposed creation of an archive. The discussion of this curatorial activity draws attention to the processes through which people try to control the chaos which terrorist activity represents. Raad deliberately employs the codes of a lecture with its logical organization and delivery of information. The PowerPoint presentation is a key aspect of the work. Raad displays graphs and charts, highlighting the fetishizing dynamics of information about terrorist attacks through its excessive, carnivalesque manner. The audience is bombarded with information and images and text build-up on the screen into an overwhelming collage. Just as the trauma of witnessing events is being repeated in a way that Freud might identify as the return of the repressed, so the images repeat themselves and proliferate. There is a sense of everything being out of control as the audience are invited to witness and make sense of overwhelming and nonsensical information. Raad ended that section of the presentation with the words "I think that was all clear," which prompted a laugh from the audience in recognition of the playful irony of the comment that appeared to recognize their difficulties in engaging with what was being presented (2004). In this way Raad notes the significance of readership to his project.

Both Anderson and Raad deal knowingly with their audience. The context of the ICA (Institute of Contemporary Arts) in London provided Raad's work with a public forum that has a reputation for engagement with vital contemporary issues; but it is also a site that is recognized for its avant-garde practices and the license to experiment with form and content. Initially the audience appeared unsure as to how to read the piece and there was a hesitance about laughing but, as the carnivalesque element developed, so did the audience response and the witnesses appeared to match the playful mood of the performance. Anderson is also positioned on the cutting edge of the mainstream and the staging of her work as part of BITE (Barbican International Theatre Events) signaled the recognition of its significance within the international avant-garde. Anderson has a reputation as an experimental artist and the audience for the event, which filled the Barbican Theatre, may have been drawn to the work because of the status of its maker, wanting to hear about her response to the events of 9/11 in a piece that she described as her most autobiographical work.

It appears that the audience for the type of autobiographical performance that Anderson and Raad present are looking to make an "authentic" connection with the material, which is problematized by the fact that the pieces are a creative mixture of fact and fiction. Anderson's storytelling shapes her material into entertaining narratives and Raad's work, which purports to inhabit the factual domain of the documentary archive, is also a blend of fact and fiction. Taylor describes the Atlas Group archive as a "sort of fictional investigation bureau" (2004). The conceit is that it is seeking to document events but, in effect, Raad the artist is creating new documents that represent possible responses to the events. Townshend notes that when terrorist acts are left "unsigned," gaps in understanding are left to be filled in (2002: 9). The car bomb was not attributed and Raad seeks to fill in the blanks with fabrication. Searle states that *My Neck Is Thinner Than a Hair* is "a provocation, a fiction, a dismaying response to an impossible situation" (2004). I would suggest a more positive reading in that it offered the pleasure of the possibility to express and explore the effects of terrorism with provocation on an emotional rather than a political level, which encourages the viewer to reassess their psychic landscape.

Conclusion

Kubiak notes that, in contemporary culture, there is a desire to be able to make a connection between what is demonstrated within the theater and "the real terrorisms of ruptured bodies and wounded minds" (1991: 4). *Happiness* and *My Neck Is Thinner Than a Hair* seek to explore the psychic after-shock of terrorist activity and to make sense of what it is to witness wounding and trauma. Anderson and Raad recognize the limits of the theatrical format, which cannot provide mimetic representations of events, and use their anti-mimetic strategies of working with absence and silence to maximize theater's ability to gesture toward that which cannot be represented.

The artists use their personal experience to shape and substantiate the work, drawing their audience into an intimate reflection upon the emotional experience of being a witness to terrorism and allowing for an exploration of pity and fear. The audience are witness to the artists' acts of witnessing and, as such, are actively engaged with the material – but in a way which allows space for reflection. The audience are not witness to events which may be perceived as being threatening to them but are given an account of events once removed, with the artist acting as a mediator for the material. The blending in of fictional material also provides distancing, which may make it safe for audience members to truly enter into the experience. Layered witnessing – where an artist relays what s/he has witnessed for the audience to witness – can be seen to be an effective way in which to negotiate traumatic material. This intervention into a dynamic of cause and effect can be seen to allow a more complex response to the relationship between acts of terror and counter-terror. Audience members are offered an aestheticized space for reflection which recognizes how conventional mediatized responses are constructed yet resists such principles of fear and anxiety and allows for a more critical dialogue with the experience of terror. Pieces that work in this way retain an element of authenticity and directly connect with spectators whilst also functioning as effective pieces of art which provide a space for reflection upon life outside the theater.

References and Further Reading

Anderson, Laurie. (2003a) "Artist Statement," *Barbican Programme*. London.

Anderson, Laurie. (2003b) *Happiness*. London: Barbican Theatre, May 8, 2003.

Aristotle. (1992) *Poetics*, trans. Theodore Buckley. New York: Prometheus Books.

The Atlas Group. (2004) *My Neck Is Thinner Than a Hair: A History of the Car Bomb in the 1975–1991 Lebanese Wars Volume 1: January 21, 1986*. London: ICA, June 7, 2004.

Betancourt, Michael. (2002) *Totentanz Transformation*. Online. Available http://www.miamiartexchange.com/pages/2002/05/betancourt_05. Accessed July 27, 2003.

Clements, Andrew. (2003) "Laurie Anderson," *Guardian*, May 9. Accessed via CD ROM.

Connor, Steven. (1992) "Aesthetics, Pleasure and Value," in Stephen Reagan, (ed.), *The Politics of Pleasure*, pp. 203–20. Buckingham, UK: Open University Press.

Eller, Thomas. (2004) *Letter from Hamburg*. Online. Available http://www.artnet.com/magazine/features/eller/eller3-15-04.asp. Accessed August 10, 2004.

Eysenck, Michael. (2002) *Happiness: Facts and Myths*. Hove: Lawrence Erlbaum Associates.

Freud, Sigmund. (1984; 1991) "Beyond the Pleasure Principle," in *On Metapsychology*, trans. James Strachey, pp. 275–338. Harmondsworth: Penguin.

Howell, John. (1999) "Acting and Nonacting," in Bonnie Marranca and Gautam Dasgupta (eds.), *Conversations on Art and Performance*, pp. 394–409. Baltimore: Johns Hopkins University Press.

Kernebone, Fenella. (2003) *Laurie Anderson on Happiness*. Online. Available http://www.abc.net.au/arts/performance/stories/s797452.htm. Accessed August 6, 2003.

Kubiak, Anthony. (1991) *Stages of Terror: Terrorism, Ideology and Coercion and Theatre History*. Bloomington: Indiana University Press.

May, Krista. (2002) *Some Thoughts on Happiness*. Online. Available http://www.popmatters.com/music/concerts/a/anderson-laurie-02. Accessed July 27, 2003.

Miller, Jacques-Alain, ed. (1991) *The Seminar of Jacques Lacan: Book II The Ego in Freud's Theory and the Technique of Psychoanalysis*, trans. Sylvana Tomaselli. London: W. W. Norton and Company.

Orr, John and Dragan Klaic, eds. (1990) *Terrorism and Modern Drama*. Edinburgh: Edinburgh University Press.

Raad, Walid. (2004) Personal communication with the author, June 21.

Schlesinger, Philip, Graham Murdock, and Philip Elliott. (1983) *Televising Terrorism: Political Violence in Popular Culture*. London: Comedia Publishing Group.

Searle, Adrian. (2004) "The Atlas Group," *Guardian*, June 8. Accessed via CD ROM.

Taylor, Paul. (2004) "Laughter in the Dark," *Independent*, June 3. Accessed via CD ROM.

Townshend, Charles. (2002) *Terrorism: A Very Short Introduction*. Oxford: Oxford University Press.

Whittaker, David, ed. (2003) *The Terrorism Reader*. London: Routledge.

Wilson-Goldie, Kaelen. (2003) "Beirut Artists Dampen Western Fantasies at Venice Biennale," *The Daily Star*, August 19. http://www.dailystar.com.lb/features/19_08_03_b.asp. Accessed August 10, 2004.

Index

Note: page references in **bold** refer to contributors' chapters.